D1210699

GAME BASICS

Final Fantasy: The 4 Heroes of Light represents a new chapter in the Final Fantasy series of games. Many elements of the game experience should feel familiar to anyone who has played another Final Fantasy game, but there are some new elements as well.

Some of the biggest changes include the lack of an Options Menu, only one game save allowed per cartridge, and no Main Menu. The Main Menu functions still exist, but they are spread out between the characters you control and some of the NPCs that populate the game world.

CAUTION! This game has a single slot for saving progress. If you save a new game, YOU WILL LOSE ALL PROGRESS AND DATA FROM YOUR OLD GAME.

Start a new game from the beginning?

Yes   No

Saving Your Progress

The only way to save your progress is to speak with the Adventurer who always appears with his companion, Friendly Fox. Fortunately, he enjoys travelling and you always seem to run into him both in towns and in dungeons.

THE CHARACTER SCREEN

Press the X button while you have control of a character (or tap the word Menu with the stylus) to bring up the portraits of all the current party members at the top of the screen. Selecting a character brings up three options: Items, Abilities, and Crowns.

Items

The Items screen serves several purposes. First, the top half of the screen displays a summary of your character's current status. It shows level, HP, AP, how much experience is needed to reach the next level, stats, and currently equipped items. The bottom half of the screen shows that character's current inventory.

Limited Inventory Space

Each character has 15 total inventory spaces available. Equipped items still take up an inventory space, as do Magic Tomes. Available space is limited, especially when the party has only one or two characters, so you must remember to visit Storage Shops when you have the opportunity.

Use the Items screen to Equip, Remove, Give, or Discard items in your inventory. When you Equip or Remove items, the character summary screen shows how that action impacts the character. Green numbers indicate an improvement in stats, while red numbers indicate a decrease in stats. Use Give to transfer an item between characters, and Discard to get rid of the selected item.

Abilities

The top half of the Abilities screen displays the same character summary information as the Items screen. The bottom half shows the character's currently available abilities. The six slots for each character can be filled with Crown-based abilities or spells.

Crown-based abilities are tied to a character's current Crown choice, and how much the character has improved that Crown (more on that soon). To use a spell, the character must have the corresponding Magic Tome in his or her inventory.

To set an ability or spell as available for battle, select a slot, which takes you to a screen with every spell and ability available to the character. Select the spell or ability to assign it to the chosen spot. You can't repeat abilities or spells (even if you have a pair of identical Magic Tomes) in your ability list. If you select a previously assigned ability, it will appear only in the last slot for which it was selected. Its previous location will become empty.

Be Informed

The Abilities screen provides a great deal of information in a compact fashion. Since the information won't appear in battle, it's important to remember what appears in the Summary Box just above the six ability slots. The color of the circle next to the name of the ability or spell tells you what element the spell uses.

The number of orange circles in the top left corner tells you how many AP are required to use the ability. The color of the text in the bottom right corner tells you whether it affects allies (blue) or enemies (red). If the red text says FRNT or REAR, that means it affects a single enemy target in the front line or back line, respectively. The significance of the colors and shapes that appear in some of the ability boxes is discussed later in this chapter.

Crowns

There are two actions available to you on the Crown screen: Wear Crown and Enhance Crown. Wear Crown simply switches the character's current Crown for a different one. When you select a Crown, the top half of the screen shows the statistical changes that occur if you make the switch and what abilities become available to the current character upon making the switch.

Enhance Crown takes you to a new screen where you place gems collected from fallen enemies into matching slots on the Crown. The top screen displays the new ability which will be available after upgrading the Crown. To learn more about Crowns, check out the Crowns chapter of this guide.

THE BASICS OF BATTLE

Whenever the party is on the World Map, exploring a dungeon, or (in same rare cases) even in town, there's a chance of entering battle with random enemies. Some enemy encounters, mainly boss encounters, occur at predetermined locations.

During Battles

Before each round of combat, you select the actions for each character in your party. Each character has the following choices for actions:

ATTACK	Attack requires 1 AP to execute. The character attacks with his or her equipped weapon. Attack targets a single enemy, and the type of weapon determines whether the preferred target is in the front or rear row.
BOOST	Boost puts a character in a guarded position and restores an additional AP. Characters who choose to Boost on a turn take reduced damage from physical attacks.
ITEM	Item allows a character to use an item from his or her inventory at the cost of 1 AP. Not all items are usable in battle.
ABILITIES/ SPELLS	With sufficient AP, the character can execute any ability or spell that appears in his or her listing. Abilities and spells have different AP costs and targets.

One important thing to keep in mind during battle is that you have almost no control over which enemy or ally becomes the target of each character's chosen action. Your choice of ability, spell, or weapon allows you to focus on enemies in the front or rear row, but that's as much control as you have over targeting enemies. For restorative spells and items, the game selects the character in greatest need of healing or removal of a negative status effect.

DETERMINING THE ORDER OF ACTION

A number of factors determine the order in which party members and enemies act. The higher the Action Value for the following formulae, the quicker the characters and enemies execute their selected action.

Other Factors

The Scholar ability Restrain and the Musician ability March impact the results of the following formulae. In addition, equipping the accessories Old Shoes and Hermes Sandals supersedes the Action Value formula. Anyone equipped with Old Shoes always acts last each round, while Hermes Sandals cause their user to act first.

The values for Ability Speed for characters are included with the Magic Tome and Crown sections of the guide. The Ability Speed values for enemies are included in the bestiary.

FOR CHARACTERS	Action Value = character's level + ([current HP value ÷ HP max value] x 100) + (remaining AP x 10) + Ability Speed
FOR ENEMIES WITH ONE ACTION PER TURN	Action Value = Level + (HP current ÷ HP max value x 100) + Ability Speed

Some enemies act more than one time per turn. The timing of each of their actions uses the following formulae:

1ST ACTION	Action Value = Level + (HP current value ÷ HP max value x 100) + Ability Speed
2ND ACTION	Level + (HP current value ÷ HP max value x 100) + Ability Speed - weight
3RD ACTION	Action Value = Level + (HP current value ÷ HP max value x 100) + Ability Speed — (weight x 2)
4TH ACTION	Action Value = Level + (HP current value ÷ HP max value X 100) + Ability Speed — (weight X 3)

HOW ENEMIES DETERMINE THEIR TARGET

Each action a character takes builds up his or her aggregate Target Value. With a few exceptions, the character with the highest aggregate Target Value is the target of enemy attacks.

Each character action taken during a combat round has a Fixed Target Value and a Reduced Target Value. The Fixed Target Value is the initial number listed when a Target Value is given for an action or ability. The Reduced Target Value is the number shown in parentheses next to the Fixed Target Value. The highest score for either Target Value is 1000, meaning no character can exceed 2000 aggregate Target Value.

Each time a character takes an action, his or her aggregate Target Value is increased by the sum of the Fixed Target Value and the Reduced Target Value. If that character is attacked, the Reduced Target Value decreases by 50%. At the end of each round of combat, every character's Reduced Target Value decreases by 20%. If a character is killed during combat and brought back to life, his or her aggregate Target Value resets to 0. At the end of every battle, all characters' aggregate Target Values reset to 0.

When Enemies Ignore the Numbers

The game's AI ignores the numbers when it's appropriate. Attempts to use Silence, for example, tend to avoid characters who don't depend on spells in favor of characters like White Mages and Black Mages. Enemies won't often try to inflict the same negative status ailment on a character who already has it.

For example, Brandt performs an action that has 50 Fixed Target Value and 50 Reduced Target Value for 100 aggregate Target Value. If he's attacked, his new aggregate Target Value is 75 (50 Fixed + [50 x .5] or 25 Reduced). If the turn ends with no more actions taken against Brandt, his aggregate Target Value will be 55 (50 Fixed + [25 x .2] or 5 Reduced).

GETTING PSYCHED UP

At certain points during battle, characters in the party may enter a state known as Psyched Up. When characters become Psyched Up, their Strength, Intellect, and Spirit are increased by 50%, and they gain an extra AP at the start of that round. When multiple characters become Psyched Up at the same time, there's an opportunity to have those characters team up to attack or cast identical spells. For a list of spells Psyched Up characters may cast simultaneously, take a look at the Magic Tomes chapter of this guide.

Psyched Up characters don't always attack or use spells simultaneously. If it's to your benefit, the game sometimes decides to keep characters attacking individually.

The following table shows how certain actions or status changes affect a character's Psyched Up level. When a character accumulates 100 points (it's possible to accumulate more than 100, but only 100 are necessary to enter the state), he or she is considered Psyched Up for that round of combat. The lowest a character's Psyched Up value can become is -100. When that happens, that character's Strength, Intellect, and Spirit are reduced by 50%.

SITUATION	PSYCHED UP CHANGE
CHARACTER HAS LESS THAN 4 AP	+15
CHARACTER TAKES DAMAGE	-10
AN ALLY IS KO'D	+50
ALLY KO'D, 1 CHARACTER LEFT IN PARTY	+20
AN ENEMY UNDERGOES A STATUS CHANGE	+10
BATTLE ENDS	X 0.8
A CHARACTER BOOSTS	+30
A CHARACTER USES AN ABILITY	+20
PERFORMING AN ACTION OTHER THAN BOOST WHEN PSYCHED UP	RESETS TO 0
ATTACK ENEMY'S WEAKNESS	+25
KILL ENEMY	+40
ENEMY EVADES YOUR ATTACK	-15
AVOID ENEMY'S ATTACK	+10

Elemental Factors

Proper application of the six elements (Air, Dark, Earth, Fire, Light, Water) is a vital part of combat in *Final Fantasy: The 4 Heroes of Light*. Hit an enemy with the correct element and the damage you inflict is magnified by an impressive amount. Protect your characters from an enemy's favored element and watch its attacks restore the health of your party.

WEAKNESSES

If an enemy has a weakness to a certain element, you can exploit it for extra damage if you hit it with that element. Stack Physical Attacks with a weapon that is boosted with an element or a gauntlet with the same element, or apply Aura. For spells, most are considered Level 1, but a handful are Level 2 and inflict greater damage.

LEVEL	HOW ACHIEVED	RESULT
LV. 1	DO ANY ONE OF THE FOLLOWING: EQUIP WEAPON OR GAUNTLET, OR APPLY AURA	1.25 DAMAGE
LV. 2	EQUIP EITHER WEAPON OR GAUNTLET, AND APPLY AURA	1.5 DAMAGE
LV. 3	EQUIP BOTH WEAPON AND GAUNTLET, AND APPLY AURA	INSTANT KILL

Works for Enemies, Too

For details on enemies' elemental weaknesses or resistances, flip to the Enemy Data chapter of this guide.

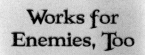

RESISTANCES

If an enemy uses a spell or attack with an elemental attribute, you can reduce damage.

LEVEL	HOW ACHIEVED	RESULT
LV. 1	ANY ONE OF: WEAR ELEMENTALIST CROWN, EQUIP PROPER SHIELD, EQUIP PROPER CAPE, APPLY MYSTERIO	RESIST MOST DAMAGE (HALF DAMAGE FOR ELEMENTALIST)
LV. 2	ANY TWO OF: WEAR ELEMENTALIST CROWN, EQUIP PROPER SHIELD, EQUIP PROPER CAPE, APPLY MYSTERIO	TAKE NO DAMAGE
LV. 3	ANY THREE OF: WEAR ELEMENTALIST CROWN, EQUIP PROPER SHIELD, EQUIP PROPER CAPE, APPLY MYSTERIO	ABSORB DAMAGE (HEALS CHARACTER)
LV. 4	WEAR ELEMENTALIST CROWN, EQUIP PROPER SHIELD, EQUIP PROPER CAPE, APPLY MYSTERIO	REFLECTS SPELL

Negative Status Effects

The following negative status effects can be applied by enemies to party members, or by Dark Magic spells to enemies. All negative status effects, except for Death, can be removed with a Remedy, the White Magic spell Esuna, and the items listed in the last column in the table. To restore a character from the Death status, use the White Magic spells Raise or Arise, or a Phoenix Down.

At the end of a battle, the following negative status effects immediately fade: Blindness, Confusion, Curse, Paralyzed, Silenced, and Sleep.

Ignore It and It May Go Away

There's a chance during each round of combat that some negative status effects will dissipate on their own. The following table applies to Poison, Paralyzed, Silenced, Sleep, Blindness, Cursed, or Confused.

FIRST ROUND	0%
SECOND ROUND	25%
THIRD ROUND	50%
FOURTH ROUND	75%
FIFTH ROUND	100%

STATUS		DESCRIPTION	DARK MAGIC SPELL	REMOVED WITH
BLINDNESS		REDUCES HIT RATE BY 50%.	FLASH	EYE DROPS, ELIXIR
CURSED		CROWN ABILITES UNAVAILABLE.	CURSE	CROSS
CONFUSED		UNABLE TO CONTROL CHARACTER, CHARACTER WILL ACT RANDOMLY.	CONFUSE	TAKING DAMAGE, TRANQULIZER, ELIXIR
DEAD		CHARACTER'S HP REACHES 0.	DEATH	PHOENIX DOWN
PARALYZED		50% CHANCE OF BEING INCAPACITATED PER TURN.	—	ANIMATE TONIC, ELIXIR
PETRIFIED		INCAPACITATED. IF ENTIRE PARTY BECOMES PETRIFIED, IT IS CONSIDERED THE SAME AS ALL CHARACTERS DYING.	BREAK	GOLD NEEDLE, ELIXIR
POISONED		LOSE 3% OF MAX HP EACH ROUND OF COMBAT, OR 3 HP PER STEP ON THE WORLD MAP	POISON	ANTIDOTE, ELIXIR
SILENCED		MAGIC SPELLS UNAVAILABLE.	SILENCE	ECHO HERB, ELIXIR
SLEEP		INCAPACITATED, WILL RECEIVE DOUBLE DAMAGE.	SLEEP	ALARM CLOCK, ELIXIR

Other Status Effects

The following table shows other status effects, and what spells or abilities inflict the status. Most of these effects are beneficial, but read the description column for more information on each status effect.

Inner Animal

Early in the adventure, the party gains an item called the Transform Staff that changes characters into an animal form. Being changed to animal form has some positive effects, but the downside is that Strength, Intellect, and Spirit are all reduced to 70% of their original values, unless there's a Beastmaster included in the party.

STATUS	DESCRIPTION	SPELL/ABILITY
ATTACK UP	INCREASES ATTACK BY 50% FOR 4 TURNS	BERSERK
DEFENSE UP	INCREASES DEFENSE BY 50% FOR 4 TURNS	PROTECT
MAGIC ATTACK UP	INCREASES MAGIC ATTACK BY 50% FOR 4 TURNS	MAGICK
MAGIC DEFENSE UP	INCREASES MAGIC DEFENSE BY 50% FOR 4 TURNS	SHELL
EVASION UP	DOUBLES EVASION FOR 4 TURNS	INVISIBLE
REGEN	RECOVERS 10% OF MAXIMUM HP AT THE END OF EACH TURN	REGEN
REFLECT	REFLECTS ALL MAGIC SPELLS FOR 4 TURNS	MIRROR
LUX	INCREASES ATTACK, MAGIC ATTACK, AND MAGIC DEFENSE BY 50%; RESTORES 10% OF TOTAL HP AT THE END OF EACH TURN; AND BOOSTS HP BY 50% FOR THE DURATION OF BATTLE OR UNTIL THE CHARACTER DIES	LUX
AP UP	FOR 3 OR 4 TURNS, AP RECOVERY INCREASES BY 1	DANCE, PERFORM
STATUS UP	INCREASES STATUS LEVELS BY 10% FOR 4 TURNS	AURA
HASTE	ACT FASTER FOR 3 TURNS	MARCH
SLOW	ACT SLOWER FOR 3 TURNS	RESTRAIN (TARGETS ENEMIES)
STOP	INCAPACITATED FOR 1 TURN	FUGUE (TARGETS ENEMIES)
STATUS DOWN	DECREASES STATUS LEVELS BY 10% FOR 4 TURNS	SUPPRESS (TARGETS ENEMIES)
INSTANT DEATH	KILLS ENEMY INSTANTLY	DEATH, SMASHING BLOW (BOTH TARGET ENEMIES)

Calculating Damage Done

The damage done by physical attacks, magic attacks (including healing), and items are calculated with different formulae. Additionally, the game performs other calculations that relate to damage: Items have a hit rate, physical attacks have a hit rate (attacks that miss inflict no damage, after all) and a critical rate (which increases damage), and magic attacks have a resist rate (which potentially reduces damage).

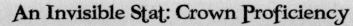

An Invisible Stat: Crown Proficiency

There is a hidden stat tied to characters using the same Crown for extended periods of time. For every 50 battles won while wearing a Crown, the character's skill level with that Crown increases by 1, up to a maximum of level 99. Each increase in level boosts that character's damage and healing output while wearing that Crown. Crown Proficiency is a subtle aspect of the adventure, so if you choose to ignore it, it should not negatively impact your game experience.

PHYSICAL ATTACKS

When a character Attacks, or chooses an ability that inflicts physical damage, use the following formulae to determine hit rate, critical rate, and damage done. To increase physical damage, use equipment that boosts the character's Strength and Attack Power. If an enemy has an elemental weakness, use a weapon that deals that type of damage if it's possible.

HIT RATE = (character's Strength + weapon Accuracy) – (target's level + target's evasion) x Attack Proficiency[1] x (100 ÷ Ability Accuracy) %

DAMAGE DONE = (character's Strength x attack + Crown Proficiency) ÷ target defense x Elemental Factor x Critical Factor x Attack Proficiency[1] x Diminished Effect

CRITICAL RATE = (character's level – target level + 10)%

Normally, Critical Rate is capped at 20%, but the Fighter ability Combat pushes the limit to 50%. If a character scores a critical hit, the attack automatically hits the target. The Critical Factor in the Damage Done formula (which is normally 1) is set to 2.

MAGIC SPELLS

To get the most out of Magic Spells, equip items with high Magic Attack power, then focus on Intellect (for damage) or Spirit (for healing).

DAMAGE DONE = character's Intelligence + (equipment's Magic Attack + Magic/Ability's Magic Attack value) + Crown Proficiency ÷ target Magic Defense x Elemental Factor x Magic Proficiency[1] x Diminished Effect

HEALING DONE = (equipment's Magic Attack + Magic/Ability's Magic Attack value + character's Spirit + Crown Proficiency x Magic Proficiency[1] x Diminished Effect

Magic attacks do not miss, but instead are tested against a resist rate, which potentially reduces the damage taken by half. Note that this does not apply to White Magic spells.

RESIST RATE = (target's Level + Magic Evade) – (character's Level + Equipment's Magic Accuracy) + 100 x Attack Proficiency[1] + (100 –Ability Accuracy)%

[1] For more information about Attack/Magic Proficiency, turn to the Crowns section of this guide

DIMINISHED EFFECT FOR MULTIPLE TARGETS

Some spells hit multiple targets and their overall effect is spread amongst all affected parties. This applies equally to Black Magic and White Magic.

Check the Spell Tomes section of this guide to see which spells are affected by Diminished Effect. The multipliers for hitting a certain number of targets is shown in the following table.

TARGETS	MULTIPLIER
1	1
2	0.7
3	0.6
4	0.5

Determining Experience Points Earned

As you progress deeper into the adventure, enemies stop having fixed level values, and scale to present a challenge to your party regardless of what level they achieve. There's a great deal more information on that in the Enemy Data section of the guide, but it's worth mentioning here since it applies to acquiring Experience Points during battle.

Enemies with fixed levels provide a fixed amount of experience. For the enemies that have variable levels, the amount of experience is calculated with the following formula:

Experience Points Earned = [(average level of characters in party – defeated monster's level) x 3] + base experience points

It's important to note that you never earn less than the base experience point value for defeating enemies! If the first half of the equation results in a negative number, the game changes that value to zero.

Auto-Mode Combat

When selecting your characters' actions, you have the option to press the X button and enter Auto-Mode for combat. Any commands entered for characters are wiped out, and you're returned to the ability menu for the first character in line.

After you select an action for each character, the game takes over and continues to execute that action each round of combat. If a character has insufficient AP to perform the selected action, he or she defaults to Boost. Auto-Mode continues to work in this fashion for every encounter until you cancel it by pressing the X button again. Auto-Mode is great for areas where you're easily defeating enemies, but you should keep control of your characters when enemies are closer to the level of your group.

After Battles

At the conclusion of each battle, the scene shifts to a loot screen. The loot screen shows the items and gems obtained upon defeating the monsters in battle. Items must be distributed to characters who have free inventory spots (displayed on the top half of the lower screen), and selecting Distribute accomplishes this automatically. Any items remaining in the Items row when you select OK are discarded.

The lower row shows the gems obtained after the battle. You don't need to worry about distributing these gems. It doesn't matter who's in the party; all gems go into the same communal storage system accessible by all characters. Your party can hold up to 99 copies of each type of gem in that communal storage system.

Characters are awarded experience points at this time as well. When characters level up, they hold a quick celebration in the top screen and may gain additional Strength, Intellect, Spirit, or HP.

Between Battles

Some recovery items and Magic Tomes can be used outside of battle to restore health or remove negative status effects from characters. To use an item or a Magic Tome, go into the inventory screen, select the item or Magic Tome, then apply it to the character in need. Applying a restorative item doesn't consume any AP, but using a Magic Tome does.

The downtime between battles is also a good time to reassign items that characters have in their inventories, especially with a Bandit in the party. Bandits have a tendency to fill up their inventories in a hurry, and most of their special abilities require some inventory space to work. As a rule of thumb, try to keep at least one Phoenix Down in each character's inventory, although it's less important for characters who have a Raise Tome.

EXPLORING TOWNS

The many towns around the world are safe havens that offer Inns, Item shops, and other helpful locations such as Storage Shops. In addition, the people and animals around town offer you glimpses into current events, or hints about your next destination. Each town has something different to offer, so each time you discover one, explore everywhere, speak with everyone, and see what is for sale at the shops.

Types of Shops

BUILDING SIGN	BUILDING TYPE	DESCRIPTION
	ITEM	ITEM SHOPS MAINLY SELL RECOVERY ITEMS, BUT IN SOME LOCATIONS THE ITEM SHOP BECOMES A ONE-STOP SHOP FOR ALL YOUR ADVENTURING NEEDS
	ARMOR	ARMOR SHOPS SELL ARMOR AND SHIELDS
	WEAPON	WEAPON SHOPS CARRY ONLY WEAPONS
	ACCESSORY	ACCESSORY SHOPS DEAL ONLY IN ACCESSORIES, BUT CARRY MULTIPLE TYPES (CAPES, RINGS, ETC.)
	MAGIC	BLACK, DARK, OR WHITE MAGIC, THIS SHOP CARRIES THEM ALL
	STORAGE SHOP	STORAGE SHOPS ACT AS A STORAGE SYSTEM. EACH STORAGE SHOP IS LINKED TO ALL OTHERS. REGARDLESS OF THE TOWN IN WHICH YOU MADE A DEPOSIT, YOU CAN WITHDRAW THAT ITEM FROM ANY OTHER STORAGE SHOP IN THE WORLD.
	UPGRADE SHOP	UNIQUE TO THE TOWN OF URBETH, THIS SHOP USES GEMS TO IMPROVE YOUR EQUIPMENT
	MULTIPLAYER	THE VENDOR IN THIS TYPE OF BUILDING INITIATES MULTIPLAYER SESSIONS AND EXCHANGES MULTIPLAYER POINTS FOR VARIOUS ITEMS
	INN	SPEND A NIGHT AT THE INNS AROUND THE WORLD TO RESTORE EVERYONE'S HP AND AP

Multiplayer Points

Even if you play through *Final Fantasy: The 4 Heroes of Light* alone, you still earn Multiplayer Points that are spent in the Multiplayer Shop. Spending time playing Multiplayer with friends earns points faster.

On your own, winning a random battle is worth 5 points. Defeating a boss rewards you with 30 points. While playing with others, you get bonus points based on the following formula:

Points = Communication Time (in seconds) ÷ 10 x # of people playing together

For example, playing for one hour with four people results in a total of 1440 points ([3600 ÷ 10] x 4). You also get a bonus of 305 points when you defeat a boss in a Multiplayer group.

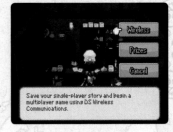

Save your single-player story and begin a multiplayer game using DS Wireless Communications.

Multiplayer Points allow you access to powerful weapons earlier in the game than what you may be used to and they're required to unlock one Crown. Additionally, some items are unique to the Multiplayer Shop, which comes into play if you're looking to unlock all the load screen images.

Unlocking the Load Screen Images

The first screen you see after starting a new game or loading your game save slowly fills with pictures of people and places. There are 23 total images to unlock. Sixteen of them are unlocked as you complete more of the adventure. The final seven, however, require a great deal of effort. If you're interested in acquiring all these images, check out the Extras section now!

CHARACTERS

Aire, Brandt, Jusqua, and Yunita are the constants in the adventure. At least one of these characters is in your party at all times.

 ## BRANDT

STATS BY LEVEL

LV	HP	STRENGTH	INTELLECT	SPIRIT
1	30	3	2	2
10	51	9	7	8
20	81	16	12	14
30	117	23	18	21
40	160	30	23	27
50	210	36	28	34
60	266	43	34	40
70	329	50	39	46
80	399	57	45	53
90	475	64	50	59
99	549	70	55	65

Brandt is your party's robust strongman. He sports the highest Strength and HP values of the group, making him an excellent choice for Crowns that deal damage with physical attacks, such as Ninja and Fighter. He's the worst choice for dealing damage with magic (don't make him a Black Mage!), but functions reasonably well when assigned to healing.

 ## JUSQUA

STATS BY LEVEL

LV	HP	STRENGTH	INTELLECT	SPIRIT
5	35	5	5	5
10	47	8	8	8
20	77	14	14	14
30	113	21	21	21
40	156	27	27	27
50	206	34	34	34
60	262	40	40	40
70	325	46	46	46
80	395	53	53	53
90	471	59	59	59
99	545	65	65	65

Jusqua's base stats remain equal to each other during the entire adventure, making him decent at everything. Unfortunately, it also means he doesn't stand out in any role, so proper gear selection is important in getting the most out of Jusqua in his designated role.

YUNITA

STATS BY LEVEL

LV	HP	STRENGTH	INTELLECT	SPIRIT
8	39	6	6	8
10	44	8	8	9
20	72	14	14	16
30	107	21	21	23
40	147	27	27	30
50	193	34	34	36
60	245	40	40	43
70	303	46	46	50
80	367	53	53	57
90	437	59	59	64
99	504	65	65	70

Yunita's Spirit is top-notch, making her the primary choice for healing duty. Her Strength and Intellect remain equal through all levels, so she's capable of filling any role provided she is decked out in the proper gear.

AIRE

STATS BY LEVEL

LV	HP	STRENGTH	INTELLECT	SPIRIT
5	30	3	4	4
10	42	6	7	7
20	70	11	14	13
30	103	17	21	20
40	142	22	28	26
50	187	28	36	33
60	237	34	43	40
70	293	39	50	46
80	355	45	57	53
90	422	50	64	59
99	486	55	70	65

With high Intellect, Aire's role quickly becomes clear. Load her up with damage-dealing spells and let her run roughshod in enemy encounters. In areas with magic-resistant enemies, fill her ability slots with healing spells, because her Strength score is the lowest of the group and her Spirit is fairly good.

TEMPORARY ALLIES

During the adventure, the following characters temporarily join your party. You aren't able to change their Crowns, and they each possess only a single ability. In addition, any items in their inventories when they leave the party are lost to you.

Krinjh

STATS UPON JOINING THE PARTY

LEVEL	12
HP	63
STRENGTH	12
INTELLECT	11
SPIRIT	11

Krinjh is an enigmatic young man who joins the party in the desert. Krinjh has the Spell Fencer ability Magic Sword at his disposal, and a few Black Magic spells.

EQUIPMENT KRINJH'S SWORD (ATTACK +4, MAGIC ATTACK +2), WOOD SHIELD, KRINJH'S ROBE (DEFENSE +3, MAGIC DEFENSE +4)

Torte

STATS UPON JOINING THE PARTY

LEVEL	15
HP	57
STRENGTH	4
INTELLECT	11
SPIRIT	13

Torte's animalistic appearance disguises his true nature. Regardless of his form, Torte is a powerful Sage with the Spell Again ability that he can use with either the healing (Cure and Cura) spells or damage (Blizzard and Blizzara) spells at his disposal.

EQUIPMENT TORTE'S CLOTHES (DEFENSE +4, MAGIC DEFENSE +3), SACRED TREE STAFF (ATTACK +2, MAGIC ATTACK +2), CURE TOME, CURA TOME, BLIZZARD TOME, BLIZZARA TOME.

Rekoteh

STATS UPON JOINING THE PARTY

LEVEL	18
HP	30
STRENGTH	16
INTELLECT	13
SPIRIT	19

Rekoteh hails from the frigid land of Invidia and assists Jusqua in a time of need. Rekoteh has the Dancer ability, Dance, along with a handful of White Magic spells.

EQUIPMENT REKOTEH'S CLOTHES (DEFENSE +6, MAGIC DEFENSE +4), SHARK LANCE (ATTACK +6 (WATER))

Rolan

STATS UPON JOINING THE PARTY

LEVEL	20
HP	93
STRENGTH	18
INTELLECT	16
SPIRIT	19

Rolan is a conflicted man, struggling with his role as a hero to his people, who joins with the party briefly. He uses the Hero ability Reckless, along with a Cure Tome and a Thundara Tome, to help the party through a rough patch of the adventure.

EQUIPMENT WOOD SHIELD, ROLAN'S CLOTHES (DEFENSE +8, MAGIC DEFENSE +7), SHINING BLADE (ATTACK +7 (LIGHT))

CROWNS

The Crown system of *The 4 Heroes of Light* allows each character access to a set of abilities that you can expand through the use of gems. Each Crown, with one exception, imparts one passive ability and one default ability. The default ability—and subsequent abilities—must be assigned a spot in the character's Abilities menu in order to be used in combat.

Increasing Crown Levels

Every character has access to the base version of each Crown (and the ability that goes with it) as soon as you meet the conditions to unlock it. Most Crowns are made available through the course of the adventure, but some are unlocked in other ways.

To boost a Crown to Level 1, you must place two sets of five gems into the proper slots. The gems used for each Crown are predetermined, and could be any type of gem, save Amethyst and Diamond.

To boost a Crown to Level 2, you must place exactly one Amethyst and 14 other gems (each Crown has specific gem requirements), save Diamonds. To unlock Level 3 requires exactly two Amethyst, one Diamond and 17 other gems determined by the individual Crowns.

For each additional Crown level unlocked, the character whose Crown was upgraded gets access to a new ability. It's important to remember that increasing a Crown's level applies to one character only! The one exception to this rule is the Storyteller Crown, which is a special case that's discussed in greater depth in its own section.

Individual Crowns

The following pages break down each of the 28 Crowns available for the adventure. The information includes everything you need to know about the Crowns.

Weapon Proficiencies and Magic Use are used in calculating Hit Rate and Damage Done (in the formulae shown in the Game Basics, they are lumped together as 'Attack Proficiency.') **A** means most proficient, **C** means least proficient.

WEAPON PROFICIENCIES

✏	SHORT SWORD	A
🗡	SWORD	A
🏹	BOW	B
🔨	STAFF	C
🗡	SPEAR	C
🪓	AXE	C
📕	BOOK	C
🎼	HARP	C

Each star represents the number of times a Crown must be upgraded to gain the use of the listed ability.

⭐⭐⭐ **MIRACLE:** **GIVE YOUR ALLIES A BIG HP BOOST AND CURE ALL THEIR AILMENTS.**

ACTION POINTS	5
ABILITY SPEED	5
TARGET	ALL ALLIES
TARGET VALUE	20 (100)

🔵	3	🔻	7
⬜	7	🌙	–
🟦	–	🌚	2
⬡	–	💎	1

For more information about Action Points, Ability Speed, and Target Value, check out the Game Basics.

This table shows the number and types of gems needed to upgrade the Crown to improve it to a given level.

FREELANCER

At the start of the game, you're forced to play everyone as a Free-lancer (it's the only crown available until you defeat the boss in the Witch's Mansion). The Freelancer crown cannot be upgraded, so the only benefit to bringing one along only comes into play if your party is wiped out.

CROWN OBTAINED	AVAILABLE FROM THE START
SPECIAL ABILITY	KEEP ALL YOUR GEMS WHEN YOUR PARTY DIES!

STATISTICAL MODIFIERS

HP	1.0
STRENGTH	1.0
INTELLECT	1.0
SPIRIT	1.0

WEAPON PROFICIENCIES

✏	SHORT SWORD	C
🗡	SWORD	C
🏹	BOW	C
🔨	STAFF	C
🗡	SPEAR	C
🪓	AXE	C
📕	BOOK	C
🎼	HARP	C

DEFENSIVE ABILITY

EVADE	C
MAGIC EVADE	C

MAGIC USE

OFFENSIVE MAGIC	C
RECOVERY MAGIC	C

PASSIVE ABILITY

If your entire party is rendered either dead or petrified, you must sacrifice half of your stockpile of a certain type of gem in order to continue the game without resorting to shutting down the game and starting from your last save point. With a Freelancer in the party, there's no real penalty for dying, other than lost time.

 WAYFARER

CROWN OBTAINED	DEFEAT GREAPS IN WITCH'S MANSION
SPECIAL ABILITY	RECOVERY ITEMS WORK BETTER!

Wayfarers represent a nice upgrade over Freelancers in almost every way. Their stats (save HP) are all better, and they have greater skill with every type of weapon, although they remain poor spellcasters.

STATISTICAL MODIFIERS

HP	1.0
STRENGTH	1.2
INTELLECT	1.2
SPIRIT	1.2

WEAPON PROFICIENCIES

	SHORT SWORD	B
	SWORD	B
	BOW	B
	STAFF	B
	SPEAR	B
	AXE	B
	BOOK	B
	HARP	B

MAGIC USE

EVADE	B
MAGIC EVADE	C

DEFENSIVE ABILITY

OFFENSIVE MAGIC	C
RECOVERY MAGIC	C

CROWN ARMOR: Traveler's Garb (Strength/Intellect/Spirit +5%)

Best attack/weapon type	None

PASSIVE ABILITY

When a Wayfarer uses a Potion, Hi-Potion, X-Potion, or Remedy, it restores twice as much health as any other character who administers a similar recovery item. This ability also applies to Ether use, restoring twice as much AP as normal.

RUNAWAY: RUN AND LIVE TO FIGHT ANOTHER DAY.

ACTION POINTS	1
ABILITY SPEED	150
TARGET	N/A
TARGET VALUE	5 (10)

If the fight doesn't look winnable, don't be afraid to leave it through the use of Runaway. Unfortunately, Runaway isn't a guaranteed escape, and works about 50% of the time (the formula is [50 + character level - average enemy level]). Once you learn Escape, you can safely skip Runaway in your active ability slots.

⭐ ESCAPE: ESCAPE THE BATTLE SO YOU CAN CONTINUE THE ADVENTURE—GUARANTEED!

ACTION POINTS	2
ABILITY SPEED	200
TARGET	N/A
TARGET VALUE	5 (10)

○	5	▽	—
▢	5	◖	—
▯	—	☾	—
◇	—	◈	—

Just as the name implies, you can escape most battles (the exceptions are boss fights). Escape comes in handy if you get in over your head, or if your party barely survived a battle and you wander into another encounter before you can restore everyone's health and Action Points. There's nothing to lose in running from a fight, so don't hesitate to get out of there!

⭐⭐ RECOVERY: RECOVER SOME HP EACH TURN.

ACTION POINTS	3
ABILITY SPEED	15
TARGET	SELF
TARGET VALUE	5 (10)

○	6	▽	—
▢	—	◖	6
▯	2	☾	1
◇	—	◈	—

Recovery restores 30% of the character's maximum HP at the end of each turn. The effect lasts the entire battle, or until the character dies. This effect stacks with Regen or Lux.

⭐⭐⭐ FRIEND IN NEED: SUMMON YOUR TRAVEL COMPANION TO ATTACK THE FOE.

ACTION POINTS	4
ABILITY SPEED	5
TARGET	ONE ENEMY, FRONT
TARGET VALUE	5 (100)

○	7	▽	3
▢	—	◖	—
▯	—	☾	2
◇	7	◈	1

Friend in Need's attack power is equal to the character's attack power plus twice the character's level. There's an additional multiplier factored into the final damage amount, making Friend in Need an incredibly powerful physical attack.

AVOIDING BATTLE

If you're ever in a situation where you don't want to deal with random battles (for example, you just completed a tough battle and everyone's HP and AP are essentially exhausted) put two Wayfarers with level 1 Crowns in the party. If you are caught in a random encounter, simply set everyone to Boost, except for one of the Wayfarers, who should use Escape.

If you stumble into another unwanted encounter, do the same thing, but have the second Wayfarer use escape. So long as you alternate who uses Escape, everyone should be able to rebuild their AP over time.

WHITE MAGE

CROWN OBTAINED	DEFEAT SAND DEVIL IN QUICKSAND CASTLE
SPECIAL ABILITY	AP COST FOR WHITE MAGIC REDUCED BY ONE!

White Mage is the best healing job in the game. Their ability to use recovery magic is unmatched, and their Spirit (the stat that contributes to healing) bonus is the best. While White Mages deal passable damage with offensive magic, their greatest contribution to killing enemies is boosting allies with abilities like Magic and Berserk.

CROWN ARMOR: White Robe (Spirit +20%)

Best attack/weapon type	Staff

STATISTICAL MODIFIERS

HP	1.0
STRENGTH	0.7
INTELLECT	1.3
SPIRIT	1.6

WEAPON PROFICIENCIES

	SHORT SWORD	C
	SWORD	C
	BOW	C
	STAFF	B
	SPEAR	C
	AXE	C
	BOOK	C
	HARP	C

MAGIC USE

OFFENSIVE MAGIC	B
RECOVERY MAGIC	A

DEFENSIVE ABILITY

EVADE	C
MAGIC EVADE	A

PASSIVE ABILITY

The lowered AP cost for White Magic allows White Mages to use better restorative spells more often. This means more heals and more buffs for your party in fewer rounds.

HEALTHGIVER: MAKE YOUR NEXT HEALING SPELL WORK ON ALL YOUR ALLIES.

ACTION POINTS	1
ABILITY SPEED	10
TARGET	SELF
TARGET VALUE	5 (10)

Healthgiver works in conjunction with spells that restore HP, including Raise and Arise, but not Regen. It's great to have an ability that can turn the tide in a battle on the verge of being lost!

⭐ LIFEGIVER: MAKE YOUR NEXT HEALING SPELL MORE POWERFUL AND WORK ON ALL YOUR ALLIES.

ACTION POINTS	2	⚪ –	🔻	5
ABILITY SPEED	10	⬜ –	🌓	5
TARGET	SELF	▯ –	🌙	–
TARGET VALUE	5 (10)	🔶 –	💎	–

Lifegiver is an improved version of Healthgiver that's a nice boost to any spell that restores HP. Anytime this isn't active on your White Mage, and no one is in immediate need of healing, you should spend that round's action to activate either Lifegiver or Healthgiver.

⭐⭐ HIDE: HIDE FROM THE FOES SO THEY WILL NOT ATTACK YOU.

ACTION POINTS	2	⚪ –	🔻	6
ABILITY SPEED	100	⬜ –	🌓	–
TARGET	SELF	▯ 2	🌙	1
TARGET VALUE	0 (0)	🔶 6	💎	–

Since the White Mage's job is to keep everyone else in fighting shape, it's sound strategy to avoid being the target of monsters. Hide sets the character's Target Values to 0, but doesn't grant invulnerability to attacks that hit the entire group.

⭐⭐⭐ MIRACLE: GIVE YOUR ALLIES A BIG HP BOOST AND CURE ALL THEIR AILMENTS.

ACTION POINTS	5	⚪ 3	🔻	7
ABILITY SPEED	5	⬜ 7	🌓	–
TARGET	ALL ALLIES	▯ –	🌙	2
TARGET VALUE	20 (100)	🔶 –	💎	1

Don't use Miracle too early. It's nice that everyone else is fully healed and has their negative status effects removed, but after performing Miracle, your White Mage will almost certainly need a few rounds of combat to build up additional Action Points. That's a big problem if the enemy follows up with lethal attacks that drop some characters; you may have no way to restore them immediately!

WHITE MAGIC SPELLS NOT FOR WHITE MAGES?

When it comes to the White Magic spells that boost a character's status, the White Mage is not the best choice for many of the Magic Tomes. The first target for these spells is typically the character who casts it, meaning a White Mage would need to use a spell like Berserk twice before you have a chance to buff a Fighter or Ninja.

Stock up the White Mage with Cure-type spells, Raise, and Arise, and use Hide until it's time to pop up and restore someone's HP.

BLACK MAGE

CROWN OBTAINED	DEFEAT SAND DEVIL IN QUICKSAND CASTLE
SPECIAL ABILITY	AP COST FOR BLACK MAGIC REDUCED BY ONE!

Black Mages are deadly at dealing damage, and no character exploits elemental weaknesses in enemies like a Black Mage. Their ability to inflict damage with offensive magic is matched only by Sages, but Sages lack the Black Mages' abilities that boost elemental damage capabilities. Mirror is an effective defensive tool in fights against powerful enemies who rely on inflicting damage with spells.

CROWN ARMOR: *Black Robe (Intellect/Magic Attack Power +10%)*

	Best attack/weapon type	Black Magic

PASSIVE ABILITY

The Action Point saved each time a Black Mage uses a Black Magic spell makes it possible to cast higher-damage spells more often.

STATISTICAL MODIFIERS

HP	1.0
STRENGTH	0.8
INTELLECT	1.6
SPIRIT	1.2

WEAPON PROFICIENCIES

SHORT SWORD	C
SWORD	C
BOW	C
STAFF	B
SPEAR	C
AXE	C
BOOK	C
HARP	C

MAGIC USE

OFFENSIVE MAGIC	A
RECOVERY MAGIC	B

DEFENSIVE ABILITY

EVADE	C
MAGIC EVADE	A

MAGIC MOJO: MAKE YOUR NEXT ATTACK SPELL INFLICT MORE DAMAGE THAN USUAL.

ACTION POINTS	1
ABILITY SPEED	15
TARGET	SELF
TARGET VALUE	5 (10)

The good news is that Magic Mojo doubles the damage inflicted with element-based spells. The bad news is that you can apply it only once. Any attempts to double up on Magic Mojo result in a miss.

⭐ SPELL FOCUS: MAKE YOUR NEXT ATTACK SPELL INFLICT A LOT MORE DAMAGE THAN USUAL.

ACTION POINTS	2
ABILITY SPEED	15
TARGET	SELF
TARGET VALUE	5 (10)

●	—	▽	—
▢	—	◖	—
▯	5	☾	—
◈	5	✦	—

Spell Focus is twice as effective as Magic Mojo, quadrupling damage done with element-based spells. Unfortunately, it also shares Magic Mojo's inability to double up on itself.

⭐⭐ MIRROR: ENABLE YOUR ENTIRE PARTY TO DEFLECT SPELLS BACK AT THE ENEMY.

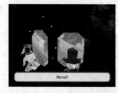

ACTION POINTS	3
ABILITY SPEED	15
TARGET	ALL ALLIES
TARGET VALUE	10 (20)

●	2	▽	—
▢	6	◖	—
▯	6	☾	1
◈		✦	

Mirror reflects all spells (Black, Dark, and White) for three turns. It doesn't matter if the spells are designed to harm or heal. Any spells designed to hit entire party are reflected to only one target. The damage done (or healing received) from a reflected spell is half as effective as it would be normally.

⭐⭐⭐ MAGIC MIGHT: CAST A MIGHTY ATTACK SPELL AGAINST ALL YOUR FOES.

ACTION POINTS	4
ABILITY SPEED	5
TARGET	ALL ENEMIES
TARGET VALUE	10 (100)

●	—	▽	3
▢	—	◖	7
▯	7	☾	2
◈	—	✦	1

Magic Might is an impressive spell that does non-elemental damage (meaning no boosting its effect with Magic Mojo or Spell Focus). Its Magic Attack strength is 170, and the damage it deals receives a 1.5 multiplier boost.

THE BIG BOOST

While you can't build up multiple charges of either Magic Mojo or Spell Focus, you can combine their effects! Use one turn to activate Magic Mojo, then the next for Spell Focus. Your next element-based spell will be eight times as effective! Note that not all damage spells inflict elemental damage, so watch the combat messages to see if the effects of Spell Focus and Magic Mojo wear off before you waste a few turns reapplying them.

 BANDIT

CROWN OBTAINED	OBTAIN LILIBELLE'S WINGS IN THE ANIMAL BURROW
SPECIAL ABILITY	MONSTERS DROP BETTER ITEMS!

Bandits provide solid physical damage output in battle, and possess special abilities that keep your inventory stocked up with items. Not only does having a Bandit in the party encourage enemies to drop better items, but Bandits also have multiple abilities designed to take extra items during battle.

CROWN ARMOR: Bandit Gear (Accuracy +20%)

	Best attack/weapon type	Short Sword / Sword

STATISTICAL MODIFIERS

HP	1.3
STRENGTH	1.3
INTELLECT	1.2
SPIRIT	1.1

WEAPON PROFICIENCIES

	SHORT SWORD	A
	SWORD	A
	BOW	B
	STAFF	C
	SPEAR	C
	AXE	C
	BOOK	C
	HARP	C

MAGIC USE

OFFENSIVE MAGIC	C
RECOVERY MAGIC	C

DEFENSIVE ABILITY

EVADE	B
MAGIC EVADE	C

PASSIVE ABILITY

Defeated enemies have a chance to drop up to four items at the conclusion of a battle. In the enemy listing in the back of the guide, these items are listed with the percent chance the enemy drops them. The following table shows the additional chance an enemy will drop an item in each slot with a Bandit in the party (there's no benefit in having multiple Bandits in the party):

SLOT 1	SLOT 2	SLOT 3	SLOT 4
0%	+15%	+10%	+5%

STEAL: TRY TO STEAL AN ITEM FROM ONE OF THE FOES.

ACTION POINTS	1
ABILITY SPEED	10
TARGET	ONE ENEMY
TARGET VALUE	5 (10)

The enemy listing in the back of the guide lists up to three items that a given enemy type may have available for Steal attempts. While there are three potential items, a specific enemy carries only one item. If you successfully steal an item from an enemy, any further attempts to steal result in a miss.

☆ PLUNDER: TRY TO STEAL AN ITEM FROM ALL THE FOES.

ACTION POINTS	2
ABILITY SPEED	10
TARGET	ALL ENEMIES
TARGET VALUE	5 (10)

●	—	▽	—
☐	—	◁	—
▯	5	☾	—
◇	5	⊕	—

Plunder is a great way to stock up on items quickly if your reserves are low. Hand over unnecessary items to the characters who consume them (such as Seamstresses, Alchemists, and Salve-makers) or sell extra items to make gil.

☆☆ DEADLY BLOW: POSSIBLY INFLICT SUDDEN DEATH ON A FOE WHEN YOU ATTACK.

ACTION POINTS	3
ABILITY SPEED	5
TARGET	ONE ENEMY
TARGET VALUE	20 (5)

●	2	▽	—
☐	6	◁	—
▯	6	☾	1
◇	—	⊕	—

The chance Deadly Blow has to inflict an immediately lethal attack is equal to [40 + your characters level - target's level]. Even if the Deadly Blow fails to kill the target immediately, it still inflicts 1.5 times normal attack damage.

☆☆☆ PILLAGE: STEAL AN ITEM FROM A FOE - GUARANTEED.

ACTION POINTS	4
ABILITY SPEED	5
TARGET	ONE ENEMY
TARGET VALUE	10 (20)

●	—	▽	3
☐	—	◁	7
▯	7	☾	2
◇	—	⊕	1

Pillage is only a necessity for fights against bosses who are the only source of a rare item. (For example, the final bosses in the Extra Dungeons generally carry an item unavailable elsewhere in the game.) Outside of these encounters, you're better off using Steal or Pillage.

KEEP AN EYE ON INVENTORY

While you're having fun stealing and pillaging from enemies, remember to check your Bandit's inventory between battles. Pillage in particular can fill your inventory quickly, so either use or trade items to make room for future sticky-fingered endeavors.

 # BARD

CROWN OBTAINED	OBTAIN LILIBELLE'S WINGS IN THE ANIMAL BURROW
SPECIAL ABILITY	GET THE MOST OUT OF EQUIPPED INSTRUMENTS!

The Bard's life is a selfless one. Bards will never be your group's top damage dealers or healers, but they provide invaluable support to the entire party in the form of boosted Attack power, Defense, and status attributes.

CROWN ARMOR: *Poet Tunic (Intellect/Spirit +10%)*

 Best attack/weapon type	Harp

STATISTICAL MODIFIERS

HP	1.1
STRENGTH	1.0
INTELLECT	1.3
SPIRIT	1.3

WEAPON PROFICIENCIES

	SHORT SWORD	C
	SWORD	C
	BOW	C
	STAFF	C
	SPEAR	C
	AXE	C
	BOOK	C
	HARP	B

MAGIC USE

OFFENSIVE MAGIC	B
RECOVERY MAGIC	C

DEFENSIVE ABILITY

EVADE	C
MAGIC EVADE	C

PASSIVE ABILITY

With a Harp equipped, a Bard's Strength, Intellect, and Spirit are increased by 10%. HP is not affected.

DITTY: SING A SONG TO RAISE YOUR PARTY'S ATTACK POWER. LASTS 3 TURNS.

ACTION POINTS	2
ABILITY SPEED	100
TARGET	ALL ALLIES
TARGET VALUE	10 (10)

For three turns, the party's Attack and Magic Attack power are doubled. For many random encounters, an ability like Ditty doesn't often come into play. When you're set to encounter a boss, Ditty becomes an invaluable tool. Keep it active to shorten big fights as much as possible.

⭐ MOTET: SING A SONG TO RAISE YOUR PARTY'S DEFENSE. LASTS 3 TURNS.

ACTION POINTS	2
ABILITY SPEED	100
TARGET	ALL ALLIES
TARGET VALUE	10 (10)

⬤	–	▽	5
◼	–	◐	5
◗	–	☾	–
⬢	–	◈	–

For three turns, the entire party's Defense and Magic Defense are doubled. Motet, like Ditty, has greater value in battles against stronger enemies. Keep it active on your characters to boost their survivability.

⭐⭐ ARIA: SING A SONG TO RAISE YOUR PARTY'S STATUS ATTRIBUTES. LASTS 3 TURNS.

ACTION POINTS	2
ABILITY SPEED	100
TARGET	ALL ALLIES
TARGET VALUE	10 (10)

⬤	–	▽	6
◼	–	◐	–
◗	2	☾	1
⬢	6	◈	–

For three turns, the entire party's Strength, Intellect, and Spirit are increased by 50%. Keep in mind that Aria stacks with Lux, making it even more important to maintain Aria's effect on the party during boss fights.

⭐⭐⭐ FUGUE: SING A SAD SONG THAT STOPS YOUR FOES IN THEIR TRACKS. LASTS ONLY ONE TURN.

ACTION POINTS	4
ABILITY SPEED	5
TARGET	ALL ENEMIES
TARGET VALUE	10 (100)

⬤	3	▽	7
◼	7	◐	–
◗	–	☾	2
⬢	–	◈	1

Don't be overly concerned with Fugue's lack of speed. It doesn't take effect until the turn after it's executed. Here's the timeline for Fugue: On the turn when Fugue is executed, there is no immediate effect. During the following turn, all enemies are incapacitated and take no actions; this is an ideal turn for restoring HP and AP. On the second turn after Fugue was executed, enemy actions return to normal.

BARD ABILITY PRIORITY

The most important decision Bards face in every major encounter is the order in which to execute abilities. Generally speaking, it's best to start off with Motet since it's the ability designed to boost survivability. Ditty and Aria are designed to boost damage and healing output, but they're just icing on the cake. Motet helps keep everyone alive and in the fight; after all, boosting the party's abilities doesn't amount to much if they're taken out in the first few turns of a battle.

MERCHANT

CROWN OBTAINED	DEFEAT DEMON IN THE TOWN OF URBETH
SPECIAL ABILITY	FIND MORE GEMS!

Until you reach the point in the game where money no longer matters, Merchants exist to do one thing: get more gems for you to upgrade Crowns and equipment. After you stockpile a great deal of gil and you no longer have any use for it, Merchants become harder to kill and able to inflict a healthy amount of damage.

CROWN ARMOR: Merchant Tunic (Intellect/Spirit +10%)

Best attack/weapon type	None

STATISTICAL MODIFIERS

HP	1.3
STRENGTH	1.1
INTELLECT	1.3
SPIRIT	1.2

WEAPON PROFICIENCIES

SHORT SWORD	C
SWORD	C
BOW	C
STAFF	C
SPEAR	C
AXE	C
BOOK	C
HARP	C

MAGIC USE

OFFENSIVE MAGIC	C
RECOVERY MAGIC	C

DEFENSIVE ABILITY

EVADE	C
MAGIC EVADE	C

PASSIVE ABILITY

With a Merchant in the party, enemies are more likely to drop gems after battles. Since gems are used to upgrade Crowns, armor, weapons, and shields, Merchants are always in demand. Including additional Merchants to the party doesn't increase the likelihood of obtaining extra gems.

FINDER: FIND GEMS IN THE MIDST OF BATTLE.

ACTION POINTS	1
ABILITY SPEED	10
TARGET	ONE ENEMY
TARGET VALUE	2 (5)

Finder allows a Merchant to dig up a gem from the field of battle. There's only ever one gem to dig up per battle, regardless of the number of monsters facing the party. The success rate with Finder is (70 + character's level) ÷ 10.

⭐ KEEPER: FIND GEMS IN THE MIDST OF BATTLE MORE EFFECTIVELY THAN WITH FINDER... MAYBE

ACTION POINTS	2
ABILITY SPEED	10
TARGET	ONE ENEMY
TARGET VALUE	5 (10)

🔵	5	▽	—
⬜	5	◖	—
▯	—	☾	—
⬠	—	💎	—

Keeper works the same as Finder, and has the same restrictions (only one gem per battle, gems must be in the enemy's drop table). The success rate with Keeper is (90 + character's level) ÷ 10. There are some battles, particularly with bosses, where there are no gems to obtain through the use of Finder or Keeper.

⭐⭐ RANSOM: EACH TIME YOU ARE STRUCK BY AN ATTACK, PAY A RANSOM INSTEAD OF TAKING DAMAGE.

ACTION POINTS	3
ABILITY SPEED	100
TARGET	SELF
TARGET VALUE	7 (15)

🔵	6	▽	—
⬜	—	◖	6
▯	2	☾	1
⬠	—	💎	—

With Ransom active, any damage dealt to the Merchant depletes gil instead of HP. The exchange is 1 to 1, meaning that if the Merchant is hit for 100 damage, 100 gil is lost instead of 100 HP.

⭐⭐⭐ MONEY TALKS: INFLICT DAMAGE IN PROPORTION TO THE AMOUNT OF MONEY YOU OWN.

ACTION POINTS	4
ABILITY SPEED	5
TARGET	ONE ENEMY
TARGET VALUE	20 (100)

🔵	7	▽	3
⬜	—	◖	—
▯	—	☾	2
⬠	7	💎	1

When Money Talks is used, the Merchant spends 1000 gil to deal damage equal to 1 percent of your accumulated gil. For example, with 150,000 gil, Money Talks would deal 1500 damage.

WHEN MONEY NO LONGER MATTERS

When gil is no longer a concern because you have so much saved up, Merchants become much more valuable to the group during battles. Give a Merchant the tools to raise and heal allies, and equipment to avoid negative status effects. Ransom blocks damage, but does nothing to stave off being incapacitated! Using a Merchant in this way is extremely expensive, so don't try it until your bank account is overflowing.

SALVE-MAKER

CROWN OBTAINED	DEFEAT DEMON IN THE TOWN OF URBETH
SPECIAL ABILITY	USE ITEMS WITHOUT CONSUMING AP!

Think of Salve-makers as White Mages who happen to use items instead of spells for healing, and who can also use healing items to damage enemies. Don't expect much from Salve-makers damage-wise; their physical attacks suffer from a combination of low Strength and lackluster weapon skills, while their Offensive Magic ability is poor. Things perk up for Salve-makers as soon as you pick up your first Elixir, but that won't happen until late in the adventure.

STATISTICAL MODIFIERS

HP	1.2
STRENGTH	0.9
INTELLECT	1.3
SPIRIT	1.4

WEAPON PROFICIENCIES

SHORT SWORD	C
SWORD	C
BOW	C
STAFF	C
SPEAR	C
AXE	C
BOOK	C
HARP	C

MAGIC USE

OFFENSIVE MAGIC	C
RECOVERY MAGIC	C

DEFENSIVE ABILITY

EVADE	C
MAGIC EVADE	C

CROWN ARMOR: *Salve-maker Robe (Intellect +10%, Evasion/Magic Evasion +5%)*

Best attack/weapon type	None

PASSIVE ABILITY

Using an item in combat costs Salve-makers 0 AP. This trait allows them to build up AP while using recovery items to heal others in party.

DISPENSARY: DO NOT CONSUME RECOVERY ITEMS WHEN YOU USE THEM. LASTS 4 TURNS.

ACTION POINTS	1
ABILITY SPEED	10
TARGET	SELF
TARGET VALUE	10 (5)

Unless there's a dire emergency, always activate Dispensary before doing anything else as a Salve-maker. Dispensary allows you to keep re-using the same items, which is extremely beneficial with each character's limited inventory space. After picking up your first Remedy, it helps alleviate any inventory problems.

☆ HEALTHCARE: MAKE RECOVERY ITEMS WORK ON EVERYONE IN THE PARTY.

ACTION POINTS	2	●	–	▽	5
ABILITY SPEED	10	□	–	◖	5
TARGET	SELF	▯	–	☾	–
TARGET VALUE	10 (10)	◈	–	◇	–

Healthcare allows a Salve-maker to apply the benefit of a recovery item to the entire party at the same time. The effect works with the following items: Potion, Hi-Potion, X-Potion, Elixir, Phoenix Down, Remedy.

☆☆ POISON PILL: CHANGE RECOVERY ITEMS INTO POISON AND USE THEM TO INFLICT DAMAGE.

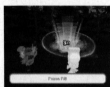

ACTION POINTS	3	●	–	▽	6
ABILITY SPEED	10	□	–	◖	–
TARGET	ONE ENEMY	▯	2	☾	1
TARGET VALUE	10 (20)	◈	6	◇	–

An active Bandit is a Salve-maker's best friend. Poison Pill is a good way to dispose of the extra healing items that are stolen by a Bandit. The following chart shows the items that can be used with Poison Pill, and the damage they inflict.

ITEM	DAMAGE
POTION	50
HI-POTION	80
REMEDY	100
X-POTION	160
ELIXIR	999

☆☆☆ LEVEL SERUM: RAISE THE PARTY'S LEVEL BY ONE FOR THE DURATION OF THE BATTLE.

ACTION POINTS	4	●	3	▽	7
ABILITY SPEED	5	□	7	◖	–
TARGET	ALL ALLIES	▯	–	☾	2
TARGET VALUE	10 (50)	◈	–	◇	1

Level Serum is a great ability at low levels because you can keep adding levels to the party, so long as the Salve-maker has enough AP. The downside to Level Serum is that it can't raise the party beyond Level 99.

ENDLESS ITEMS

It's important to keep Dispensary active because it works with both Healthcare and Poison Pill. With Dispensary active, you can use the same item over and over (unless your goal is to clear inventory space so the Bandit can keep stealing items). After picking up your first Elixir, the importance of maintaining Dispensary's effect is magnified. Elixir allows a Salve-maker to heal everyone to full health every turn, or deal 999 damage to one enemy. You don't want to give that up by mistake!

ELEMENTALIST

CROWN OBTAINED	DEFEAT ARBAROC IN THE GREAT TREE
SPECIAL ABILITY	ELEMENTAL DAMAGE IS REDUCED BY HALF!

It's hard to overstate the value of including an Elementalist in your party. With so many enemies, especially bosses, that use spells and attacks enhanced with elemental damage, Mysterio becomes a borderline necessity for your party from the moment you earn the Elementalist Crown until you face the final boss. It's possible to get through tricky encounters without one, but including an Elementalist makes everything so much easier.

CROWN ARMOR: *Elementalist Robe (Magic Accuracy/Intellect +10%)*

	Best attack/weapon type	Harp

PASSIVE ABILITY

The damage Elementalists receive from any attack with an elemental component is halved. This applies to spells and physical attacks enhanced with an element.

STATISTICAL MODIFIERS

HP	1.0
STRENGTH	1.1
INTELLECT	1.4
SPIRIT	1.1

WEAPON PROFICIENCIES

SHORT SWORD	C
SWORD	C
BOW	C
STAFF	C
SPEAR	C
AXE	C
BOOK	C
HARP	A

MAGIC USE

OFFENSIVE MAGIC	B
RECOVERY MAGIC	B

DEFENSIVE ABILITY

EVADE	C
MAGIC EVADE	B

AUGMENT: *ENHANCE THE EFFECTS OF ALLIES' ELEMENT ATTACKS. LASTS 4 TURNS.*

ACTION POINTS	1
ABILITY SPEED	10
TARGET	ALL ALLIES
TARGET VALUE	5 (5)

Augment boosts any attack's elemental component for four turns, which is a nice bonus. There's more good news waiting for you in the Elementalist's next ability.

☆ AMPLIFY: *GREATLY ENHANCE THE EFFECTS OF ALLIES' ELEMENT ATTACKS. LASTS 4 TURNS.*

ACTION POINTS	2
ABILITY SPEED	10
TARGET	ALL ALLIES
TARGET VALUE	5 (10)

🔴	5	🔻	–
⬜	5	🌙	–
⬛	–	☾	–
🔶	–	💎	–

Amplify has double the effect of Augment for double the AP cost. What's the good news, then? Amplify and Augment combine to boost your party's elemental damage through the roof, particularly if there's a Black Mage present.

☆☆ MYSTERIO: *ENHANCE YOUR PARTY'S RESISTANCE TO ELEMENT ATTACKS.*

ACTION POINTS	3
ABILITY SPEED	25
TARGET	ALL ALLIES
TARGET VALUE	5 (15)

🔴	6	🔻	–
⬜	–	🌙	6
⬛	2	☾	1
🔶	–	💎	–

It bears repeating here: Mysterio is among the best abilities you can add to your party's defensive repertoire. Its effect fades after four turns, so always have 3 AP saved up when it fades so you can immediately reapply it.

☆☆☆ ELEMENTAL: *UNLEASH A STORM OF ELEMENT ATTACKS AGAINST THE FOE.*

ACTION POINTS	4
ABILITY SPEED	5
TARGET	ALL ENEMIES
TARGET VALUE	20 (100)

🔴	7	🔻	3
⬜	–	🌙	–
⬛	–	☾	2
🔶	7	💎	1

The Elementalist unleashes Fire, Water, Aero, Quake, Dark, and Banish in rapid succession. If there are multiple enemies, the spells target them at random.

ELEMENTAL RESISTANCE TO ABSORPTION

Elementalists begin with an inherent resistance to elemental damage. With Mysterio active, they take no damage from spells, and greatly reduced damage from physical attacks with an elemental component. Add a third layer of protection, whether it's an accessory or a shield, and suddenly elemental attacks restore health to the Elementalist. If you know which element an upcoming boss favors, equip the Elementalist with the right accessory or shield and laugh in the face of that boss's most powerful spells.

 # RANGER

CROWN OBTAINED	DEFEAT ARBAROC IN THE GREAT TREE
SPECIAL ABILITY	DELIVER EXTRA DAMAGE WITH BOWS AND ARROWS!

Having a hard time with flying enemies? Add a Ranger with a bow into the party. Bows inflict 1.4 times damage to flying enemies, and no one is handier with bows than a Ranger. Facing enemies with high evasion rates? Rangers also have two abilities that guarantee hits on selected targets.

CROWN ARMOR: *Ranger Outfit (Strength/Accuracy +10%)*

	Best attack/weapon type	Bow

PASSIVE ABILITY

Rangers with bows hit hard, but keep in mind that bows initially target the back row if you're trying to focus damage on single enemies at a time.

STATISTICAL MODIFIERS

HP	1.3
STRENGTH	1.4
INTELLECT	1.0
SPIRIT	1.2

WEAPON PROFICIENCIES

SHORT SWORD	B
SWORD	B
BOW	A
STAFF	C
SPEAR	C
AXE	C
BOOK	C
HARP	C

MAGIC USE

OFFENSIVE MAGIC	C
RECOVERY MAGIC	C

DEFENSIVE ABILITY

EVADE	B
MAGIC EVADE	C

TARGET: ENSURE THAT EVERY ATTACK STRIKES ITS TARGET.

ACTION POINTS	1
ABILITY SPEED	10
TARGET	ONE ENEMY
TARGET VALUE	5 (10)

Attack costs 1 AP. Target costs 1 AP and doesn't miss. If you're simply attacking with a Ranger, always use Target.

☆ SNIPE: ENSURE THAT EVERY ATTACK STRIKES ITS TARGET – WITH EXTRA DAMAGE.

ACTION POINTS	2
ABILITY SPEED	10
TARGET	ONE ENEMY
TARGET VALUE	7 (15)

●	5	▽	–
☐	5	◑	–
⬙	–	☾	–
◈	–	◉	–

Snipe deals 50% more damage than Target for one additional AP. It's a good trade-off, especially if any abilities that boost AP recovery are active.

☆☆ COVERING FIRE: INFLICT HEAVY DAMAGE ON ALL THE FOES AT THE BEGINNING OF THE NEXT TURN.

ACTION POINTS	3
ABILITY SPEED	10
TARGET	ALL ENEMIES
TARGET VALUE	10 (20)

●	6	▽	–
☐	–	◑	6
⬙	2	☾	1
◈	–	◉	–

For three AP, a Ranger can inflict double normal damage to every enemy in one deadly rain of arrows. The only downside to this ability is that the attack occurs one turn after the ability is executed.

☆☆☆ SMASHING BLOW: DELIVER A SINGLE, MIGHTY BLOW AGAINST THE ENEMY.

ACTION POINTS	4
ABILITY SPEED	5
TARGET	ONE ENEMY
TARGET VALUE	12 (200)

●	7	▽	3
☐	–	◑	–
⬙	–	☾	2
◈	7	◉	1

It's pricey at 4 AP, but there's a 25% chance of an instant kill should this attack hit. If the attack isn't instantly fatal, it still inflicts three times normal damage.

WITH A LITTLE HELP

Some Crowns are designed to support the party; this is not the case with Ranger. Rangers have exactly zero abilities that enhance others in the group, but that's okay. What Rangers provide is damage in frightening quantities. Think of the Ranger as your superweapon, and the other characters in the party as the maintenance team. Buff a Ranger with Berserk, Ditty, or any ability with similar effects, then sit back and watch the health fly off enemies in big chunks. Keep the Ranger healthy enough to continue firing arrows each round and most battles will end quickly.

FIGHTER

CROWN OBTAINED	DEFEAT ICE DRAGON IN THE INVIDIA UNDERGROUND
SPECIAL ABILITY	DELIVER EXTRA BARE-HANDED DAMAGE!

Another physical damage dynamo, Fighters believe less is more when it comes to weapons. They fight best with bare fists and as much Strength as possible. If you want to add element-based damage to a Fighter's attacks, your only real option is to equip a gauntlet accessory.

CROWN ARMOR: *Fighter Gi (HP/Strength +10%)*

Best attack/weapon type	Fists

STATISTICAL MODIFIERS

HP	1.5
STRENGTH	1.4
INTELLECT	0.9
SPIRIT	1.2

WEAPON PROFICIENCIES

	SHORT SWORD	C
	SWORD	C
	BOW	B
	STAFF	B
	SPEAR	B
	AXE	C
	BOOK	C
	HARP	C

MAGIC USE

OFFENSIVE MAGIC	C
RECOVERY MAGIC	C

DEFENSIVE ABILITY

EVADE	B
MAGIC EVADE	C

PASSIVE ABILITY

A Fighter's Attack power is equal to his or her strength, so long as a weapon is not equipped. Even though it technically uses a hand, equipping a shield has no effect on damage, so always equip a shield for its defensive properties.

COMBAT: *INCREASE THE ODDS OF LANDING A CRITICAL HIT. LASTS 4 TURNS.*

ACTION POINTS	1
ABILITY SPEED	10
TARGET	SELF
TARGET VALUE	5 (5)

For four turns after activating Combat, the Fighter's critical rate is 30% higher. Where other characters cap out at 20% critical rate, Fighters under the effect of Combat max out at 50%.

☆ JUGULAR: *STRIKE THE FOE WITH A CRITICAL HIT.*

ACTION POINTS	2
ABILITY SPEED	10
TARGET	ONE ENEMY
TARGET VALUE	5 (10)

●	5	▽	—
■	5	◖	—
▯	—	☾	—
◓	—	◈	—

The Fighter's Attack power is boosted by 50% and lands a guaranteed critical strike. Its 2 AP cost is a trivial concern relative to the amount of damage it deals.

☆☆ CHAKRA: *DOUBLE YOUR OWN HP FOR THE DURATION OF THE BATTLE.*

ACTION POINTS	3
ABILITY SPEED	100
TARGET	SELF
TARGET VALUE	5 (15)

●	6	▽	—
■	—	◖	6
▯	2	☾	1
◓	—	◈	—

Chakra starts out as a huge advantage, but as you gain levels and additional abilities that boost everyone's HP, it loses some steam.

☆☆☆ FRENZY FU: *HIT THE FOE WITH REPEATED ATTACKS. THE STRONGER YOU ARE, THE LONGER THE CHAIN.*

ACTION POINTS	4
ABILITY SPEED	10
TARGET	ONE ENEMY
TARGET VALUE	5 (100)

●	7	▽	3
■	—	◖	—
▯	—	☾	2
◓	7	◈	1

The number of attacks executed is equal to (3 + character's Strength ÷ 10), with a maximum value of 8. The initial punches all strike for 40% of regular damage, but the final punch deals 10 times normal damage.

SINGLE-TARGET SLAYER

Fighters are designed to crush single enemies under an avalanche of empty-handed blows. Equip a Fighter with equipment that boosts Strength, and use Frenzy-Fu and Jugular as often as possible. As with the Ranger, Fighters don't boost other characters in the group, but they excel at demolishing enemies in short order. Early in the game, rely on Chakra's HP boost for help in surviving boss encounters. As HP totals increase, just forget about that and focus on dealing damage. After all, that's what a Fighter is there to do!

 # SCHOLAR

CROWN OBTAINED	DEFEAT ICE DRAGON IN THE INVIDIA UNDERGROUND
SPECIAL ABILITY	MAKE THE MOST OF EQUIPPED BOOKS!

Scholar is a support Crown designed to reduce incoming damage and soften up enemies. Outside of Tame, Scholar abilities are among the first actions performed in a round of combat and are relatively cheap in terms of AP requirements.

CROWN ARMOR: *Scholar Gown (Intellect +20%)*

Best attack/weapon type	Book

PASSIVE ABILITY

A Scholar with a book equipped gets a 10% increase in Strength, Intellect, and Spirit. HP is unaffected by this ability.

STATISTICAL MODIFIERS

HP	1.0
STRENGTH	0.8
INTELLECT	1.5
SPIRIT	1.3

WEAPON PROFICIENCIES

	SHORT SWORD	C
	SWORD	C
	BOW	C
	STAFF	C
	SPEAR	C
	AXE	C
	BOOK	B
	HARP	C

MAGIC USE

OFFENSIVE MAGIC	B
RECOVERY MAGIC	B

DEFENSIVE ABILITY

EVADE	C
MAGIC EVADE	B

QUELL: REDUCE THE ATTACK POWER OF ALL FOES BY HALF. LASTS 3 TURNS.

ACTION POINTS	2
ABILITY SPEED	100
TARGET	ALL ENEMIES
TARGET VALUE	5 (5)

Quell is a big help when your party's armor isn't keeping everyone safe. Use Quell to help the group stay alive long enough to return to town and improve defenses!

☆ SUBDUE: REDUCE THE DEFENSE OF ALL FOES BY HALF. LASTS 3 TURNS.

ACTION POINTS	2
ABILITY SPEED	100
TARGET	ALL ENEMIES
TARGET VALUE	5 (10)

●	–	▽	5
▢	–	◖	5
▯	–	☾	–
◇	–	◈	–

Subdue reduces enemy Defense and Magic Defense. With Subdue active on enemies, your party's attacks hit much harder and shorten fights considerably.

☆☆ RESTRAIN: SLOW THE MOVEMENTS OF ALL FOES. LASTS 3 TURNS.

ACTION POINTS	2
ABILITY SPEED	100
TARGET	ALL ENEMIES
TARGET VALUE	5 (10)

●	–	▽	6
▢	–	◖	–
▯	2	☾	1
◇	6	◈	–

Restrain doesn't reduce the number of actions each enemy takes per round, only the speed at which they take the actions. Unless you're frustrated that an enemy is consistently performing its actions before your party does, it's best to save a Scholar's AP for other abilities.

☆☆☆ TAME: REDUCE THE ATTACK AND DEFENSE OF ALL FOES TO 1. APPLIES ONLY FOR THAT TURN.

ACTION POINTS	5
ABILITY SPEED	5
TARGET	ALL ENEMIES
TARGET VALUE	10 (200)

●	3	▽	7
▢	7	◖	–
▯	–	☾	2
◇	–	◈	1

Tame is a potentially powerful tool, so each enemy's vulnerability to Tame is given in its bestiary listing (in the Enemy Data section of this guide). The bad news is that most enemies vulnerable to Tame aren't enough of a threat to warrant using it. To get the most out of Tame, equip the Hermes Sandals accessory on your Scholar.

A GOOD COMBO

Bard and Scholar abilities work together wonderfully. Bards boost the party's capabilities while Scholars weaken the enemy. At least one of the other two characters should use a Crown that's designed to inflict damage (Ranger or Black Mage, for example) to take advantage of the conditions created by the Bard/Scholar combo.

PARTY HOST

CROWN OBTAINED	DEFEAT ROLAN IN ROLAN'S SOUL
SPECIAL ABILITY	DEAL MORE DAMAGE WITH JOINT ATTACKS!

Party Hosts are used to get the party to join forces for their attacks. The Crown's passive ability boosts damage done with joint attacks, while three of the four active abilities deal with psyching up the party. If you like cooperative attacks, include a Party Host.

CROWN ARMOR: *Party Host Wear (Intellect/Spirit/Evasion/Magic Evasion +5%)*

	Best attack/weapon type	Harp

STATISTICAL MODIFIERS

HP	1.1
STRENGTH	1.1
INTELLECT	1.1
SPIRIT	1.1

WEAPON PROFICIENCIES

✏	SHORT SWORD	C
🗡	SWORD	C
🏹	BOW	C
🔨	STAFF	C
🔱	SPEAR	C
🪓	AXE	C
📕	BOOK	C
🎵	HARP	B

MAGIC USE

OFFENSIVE MAGIC	C
RECOVERY MAGIC	C

DEFENSIVE ABILITY

EVADE	B
MAGIC EVADE	B

PASSIVE ABILITY

With a Party Host in the group, the damage dealt by joint attacks is increased by a multiplier, even if the Party Host isn't involved in the joint attack. If two characters act together, the damage is multiplied by 1.2. If three characters act together, the multiplier is 1.4. If all four characters attack simultaneously, the damage is doubled.

CHARM: PSYCH UP A SINGLE ALLY.

ACTION POINTS	1
ABILITY SPEED	100
TARGET	ONE ALLY
TARGET VALUE	10 (10)

Charm is a tough ability to use efficiently. It does psyche up one member of the party, but in order for that to be useful for an attack, another party member needs to be psyched up, and using the same attack. As soon as you learn Rouse, you can safely leave this ability behind.

☆ ROUSE: PSYCH UP EVERYONE IN THE PARTY.

ACTION POINTS	2
ABILITY SPEED	100
TARGET	ALL ALLIES
TARGET VALUE	10 (15)

🔵	–	🔻	5
⬜	–	💧	–
🔲	–	🌙	–
◈	5	💎	–

Rouse boosts every character's pysche up level by 50. Because of its speed, it should be activated early in the round, allowing your other characters the opportunity to strike simultaneously.

☆☆ POT LUCK: SOMETHING WILL HAPPEN, THAT'S FOR SURE.

ACTION POINTS	3
ABILITY SPEED	20
TARGET	ALL ALLIES AND ENEMIES
TARGET VALUE	10 (20)

🔵	2	🔻	–
⬜	6	💧	–
🔲	6	🌙	1
◈	–	💎	–

There are eight possible outcomes when Pot Luck is used.

❶ NOTHING HAPPENS	❺ EVERYONE AT MAX AP
❷ ALL PHYSICAL ATTACKS ARE CRITICAL HITS	❻ EVERYONE LOSES ALL AP
❸ EVERYONE AT MAX HP	❼ RECOVER FROM ALL STATUS EFFECTS
❹ FOES RECOVER HP	❽ ALL ENEMIES DEAD

☆☆☆ GO TEAM GO!: PSYCH UP EVERYONE IN THE PARTY – A LOT!

ACTION POINTS	3
ABILITY SPEED	5
TARGET	ALL ALLIES
TARGET VALUE	20 (150)

🔵	–	🔻	3
⬜	–	💧	7
🔲	7	🌙	2
◈	–	💎	1

For 3 AP, you can psyche up everyone in the party instantly. Hermes Sandals are a big help if you're trying to get everyone to act together in that same turn. Add a Dancer (and Applaud) to the mix, and you can have two powerful allies acting together every turn!

POT LUCK POTHOLES

Pot Luck is a desperation move that should only be used as a last-ditch effort to save a battle. Not only are the possible outcomes randomly determined, but some do more harm than good! On the flip side, if you hit the right outcome, it could mean the difference between restarting at an old save point and claiming victory in a hard-fought battle. Try it out in random fights on the World Map before you start using it in boss fights.

HERO

CROWN OBTAINED	DEFEAT ROLAN IN ROLAN'S SOUL
SPECIAL ABILITY	GET PSYCHED UP MORE OFTEN!

Outside of Books and Swords, the Hero is equally adept with every weapon and magic type. To get the most out of Heroes, equip swords and let them swing away. Heroes are a good choice for back-up healing, so stick a Cure-style spell in any empty ability slot.

CROWN ARMOR: Hero Armor (Strength/Intellect/Spirit +10%)

⚔ Best attack/weapon type	Sword

PASSIVE ABILITY

Heroes gain psyche up level at a faster rate than other characters.

STATISTICAL MODIFIERS

HP	1.3
STRENGTH	1.3
INTELLECT	1.2
SPIRIT	1.2

WEAPON PROFICIENCIES

✏	SHORT SWORD	B
⚔	SWORD	A
⟋	BOW	B
⚒	STAFF	B
⚔	SPEAR	B
⚒	AXE	B
▦	BOOK	C
◗	HARP	B

MAGIC USE

OFFENSIVE MAGIC	B
RECOVERY MAGIC	B

DEFENSIVE ABILITY

EVADE	B
MAGIC EVADE	B

RECKLESS: THROW EVERYTHING YOU HAVE INTO AN ATTACK, BUT WEAKEN YOUR DEFENSE.

ACTION POINTS	2
ABILITY SPEED	10
TARGET	ONE ENEMY, FRONT
TARGET VALUE	7 (15)

Reckless deals twice normal damage to a single enemy. The trade-off is a reduction in Defense to 70% of its value for one turn.

☆ BLADEBLITZ: STRIKE AT THE ENTIRE ENEMY PARTY.

ACTION POINTS	2
ABILITY SPEED	10
TARGET	ALL ENEMIES
TARGET VALUE	7 (15)

●	–	▽	5
■	–	◖	5
▯	–	☾	–
◈	–	✦	–

Bladeblitz deals 2.5 times normal physical damage, but that damage is divided equally among the enemy targets. The more enemies there are, the less damage this ability does to each one.

☆☆ WRATH: DELIVER MASSIVE MAGIC DAMAGE TO A SINGLE FOE.

ACTION POINTS	3
ABILITY SPEED	5
TARGET	ONE ENEMY, REAR
TARGET VALUE	10 (20)

●	–	▽	6
■	–	◖	–
▯	2	☾	1
◈	6	✦	–

Wrath hits with Magic Attack power of 150 and deals non-elemental damage to a single target.

☆☆☆ FINALE: COMBINE WITH YOUR ALLIES TO DELIVER A COMBINATION ATTACK.

ACTION POINTS	4
ABILITY SPEED	5
TARGET	20 (100)
TARGET VALUE	ONE ENEMY, FRONT

●	3	▽	7
■	7	◖	–
▯	–	☾	2
◈	–	✦	1

Think of Finale as a controlled version of allies joining forces in attacks after being psyched up. Each ally attacks the same target, with the Hero acting last. The damage done is entirely based on Attack Power, so Finale is more effective with Crowns like Fighter and Ninja in the party.

GEAR CHOICE IS VITAL

Statistically, Heroes are well-rounded, but their abilities lean toward physical damage. To get the most out of the Hero's abilities (Wrath is the exception, but it hits with a static Magic Attack power, so gearing for it isn't helpful anyway), pair Strength- and Attack Power-boosting gear with Swords to create a physical damage dynamo ready to pound enemies at the end of a Finale.

SPELL FENCER

CROWN OBTAINED	DEFEAT ASMODEUS IN QUICKSAND CASTLE
SPECIAL ABILITY	FOLLOW UP A SPELL WITH AN ATTACK FOR EXTRA DAMAGE!

Spell Fencers shine in areas where enemies you encounter have a variety of elemental weaknesses. Spell Fencers imbue their weapons with Black Magic to boost their damage output. On defense, they sport an ability that allows them to avoid all spell damage!

CROWN ARMOR: *Spell Fencer Armor (Strength/Intellect +10%)*

⚔️🗡️ Best attack/weapon type	Sword, Spear

STATISTICAL MODIFIERS

HP	1.3
STRENGTH	1.4
INTELLECT	1.3
SPIRIT	1.0

WEAPON PROFICIENCIES

	SHORT SWORD	B
	SWORD	A
	BOW	B
	STAFF	B
	SPEAR	A
	AXE	B
	BOOK	C
	HARP	C

MAGIC USE

OFFENSIVE MAGIC	B
RECOVERY MAGIC	C

DEFENSIVE ABILITY

EVADE	B
MAGIC EVADE	B

PASSIVE ABILITY

If a Spell Fencer attacks an enemy that was just hit by a spell, the damage dealt is doubled. The one condition that must be met is that the Spell Fencer's weapon must be imbued with the same elemental type as the spell that was used.

MAGIC SWORD: *CHANGE WEAPON ELEMENT AND STRIKE WITH ATTACK SPELLS.*

ACTION POINTS	1
ABILITY SPEED	10
TARGET	SELF
TARGET VALUE	5 (5)

The Spell Fencer spends one turn applying a Black Magic spell to his or her weapon. The effect (regardless of the spell used) is considered Level 1, and it inflicts 1.3 times damage.

⭐ MYSTIC SWORD: *CHANGE WEAPON ELEMENT. A MORE POWERFUL VERSION OF MAGIC SWORD.*

ACTION POINTS	2
ABILITY SPEED	10
TARGET	SELF
TARGET VALUE	5 (10)

●	5	▽	–
■	5	◗	–
▯	–	☾	–
◇	–	◈	–

The Spell Fencer spends one turn applying a Black Magic spell to his or her weapon. The effect (regardless of the spell used) is considered Level 2 and inflicts 1.6 times damage.

⭐⭐ MAGIC THWART: *NULLIFY THE EFFECTS OF ATTACK SPELLS CAST AGAINST YOU. LASTS 4 TURNS.*

ACTION POINTS	3
ABILITY SPEED	10
TARGET	SELF
TARGET VALUE	7 (15)

●	6	▽	–
■	–	◗	6
▯	2	☾	1
◇	–	◈	–

For four turns, the Spell Fencer becomes immune to any direct damage spells. White Magic continues to work normally, as do spells that inflict negative status effects, including Drain and Poison.

⭐⭐⭐ MAGIC INFUSE: *CAST AN ATTACK SPELL AND STRIKE WITH YOUR WEAPON AT THE SAME TIME.*

ACTION POINTS	3
ABILITY SPEED	5
TARGET	ONE ENEMY, FRONT
TARGET VALUE	10 (100)

●	7	▽	3
■	–	◗	–
▯	–	☾	2
◇	7	◈	1

The first stage of this double attack strikes with Magic Attack power of 130, with the weapon swing following up immediately afterward. For 3 AP, you can't beat the amount of damage this ability inflicts.

MAGIC SWORD AND MYSTIC SWORD SPELLS

The amount of damage dealt doesn't depend on which version of the elemental spell you use, just on which ability (Magic Sword or Mystic Sword) is used. You can apply any of the following twelve spells:

Fire	Fira	Firaga
Water	Watera	Waterga
Aero	Aeora	Aeroga
Quake	Quakra	Quaga

 # MONK

CROWN OBTAINED	DEFEAT BELPHEGOR IN MT. GULG
SPECIAL ABILITY	GROW STRONGER WITH EVERY RESURRECTION!

Monk is an odd Crown to include in a party. Wearers of this Crown don't use any weapon particularly well, nor are they adept at using magic (despite Intellect and Spirit being the Monk's strongest stats). In addition, their abilities rely on the Monk dying, or the other characters in the party dying.

CROWN ARMOR: *Monk Robe (Intellect/Spirit +10%)*

Best attack/weapon type	None

PASSIVE ABILITY

Each time a Monk falls in battle, his or her Intellect and Spirit increase by 2, improving both healing and attack spell power. The added stats are lost when the battle ends.

STATISTICAL MODIFIERS

HP	1.0
STRENGTH	0.9
INTELLECT	1.3
SPIRIT	1.3

WEAPON PROFICIENCIES

✎	SHORT SWORD	C
⚔	SWORD	C
⌒	BOW	C
↗	STAFF	C
➳	SPEAR	C
⚒	AXE	C
📕	BOOK	C
♘	HARP	C

MAGIC USE

OFFENSIVE MAGIC	C
RECOVERY MAGIC	C

DEFENSIVE ABILITY

EVADE	C
MAGIC EVADE	B

TOOL: GIVE A DEAD ALLY THE ABILITY TO ATTACK THE FOE.

ACTION POINTS	1
ABILITY SPEED	10
TARGET	ONE ALLY
TARGET VALUE	5 (10)

Should an ally fall in battle when you lack the resources to bring him or her back to life, using Tool at least gives that character the chance to strike back at enemies.

⭐ IMPLEMENT: GIVE A DEAD ALLY THE ABILITY TO USE MAGIC

ACTION POINTS	2
ABILITY SPEED	5
TARGET	ONE ALLY
TARGET VALUE	5 (10)

●	—	▽	—
▢	—	◖	—
▯	5	☾	—
◈	5	✦	—

Should an ally fall in battle, and can't be revived, use Implement to give that ally the ability to use magic spells. For more information about which spells are eligible for use while under the influence of Implement, check out the Magic Tomes section of this guide.

⭐⭐ KAMIKAZE: ATTACK FOES AS YOU DIE. THE MORE TIMES YOU HAVE DIED, THE GREATER THE DAMAGE.

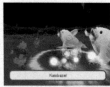

ACTION POINTS	1
ABILITY SPEED	10
TARGET	ALL ENEMIES
TARGET VALUE	5 (15)

●	2	▽	—
▢	6	◖	—
▯	6	☾	1
◈	—	✦	—

The Monk sacrifices his or her life to damage all enemies. The amount of damage inflicted is determined by the following formula: character's level x (four + the number of times the character has died during the current fight).

⭐⭐⭐ GHOST ARMY: SUMMON AN ARMY OF GHOSTS THAT ATTACKS ALL FOES AND DEALS DEVASTATING DAMAGE.

ACTION POINTS	3
ABILITY SPEED	5
TARGET	ALL ENEMIES
TARGET VALUE	10 (50)

●	—	▽	3
▢	—	◖	7
▯	7	☾	2
◈	—	✦	1

Ghost Army deals Magic Damage with a Magic Attack power of 160, with the damage multiplier rate determined by the following formula: (1 + [# of times the Monk has died during the battle ÷ 10])

LIFE AND DEATH

If you can plan ahead properly and continually raise the Monk from the dead after Kamikaze, the Monk character can build up to some increasingly impressive damage numbers. Kamikaze costs only one Action Point, so it can be used the round that immediately follows the Monk's resurrection.

DANCER

CROWN OBTAINED	DEFEAT LEVIATHAN ON THE WORLD MAP
SPECIAL ABILITY	DEAL EXTRA DAMAGE WHEN USING A SHORT SWORD!

The Dancer works best in a support role, restoring AP each round to a character who uses a powerful, high AP-cost ability so it can be used repeatedly.

CROWN ARMOR: Dancer Clothes (Evasion/Spirit +10%)

	Best attack/weapon type	Short Sword

PASSIVE ABILITY

Although dealing damage is not the best use of their AP, the best way to inflict damage as a Dancer is to equip a Short Sword and use Attack.

STATISTICAL MODIFIERS

HP	1.3
STRENGTH	1.3
INTELLECT	1.0
SPIRIT	1.3

WEAPON PROFICIENCIES

SHORT SWORD	A
SWORD	B
BOW	C
STAFF	C
SPEAR	C
AXE	C
BOOK	C
HARP	C

MAGIC USE

OFFENSIVE MAGIC	C
RECOVERY MAGIC	C

DEFENSIVE ABILITY

EVADE	B
MAGIC EVADE	C

DANCE: RECOVER AP MORE QUICKLY THAN USUAL. LASTS 3 TURNS.

ACTION POINTS	1
ABILITY SPEED	10
TARGET	SELF
TARGET VALUE	10 (10)

Dance boosts the Dancer's AP recovery for three turns. The effect of Dance does not stack with either Lux or Perform. Once a character learns Perform (or you obtain Lux), Dance should be set aside.

☆ PERFORM: MAKE YOUR ALLIES RECOVER THEIR AP MORE QUICKLY THAN USUAL. LASTS 3 TURNS.

ACTION POINTS	3	⬤	5	▽	—
ABILITY SPEED	10	◻	5	◗	—
TARGET	ALL ALLIES	▯	—	☾	—
TARGET VALUE	10 (15)	◈	—	◆	—

Perform causes characters to recover AP twice as fast as normal for three turns. Since Lux provides the same effect (in addition to many others), there's no need to use Perform once Lux has been obtained.

☆☆ APPLAUD: INCREASE ONE ALLY'S AP BY 3 POINTS.

ACTION POINTS	1	⬤	6	▽	—
ABILITY SPEED	5	◻	—	◗	6
TARGET	ONE ALLY	▯	2	☾	1
TARGET VALUE	10 (100)	◈	—	◆	—

Sacrificing one of a Dancer's AP to give an ally three AP is a wonderful trade. The target of Applaud is always the character with the lowest AP level when the ability is executed.

☆☆☆ OVATION: RESTORE ALL OF ONE ALLY'S AP.

ACTION POINTS	2	⬤	7	▽	3
ABILITY SPEED	5	◻	—	◗	—
TARGET	ONE ALLY	▯	—	☾	2
TARGET VALUE	10 (50)	◈	7	◆	1

If trading one AP for three seems like a good idea, trading two AP for five is an even better one! Just like Applaud, Ovation's target is the character with the least amount of AP when the ability is executed.

PROPER AP RESTORATION

The toughest thing about using Ovation and Applaud to restore AP is timing the abilities to execute after the other characters act. Both Ovation and Applaud have low speed values, but so do the big-hitting abilities being used by the characters whose AP you wish to restore. The easiest way to ensure that the effects of Ovation or Applaud aren't wasted on a character who hasn't acted yet is to equip Old Shoes. Otherwise, follow the acting priority forumla included in the Game Basics section to ensure your Dancer acts as late in a round as possible.

 # PALADIN

CROWN OBTAINED	DEFEAT ARCH DEMON IN ROLAN'S SOUL
SPECIAL ABILITY	DEFEND YOURSELF EVEN BETTER WHEN EQUIPPED WITH A SHIELD!

No Crown comes close to matching a Paladin's 1.7 HP multiplier. The extra health is a necessity for Paladins, since their job is to take blows aimed at other characters. Paladins can do decent physical damage, combining Sword and Spear proficiency with above-average Strength.

CROWN ARMOR: Paladin Armor (HP +20%)

⚔️⚔️	Best attack/weapon type	Sword/Spear

STATISTICAL MODIFIERS

HP	1.7
STRENGTH	1.4
INTELLECT	0.9
SPIRIT	1.0

WEAPON PROFICIENCIES

	SHORT SWORD	C
	SWORD	A
	BOW	C
	STAFF	B
	SPEAR	A
	AXE	C
	BOOK	C
	HARP	C

MAGIC USE

OFFENSIVE MAGIC	C
RECOVERY MAGIC	C

DEFENSIVE ABILITY

EVADE	B
MAGIC EVADE	C

PASSIVE ABILITY

When a Paladin equips a shield, his or her Defense is improved by 50%. When you throw yourself in front of enemy attacks, you want as much protection as possible!

COVER: SHELTER A FRIEND FROM ATTACK AND TAKE THE DAMAGE YOURSELF.

ACTION POINTS	1
ABILITY SPEED	200
TARGET	ONE ALLY
TARGET VALUE	0 (0)

When you use Cover, the Paladin selects an ally to protect from one single-target attack. It's a nice gesture, but when Bait becomes available you can mostly forget about Cover.

⭐ BAIT: DRAW THE FOE'S ATTENTION SO YOU BECOME THE TARGET OF THEIR ATTACKS.

ACTION POINTS	2		⬤	—	▽	5
ABILITY SPEED	200		⬛	—	🌙	5
TARGET	ALL ENEMIES		▯	—	☾	—
TARGET VALUE	20 (500)		⬡	—	💎	—

Bait taunts all enemies to focus their attacks on the Paladin. It won't hold their attention for long, however. Each attack drops 50% off the 500-point Reduced Target Value of this ability. Depending on the number of enemies attacking, you may need to refresh Bait every other turn.

⭐⭐ AVENGE: INCREASE THE DAMAGE YOU INFLICT THE MORE YOU ARE TARGETED FOR ATTACK.

ACTION POINTS	3		⬤	—	▽	6
ABILITY SPEED	5		⬛	—	🌙	—
TARGET	SELF		▯	2	☾	1
TARGET VALUE	0 (0)		⬡	6	💎	—

Avenge builds up every time the Paladin takes damage. When activated, Avenge deals damage equal to (damage taken) x (the number of times the Paladin was targeted ÷ 100). When Avenge is used, all these values reset to zero, so wait a few turns before using it.

⭐⭐⭐ LAST STAND: HANG ON TO LIFE FOR SEVERAL TURNS AT HP 1.

ACTION POINTS	4		⬤	3	▽	7
ABILITY SPEED	20		⬛	7	🌙	—
TARGET	SELF		▯	—	☾	2
TARGET VALUE	10 (100)		⬡	—	💎	1

Last Stand allows the Paladin to remain alive with 1 HP after being struck with an attack that would otherwise be fatal. There's a 20% chance each turn that the effect will wear off. Last Stand only works against direct damage attacks; Last Stand does not save the Paladin from attacks that petrify and cause instant death.

A LIVING SHIELD

Try to activate Last Stand first, then Bait enemies into focusing on the Paladin. After a few rounds of absorbing enemy attacks, unleash Avenge for a measure of payback. Sneak in a few Attacks when possible, but since the Paladin's job is to absorb damage, expect to spend more than a few rounds using Boost to blunt the effect of incoming attacks.

ALCHEMIST

CROWN OBTAINED	DEFEAT BEELZEBUB IN THE SKY TOWER
SPECIAL ABILITY	BOOST THE DAMAGE INFLICTED BY ATTACK ITEMS!

Attack Items, such as Bomb Fragments and Raven's Yawns, are the Alchemist's playground. Every Alchemist ability includes their use, creation, or modification. If you don't mind constant inventory juggling, then Alchemist is a fun Crown to try.

CROWN ARMOR: Alchemist Gown (Defense/Magic Defense/Accuracy/Magic Accuracy +5%)

🎒 Best attack/weapon type	Items

PASSIVE ABILITY

Attack Items inflict 50% more damage when used by an Alchemist.

STATISTICAL MODIFIERS

HP	1.2
STRENGTH	1.0
INTELLECT	1.5
SPIRIT	1.3

WEAPON PROFICIENCIES

	SHORT SWORD	C
	SWORD	C
	BOW	C
	STAFF	C
	SPEAR	C
	AXE	C
	BOOK	C
	HARP	C

MAGIC USE

OFFENSIVE MAGIC	C
RECOVERY MAGIC	C

DEFENSIVE ABILITY

EVADE	C
MAGIC EVADE	B

EXPERIMENT: TRANSFORM AN ITEM IN YOUR POSSESSION INTO ANOTHER KIND OF ITEM.

ACTION POINTS	1
ABILITY SPEED	5
TARGET	SELF
TARGET VALUE	5 (5)

Not carrying the Attack Item you need to hit an enemy's weak spot? Just spend an AP changing it into something else! Your success rate for conversion is (80 + [character's level ÷ 6])%.

☆ FORGE: CREATE A RANDOM ATTACK ITEM AND ADD IT TO YOUR BELONGINGS.

ACTION POINTS	1
ABILITY SPEED	5
TARGET	SELF
TARGET VALUE	5 (5)

🔵	–	🔻	–
⬜	–	🍃	–
🟦	5	🌙	–
🔶	5	💎	–

Did you use up your Attack Items in the last battle and didn't get a chance to restock? No worries! You can create one item per turn with Forge. Your success rate for creation is (80 + [character's level ÷ 10])%.

☆☆ SMELT: COMBINE ITEMS FOR A VARIETY OF DIFFERENT EFFECTS.

ACTION POINTS	3
ABILITY SPEED	15
TARGET	ONE ENEMY
TARGET VALUE	5 (15)

🔵	2	🔻	–
⬜	6	🍃	–
🟦	6	🌙	1
🔶	–	💎	–

SMELT RESULTS TABLE

ATTACK ITEMS	RESULTING ATTACK	ELEMENT	DAMAGE MULTIPLIER
BOMB FRAGMENT + BOMB FRAGMENT	CLUSTER OF BOMBS	FIRE	3
ANTARCTIC WIND + ANTARCTIC WIND	POLAR WIND	WATER	3
GAIA DRUM + GAIA DRUM	GROUND CONVULSION	EARTH	3
RAVEN'S YAWN + RAVEN'S YAWN	OGRE'S SNEEZE	AIR	3
GREAT TREE LOG + GREAT TREE LOG	GREAT TREE FRUIT	NONE	4
ZEUS'S WRATH + ZEUS'S WRATH	RAGE OF ZEUS	LIGHT	4
DARK SIGH + DARK SIGH	SIGH OF DARKNESS	DARK	3
HOLY BREATH + HOLY BREATH	HOLY SHOWER	LIGHT	3
HOLY BREATH + DARK SIGH	WHIRLPOOL OF CHAOS	DARK	5
ANY OTHER COMBINATION	STRANGE LIQUID	NONE	2

☆☆☆ CAST: THROW ALL THE ATTACK ITEMS YOU CARRY AT THE FOE.

ACTION POINTS	4
ABILITY SPEED	5
TARGET	ONE ENEMY
TARGET VALUE	20 (50)

🔵	–	🔻	3
⬜	–	🍃	7
🟦	7	🌙	2
🔶	–	💎	1

This is the super-ultimate Alchemist ability! Every Attack Item in the Alchemist's inventory is launched at a single target. The only thing Cast lacks is the Alchemist shouting the name of each item as it is thrown at the enemy.

DAMAGE DEALT BY SMELT

The formula for calculating damage done by Smelt is as follows:

Damage = 100 x Element Factor x Smelt Damage Multiplier x random factor (a number between 1.0 and 1.25)

 # SHAMAN

CROWN OBTAINED	DEFEAT MAMMON IN THE SUN TEMPLE
SPECIAL ABILITY	AP COST FOR DARK MAGIC REDUCED BY ONE!

The master of Dark Magic is a powerful addition to parties, especially in boss fights. Many bosses are vulnerable to Dark Magic's effects, and Poison's consistent 3% damage per round really adds up in a battle against enemies with health in the thousands.

CROWN ARMOR: *Shaman Robe (Accuracy/Intellect +10%)*

Best attack/weapon type	Dark Magic

PASSIVE ABILITY

The Action Point saved each time a Shaman uses a Dark Magic spell allows you to apply more negative status effects to bosses than with any other Crown.

STATISTICAL MODIFIERS

HP	1.2
STRENGTH	0.9
INTELLECT	1.5
SPIRIT	1.2

WEAPON PROFICIENCIES

SHORT SWORD	C
SWORD	C
BOW	C
STAFF	B
SPEAR	C
AXE	C
BOOK	C
HARP	C

MAGIC USE

OFFENSIVE MAGIC	B
RECOVERY MAGIC	C

DEFENSIVE ABILITY

EVADE	C
MAGIC EVADE	B

RITUAL: MAKE YOUR NEXT DARK MAGIC SPELL AFFECT ALL YOUR FOES.

ACTION POINTS	1
ABILITY SPEED	10
TARGET	SELF
TARGET VALUE	5 (5)

Whenever there are multiple enemies in the field, use Ritual before delivering any Dark Magic spell. The loss of the one turn necessary to active Ritual to hit four enemies at once is a good trade-off.

⭐ HEX: MAKE YOUR NEXT DARK MAGIC SPELL MORE POWERFUL AND AFFECT ALL YOUR FOES.

ACTION POINTS	2
ABILITY SPEED	10
TARGET	SELF
TARGET VALUE	5 (10)

●	—	▽	—
▢	—	◖	—
▯	5	☾	—
⬠	5	◈	—

Hex doesn't necessarily make Dark Magic spells hit harder (not many deal direct damage); it generally makes it more likely for the effect of the spell to take hold.

⭐⭐ SPELLBOUND: PREVENT BOTH FRIEND AND FOE ALIKE FROM TAKING ANY ACTIONS. LASTS SEVERAL TURNS.

ACTION POINTS	3
ABILITY SPEED	10
TARGET	ALL ALLIES AND ENEMIES
TARGET VALUE	5 (15)

●	2	▽	—
▢	6	◖	—
▯	6	☾	1
⬠	—	◈	—

Save Spellbound for use immediately after applying spells like Lux, Regen, or anything that restores HP (there's no AP recovery for characters while under the effect of Spellbound). Each combatant (friend and foe) affected by Spellbound has a 20% chance, each turn, to shake off its effect.

⭐⭐⭐ FORBIDDEN ART: REDUCE THE HP OF FRIEND AND FOE ALIKE TO 1.

ACTION POINTS	4
ABILITY SPEED	5
TARGET	ALL ALLIES AND ENEMIES
TARGET VALUE	30 (200)

●	—	▽	3
▢	—	◖	7
▯	7	☾	2
⬠	—	◈	1

Not all enemies are vulnerable to this ability, so check the enemy listing before you try out Forbidden Art. Ideally, you would inflict Poison on all the enemies, then hit them with Forbidden Art as the last action in a turn. It's also in your interest to have Regen or Lux active so your party gets in a tick of healing before another round of combat begins (in the event an enemy resists Forbidden Art).

HEX AND RITUAL

With Hex or Ritual active (you never need to have both active at the same time), the following Dark Magic spells can be applied to all enemies:

Break	Flash
Confuse	Poison
Curse	Silence
Death	Sleep
Drain	Suppress

DARK FENCER

CROWN OBTAINED	DEFEAT SATAN IN THE MAGIC LABORATORY
SPECIAL ABILITY	DEAL EXTRA DAMAGE WHEN USING A SWORD!

How good are Dark Fencers at dealing damage? That depends on how good you are at keeping them healed. There are three Dark Fencer abilities allowing them to sacrifice their own HP to deal extra damage to enemies. If they aren't healed after their HP-depleting attacks, they become far less effective.

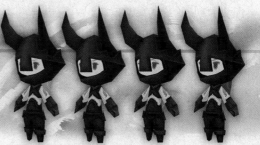

CROWN ARMOR: Dark Fencer Armor (Attack Power/Strength +10%)

Best attack/weapon type	Sword

PASSIVE ABILITY

Dark Fencers love swords, and are very effective with them. That being said, don't shy away from the use of Axes when one with Attack Power far superior to any Swords becomes available.

STATISTICAL MODIFIERS

HP	1.3
STRENGTH	1.6
INTELLECT	1.0
SPIRIT	1.0

WEAPON PROFICIENCIES

SHORT SWORD	A
SWORD	A
BOW	C
STAFF	B
SPEAR	B
AXE	A
BOOK	C
HARP	C

MAGIC USE

OFFENSIVE MAGIC	C
RECOVERY MAGIC	C

DEFENSIVE ABILITY

EVADE	B
MAGIC EVADE	C

DARKSIDE: SACRIFICE SOME OF YOUR OWN HP TO DEAL HEAVY DAMAGE TO A FOE.

ACTION POINTS	1
ABILITY SPEED	10
TARGET	ONE ENEMY
TARGET VALUE	10 (10)

The Dark Fencer sacrifices 20% of his or her maximum HP to increase damage output against a single enemy. If the Dark Fencer is under 20% of maximum HP, the attack results in the character's death.

⭐ DARKER SIDE: SACRIFICE SOME OF YOUR OWN HP TO DEAL HEAVY DAMAGE TO ALL FOES.

ACTION POINTS	2
ABILITY SPEED	10
TARGET	ALL ENEMIES
TARGET VALUE	10 (15)

🔵	–	🔻	–
🟦	–	💧	–
🟧	5	🌙	–
🔷	5	💎	–

The Dark Fencer sacrifices 30% of his or her maximum HP to increase damage output and attack all enemies. If the Dark Fencer is under 30% of maximum HP, the attack results in the character's death.

⭐⭐ EYE FOR AN EYE: MAKE YOUR ATTACKS STRONGER AS YOUR HP FALLS.

ACTION POINTS	3
ABILITY SPEED	10
TARGET	SELF
TARGET VALUE	10 (20)

🔵	2	🔻	–
🟦	6	💧	–
🟧	6	🌙	1
🔷	–	💎	–

The lower the Dark Fencer's HP is (in relation to maximum HP), the more damage he or she deals. The damage scales up as HP drops, but it caps out at double damage.

⭐⭐⭐ AMOK: UNLEASH DARKSIDE REPEATEDLY UNTIL ALL YOUR HP IS CONSUMED.

ACTION POINTS	5
ABILITY SPEED	5
TARGET	ALL ENEMIES
TARGET VALUE	30 (200)

🔵	–	🔻	3
🟦	–	💧	7
🟧	7	🌙	2
🔷	–	💎	1

Amok works better the closer the Dark Fencer's HP is to maximum. At most, the Dark Fencer performs five attacks. Regardless of how many attacks are performed, the Dark Fencer always ends with 1 HP left after using Amok.

MAINTENANCE OF YOUR SELF-DESTRUCTIVE FRIEND

When a Dark Fencer's health is close to full, use Amok. Depending on how many enemies are on the field, use Darkside or Darker side between 40% and 60% health. With health below 40%, use Eye for an Eye and demand some healing!

As with all character who damage themselves, exercise extreme caution with big attacks, since you're only one negative status effect away from your designated healer being unable to restore the Dark Fencer's health.

SEAMSTRESS

CROWN OBTAINED	EARN 20,000 GIL IN ONE SESSION AT THAUZAND'S SHOP IN THE TOWN OF URBETH
SPECIAL ABILITY	ATTACK WITH GREATER POWER WHEN EQUIPPED WITH A NEEDLE!

Unless you've been fortunate with weapon and armor drops from enemies, Seamstress is an expensive Crown to use. Until a needle is obtained, Seamstress is more of a "for fun" Crown to use. Their abilities are just that odd, and their damage is dependent on using a needle as a weapon.

CROWN ARMOR: *Seamstress Clothes (Defense +7, Magic Defense +7, Defense/Magic Defense/Evade/Magic Evade +5%)*

STATISTICAL MODIFIERS

HP	1.2
STRENGTH	1.0
INTELLECT	1.3
SPIRIT	1.3

WEAPON PROFICIENCIES

✏️	SHORT SWORD	C
🗡️	SWORD	C
🏹	BOW	C
🔱	STAFF	C
🔱	SPEAR	C
🪓	AXE	C
📖	BOOK	C
🎵	HARP	C

MAGIC USE

OFFENSIVE MAGIC	C
RECOVERY MAGIC	C

DEFENSIVE ABILITY

EVADE	B
MAGIC EVADE	B

✏️	Best attack/weapon type	Needle

PASSIVE ABILITY

A Seamstress wielding a needle does triple damage. Needles are hard to obtain (they're available only in the Extra Dungeons) but worth the effort if you want to include a Seamstress in your party.

PATCHED UP: PATCH ALL YOUR NON-UPGRADED ARMOR TOGETHER FOR BETTER PROTECTION.

ACTION POINTS	1
ABILITY SPEED	10
TARGET	SELF
TARGET VALUE	10 (10)

Seamstresses use Patched Up to layer armor and shields to their existing equipment for a defensive boost. The attached item must be in the Seamstress's inventory, and it's consumed as soon as it is attached. Note that this upgrade applies to Defense only, Magic Defense is not affected.

⭐ STITCHED UP: PATCH ALL YOUR NON-UPGRADED WEAPONS TOGETHER FOR A STRONGER ATTACK.

ACTION POINTS	2		🔵	–	▽	5
ABILITY SPEED	10		🟫	–	💧	5
TARGET	SELF		🔘	–	🌙	–
TARGET VALUE	10 (15)		⬠	–	💎	–

Stitched Up works similarly to Patched Up, except with weapons. A weapon from the Seamstress's inventory is temporarily attached to the character's current weapon, and is consumed in the process. The increase applies only to Attack Power, not Magic Attack Power.

⭐⭐ REFURBISH: BRING ONE ALLY BACK TO LIFE.

ACTION POINTS	3		🔵	–	▽	6
ABILITY SPEED	10		🟫	–	💧	–
TARGET	ONE ALLY		🔘	2	🌙	1
TARGET VALUE	10 (20)		⬠	6	💎	–

Refurbish works just like the White Magic spell Arise, but for one less AP. The revived character comes back to life with full HP.

⭐⭐⭐ SEW TOGETHER: SEW YOURSELF AND AN ALLY TOGETHER TO COMBINE YOUR STATUS LEVELS.

ACTION POINTS	5		🔵	3	▽	7
ABILITY SPEED	5		🟫	7	💧	–
TARGET	ONE ALLY		🔘	–	🌙	2
TARGET VALUE	30 (200)		⬠	–	💎	1

Sew Together fuses the Seamstress and one other party member into a character with much higher stats. The lower-level character involved in Sew Together fades from the screen until the end of the battle.

MORE INVENTORY CLEARING

Salve-makers use up extra restorative items, and Alchemists go through Attack Items in bunches, leaving equipment for Seamstresses. If you don't have extra Weapons, Shields, or Armor to sacrifice to Seamstress abilities, it reduces their effectiveness significantly. Equip a needle and stuff a few extraneous weapons into the Seamstress's inventory, though, and it's a different story.

BEASTMASTER

CROWN OBTAINED	SCORE 250 POINTS AT THE MATH GAME IN INVIDIA
SPECIAL ABILITY	MAKE YOUR ALLIES STRONGER WHEN IN ANIMAL FORM!

If you enjoy running around with all your characters in animal form, you should always have one character set as a Beastmaster. To get the most out of a party comprising three animals and a Beastmaster, choose mainly physical attack Crowns, such as Fighter or Paladin. The damage from Command is physical, not magical.

CROWN ARMOR: **Beastmasters Coast (Defense/Magic Defense +5%, Strength +10%)**

Best attack/weapon type	Axe

STATISTICAL MODIFIERS

HP	1.3
STRENGTH	1.3
INTELLECT	1.1
SPIRIT	1.1

WEAPON PROFICIENCIES

SHORT SWORD	B
SWORD	B
BOW	C
STAFF	C
SPEAR	C
AXE	A
BOOK	C
HARP	C

MAGIC USE

OFFENSIVE MAGIC	C
RECOVERY MAGIC	C

DEFENSIVE ABILITY

EVADE	B
MAGIC EVADE	C

PASSIVE ABILITY

In animal form each character's Strength, Intellect, and Spirit are reduced to 70% of the regular values. With a Beastmaster in the party, characters in animal form have their stats doubled, meaning they're 40% higher than the stats they'd have in human form.

CAPTURE: **CAPTURE A MONSTER. WEAKENED MONSTERS ARE EASIER TO CATCH.**

SIC: **MAKE A CAPTURED MONSTER ATTACK THE ENEMY.**

ACTION POINTS	1
ABILITY SPEED	10
TARGET	ONE ENEMY
TARGET VALUE	5 (10) / 10 (20)

When an enemy has less than 10% of its maximum HP, use Capture to tuck that creature away for later use. When that happens, the Capture command is switched with Sic. Use Sic to send your Captured enemy to attack other creatures. Each Captured enemy can be used for Sic three times.

☆ GENTLE: **ATTACK THE FOE WITHOUT KILLING IT.**

ACTION POINTS	2
ABILITY SPEED	10
TARGET	ONE ENEMY
TARGET VALUE	10 (15)

	–		–
	–		–
	5		–
	5		–

Use Gentle when there's a particular enemy you want to Capture, but it's too close to death to risk hitting it with a regular attack.

☆☆ COMMAND: **MAKE ALL PARTY MEMBERS IN ANIMAL FORM ATTACK THE ENEMY.**

ACTION POINTS	3
ABILITY SPEED	10
TARGET	ALL ENEMIES
TARGET VALUE	7 (15)

	2		–
	6		–
	6		1
	–		–

When Command is used, all party members in animal form attack an enemy, with the Beastmaster (who can remain in human form) delivering a final blow. Just think of it as the furry version of the Hero ability Finale. All other characters will still perform their own actions in addition to joining in on Command.

☆☆☆ TURNCOAT: **MAKE A CAPTURED MONSTER ATTACK ITS OWN.**

ACTION POINTS	4
ABILITY SPEED	5
TARGET	ONE ENEMY
TARGET VALUE	10 (100)

	–		3
	–		7
	7		2
	–		1

Turncoat is a more powerful version of Sic. It deals four times as much damage, but the captured enemy is used up in the process. The good news is that the creature does the same amount of damage regardless of having been used for Sic previously.

ANIMALS, ANIMALS, ANIMALS EVERYWHERE

With a Beastmaster in the party, every other character should be set to their animal form at all times. They enjoy increased stats, making Command deal serious damage. Just don't let the cuteness of puppies, bunnies, and kittens distract you from your mission!

 MUSICIAN

CROWN OBTAINED	BUY MUSICAL SCORE FROM MP SHOP IN LIBERTE TOWN
SPECIAL ABILITY	ENJOY ENHANCED STATS WHEN IN THE PRESENCE OF A BARD!

While Musicians are slightly better in groups that focus on magic damage, the buffs they provide are incredible. Best of all, the benefits of their three initial abilities stack with what is provided through Oratorio!

CROWN ARMOR: Musician Robes (Spirit +10%, Evade/Magic Evade +5%)

Best attack/weapon type	Harp

PASSIVE ABILITY

Anytime a Bard is in the same group as a Musician, the Musician's Strength, Intellect, and Spirit are increased by 10%.

STATISTICAL MODIFIERS

HP	1.1
STRENGTH	0.9
INTELLECT	1.4
SPIRIT	1.4

WEAPON PROFICIENCIES

	SHORT SWORD	C
	SWORD	C
	BOW	C
	STAFF	C
	SPEAR	C
	AXE	C
	BOOK	C
	HARP	A

MAGIC USE

OFFENSIVE MAGIC	C
RECOVERY MAGIC	C

DEFENSIVE ABILITY

EVADE	C
MAGIC EVADE	C

SERENADE: GRANT REGEN TO YOUR WHOLE PARTY FOR 3 TURNS.

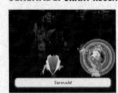

ACTION POINTS	2
ABILITY SPEED	15
TARGET	ALL ALLIES
TARGET VALUE	3 (5)

For three turns, each member of the party regenerates 20% of their total HP at the start of each turn. Even better, it stacks with other HP-regenerating abilities.

☆ NOCTURNE: RAISE YOUR PARTY'S MAGIC ATTACK POWER FOR 3 TURNS.

ACTION POINTS	2
ABILITY SPEED	100
TARGET	ALL ALLIES
TARGET VALUE	3 (10)

icon	value	icon	value
●	—	▽	5
■	—	◑	—
▯	—	☽	—
◇	5	◈	—

For three turns, Nocturne doubles the party's Magic Attack power. Nocture works well with Ditty, and you always have a Bard in the group with your Musician, right?

☆☆ MARCH: INCREASE YOUR PARTY'S MOVEMENT SPEED FOR 3 TURNS.

ACTION POINTS	3
ABILITY SPEED	30
TARGET	ALL ALLIES
TARGET VALUE	5 (15)

icon	value	icon	value
●	—	▽	6
■	—	◑	—
▯	2	☽	1
◇	6	◈	—

For three turns, March increases everyone's Action Value by 60. That's a big boost, and allows your characters to act before most enemies as long as it's active.

☆☆☆ ORATORIO: GRANT YOUR PARTY REGEN. BOOST ATTACK, MAGIC ATTACK, AND SPEED FOR 5 TURNS.

ACTION POINTS	5
ABILITY SPEED	5
TARGET	ALL ALLIES
TARGET VALUE	10 (100)

icon	value	icon	value
●	3	▽	7
■	7	◑	—
▯	—	☽	2
◇	—	◈	1

For five turns, Oratorio restores 10% of everyone's maximum HP, Attack and Magic Attack power are increased by 50%, and Action Value is increased by 30.

WORKS WELL WITH OTHERS

The effects from Oratorio combine with Serenade, Nocturne, and March, which means 30% HP recovery, 250% increase in Magic Attack, and an additional 90 Action Value when everything is up. Toss in Bard abilities (since you have a Bard in the group with the Musician, right?) and the other two characters in the group are ready to annihilate anything that dares face your party in combat.

NINJA

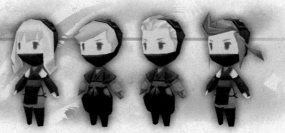

CROWN OBTAINED	DEFEAT KRINJH IN MOONSAND RUINS
SPECIAL ABILITY	ENCOUNTER FEWER MONSTERS!

Placing a Ninja in your party adds powerful sword attacks and a reduction in the number of random enemy encounters. Ninja thrive when their Evasion is boosted to the point where they're almost untouchable. Evasion helps out two of their powerful abilities, so it's worth it to boost it through equipment as much as possible.

CROWN ARMOR: *Ninja Uniform (Evasion +20%)*

⚔ Best attack/weapon type	Sword

PASSIVE ABILITY

It's great that you can go through dungeons and have fewer random encounters when all you want is to get to the next staircase or find the next boss fight. The downside is that you can't turn off this ability. If you're wandering the World Map because you want to get some experience or gather some extra gems, keep the Ninja at home.

STATISTICAL MODIFIERS

HP	1.3
STRENGTH	1.4
INTELLECT	1.2
SPIRIT	1.0

WEAPON PROFICIENCIES

SHORT SWORD	B
SWORD	A
BOW	C
STAFF	B
SPEAR	C
AXE	C
BOOK	C
HARP	C

MAGIC USE

OFFENSIVE MAGIC	C
RECOVERY MAGIC	C

DEFENSIVE ABILITY

EVADE	A
MAGIC EVADE	C

MOVING TARGET: BOOST YOUR OWN ABILITY TO EVADE ATTACKS.

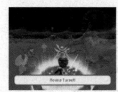

ACTION POINTS	1
ABILITY SPEED	15
TARGET	SELF
TARGET VALUE	5 (10)

Moving Target increases the Ninja's Evasion score by an increasing amount. The first application boosts Evasion by 10%, the second by 20%, and the third (and final) increase is by 40%. All three effects stack, resulting in a total 70% increase. Even better, the effect lasts the duration of the battle.

☆ TARGET DUMMY: CREATE A COPY OF YOURSELF SO YOU CAN EVADE PHYSICAL ATTACKS. MAKES 2 COPIES.

ACTION POINTS	2
ABILITY SPEED	100
TARGET	SELF
TARGET VALUE	7 (15)

○	–	▽	–
□	–	◐	–
▯	5	☾	–
◇	5	◈	–

Target Dummy creates two shadowy copies that draw physical attacks away from the Ninja. So long as this ability is active (each miss removes a copy), the Ninja is immune to physical attacks. The downside is that you must wait for the entire effect to fade before it can be reapplied. This sometimes causes problems when you're facing bosses that act multiple times per turn.

☆☆ COUNTER: UNLEASH A COUNTER-ATTACK WHENEVER YOU EVADE A BLOW. LASTS 4 TURNS.

ACTION POINTS	3
ABILITY SPEED	10
TARGET	SELF
TARGET VALUE	10 (20)

○	2	▽	–
□	6	◐	–
▯	6	☾	1
◇	–	◈	–

Reason number one to boost a Ninja's evasion: for four turns, any physical attack directed at the Ninja that a misses triggers an immediate counterattack.

☆☆☆ LIGHTNING FISTS: UNLEASH REPEATED ATTACKS. THE BETTER YOUR EVASION, THE LONGER THE CHAIN.

ACTION POINTS	4
ABILITY SPEED	5
TARGET	ONE ENEMY
TARGET VALUE	20 (100)

○	–	▽	3
□	–	◐	7
▯	7	☾	2
◇	–	◈	1

Lightning Fists attacks 2 + (Evasion ÷ 5) times, up to a maximum of five times. While each strike hits a single enemy, the attack will change targets should the first enemy fall before the Ninja reaches the number of attacks from Lightning Fists.

SETTING UP NINJA ABILITIES

To get the most out of Lightning Fists, perform one or two (a third application is overkill) iterations of Moving Target. You really only need a total of 15 Evasion to max out the number of Lightning Fists strikes.

Counter also works well with Moving Target, but it is most effective after you reach the maximum Evasion bonus of 70%. Even better, follow up Counter with Moving Target. That's two guaranteed counterattacks every time you use Moving Target while Counter is still active.

 # SAGE

CROWN OBTAINED	DEFEAT TORTE IN HOLY TREE TOWER
SPECIAL ABILITY	BOOST THE EFFECTS OF MAGIC BOTH BLACK AND WHITE!

They're not the hardiest of characters, but Sages are versatile magic-wielding dynamos. They're equally adept with Black Magic and White Magic, and their Intellect and Spirit multipliers are identical!

CROWN ARMOR: *Sage Robe (Magic Accuracy +20%)*

⚔ Best attack/weapon type	Black Magic

STATISTICAL MODIFIERS

HP	1.0
STRENGTH	0.7
INTELLECT	1.5
SPIRIT	1.5

WEAPON PROFICIENCIES

SHORT SWORD	C
SWORD	C
BOW	C
STAFF	B
SPEAR	C
AXE	C
BOOK	C
HARP	C

MAGIC USE

OFFENSIVE MAGIC	A
RECOVERY MAGIC	A

DEFENSIVE ABILITY

EVADE	C
MAGIC EVADE	C

PASSIVE ABILITY

Only Sages have top ratings with both Black Magic and White Magic. You can set them up to be more than adequate with either type of magic, and they won't disappoint you.

SPELL AGAIN: KEEP CASTING SPELLS UNTIL ALL YOUR AP IS CONSUMED. APPLIES NEXT TURN ONLY.

ACTION POINTS	1
ABILITY SPEED	10
TARGET	SELF
TARGET VALUE	5 (5)

In the turn after Spell Again is used, you must cast a combination of spells that have an aggregate AP cost of five. You could potentially cast five spells, provided they're all one-AP spells. Duplicating a spell is permitted.

☆ DILIGENCE: DURING THE BATTLE, REDUCE BLACK MAGIC AP CONSUMPTION BY 1.

ACTION POINTS	2
ABILITY SPEED	10
TARGET	SELF
TARGET VALUE	5 (10)

●	5	▽	—
■	5	◖	—
▮	—	☾	—
◇	—	💎	—

If your Sage is more offensively minded, Diligence is the way to go. The lowered AP cost for Black Magic spells goes a long way when combined with Spell Again.

☆☆ BETTERMENT: DURING THE BATTLE, REDUCE WHITE MAGIC AP CONSUMPTION BY 1.

ACTION POINTS	2
ABILITY SPEED	10
TARGET	SELF
TARGET VALUE	5 (15)

●	6	▽	—
■	—	◖	6
▮	2	☾	1
◇	—	💎	—

The Sage takes a page out of the White Mage's playbook with Betterment. If you plan on using White Magic fairly often through the battle, activate this ability as early as possible.

☆☆☆ GOOD AND EVIL: SUMMON A HOLY LIGHT TO DAMAGE ALL FOES AND HEAL ALL ALLIES.

ACTION POINTS	4
ABILITY SPEED	5
TARGET	ALL ALLIES AND ENEMIES
TARGET VALUE	20 (150)

●	7	▽	3
■	—	◖	—
▮	—	☾	2
◇	7	💎	1

The initial portion of the spell strikes all enemies with 120 Magic Attack power and Light-based damage. The damage done is increased by an additional 50%. After the attack, the damage done to the enemies is transferred to the party in the form of restored HP.

LIMITED BY ABILITY SLOTS

Sages are incredibly versatile, but with only six ability slots available, you really should focus on either Black Magic or White Magic. If you don't, you're stuck with a Sage who either misses out on some great Crown abilities, or has an incredibly limited pool of spells.

Pick one type of magic, drop either Diligence or Betterment (whichever one you don't need) and fill out the three open spots with either appropriate restoration spells or deadly Black Magic spells. Let upcoming encounters guide your choices, but try to keep at least one spell that costs only 2 AP. With Spell Again, you can always use it multiple times!

# SCRIBE

CROWN OBTAINED	DEFEAT ADVENTURER AND FAITHFUL FOX IN TRIAL TOWER
SPECIAL ABILITY	GROW MORE POWERFUL THE MORE TIME YOU SPEND PLAYING THE GAME!

Scribes thrive on the metaphysical aspects of the game. Instead of drawing their power from the magic or weapons of the world, they become more powerful in relation to the amount of time you spend playing the game!

CROWN ARMOR: *Scribe Gown (Strength/Intellect/Spirit +5%)*

Best attack/weapon type	None

PASSIVE ABILITY

A Scribe's Strength, Intellect, and Spirit increase as you play the game and perform certain functions.

- STRENGTH BONUS: # of battles divided by 499
- INTELLECT BONUS: # of searches divided by 499
- SPIRIT BONUS: # of steps divided by 4999

STATISTICAL MODIFIERS

HP	1.0
STRENGTH	1.0
INTELLECT	1.0
SPIRIT	1.0

WEAPON PROFICIENCIES

SHORT SWORD	B
SWORD	B
BOW	B
STAFF	B
SPEAR	B
AXE	B
BOOK	B
HARP	B

MAGIC USE

OFFENSIVE MAGIC	C
RECOVERY MAGIC	C

DEFENSIVE ABILITY

EVADE	B
MAGIC EVADE	B

TIME: UNLEASH A POWERFUL ATTACK. WORKS BETTER THE LONGER YOU HAVE PLAYED THE GAME.

ACTION POINTS	2
ABILITY SPEED	10
TARGET	ONE ENEMY
TARGET VALUE	10 (20)

Time initiates a string of 10 physical strikes. The success of your attacks is equal to (character's level + playing time [rounded to a full minute] ÷ 2)%.

⭐ WIRELESS: UNLEASH A MAGIC ATTACK. WORKS BETTER THE LONGER YOU PLAY MULTIPLAYER.

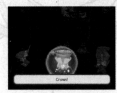

ACTION POINTS	2
ABILITY SPEED	10
TARGET	ONE ENEMY
TARGET VALUE	10 (20)

●	—	▼	5
■	—	◐	5
▯	—	☾	—
◆	—	✺	—

The Magic Attack power of Wireless is equal to your total battle points ÷ 15. Keep in mind that your total battle points is not your current total, but the total you have earned playing multiplayer.

⭐⭐ CROWN: HEAL ONE ALLY'S HP. AMOUNT RECOVERED DEPENDS ON EVERYONE'S CROWN LEVELS.

ACTION POINTS	2
ABILITY SPEED	10
TARGET	ONE ALLY
TARGET VALUE	10 (20)

●	—	▼	6
■	—	◐	—
▯	2	☾	1
◆	6	✺	—

Crown clears all negative status effects (save death) and also restores HP to its target. The amount of HP restored is related to how much that character has enhanced his or her crowns. If all Crowns are at Level 3, then he or she will have 100% HP recovery.

⭐⭐⭐ COMPLETION: BOOST YOUR STATUS LEVELS. WORKS BETTER AS YOU COMPLETE MORE OF THE GAME.

ACTION POINTS	4
ABILITY SPEED	5
TARGET	SELF
TARGET VALUE	10 (20)

●	3	▼	7
■	7	◐	—
▯	—	☾	2
◆	—	✺	1

The improvements from Completion are tied to your progress on the loading screen. Meeting each of the following requirements improves your Completion score:

- 9,999,999 gil on hand
- Clear all Extra Dungeons
- Have every Crown at Level 3
- Strengthen any Armor, Shield, or Weapon to +99
- Open 100% of treasure chests
- Get one of every item
- While in animal form, speak to every animal

MORE TIME MEANS MORE POWER

To get the most out of a Scribe, you must invest a great deal of effort into completing every aspect of the game, from playing multiplayer to finding animals for conversation to gathering a staggering amount of gems. If your interest is in getting through the adventure only, Scribe is not the Crown for you.

STORYTELLER

CROWN OBTAINED	DEFEAT REKOTEH AND ROLAN IN MYSTERIOUS TOWER
SPECIAL ABILITY	MAKE THE MOST OF YOUR ABILITIES!

The trick with Storytellers is to figure out combinations of abilities that work well together. Characters can only use abilities they have unlocked for themselves. Use the tips from the other Crown sections to build powerful Storytellers. After you make your ability choices, select equipment that complements them best.

Crown Armor: *Storyteller Robe (Defense +5, Magic Defense +4, All Stats +5%)*

Best attack/weapon type	None

PASSIVE ABILITY

Storytellers have no abilities of their own, but they allow a character to use the abilities unlocked by improving other Crowns.

STATISTICAL MODIFIERS

HP	1.0
STRENGTH	1.0
INTELLECT	1.0
SPIRIT	1.0

WEAPON PROFICIENCIES

SHORT SWORD	B
SWORD	B
BOW	B
STAFF	B
SPEAR	B
AXE	B
BOOK	B
HARP	B

MAGIC USE

OFFENSIVE MAGIC	B
RECOVERY MAGIC	B

DEFENSIVE ABILITY

EVADE	B
MAGIC EVADE	B

THE FOLLOWING ABILITIES ARE AVAILABLE TO EVERYONE, PROVIDED YOU HAVE UNLOCKED THE PROPER CROWN.

★

● 5	▽ —
▢ 5	◗ —
▯ —	☾ —
◈ —	◆ —

★★

● 6	▽ —
▢ —	◗ 6
▯ 2	☾ 1
◈ —	◆ —

★★★

● 7	▽ 3
▢ —	◗ —
▯ —	☾ 2
◈ 7	◆ 1

BUILDING A BETTER STORYTELLER

You can make an essentially immortal Storyteller with one ability, the right equipment, and a huge bank account. The Merchant abilty Ransom and sufficient gil means the Storyteller will never die as a result of damage done by attacks, abilities, or spells. Equip a Ribbon or the Shield of Light and the Storyteller is immune to negative status effects. The Monk abilities Tool and Implement are worth investigating in this setup as well. In a nasty boss fight, it saves you the effort of bringing allies back to life just to watch them die again in the same round.

The following table is a quick summary of the abilities available to the Storyteller, listed by Crown and Crown Level.

CROWN	DEFAULT ABILITY	DESCRIPTION	★	DESCRIPTION	★★	DESCRIPTION	★★★	DESCRIPTION
Alchemist	Experiment	Transform an item in your possession into another kind of item.	Forge	Create a random attack item and add it to your belongings.	Smelt	Combine items for a variety of different effects.	Cast	Throw all the attack items you carry at the foe.
Bandit	Steal	Try to steal an item from one of the foes.	Plunder	Try to steal an item from all the foes.	Deadly Blow	Possibly inflict sudden death on a foe when you attack.	Pillage	Steal an item from a foe - guaranteed.
Bard	Ditty	Sing a song to raise your party's attack power. Lasts 3 turns.	Motet	Sing a song to raise your party's defense. Lasts 3 turns.	Aria	Sing a song to raise your party's status attributes. Lasts 3 turns.	Fugue	Sing a sad song that stops your foes in their tracks. Lasts only one turn.
Beastmaster	Capture/ Sic	Make a captured monster attack the enemy.	Gentle	Attack the foe without killing it.	Command	Make all party members in animal form attack the enemy.	Turncoat	Make a captured monster attack its own.
Black Mage	Magic Mojo	Make your next attack spell inflict more damage than usual.	Spell Focus	Make your next attack spell inflict a lot more damage than usual.	Mirror	Enable your entire party to deflect spells back at the enemy.	Magic Might	Cast a mighty attack spell against all your foes.
Dancer	Dance	Recover AP more quickly than usual. Lasts 3 turns.	Perform	Make your allies recover their AP more quickly than usual. Lasts 3 turns.	Applaud	Increase one ally's AP by 3 points.	Ovation	Restore all of one ally's AP.
Dark Fencer	Darkside	Sacrifice some of your own HP to deal heavy damage to a foe.	Darker Side	Sacrifice some of your own HP to deal heavy damage to all foes!	Eye for an Eye	Make your attacks stronger as your HP falls.	Amok	Unleash Darkside repeatedly until all your HP is consumed.
Elementalist	Augment	Enhance the effects of allies' element attacks. Lasts 4 turns.	Amplify	Greatly enhance the effects of allies' element attacks. Lasts 4 turns.	Mysterio	Enhance your party's resistance to element attacks.	Elemental	Unleash a storm of element attacks against the foe.
Fighter	Combat	Increase the odds of landing a critical hit. Lasts 4 turns.	Jugular	Strike the foe with a critical hit.	Chakra	Double your own HP for the duration of the battle.	Frenzy-Fu	Hit the foe with repeated attacks. The stronger you are, the longer the chain.
Hero	Reckless	Throw everything you have into an attack, but weaken your defense.	Bladeblitz	Strike at the entire enemy party.	Wrath	Deliver massive magic damage to a single foe.	Finale	Combine with your allies to deliver a combination attack.
Merchant	Finder	Find gems in the midst of battle.	Keeper	Find gems in the midst of battle more effectively than with Finder… Maybe.	Ransom	Each time you are struck by an attack, pay a ransom instead of taking damage.	Money Talks	Inflict damage in proportion to the amount of money you own.
Monk	Tool	Give a dead ally the ability to attack the foe.	Implement	Give a dead ally the ability to use magic	Kamikaze	Attack foes as you die. The more times you have died, the greater the damage.	Ghost Army	Summon an army of ghosts that attacks all foes and deals devastating damage.
Musician	Serenade	Grant Regen to your whole party for 3 turns.	Nocturne	Raise your party's magic attack power for 3 turns.	March	Increase your party's movement speed for 3 turns.	Oratorio	Grant your party Regen. Boost attack, magic attack, and speed for 5 turns.
Ninja	Moving Target	Boost your own ability to evade attacks.	Target Dummy	Create a copy of yourself so you can evade physical attacks. Makes 2 copies.	Counter	Unleash a counter-attack whenever you evade a blow. Lasts 4 turns.	Lightning Fists	Unleash repeated attacks. The better your evasion, the longer the chain.
Paladin	Cover	Shelter a friend from attack and take the damage yourself.	Bait	Draw the foe's attention so you become the target of their attacks.	Avenge	Increase the damage you inflict the more you are targeted for attack.	Last Stand	Hang on to life for several turns at HP 1.
Party Host	Charm	Psych up a single ally.	Rouse	Psych up everyone in the party.	Pot Luck	Something will happen, that's for sure.	Go Team Go!	Psych up everyone in the party - a lot!
Ranger	Target	Ensure that every attack strikes its target.	Snipe	Ensure that every attack strikes its target - with extra damage.	Covering Fire	Inflict heavy damage on all the foes at the beginning of the next turn.	Smashing Blow	Deliver a single, mighty blow against the enemy.
Sage	Spell Again	Keep casting spells until all your AP is consumed. Applies next turn only.	Diligence	During the battle, reduce black magic AP consumption by 1.	Betterment	During the battle, reduce white magic AP consumption by 1.	Good and Evil	Summon a holy light to damage all foes and heal all allies.
Salve-maker	Dispensary	Do not consume recovery items when you use them. Lasts 4 turns.	Healthcare	Make recovery items work on everyone in the party.	Poison Pill	Change recovery items into poison and use them to inflict damage.	Level Serum	Raise the party's level by one for the duration of the battle.
Scholar	Quell	Reduce the attack power of all foes by half. Lasts 3 turns.	Subdue	Reduce the defense of all foes by half. Lasts 3 turns.	Restrain	Slow the movements of all foes. Lasts 3 turns.	Tame	Reduce the attack and defense of all foes to 1. Applies only for that turn.
Scribe	Time	Unleash a powerful attack. Works better the longer you have played the game.	Wireless	Unleash a magic attack. Works better the longer you play multiplayer.	Crown	Heal one ally's HP. Amount recovered depends on everyone's crown levels.	Completion	Boost your status levels. Works better as you complete more of the game.
Seamstress	Patched up	Patch all your non-upgraded armor together for better protection.	Stitched up	Patch all your non-upgraded weapons together for a stronger attack.	Refurbish	Bring one ally back to life.	Sew Together	Sew yourself and an ally together to combine your status levels.
Shaman	Ritual	Make your next dark magic spell affect all your foes.	Curse	Make your next dark magic spell more powerful and affect all your foes.	Spellbound	Prevent both friend and foe alike from taking any actions. Lasts several turns.	Forbidden Art	Reduce the HP of friend and foe alike to 1.
Spell Fencer	Magic Sword	Change weapon element and strike with attack spells.	Mystic Sword	Change weapon element. A more powerful version of Magic Sword.	Magic Thwart	Nullify the effects of attack spells cast against you. Lasts 4 turns.	Magic Infuse	Cast an attack spell and strike with your weapon at the same time.
Wayfarer	Runaway	Run and live to fight another day.	Escape	the battle so you can continue the adventure-guaranteed!	Recovery	Recover some HP each turn.	Friend in Need	Summon your travel companion to attack the foe.
White Mage	Healthgiver	Make your next healing spell work on all your allies.	Lifegiver	Make your next healing spell more powerful and work on all your allies.	Hide	Hide from the foes so they will not attack you.	Miracle	Give your allies a big HP boost and cure all their ailments.

WEAPONS

Even though every character can equip every type of weapon,
it pays to know which weapons each job type uses best.
Use the information on the following pages, as well as the
Crowns section of the
guide, to match the best
weapons to your party's
Crown choices.

Weapons bought with Multiplayer Points

For any weapon marked for sale from the Mutiplayer Shop, the value in the 'Buy' column indicates how many multiplayer points are required to purchase the item. These items can't be sold to vendors, but otherwise work the same as the other weapons.

All weapon types have a preferred initial target line (Front or Rear). If you're concerned about focusing your efforts on defeating one enemy at a time, equip weapons that attack the same line.

AXES

BEST AXE CROWNS	DARK FENCER, BEASTMASTER
FIRST TARGET	FRONT

Axes are consistently at the top of the attack value chart whenever you find one during the adventure, but they have low accuracy scores. If you want to use an Axe effectively, consider items that boost Accuracy (such as Bandit Gear or a Sniper Ring) to go along with it.

ARES

ATTACK	19
MAGIC ATTACK	—
ACCURACY	90
MAGIC ACCURACY	100
ELEMENTAL MODIFIER	—
INFLICTS	—

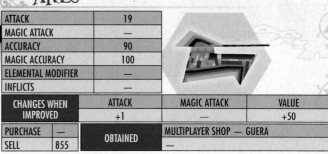

CHANGES WHEN IMPROVED	ATTACK	MAGIC ATTACK	VALUE
	+1	—	+50

PURCHASE	—	OBTAINED	MULTIPLAYER SHOP — GUERA
SELL	855		—

 EARTH AXE

ATTACK	6
MAGIC ATTACK	—
ACCURACY	85
MAGIC ACCURACY	85
ELEMENTAL MODIFIER	EARTH LV.1
INFLICTS	—

CHANGES WHEN IMPROVED	ATTACK	MAGIC ATTACK	VALUE
	+1	—	+50

PURCHASE	—	OBTAINED	CHEST — QUICKSAND CASTLE
SELL	102		DROP — ROCK GOLEM [A]

 FIRE AXE

ATTACK	12
MAGIC ATTACK	—
ACCURACY	85
MAGIC ACCURACY	85
ELEMENTAL MODIFIER	FIRE LV.1
INFLICTS	—

CHANGES WHEN IMPROVED	ATTACK	MAGIC ATTACK	VALUE
	+1	—	+50

PURCHASE	1220	OBTAINED	SOLD — LIBERTE TOWN
SELL	244		SOLD — INVIDIA

HATCHET

ATTACK	3
MAGIC ATTACK	—
ACCURACY	85
MAGIC ACCURACY	85
ELEMENTAL MODIFIER	—
INFLICTS	—

CHANGES WHEN IMPROVED	ATTACK	MAGIC ATTACK	VALUE
	+1	—	+50

PURCHASE	255	OBTAINED	SOLD — URBETH
SELL	51		CHEST — NORTH CAVES

 # HERCULES

ATTACK	50
MAGIC ATTACK	—
ACCURACY	10
MAGIC ACCURACY	10
ELEMENTAL MODIFIER	—
INFLICTS	—

CHANGES WHEN IMPROVED	ATTACK	MAGIC ATTACK	VALUE
	+1	—	+50

PURCHASE	—	OBTAINED	MULTIPLAYER SHOP — GUERA
SELL	1500		—

HYDRAXE

ATTACK	8
MAGIC ATTACK	—
ACCURACY	85
MAGIC ACCURACY	85
ELEMENTAL MODIFIER	WATER LV.1
INFLICTS	—

CHANGES WHEN IMPROVED	ATTACK	MAGIC ATTACK	VALUE
	+1	—	+50

PURCHASE	—	OBTAINED	STEAL — TROLLUD [A]
SELL	176		FOUND — URBETH

 # MJOLLNIR

ATTACK	13
MAGIC ATTACK	—
ACCURACY	85
MAGIC ACCURACY	100
ELEMENTAL MODIFIER	—
INFLICTS	—

CHANGES WHEN IMPROVED	ATTACK	MAGIC ATTACK	VALUE
	+1	—	+50

PURCHASE	—	OBTAINED	MULTIPLAYER SHOP — GUERA
SELL	550		—

 # MYTHRIL HAMMER

ATTACK	11
MAGIC ATTACK	—
ACCURACY	90
MAGIC ACCURACY	90
ELEMENTAL MODIFIER	—
INFLICTS	—

CHANGES WHEN IMPROVED	ATTACK	MAGIC ATTACK	VALUE
	+1	—	+50

PURCHASE	—	OBTAINED	EVENT — EXCHANGED FOR MYTHRIL IN INVIDIA
SELL	198		

SHINING AXE

ATTACK	11
MAGIC ATTACK	—
ACCURACY	85
MAGIC ACCURACY	85
ELEMENTAL MODIFIER	LIGHT LV.1
INFLICTS	—

CHANGES WHEN IMPROVED	ATTACK	MAGIC ATTACK	VALUE
	+1	—	+50

PURCHASE	1135	OBTAINED	SOLD — SPELVIA
SELL	227		CHEST — SPELVIA DUNGEONS

STORMAXE

ATTACK	12
MAGIC ATTACK	—
ACCURACY	85
MAGIC ACCURACY	85
ELEMENTAL MODIFIER	WIND LV.1
INFLICTS	—

CHANGES WHEN IMPROVED	ATTACK	MAGIC ATTACK	VALUE
	+1	—	+50

PURCHASE	1220	OBTAINED	SOLD — TOWN OF HORNE
SELL	244		—

THUNDER AXE

ATTACK	6
MAGIC ATTACK	—
ACCURACY	85
MAGIC ACCURACY	85
ELEMENTAL MODIFIER	LIGHT LV.1
INFLICTS	PARALYSIS(20%)

CHANGES WHEN IMPROVED	ATTACK	MAGIC ATTACK	VALUE
	+1	—	+50

PURCHASE	—	OBTAINED	CHEST — HUNTING CAVES
SELL	142		

WIZARD'S AXE

ATTACK	23
MAGIC ATTACK	—
ACCURACY	80
MAGIC ACCURACY	80
ELEMENTAL MODIFIER	—
INFLICTS	—

CHANGES WHEN IMPROVED	ATTACK	MAGIC ATTACK	VALUE
	+2	—	+100

PURCHASE	—	OBTAINED	CHEST — EXTRA DUNGEONS
SELL	368		

 # WOOD AXE

ATTACK	5
MAGIC ATTACK	—
ACCURACY	85
MAGIC ACCURACY	85
ELEMENTAL MODIFIER	—
INFLICTS	—

CHANGES WHEN IMPROVED	ATTACK	MAGIC ATTACK	VALUE
	+1	—	+50

PURCHASE	—	OBTAINED	CHEST — GUERA
SELL	85		

BOOKS

BEST BOOK CROWN	SCHOLAR
FIRST TARGET	FRONT

Except for rare exceptions, Books are better at boosting magic (both Magic Attack and Magic Accuracy values) than physical attacks. That suits Scholars just fine, since they're better off using spells and abilities instead of brute force.

AKASHIC RECORDS

ATTACK	8		
MAGIC ATTACK	14		
ACCURACY	95		
MAGIC ACCURACY	105		
ELEMENTAL MODIFIER	—		
INFLICTS	—		
CHANGES WHEN IMPROVED	ATTACK +1	MAGIC ATTACK +1	VALUE +50
PURCHASE —	OBTAINED	MULTIPLAYER SHOP — LIBERTE PORT
SELL 1115		—

AVALON SCROLLS

ATTACK	13		
MAGIC ATTACK	5		
ACCURACY	95		
MAGIC ACCURACY	105		
ELEMENTAL MODIFIER	—		
INFLICTS	—		
CHANGES WHEN IMPROVED	ATTACK +1	MAGIC ATTACK +1	VALUE +50
PURCHASE —	OBTAINED	MULTIPLAYER SHOP — LIBERTE PORT
SELL 880		—

BLACK BOOK

ATTACK	7		
MAGIC ATTACK	12		
ACCURACY	95		
MAGIC ACCURACY	105		
ELEMENTAL MODIFIER	DARK LV.1		
INFLICTS	—		
CHANGES WHEN IMPROVED	ATTACK +1	MAGIC ATTACK +1	VALUE +50
PURCHASE 865	OBTAINED	SOLD — INVIDIA
SELL 173		CHEST — MAGIC LABORATORY

BOOK OF DRYAD

ATTACK	5		
MAGIC ATTACK	8		
ACCURACY	95		
MAGIC ACCURACY	105		
ELEMENTAL MODIFIER	—		
INFLICTS	—		
CHANGES WHEN IMPROVED	ATTACK +1	MAGIC ATTACK +1	VALUE +50
PURCHASE 475	OBTAINED	SOLD — ARBOR
SELL 95		—

BOOK OF IFRIT

ATTACK	6		
MAGIC ATTACK	11		
ACCURACY	95		
MAGIC ACCURACY	105		
ELEMENTAL MODIFIER	FIRE LV.1		
INFLICTS	—		
CHANGES WHEN IMPROVED	ATTACK +1	MAGIC ATTACK +1	VALUE +50
PURCHASE 770	OBTAINED	SOLD — URBETH
SELL 154		SOLD — INVIDIA

BOOK OF RAMUH

ATTACK	4		
MAGIC ATTACK	6		
ACCURACY	95		
MAGIC ACCURACY	105		
ELEMENTAL MODIFIER	LIGHT LV.1		
INFLICTS	PARALYSIS(20%)		
CHANGES WHEN IMPROVED	ATTACK +1	MAGIC ATTACK +1	VALUE +50
PURCHASE 580	OBTAINED	SOLD — TOWN OF HORNE
SELL 116		CHEST — SPELVIA DUNGEONS

BOOK OF SECRETS

ATTACK	6		
MAGIC ATTACK	10		
ACCURACY	95		
MAGIC ACCURACY	105		
ELEMENTAL MODIFIER	—		
INFLICTS	—		
CHANGES WHEN IMPROVED	ATTACK +1	MAGIC ATTACK +1	VALUE +50
PURCHASE —	OBTAINED	MULTIPLAYER SHOP — LIBERTE PORT
SELL 810		—

BOOK OF SHIVA

ATTACK	5		
MAGIC ATTACK	9		
ACCURACY	95		
MAGIC ACCURACY	105		
ELEMENTAL MODIFIER	WATER LV.1		
INFLICTS	—		
CHANGES WHEN IMPROVED	ATTACK +1	MAGIC ATTACK +1	VALUE +50
PURCHASE 675	OBTAINED	SOLD — LIBERTE TOWN
SELL 135		CHEST — INVIDIA UNDERGROUND

BOOK OF SYLPH

ATTACK	7		
MAGIC ATTACK	13		
ACCURACY	95		
MAGIC ACCURACY	105		
ELEMENTAL MODIFIER	WIND LV.1		
INFLICTS	—		
CHANGES WHEN IMPROVED	ATTACK +1	MAGIC ATTACK +1	VALUE +50
PURCHASE 865	OBTAINED	SOLD — TOWN OF HORNE
SELL 173		SOLD — GUERA

BOOK OF TITAN

ATTACK	4
MAGIC ATTACK	7
ACCURACY	95
MAGIC ACCURACY	105
ELEMENTAL MODIFIER	EARTH LV.1
INFLICTS	—

CHANGES WHEN IMPROVED	ATTACK	MAGIC ATTACK	VALUE
	+1	+1	+50

PURCHASE	380	OBTAINED	SOLD — GUERA
SELL	76		—

ENCYCLOPEDIA

ATTACK	3
MAGIC ATTACK	4
ACCURACY	95
MAGIC ACCURACY	105
ELEMENTAL MODIFIER	—
INFLICTS	—

CHANGES WHEN IMPROVED	ATTACK	MAGIC ATTACK	VALUE
	+1	+1	+50

PURCHASE	285	OBTAINED	SOLD — URBETH
SELL	57		—

NECRONOMICON

ATTACK	7
MAGIC ATTACK	18
ACCURACY	95
MAGIC ACCURACY	105
ELEMENTAL MODIFIER	—
INFLICTS	—

CHANGES WHEN IMPROVED	ATTACK	MAGIC ATTACK	VALUE
	+1	+2	+100

PURCHASE	—	OBTAINED	CHEST — EXTRA DUNGEONS
SELL	147		STEAL — BEEZLZEBUB [B]

WHITE BOOK

ATTACK	5
MAGIC ATTACK	9
ACCURACY	95
MAGIC ACCURACY	105
ELEMENTAL MODIFIER	LIGHT LV.1
INFLICTS	—

CHANGES WHEN IMPROVED	ATTACK	MAGIC ATTACK	VALUE
	+1	+1	+50

PURCHASE	675	OBTAINED	SOLD — INVIDIA
SELL	135		SOLD — SPELVIA

BOWS

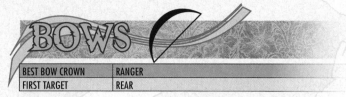

BEST BOW CROWN	RANGER
FIRST TARGET	REAR

Unless a character is a Ranger, it's generally best to use another type of weapon. Of course, Rangers shouldn't use any other type of weapon! Combine a Ranger, a Bow, and the Covering Fire ability to make short work of many random encounters. Bows also inflict 1.4 times damage against flying enemies.

ARTEMIS BOW

ATTACK	19
MAGIC ATTACK	—
ACCURACY	95
MAGIC ACCURACY	100
ELEMENTAL MODIFIER	—
INFLICTS	—

CHANGES WHEN IMPROVED	ATTACK	MAGIC ATTACK	VALUE
	+2	—	+100

PURCHASE	—	OBTAINED	CHEST — EXTRA DUNGEONS
SELL	38		—

BLOODY BOW

ATTACK	7
MAGIC ATTACK	—
ACCURACY	95
MAGIC ACCURACY	100
ELEMENTAL MODIFIER	DARK LV.1
INFLICTS	—

CHANGES WHEN IMPROVED	ATTACK	MAGIC ATTACK	VALUE
	+1	—	+50

PURCHASE	865	OBTAINED	SOLD — INVIDIA
SELL	173		DROP — BORGBEAR [B]

BLUE SHOT

ATTACK	4
MAGIC ATTACK	—
ACCURACY	95
MAGIC ACCURACY	100
ELEMENTAL MODIFIER	WATER LV.1
INFLICTS	—

CHANGES WHEN IMPROVED	ATTACK	MAGIC ATTACK	VALUE
	+1	—	+50

PURCHASE	580	OBTAINED	SOLD — URBETH
SELL	116		SOLD — ARBOR

BOLT BOW

ATTACK	8
MAGIC ATTACK	—
ACCURACY	95
MAGIC ACCURACY	100
ELEMENTAL MODIFIER	LIGHT LV.1
INFLICTS	PARALYSIS(20%)

CHANGES WHEN IMPROVED	ATTACK	MAGIC ATTACK	VALUE
	+1	—	+50

PURCHASE	960	OBTAINED	SOLD — SPELVIA
SELL	192		—

EARTH BOW

ATTACK	4
MAGIC ATTACK	—
ACCURACY	95
MAGIC ACCURACY	100
ELEMENTAL MODIFIER	EARTH LV.1
INFLICTS	—

CHANGES WHEN IMPROVED	ATTACK	MAGIC ATTACK	VALUE
	+1	—	+50

PURCHASE	—	OBTAINED	CHEST — ????
SELL	76		—

EXPUNGER

ATTACK	30
MAGIC ATTACK	—
ACCURACY	50
MAGIC ACCURACY	50
ELEMENTAL MODIFIER	—
INFLICTS	—

CHANGES WHEN IMPROVED	ATTACK	MAGIC ATTACK	VALUE
	+1	—	+50

PURCHASE	—	OBTAINED	MULTIPLAYER SHOP — INVIDIA
SELL	750		—

FAILNAUGHT

ATTACK	15
MAGIC ATTACK	15
ACCURACY	100
MAGIC ACCURACY	100
ELEMENTAL MODIFIER	—
INFLICTS	—

CHANGES WHEN IMPROVED	ATTACK	MAGIC ATTACK	VALUE
	+1	—	+50

PURCHASE	—	OBTAINED	MULTIPLAYER SHOP — INVIDIA
SELL	1500		—

HADES BOW

ATTACK	10
MAGIC ATTACK	—
ACCURACY	200
MAGIC ACCURACY	100
ELEMENTAL MODIFIER	—
INFLICTS	—

CHANGES WHEN IMPROVED	ATTACK	MAGIC ATTACK	VALUE
	+1	—	+50

PURCHASE	—	OBTAINED	MULTIPLAYER SHOP — INVIDIA
SELL	1000		—

HORNE'S BOW

ATTACK	2
MAGIC ATTACK	—
ACCURACY	95
MAGIC ACCURACY	100
ELEMENTAL MODIFIER	—
INFLICTS	—

CHANGES WHEN IMPROVED	ATTACK	MAGIC ATTACK	VALUE
	+1	—	+50

PURCHASE	190	OBTAINED	SOLD — TOWN OF HORNE
SELL	38		SOLD — GUERA

RANGER BOW

ATTACK	6
MAGIC ATTACK	—
ACCURACY	95
MAGIC ACCURACY	100
ELEMENTAL MODIFIER	—
INFLICTS	—

CHANGES WHEN IMPROVED	ATTACK	MAGIC ATTACK	VALUE
	+1	—	+50

PURCHASE	570	OBTAINED	SOLD — ARBOR
SELL	114		—

RED SHOT

ATTACK	7
MAGIC ATTACK	—
ACCURACY	95
MAGIC ACCURACY	100
ELEMENTAL MODIFIER	FIRE LV.1
INFLICTS	—

CHANGES WHEN IMPROVED	ATTACK	MAGIC ATTACK	VALUE
	+1	—	+50

PURCHASE	865	OBTAINED	SOLD — ARBOR
SELL	173		CHEST — TOWER TO THE SKY

STARDUST BOW

ATTACK	8
MAGIC ATTACK	—
ACCURACY	95
MAGIC ACCURACY	100
ELEMENTAL MODIFIER	LIGHT LV.1
INFLICTS	—

CHANGES WHEN IMPROVED	ATTACK	MAGIC ATTACK	VALUE
	+1	—	+50

PURCHASE	960	OBTAINED	SOLD — SPELVIA
SELL	192		—

WIND BOW

ATTACK	3
MAGIC ATTACK	—
ACCURACY	95
MAGIC ACCURACY	100
ELEMENTAL MODIFIER	WIND LV.1
INFLICTS	—

CHANGES WHEN IMPROVED	ATTACK	MAGIC ATTACK	VALUE
	+1	—	+50

PURCHASE	485	OBTAINED	SOLD — GUERA
SELL	97		SOLD — ARBOR

HARPS

BEST HARP CROWNS	BARD, ELEMENTALIST, MUSICIAN
FIRST TARGET	REAR

Harps start out with equal ratings for Attack and Magic Attack (when improved in Urbeth, only the harp's Magic Attack gets better) but their Accuracy and Magic Accuracy numbers are all over the place! Before you equip a newly acquired Harp, check out its stats before putting it to use. A bit more Magic Attack may not be enough to make up for a big drop in Magic Accuracy. Harps also inflict 1.4 times damage against flying enemies.

ANGEL HARP

ATTACK	12
MAGIC ATTACK	12
ACCURACY	100
MAGIC ACCURACY	150
ELEMENTAL MODIFIER	—
INFLICTS	DEATH (15%)

CHANGES WHEN IMPROVED	ATTACK	MAGIC ATTACK	VALUE
	—	+1	+50

PURCHASE	—	OBTAINED	MULTIPLAYER SHOP — SPELVIA
SELL	1100		—

APOLLO'S HARP

ATTACK	17
MAGIC ATTACK	17
ACCURACY	110
MAGIC ACCURACY	105
ELEMENTAL MODIFIER	—
INFLICTS	—

CHANGES WHEN IMPROVED	ATTACK	MAGIC ATTACK	VALUE
	—	+2	+100

PURCHASE	—	OBTAINED	CHEST — EXTRA DUNGEONS
SELL	172		—

BURNING HARP

ATTACK	7
MAGIC ATTACK	7
ACCURACY	110
MAGIC ACCURACY	105
ELEMENTAL MODIFIER	FIRE LV.1
INFLICTS	—

CHANGES WHEN IMPROVED	ATTACK	MAGIC ATTACK	VALUE
	—	+1	+50

PURCHASE	970	OBTAINED	SOLD — URBETH
SELL	194		SOLD — INVIDIA

DARKENING HARP

ATTACK	6
MAGIC ATTACK	6
ACCURACY	110
MAGIC ACCURACY	105
ELEMENTAL MODIFIER	DARK LV.1
INFLICTS	—

CHANGES WHEN IMPROVED	ATTACK	MAGIC ATTACK	VALUE
	—	+1	+50

PURCHASE	860	OBTAINED	SOLD — INVIDIA
SELL	172		CHEST — ICE CAVERNS

DAVID'S HARP

ATTACK	12
MAGIC ATTACK	12
ACCURACY	125
MAGIC ACCURACY	125
ELEMENTAL MODIFIER	—
INFLICTS	LOWERS STATUS(20%)

CHANGES WHEN IMPROVED	ATTACK	MAGIC ATTACK	VALUE
	—	+1	+50

PURCHASE	—	OBTAINED	MULTIPLAYER SHOP — SPELVIA
SELL	1000		—

FLOWING HARP

ATTACK	4
MAGIC ATTACK	4
ACCURACY	110
MAGIC ACCURACY	105
ELEMENTAL MODIFIER	WATER LV.1
INFLICTS	—

CHANGES WHEN IMPROVED	ATTACK	MAGIC ATTACK	VALUE
	—	+1	+50

PURCHASE	640	OBTAINED	SOLD — LIBERTE TOWN
SELL	128		—

GREAT TREE HARP

ATTACK	5
MAGIC ATTACK	5
ACCURACY	110
MAGIC ACCURACY	105
ELEMENTAL MODIFIER	—
INFLICTS	—

CHANGES WHEN IMPROVED	ATTACK	MAGIC ATTACK	VALUE
	—	+1	+50

PURCHASE	—	OBTAINED	CHEST — GREAT TREE ROOTS
SELL	110		—

HARP

ATTACK	2
MAGIC ATTACK	2
ACCURACY	110
MAGIC ACCURACY	105
ELEMENTAL MODIFIER	—
INFLICTS	—

CHANGES WHEN IMPROVED	ATTACK	MAGIC ATTACK	VALUE
	—	+1	+50

PURCHASE	220	OBTAINED	SOLD — LIBERTE TOWN
SELL	44		SOLD — URBETH

LAMIA HARP

ATTACK	12
MAGIC ATTACK	12
ACCURACY	150
MAGIC ACCURACY	100
ELEMENTAL MODIFIER	—
INFLICTS	PETRIFICATION (15%)

CHANGES WHEN IMPROVED	ATTACK	MAGIC ATTACK	VALUE
	—	+1	+50

PURCHASE	—	OBTAINED	MULTIPLAYER SHOP — SPELVIA
SELL	1150		—

QUAKING HARP

ATTACK	8
MAGIC ATTACK	8
ACCURACY	110
MAGIC ACCURACY	105
ELEMENTAL MODIFIER	EARTH LV.1
INFLICTS	—

CHANGES WHEN IMPROVED	ATTACK	MAGIC ATTACK	VALUE
	—	+1	+50

PURCHASE	—	OBTAINED	DROP — ARP
SELL	176		—

SHINING HARP

ATTACK	6
MAGIC ATTACK	6
ACCURACY	110
MAGIC ACCURACY	105
ELEMENTAL MODIFIER	LIGHT LV.1
INFLICTS	—

CHANGES WHEN IMPROVED	ATTACK	MAGIC ATTACK	VALUE
	—	+1	+50

PURCHASE	860	OBTAINED	SOLD — SPELVIA
SELL	172		

STUNNING HARP

ATTACK	7
MAGIC ATTACK	7
ACCURACY	110
MAGIC ACCURACY	105
ELEMENTAL MODIFIER	LIGHT LV.1
INFLICTS	PARALYSIS(20%)

CHANGES WHEN IMPROVED	ATTACK	MAGIC ATTACK	VALUE
	—	+1	+50

PURCHASE	—	OBTAINED	CHEST — LIBERTE TOWN (AFTER OBTAINING MAGIC KEY)
SELL	194		

WHISPERING HARP

ATTACK	8
MAGIC ATTACK	8
ACCURACY	110
MAGIC ACCURACY	105
ELEMENTAL MODIFIER	WIND LV.1
INFLICTS	—

CHANGES WHEN IMPROVED	ATTACK	MAGIC ATTACK	VALUE
	—	+1	+50

PURCHASE	—	OBTAINED	DROP — LILITH
SELL	216		STEAL — IMP [B]

NEEDLES

BEST NEEDLE CROWN	SEAMSTRESS
FIRST TARGET	REAR

There aren't many Needles in the game, and you don't find any until you start investigating the bonus towers scattered around the world. When you get your hands on one, put it to work immediately in the hands of any Seamstress in your party. If you don't have a Seamstress, store Needles in the bank; there are better weapon options for the other Crowns. Needles inflict 1.4 times damage versus flying enemies.

GIANT NEEDLE

ATTACK	17
MAGIC ATTACK	—
ACCURACY	110
MAGIC ACCURACY	90
ELEMENTAL MODIFIER	—
INFLICTS	—

CHANGES WHEN IMPROVED	ATTACK	MAGIC ATTACK	VALUE
	+1	—	+50

PURCHASE	25,000	OBTAINED	SOLD — TRIAL TOWER
SELL	5000		—

GIANT'S TOOTHPICK

ATTACK	18
MAGIC ATTACK	—
ACCURACY	100
MAGIC ACCURACY	100
ELEMENTAL MODIFIER	—
INFLICTS	—

CHANGES WHEN IMPROVED	ATTACK	MAGIC ATTACK	VALUE
	+2	—	+100

PURCHASE	—	OBTAINED	CHEST — EXTRA DUNGEONS
SELL	6500		FOR SALE — TRIAL TOWER

SHORT SWORDS

BEST SHORT SWORD CROWNS	BANDIT, DANCER, DARK FENCER
FIRST TARGET	FRONT

Short Swords offer a nice mix of accurate attacks, element-based damage, and negative status effects. Not all Short Swords offer the extra damage or inflict negative status effects, but put one into the hands of Dancer (or, to a lesser extent, Bandits and Dark Fencers) and you won't miss them.

BANEKNIFE

ATTACK	2
MAGIC ATTACK	2
ACCURACY	120
MAGIC ACCURACY	120
ELEMENTAL MODIFIER	WATER LV.1
INFLICTS	POISON (30%)

CHANGES WHEN IMPROVED	ATTACK	MAGIC ATTACK	VALUE
	+1	—	+50

PURCHASE	—	OBTAINED	CHEST — QUICKSAND CASTLE
SELL	88		—

CURSED BLADE

ATTACK	5
MAGIC ATTACK	5
ACCURACY	110
MAGIC ACCURACY	110
ELEMENTAL MODIFIER	DARK LV.1
INFLICTS	BLINDNESS (30%)

CHANGES WHEN IMPROVED	ATTACK	MAGIC ATTACK	VALUE
	+1	—	+50

PURCHASE	—	OBTAINED	DROP — DOPPLEGANGER [AIRE A]
SELL	150		DROP — DOPPLEGANGER [JUSQUA A]

DIRT DIRK

ATTACK	3
MAGIC ATTACK	3
ACCURACY	110
MAGIC ACCURACY	110
ELEMENTAL MODIFIER	EARTH LV.1
INFLICTS	PETRIFICATION (15%)

CHANGES WHEN IMPROVED	ATTACK	MAGIC ATTACK	VALUE
	+1	—	+50

PURCHASE	—	OBTAINED	FOUND — GUERA
SELL	130		—

FLAME DAGGER

ATTACK	3
MAGIC ATTACK	3
ACCURACY	110
MAGIC ACCURACY	110
ELEMENTAL MODIFIER	FIRE LV.1
INFLICTS	CONFUSION (30%)

CHANGES WHEN IMPROVED	ATTACK	MAGIC ATTACK	VALUE
	+1	—	+50

PURCHASE	530	OBTAINED	SOLD — LIBERTE TOWN
SELL	106		SOLD — INVIDIA

FRESH MEAT

ATTACK	10
MAGIC ATTACK	5
ACCURACY	110
MAGIC ACCURACY	110
ELEMENTAL MODIFIER	—
INFLICTS	DEATH (15%)

CHANGES WHEN IMPROVED	ATTACK	MAGIC ATTACK	VALUE
	+1	—	+50

PURCHASE	—	OBTAINED	CHEST — PIRATE HIDEOUT
SELL	220		CHEST — STAR CHAMBER

GREAT TREE DAGGER

ATTACK	4
MAGIC ATTACK	4
ACCURACY	110
MAGIC ACCURACY	110
ELEMENTAL MODIFIER	—
INFLICTS	—

CHANGES WHEN IMPROVED	ATTACK	MAGIC ATTACK	VALUE
	+1	—	+50

PURCHASE	440	OBTAINED	SOLD — ARBOR
SELL	88		—

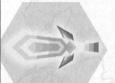

HOLY KNIFE

ATTACK	8
MAGIC ATTACK	8
ACCURACY	110
MAGIC ACCURACY	110
ELEMENTAL MODIFIER	LIGHT LV.1
INFLICTS	LOWERS STATUS (20%)

CHANGES WHEN IMPROVED	ATTACK	MAGIC ATTACK	VALUE
	+1	—	+50

PURCHASE	1080	OBTAINED	SOLD — SPELVIA
SELL	216		DROP — DOPPLEGANGER [JUSQUA B]

ICE PICK

ATTACK	4
MAGIC ATTACK	4
ACCURACY	110
MAGIC ACCURACY	110
ELEMENTAL MODIFIER	WATER LV.1
INFLICTS	SLEEP (30%)

CHANGES WHEN IMPROVED	ATTACK	MAGIC ATTACK	VALUE
	+1	—	+50

PURCHASE	640	OBTAINED	SOLD — URBETH
SELL	128		SOLD — INVIDIA

KING'S SHORTSWORD

ATTACK	2
MAGIC ATTACK	2
ACCURACY	130
MAGIC ACCURACY	130
ELEMENTAL MODIFIER	—
INFLICTS	—

CHANGES WHEN IMPROVED	ATTACK	MAGIC ATTACK	VALUE
	+2	+2	+100

PURCHASE	—	OBTAINED	[SG] AIRE
SELL	200		—

KNIFE

ATTACK	2		
MAGIC ATTACK	2		
ACCURACY	110		
MAGIC ACCURACY	110		
ELEMENTAL MODIFIER	—		
INFLICTS	—		

CHANGES WHEN IMPROVED	ATTACK	MAGIC ATTACK	VALUE
	+1	—	+50

PURCHASE	220	OBTAINED	SOLD — LIBERTE TOWN
SELL	44		SOLD — URBETH

MAIN GAUCHE

ATTACK	8		
MAGIC ATTACK	4		
ACCURACY	130		
MAGIC ACCURACY	130		
ELEMENTAL MODIFIER	—		
INFLICTS	PARALYSIS, LOWERS STATUS (25%).		

CHANGES WHEN IMPROVED	ATTACK	MAGIC ATTACK	VALUE
	+1	—	+50

PURCHASE	—	OBTAINED	MULTIPLAYER SHOP — SPELVIA
SELL	1030		—

SASUKE'S KODACHI

ATTACK	8		
MAGIC ATTACK	4		
ACCURACY	130		
MAGIC ACCURACY	130		
ELEMENTAL MODIFIER	—		
INFLICTS	CONFUSION, POISON (35%)		

CHANGES WHEN IMPROVED	ATTACK	MAGIC ATTACK	VALUE
	+1	—	+100

PURCHASE	—	OBTAINED	MULTIPLAYER SHOP — SPELVIA
SELL	780		

STILETTO

ATTACK	8		
MAGIC ATTACK	4		
ACCURACY	130		
MAGIC ACCURACY	130		
ELEMENTAL MODIFIER	—		
INFLICTS	SILENCE, BLINDNESS (35%)		

CHANGES WHEN IMPROVED	ATTACK	MAGIC ATTACK	VALUE
	+1	—	+100

PURCHASE	—	OBTAINED	MULTIPLAYER SHOP — SPELVIA
SELL	780		—

STUN STILETTO

ATTACK	3		
MAGIC ATTACK	3		
ACCURACY	110		
MAGIC ACCURACY	110		
ELEMENTAL MODIFIER	LIGHT LV.1		
INFLICTS	PARALYSIS (20%)		

CHANGES WHEN IMPROVED	ATTACK	MAGIC ATTACK	VALUE
	+1	—	+50

PURCHASE	530	OBTAINED	SOLD — ARBOR
SELL	106		—

TONBERRY KNIFE

ATTACK	8		
MAGIC ATTACK	4		
ACCURACY	130		
MAGIC ACCURACY	130		
ELEMENTAL MODIFIER	—		
INFLICTS	DEATH (30%)		

CHANGES WHEN IMPROVED	ATTACK	MAGIC ATTACK	VALUE
	+1	—	+50

PURCHASE	—	OBTAINED	MULTIPLAYER SHOP — SPELVIA
SELL	1280		—

WIND DAGGER

ATTACK	6		
MAGIC ATTACK	6		
ACCURACY	110		
MAGIC ACCURACY	110		
ELEMENTAL MODIFIER	WIND LV.1		
INFLICTS	SILENCE (30%)		

CHANGES WHEN IMPROVED	ATTACK	MAGIC ATTACK	VALUE
	+1	—	+50

PURCHASE	—	OBTAINED	DROP — RATTATOX [A]
SELL	172		DROP — CARBUNKLE

SPEARS

BEST SPEAR CROWNS	SPELL FENCER, PALADIN
FIRST TARGET	REAR

The two Crowns who excel with Spears are also experts with Swords, so it's worthwhile to compare the two types of weapon. Spears have a slight advantage in Accuracy (most of the time) but don't pack the elemental punch of Swords. Spears also deal 1.4 times damage against flying enemies. Select Spears if you're about to visit an area filled with flying enemies and save Swords for the times when inflicting elemental-based damage makes a difference.

EVIL LANCE

ATTACK	17		
MAGIC ATTACK	—		
ACCURACY	110		
MAGIC ACCURACY	90		
ELEMENTAL MODIFIER	DARK LV.1		
INFLICTS	—		

CHANGES WHEN IMPROVED	ATTACK	MAGIC ATTACK	VALUE
	+1	—	+50

PURCHASE	2070	OBTAINED	SOLD — INVIDIA
SELL	414		CHEST — MAGIC LABORATORY

FLAME SPEAR

ATTACK	4
MAGIC ATTACK	—
ACCURACY	110
MAGIC ACCURACY	90
ELEMENTAL MODIFIER	FIRE LV.1
INFLICTS	—

CHANGES WHEN IMPROVED	ATTACK	MAGIC ATTACK	VALUE
	+1	—	+50

PURCHASE	640	OBTAINED	SOLD — LIBERTE TOWN
SELL	128		CHEST — ICE CAVERNS

GAE BOLG

ATTACK	13
MAGIC ATTACK	—
ACCURACY	110
MAGIC ACCURACY	90
ELEMENTAL MODIFIER	—
INFLICTS	—

CHANGES WHEN IMPROVED	ATTACK	MAGIC ATTACK	VALUE
	+1	—	+50

PURCHASE	—	OBTAINED	MULTIPLAYER SHOP — URBETH
SELL	715		—

GUAN YU'S PIKE

ATTACK	18
MAGIC ATTACK	—
ACCURACY	110
MAGIC ACCURACY	90
ELEMENTAL MODIFIER	—
INFLICTS	—

CHANGES WHEN IMPROVED	ATTACK	MAGIC ATTACK	VALUE
	+1	—	+60

PURCHASE	55000	OBTAINED	SOLD — HOLY TREE TOWER
SELL	11000		—

GUNGNIR

ATTACK	21
MAGIC ATTACK	—
ACCURACY	110
MAGIC ACCURACY	110
ELEMENTAL MODIFIER	—
INFLICTS	—

CHANGES WHEN IMPROVED	ATTACK	MAGIC ATTACK	VALUE
	+1	—	+50

PURCHASE	65000	OBTAINED	SOLD — MOONSAND RUINS
SELL	13000		—

HOLY LANCE

ATTACK	9
MAGIC ATTACK	—
ACCURACY	110
MAGIC ACCURACY	90
ELEMENTAL MODIFIER	LIGHT LV.1
INFLICTS	—

CHANGES WHEN IMPROVED	ATTACK	MAGIC ATTACK	VALUE
	+1	—	+50

PURCHASE	—	OBTAINED	DROP — WYVERN [B]
SELL	238		

INDRA'S SPEAR

ATTACK	8
MAGIC ATTACK	—
ACCURACY	110
MAGIC ACCURACY	90
ELEMENTAL MODIFIER	LIGHT LV.1
INFLICTS	PARALYSIS(20%)

CHANGES WHEN IMPROVED	ATTACK	MAGIC ATTACK	VALUE
	+1	—	+50

PURCHASE	—	OBTAINED	FOUND — SPELVIA
SELL	216		

MAMON'S SPEAR

ATTACK	11
MAGIC ATTACK	—
ACCURACY	110
MAGIC ACCURACY	90
ELEMENTAL MODIFIER	—
INFLICTS	—

CHANGES WHEN IMPROVED	ATTACK	MAGIC ATTACK	VALUE
	+1	—	+50

PURCHASE	—	OBTAINED	STEAL — MAMMON [B]
SELL	605		MULTIPLAYER SHOP — URBETH

ROCK LANCE

ATTACK	4
MAGIC ATTACK	—
ACCURACY	110
MAGIC ACCURACY	90
ELEMENTAL MODIFIER	EARTH LV.1
INFLICTS	—

CHANGES WHEN IMPROVED	ATTACK	MAGIC ATTACK	VALUE
	+1	—	+50

PURCHASE	—	OBTAINED	CHEST — PIRATE HIDEOUT
SELL	88		STEAL — HOBGOBLIN

SHARK LANCE

ATTACK	6
MAGIC ATTACK	—
ACCURACY	110
MAGIC ACCURACY	90
ELEMENTAL MODIFIER	WATER LV.1
INFLICTS	—

CHANGES WHEN IMPROVED	ATTACK	MAGIC ATTACK	VALUE
	+1	—	+50

PURCHASE	—	OBTAINED	STEAL — ORC [B]
SELL	172		DROP — BRAINSHARK [A]

STEEL SPEAR

ATTACK	3
MAGIC ATTACK	—
ACCURACY	110
MAGIC ACCURACY	90
ELEMENTAL MODIFIER	—
INFLICTS	—

CHANGES WHEN IMPROVED	ATTACK	MAGIC ATTACK	VALUE
	+1	—	+50

PURCHASE	330	OBTAINED	SOLD — GUERA
SELL	66		SOLD — URBETH

TEMPEST PIKE

ATTACK	3
MAGIC ATTACK	—
ACCURACY	110
MAGIC ACCURACY	90
ELEMENTAL MODIFIER	WIND LV.1
INFLICTS	

CHANGES WHEN IMPROVED	ATTACK	MAGIC ATTACK	VALUE
	+1	—	+50

PURCHASE	530	OBTAINED	SOLD — TOWN OF HORNE (AFTER EVENT G-15)
SELL	106		CHEST — MOONLIGHT TOWER

TRIDENT

ATTACK	20
MAGIC ATTACK	—
ACCURACY	120
MAGIC ACCURACY	120
ELEMENTAL MODIFIER	—
INFLICTS	—

CHANGES WHEN IMPROVED	ATTACK	MAGIC ATTACK	VALUE
	+1	—	+50

PURCHASE	—	OBTAINED	MULTIPLAYER SHOP — URBETH
SELL	1200		—

WOOD LANCE

ATTACK	6
MAGIC ATTACK	—
ACCURACY	110
MAGIC ACCURACY	90
ELEMENTAL MODIFIER	
INFLICTS	—

CHANGES WHEN IMPROVED	ATTACK	MAGIC ATTACK	VALUE
	+1	—	+50

PURCHASE	660	OBTAINED	SOLD — ARBOR
SELL	132		CHEST — GREAT TREE ROOTS

ZODIAC SPEAR

ATTACK	22
MAGIC ATTACK	—
ACCURACY	120
MAGIC ACCURACY	90
ELEMENTAL MODIFIER	—
INFLICTS	—

CHANGES WHEN IMPROVED	ATTACK	MAGIC ATTACK	VALUE
	+2	+1	+100

PURCHASE	—	OBTAINED	CHEST — EXTRA DUNGEONS
SELL	3800		—

STAVES

BEST STAVES CROWNS	BLACK MAGE, SAGE
FIRST TARGET	FRONT

They're perfect fits: Black Mages and Sages are the best at inflicting damage with magic, and Staves are the best weapons for enhancing your magical damage output. Unlike other weapon choices, you can usually disregard the Elemental Modifiers found on Staves if you're about to encounter enemies with resistances. Any Crown that equips a staff should be focused on dealing magic damage, not hitting enemies with a big stick!

CLAUSTRUM

ATTACK	6
MAGIC ATTACK	14
ACCURACY	95
MAGIC ACCURACY	110
ELEMENTAL MODIFIER	—
INFLICTS	

Equipping Claustrum increases Magic Attack by 20%.

ATTACK —	MAGIC ATTACK	VALUE
	+1	+50

PURCHASE	—	OBTAINED	STEAL — MAMMON [A]
SELL	191		—

CYCLONE STAFF

ATTACK	1
MAGIC ATTACK	4
ACCURACY	95
MAGIC ACCURACY	110
ELEMENTAL MODIFIER	WIND LV.1
INFLICTS	—

CHANGES WHEN IMPROVED	ATTACK	MAGIC ATTACK	VALUE
	—	+1	+50

PURCHASE	295	OBTAINED	SOLD — URBETH
SELL	59		SOLD — TOWN OF HORNE (AFTER EVENT G-15)

DARKNESS STAFF

ATTACK	5
MAGIC ATTACK	13
ACCURACY	95
MAGIC ACCURACY	110
ELEMENTAL MODIFIER	DARK LV.1
INFLICTS	—

CHANGES WHEN IMPROVED	ATTACK	MAGIC ATTACK	VALUE
	—	+1	+50

PURCHASE	675	OBTAINED	SOLD — INVIDIA
SELL	135		CHEST — MAGIC LABORATORY

GREAT WIZARD STAVE

ATTACK	7
MAGIC ATTACK	16
ACCURACY	95
MAGIC ACCURACY	120
ELEMENTAL MODIFIER	—
INFLICTS	—

Equipping Great Wizard Stave increases Magic Attack by 20%.

CHANGES WHEN IMPROVED	ATTACK	MAGIC ATTACK	VALUE
	—	+2	+100

PURCHASE	—	OBTAINED	CHEST — EXTRA DUNGEONS
SELL	1292		—

INFERNO STAVE

ATTACK	2
MAGIC ATTACK	5
ACCURACY	95
MAGIC ACCURACY	110
ELEMENTAL MODIFIER	FIRE LV.1
INFLICTS	—

CHANGES WHEN IMPROVED	ATTACK	MAGIC ATTACK	VALUE
	—	+1	+50

PURCHASE	390	OBTAINED	CHEST — PIRATE HIDEOUT
SELL	78		DROP — CAIT SITH [A]

MAGIC STAFF

ATTACK	1
MAGIC ATTACK	3
ACCURACY	95
MAGIC ACCURACY	110
ELEMENTAL MODIFIER	—
INFLICTS	—

CHANGES WHEN IMPROVED	ATTACK	MAGIC ATTACK	VALUE
	—	+1	+50

PURCHASE	95	OBTAINED	SOLD — GUERA
SELL	19		SOLD — URBETH

MYTHRIL ROD

ATTACK	5
MAGIC ATTACK	12
ACCURACY	95
MAGIC ACCURACY	120
ELEMENTAL MODIFIER	—
INFLICTS	—

CHANGES WHEN IMPROVED	ATTACK	MAGIC ATTACK	VALUE
	—	+1	+50

PURCHASE	—	OBTAINED	MULTIPLAYER SHOP — ARBOR
SELL	958		—

OCEAN STAVE

ATTACK	1
MAGIC ATTACK	3
ACCURACY	95
MAGIC ACCURACY	110
ELEMENTAL MODIFIER	WATER LV.1
INFLICTS	—

CHANGES WHEN IMPROVED	ATTACK	MAGIC ATTACK	VALUE
	—	+1	+50

PURCHASE	295	OBTAINED	SOLD — INVIDIA
SELL	59		CHEST — PIRATE HIDEOUT

SACRED TREE STAFF

ATTACK	2
MAGIC ATTACK	5
ACCURACY	95
MAGIC ACCURACY	110
ELEMENTAL MODIFIER	—
INFLICTS	—

CHANGES WHEN IMPROVED	ATTACK	MAGIC ATTACK	VALUE
	—	+1	+50

PURCHASE	190	OBTAINED	SOLD — ARBOR
SELL	38		STEAL — NEKO NATTER

SAGE'S STAFF

ATTACK	6
MAGIC ATTACK	14
ACCURACY	95
MAGIC ACCURACY	120
ELEMENTAL MODIFIER	—
INFLICTS	—

CHANGES WHEN IMPROVED	ATTACK	MAGIC ATTACK	VALUE
	—	+1	+50

PURCHASE	—	OBTAINED	MULTIPLAYER SHOP — ARBOR
SELL	1125		—

SHINING STAFF

ATTACK	3
MAGIC ATTACK	7
ACCURACY	95
MAGIC ACCURACY	110
ELEMENTAL MODIFIER	LIGHT LV.1
INFLICTS	—

CHANGES WHEN IMPROVED	ATTACK	MAGIC ATTACK	VALUE
	—	+1	+50

PURCHASE	485	OBTAINED	SOLD — SPELVIA
SELL	97		STEAL — NEKO NATTER

SWORDS

BEST SWORD CROWNS	BANDIT, HERO, SPELL FENCER, PALADIN, DARK FENCER, NINJA
FIRST TARGET	FRONT

It's a good thing there are so many Swords available during the adventure; many jobs excel at using them, so make sure there are enough to go around! Swords have Level 2 Elemental Modifiers. That's a big help when you're facing enemies with an elemental weakness.

BLACKSWORD

ATTACK	18
MAGIC ATTACK	—
ACCURACY	100
MAGIC ACCURACY	100
ELEMENTAL MODIFIER	DARK LV.2
INFLICTS	DEATH (20%)

CHANGES WHEN IMPROVED	ATTACK	MAGIC ATTACK	VALUE
	+1	—	+50

PURCHASE	—	OBTAINED	MULTIPLAYER SHOP — TOWN OF HORNE
SELL	1600		—

BOLT SWORD

ATTACK	5
MAGIC ATTACK	—
ACCURACY	100
MAGIC ACCURACY	100
ELEMENTAL MODIFIER	LIGHT LV.1
INFLICTS	PARALYSIS (20%)

CHANGES WHEN IMPROVED	ATTACK	MAGIC ATTACK	VALUE
	+1	—	+50

PURCHASE	700	OBTAINED	SOLD — URBETH
SELL	140		CHEST — ???

DARKBRINGER

ATTACK	17		
MAGIC ATTACK	—		
ACCURACY	100		
MAGIC ACCURACY	100		
ELEMENTAL MODIFIER	DARK LV.2		
INFLICTS	—		

CHANGES WHEN IMPROVED	ATTACK	MAGIC ATTACK	VALUE
	+1	—	+50

PURCHASE	—	OBTAINED	STEAL — SATAN [A]
SELL	420		STEAL — SATAN [B]

DARKNESS BLADE

ATTACK	9		
MAGIC ATTACK	—		
ACCURACY	100		
MAGIC ACCURACY	100		
ELEMENTAL MODIFIER	DARK LV.1		
INFLICTS	—		

CHANGES WHEN IMPROVED	ATTACK	MAGIC ATTACK	VALUE
	+1	—	+50

PURCHASE	1100	OBTAINED	SOLD — INVIDIA
SELL	220		—

EARTH SWORD

ATTACK	5		
MAGIC ATTACK	—		
ACCURACY	100		
MAGIC ACCURACY	100		
ELEMENTAL MODIFIER	EARTH LV.1		
INFLICTS	—		

CHANGES WHEN IMPROVED	ATTACK	MAGIC ATTACK	VALUE
	+1	—	+50

PURCHASE	—	OBTAINED	DROP — SAND DEVIL [A]
SELL	100		—

EXCALIBUR

ATTACK	20		
MAGIC ATTACK	—		
ACCURACY	100		
MAGIC ACCURACY	100		
ELEMENTAL MODIFIER	—		
INFLICTS	—		

ATTACK+2	MAGIC ATTACK	VALUE	
	—	+100	

PURCHASE	—	OBTAINED	CHEST — EXTRA DUNGEONS
SELL	400		—

FLAMEBLADE

ATTACK	10		
MAGIC ATTACK	—		
ACCURACY	100		
MAGIC ACCURACY	100		
ELEMENTAL MODIFIER	FIRE LV.1		
INFLICTS	—		

CHANGES WHEN IMPROVED	ATTACK	MAGIC ATTACK	VALUE
	+1	—	+50

PURCHASE	—	OBTAINED	CHEST — MOUNT GULG
SELL	240		

FROST BULL

ATTACK	12		
MAGIC ATTACK	—		
ACCURACY	110		
MAGIC ACCURACY	110		
ELEMENTAL MODIFIER	WATER LV.2		
INFLICTS	—		

CHANGES WHEN IMPROVED	ATTACK	MAGIC ATTACK	VALUE
	+1	—	+50

PURCHASE	—	OBTAINED	MULTIPLAYER SHOP — TOWN OF HORNE
SELL	860		—

GRAN FISSURE

ATTACK	16		
MAGIC ATTACK	—		
ACCURACY	85		
MAGIC ACCURACY	100		
ELEMENTAL MODIFIER	EARTH LV.2		
INFLICTS	—		

CHANGES WHEN IMPROVED	ATTACK	MAGIC ATTACK	VALUE
	+1	—	+50

		OBTAINED	MULTIPLAYER SHOP — TOWN OF HORNE
			—

GREAT TREE SWORD

ATTACK	7		
MAGIC ATTACK	—		
ACCURACY	100		
MAGIC ACCURACY	100		
ELEMENTAL MODIFIER	—		
INFLICTS	—		

CHANGES WHEN IMPROVED	ATTACK	MAGIC ATTACK	VALUE
	+1	—	+50

PURCHASE	—	OBTAINED	DROP — FUNGUS
SELL	140		STEAL — CARBUNCLE

ICEBRAND

ATTACK	4		
MAGIC ATTACK	—		
ACCURACY	100		
MAGIC ACCURACY	100		
ELEMENTAL MODIFIER	WATER LV.1		
INFLICTS	—		

CHANGES WHEN IMPROVED	ATTACK	MAGIC ATTACK	VALUE
	+1	—	+50

PURCHASE	—	OBTAINED	CHEST — PIRATE HIDEOUT
SELL	120		DROP — LIZARDHAWK

INFERNO

ATTACK	14		
MAGIC ATTACK	—		
ACCURACY	100		
MAGIC ACCURACY	100		
ELEMENTAL MODIFIER	FIRE LV.2		
INFLICTS	—		

CHANGES WHEN IMPROVED	ATTACK	MAGIC ATTACK	VALUE
	+1	—	+50

PURCHASE	—	OBTAINED	MULTIPLAYER SHOP — TOWN OF HORNE
SELL	900		—

KIKU-ICHIMONJI

ATTACK	15
MAGIC ATTACK	—
ACCURACY	110
MAGIC ACCURACY	110
ELEMENTAL MODIFIER	—
INFLICTS	—

CHANGES WHEN IMPROVED	ATTACK	MAGIC ATTACK	VALUE
	+1	—	+50

PURCHASE	—	OBTAINED	CHEST — STAR CHAMBER
SELL	2000		—

KRINJH'S SWORD

ATTACK	4
MAGIC ATTACK	2
ACCURACY	110
MAGIC ACCURACY	110
ELEMENTAL MODIFIER	—
INFLICTS	—

CHANGES WHEN IMPROVED	ATTACK	MAGIC ATTACK	VALUE
	+1	—	+50

PURCHASE	—	OBTAINED	[SG] KRINJH
SELL	88		—

KRYSTA

ATTACK	15
MAGIC ATTACK	—
ACCURACY	100
MAGIC ACCURACY	100
ELEMENTAL MODIFIER	WIND LV.2
INFLICTS	—

CHANGES WHEN IMPROVED	ATTACK	MAGIC ATTACK	VALUE
	+1	—	+50

PURCHASE	—	OBTAINED	MULTIPLAYER SHOP — TOWN OF HORNE
SELL	950		—

LIGHTBRINGER

ATTACK	11
MAGIC ATTACK	11
ACCURACY	100
MAGIC ACCURACY	100
ELEMENTAL MODIFIER	LIGHT LV.2
INFLICTS	—

CHANGES WHEN IMPROVED	ATTACK	MAGIC ATTACK	VALUE
	+1	—	+50

PURCHASE	—	OBTAINED	STEAL — ROLAN [A]
SELL	300		STEAL — LUCIFER [A]

MURAMASA

ATTACK	14
MAGIC ATTACK	—
ACCURACY	115
MAGIC ACCURACY	115
ELEMENTAL MODIFIER	—
INFLICTS	LOWERS STATUS (30%)

CHANGES WHEN IMPROVED	ATTACK	MAGIC ATTACK	VALUE
	+1	—	+50

PURCHASE	9000	OBTAINED	SOLD — MYSTERIOUS LIGHTHOUSE
SELL	1800		—

MUTSUNOKAMI

ATTACK	13
MAGIC ATTACK	—
ACCURACY	110
MAGIC ACCURACY	110
ELEMENTAL MODIFIER	—
INFLICTS	—

CHANGES WHEN IMPROVED	ATTACK	MAGIC ATTACK	VALUE
	+1	—	+50

PURCHASE	10,000	OBTAINED	SOLD — URBETH
SELL	2000		—

SHINING BLADE

ATTACK	7
MAGIC ATTACK	—
ACCURACY	100
MAGIC ACCURACY	100
ELEMENTAL MODIFIER	LIGHT LV.1
INFLICTS	—

CHANGES WHEN IMPROVED	ATTACK	MAGIC ATTACK	VALUE
	+1	—	+50

PURCHASE	900	OBTAINED	SOLD — SPELVIA
SELL	180		[SG] ROLAN

STEEL SWORD

ATTACK	2
MAGIC ATTACK	—
ACCURACY	100
MAGIC ACCURACY	100
ELEMENTAL MODIFIER	—
INFLICTS	—

CHANGES WHEN IMPROVED	ATTACK	MAGIC ATTACK	VALUE
	+1	—	+50

PURCHASE	200	OBTAINED	EVENT — SPEAK WITH KING HORNE BEFORE TRIP TO NORTHERN CAVES
SELL	40		

SWORD OF LIGHT

ATTACK	17
MAGIC ATTACK	17
ACCURACY	120
MAGIC ACCURACY	120
ELEMENTAL MODIFIER	LIGHT LV.2
INFLICTS	—

CHANGES WHEN IMPROVED	ATTACK	MAGIC ATTACK	VALUE
	+1	+1	+100

PURCHASE	—	OBTAINED	EVENT — SPEAK WITH ROLAN AFTER DEFEATING LUCIFER
SELL	—		—

WIND FOIL

ATTACK	3
MAGIC ATTACK	—
ACCURACY	100
MAGIC ACCURACY	100
ELEMENTAL MODIFIER	WIND LV.1
INFLICTS	—

CHANGES WHEN IMPROVED	ATTACK	MAGIC ATTACK	VALUE
	+1	—	+50

PURCHASE	500	OBTAINED	SOLD — GUERA
SELL	100		DROP — LIZARDMAN [A]

THROWN

BEST THROWN CROWN	(SAME AS BOW?)
FIRST TARGET	REAR

Beyond inflicting 1.4 times damage against flying enemies, the Thrown weapons offer a variety of bonuses including negative status effects, and enhanced Evasion scores. In fact, if you have a Ninja in your party, equip a Shiranui and watch the damage done with Lightning Fists pile up even faster!

FUMA SHURIKEN

ATTACK	15
MAGIC ATTACK	—
ACCURACY	120
MAGIC ACCURACY	120
ELEMENTAL MODIFIER	—
INFLICTS	POISON, PARALYSIS(30%)

CHANGES WHEN IMPROVED	ATTACK	MAGIC ATTACK	VALUE
	+1	—	+50

PURCHASE	28,000	OBTAINED	SOLD — MYSTERIOUS LIGHTHOUSE
SELL	5600		—

KOGA SHURIKEN

ATTACK	15
MAGIC ATTACK	—
ACCURACY	120
MAGIC ACCURACY	120
ELEMENTAL MODIFIER	—
INFLICTS	CONFUSION, BLINDNESS (30%)

CHANGES WHEN IMPROVED	ATTACK	MAGIC ATTACK	VALUE
	+1	—	+50

PURCHASE	28,000	OBTAINED	SOLD — HOLY TREE TOWER
SELL	5600		—

KUNAI

ATTACK	10
MAGIC ATTACK	—
ACCURACY	100
MAGIC ACCURACY	150
ELEMENTAL MODIFIER	—
INFLICTS	—

CHANGES WHEN IMPROVED	ATTACK	MAGIC ATTACK	VALUE
	+1	—	+50

PURCHASE	50,000	OBTAINED	SOLD — TRIAL TOWER
SELL	10,000		—

MOONRING BLADE

ATTACK	10
MAGIC ATTACK	10
ACCURACY	120
MAGIC ACCURACY	120
ELEMENTAL MODIFIER	—
INFLICTS	DEATH (30%)

CHANGES WHEN IMPROVED	ATTACK	MAGIC ATTACK	VALUE
	+1	+1	+100

PURCHASE	22,000	OBTAINED	SOLD — HOLY TREE TOWER
SELL	4400		—

OBORO

ATTACK	20
MAGIC ATTACK	—
ACCURACY	100
MAGIC ACCURACY	150
ELEMENTAL MODIFIER	—
INFLICTS	—

Equipping Oboro increases Magic Evasion rate by 20%.

CHANGES WHEN IMPROVED	ATTACK	MAGIC ATTACK	VALUE
	+1	—	+50

PURCHASE	50,000	OBTAINED	SOLD — TRIAL TOWER
SELL	10,000		—

RISING SUN

ATTACK	3
MAGIC ATTACK	2
ACCURACY	100
MAGIC ACCURACY	110
ELEMENTAL MODIFIER	—
INFLICTS	—

CHANGES WHEN IMPROVED	ATTACK	MAGIC ATTACK	VALUE
	+1	—	+50

PURCHASE	—	OBTAINED	CHEST — MOONLIGHT TOWER
SELL	60		—

SHIRANUI

ATTACK	20
MAGIC ATTACK	—
ACCURACY	150
MAGIC ACCURACY	100
ELEMENTAL MODIFIER	—
INFLICTS	—

Equipping Shiranui increases Evasion rate by 20%.

CHANGES WHEN IMPROVED	ATTACK	MAGIC ATTACK	VALUE
	+1	—	+50

PURCHASE	50,000	OBTAINED	SOLD — MYSTERIOUS LIGHTHOUSE
SELL	10,000		—

ARMOR

Armor provides protection against physical and magic attacks, through mitigation and avoidance. In addition, Armor offers a large number of choices when it comes to boosting the abilities of your characters. Since there is an Armor type associated with each Crown (for more information, check out the Crowns section of this guide), use that Armor's Equip Bonus as a guideline when you're trying to get the most out of your characters. For example, the Black Robe (for Black Mage) boosts Intellect and Magic Attack Power. Look for weapons and accessories that boost the same attributes to create a powerful Black Mage.

Armor bought with Multiplayer Points

For any piece of Armor marked "SOLD" from the Mutiplayer Shop, the value in the "Buy" column indicates how many multiplayer points are required to purchase the item. These items can't be sold to vendors, but otherwise work the same as the other Armor pieces.

ADVENTURER'S GARB

BUY	—
SELL	440
DEFENSE	15
MAGIC DEFENSE	15
EVASION	15
MAGIC EVASION	15
EQUIP BONUS	ALL STATS +5%

CHANGES WHEN IMPROVED

DEFENSE	+1
MAGIC DEFENSE	+1
EVASION	—
VALUE	+100

WHERE OBTAINED

DROPPED BY ENEMY	ADVENTURER
STOLEN FROM ENEMY	ADVENTURER

 AFREET ROBE

BUY	1000
SELL	—
DEFENSE	2
MAGIC DEFENSE	2
EVASION	1
MAGIC EVASION	1
EQUIP BONUS	STRENGTH/INTELLECT/SPIRIT +5%

CHANGES WHEN IMPROVED

DEFENSE	+1
MAGIC DEFENSE	+1
EVASION	+1
VALUE	+50

WHERE OBTAINED

MULTIPLAYER SHOP	GUERA

 AIRE'S FROCK

BUY	—
SELL	8
DEFENSE	1
MAGIC DEFENSE	1
EVASION	—
MAGIC EVASION	—
EQUIP BONUS	—

CHANGES WHEN IMPROVED

DEFENSE	+1
MAGIC DEFENSE	+1
EVASION	—
VALUE	+100

WHERE OBTAINED

STARTING GEAR	AIRE

BANDIT GEAR

BUY	350
SELL	70
DEFENSE	4
MAGIC DEFENSE	2
EVASION	10
MAGIC EVASION	—
EQUIP BONUS	ACCURACY +20%

CHANGES WHEN IMPROVED

DEFENSE	+1
MAGIC DEFENSE	+1
EVASION	—
VALUE	+50

WHERE OBTAINED

SOLD	URBETH[A], INVIDIA[A]
SOLD	LIBERTE TOWN[B]

ALCHEMIST GOWN

BUY	850
SELL	170
DEFENSE	9
MAGIC DEFENSE	8
EVASION	—
MAGIC EVASION	—
EQUIP BONUS	DEFENSE/MAGIC DEFENSE/ACCURACY/MAGIC ACCURACY +5%

CHANGES WHEN IMPROVED

DEFENSE	+1
MAGIC DEFENSE	+1
EVASION	—
VALUE	+50

WHERE OBTAINED

SOLD	INVIDIA[B]

BEASTMASTER COAT

BUY	—
SELL	150
DEFENSE	8
MAGIC DEFENSE	7
EVASION	—
MAGIC EVASION	—
EQUIP BONUS	DEFENSE/MAGIC DEFENSE, STRENGTH +10%

CHANGES WHEN IMPROVED

DEFENSE	+1
MAGIC DEFENSE	+1
EVASION	—
VALUE	+50

WHERE OBTAINED

CHEST	EXTRA DUNGEONS

ANGEL TOGA

BUY	1000
SELL	—
DEFENSE	2
MAGIC DEFENSE	2
EVASION	1
MAGIC EVASION	1
EQUIP BONUS	STRENGTH/INTELLECT/SPIRIT +5%

CHANGES WHEN IMPROVED

DEFENSE	+1
MAGIC DEFENSE	+1
EVASION	+1
VALUE	+50

WHERE OBTAINED

MULTIPLAYER SHOP	LIBERTE PORT

BLACK ROBE

BUY	350
SELL	70
DEFENSE	3
MAGIC DEFENSE	4
EVASION	—
MAGIC EVASION	—
EQUIP BONUS	INTELLECT/MAGIC ATTACK POWER +10%

CHANGES WHEN IMPROVED

DEFENSE	+1
MAGIC DEFENSE	+1
EVASION	—
VALUE	+50

WHERE OBTAINED

SOLD	LIBERTE TOWN[A], URBETH[A], INVIDIA[A]
SOLD	GUERA[B]

ARMOR OF LIGHT

BUY	—
SELL	—
DEFENSE	12
MAGIC DEFENSE	12
EVASION	—
MAGIC EVASION	—
EQUIP BONUS	ALL STATS +10%

CHANGES WHEN IMPROVED

DEFENSE	+1
MAGIC DEFENSE	+1
EVASION	+1
VALUE	+100

WHERE OBTAINED

FOUND	SPEAK WITH INVIDIA CHIEF AFTER OBTAINING SHAMAN CROWN

BLUE JACKET

BUY	1000
SELL	—
DEFENSE	2
MAGIC DEFENSE	2
EVASION	1
MAGIC EVASION	1
EQUIP BONUS	STRENGTH/INTELLECT/SPIRIT +5%

CHANGES WHEN IMPROVED

DEFENSE	+1
MAGIC DEFENSE	+1
EVASION	+1
VALUE	+50

WHERE OBTAINED

MULTIPLAYER SHOP	LIBERTE PORT

BRANDT'S TOGS

BUY	—
SELL	8
DEFENSE	1
MAGIC DEFENSE	1
EVASION	—
MAGIC EVASION	—
EQUIP BONUS	—

CHANGES WHEN IMPROVED

DEFENSE	+1
MAGIC DEFENSE	+1
EVASION	—
VALUE	+100

WHERE OBTAINED

STARTING GEAR	BRANDT

DANCER CLOTHES

BUY	735
SELL	147
DEFENSE	7
MAGIC DEFENSE	6
EVASION	12
MAGIC EVASION	5
EQUIP BONUS	EVASION/SPIRIT +10%

CHANGES WHEN IMPROVED

DEFENSE	+1
MAGIC DEFENSE	+1
EVASION	—
VALUE	+50

WHERE OBTAINED

SOLD	SPELVIA[B]
FOUND IN CHEST	ANIMAL BURROW[B]

CAT'S CLOAK

BUY	1000
SELL	—
DEFENSE	2
MAGIC DEFENSE	2
EVASION	1
MAGIC EVASION	1
EQUIP BONUS	STRENGTH/INTELLECT/SPIRIT +5%

CHANGES WHEN IMPROVED

DEFENSE	+1
MAGIC DEFENSE	+1
EVASION	+1
VALUE	+50

WHERE OBTAINED

MULTIPLAYER SHOP	INVIDIA

DANCING WEAR

BUY	1000
SELL	—
DEFENSE	2
MAGIC DEFENSE	2
EVASION	1
MAGIC EVASION	1
EQUIP BONUS	STRENGTH/INTELLECT/SPIRIT +5%

CHANGES WHEN IMPROVED

DEFENSE	+1
MAGIC DEFENSE	+1
EVASION	+1
VALUE	+50

WHERE OBTAINED

MULTIPLAYER SHOP	LIBERTE PORT

CAT'S TUNIC

BUY	1000
SELL	—
DEFENSE	2
MAGIC DEFENSE	2
EVASION	1
MAGIC EVASION	1
EQUIP BONUS	STRENGTH/INTELLECT/SPIRIT +5%

CHANGES WHEN IMPROVED

DEFENSE	+1
MAGIC DEFENSE	+1
EVASION	+1
VALUE	+50

WHERE OBTAINED

MULTIPLAYER SHOP	LIBERTE PORT

DARK ARMOR

BUY	1000
SELL	—
DEFENSE	2
MAGIC DEFENSE	2
EVASION	1
MAGIC EVASION	1
EQUIP BONUS	STRENGTH/INTELLECT/SPIRIT +5%

CHANGES WHEN IMPROVED

DEFENSE	+1
MAGIC DEFENSE	+1
EVASION	+1
VALUE	+50

WHERE OBTAINED

MULTIPLAYER SHOP	ARBOR

CEREMONIAL ROBE

BUY	1000
SELL	—
DEFENSE	2
MAGIC DEFENSE	2
EVASION	1
MAGIC EVASION	1
EQUIP BONUS	STRENGTH/INTELLECT/SPIRIT +5%

CHANGES WHEN IMPROVED

DEFENSE	+1
MAGIC DEFENSE	+1
EVASION	+1
VALUE	+50

WHERE OBTAINED

MULTIPLAYER SHOP	TOWN OF HORNE

DARK FENCER ARMOR

BUY	850
SELL	170
DEFENSE	10
MAGIC DEFENSE	7
EVASION	—
MAGIC EVASION	—
EQUIP BONUS	ATTACK POWER/STRENGTH +10%

CHANGES WHEN IMPROVED

DEFENSE	+1
MAGIC DEFENSE	+1
EVASION	—
VALUE	+50

WHERE OBTAINED

SOLD	TOWN OF HORNE[B] (AFTER DEFEATING SATAN)

EASTERN GARB

BUY	1000
SELL	—
DEFENSE	2
MAGIC DEFENSE	2
EVASION	1
MAGIC EVASION	1
EQUIP BONUS	STRENGTH/INTELLECT/SPIRIT +5%

CHANGES WHEN IMPROVED

DEFENSE	+1
MAGIC DEFENSE	+1
EVASION	+1
VALUE	+50

WHERE OBTAINED

MULTIPLAYER SHOP	ARBOR

GARB OF KNOWLEDGE

BUY	1000
SELL	—
DEFENSE	2
MAGIC DEFENSE	2
EVASION	1
MAGIC EVASION	1
EQUIP BONUS	STRENGTH/INTELLECT/SPIRIT +5%

CHANGES WHEN IMPROVED

DEFENSE	+1
MAGIC DEFENSE	+1
EVASION	+1
VALUE	+50

WHERE OBTAINED

MULTIPLAYER SHOP	ARBOR

ELEMENTALIST ROBE

BUY	550
SELL	110
DEFENSE	5
MAGIC DEFENSE	6
EVASION	—
MAGIC EVASION	—
EQUIP BONUS	MAGIC ACCURACY/INTELLECT +10%

CHANGES WHEN IMPROVED

DEFENSE	+1
MAGIC DEFENSE	+1
EVASION	—
VALUE	+50

WHERE OBTAINED

SOLD	INVIDIA[A], SPELVIA[A]

GUNNER'S COAT

BUY	1000
SELL	—
DEFENSE	2
MAGIC DEFENSE	2
EVASION	1
MAGIC EVASION	1
EQUIP BONUS	STRENGTH/INTELLECT/SPIRIT +5%

CHANGES WHEN IMPROVED

DEFENSE	+1
MAGIC DEFENSE	+1
EVASION	+1
VALUE	+50

WHERE OBTAINED

MULTIPLAYER SHOP	INVIDIA

FENCER'S GARB

BUY	1000
SELL	—
DEFENSE	2
MAGIC DEFENSE	2
EVASION	1
MAGIC EVASION	1
EQUIP BONUS	STRENGTH/INTELLECT/SPIRIT +5%

CHANGES WHEN IMPROVED

DEFENSE	+1
MAGIC DEFENSE	+1
EVASION	+1
VALUE	+50

WHERE OBTAINED

MULTIPLAYER SHOP	TOWN OF HORNE

HERO ARMOR

BUY	750
SELL	130
DEFENSE	8
MAGIC DEFENSE	7
EVASION	—
MAGIC EVASION	—
EQUIP BONUS	STRENGTH/INTELLECT/SPIRIT +10%

CHANGES WHEN IMPROVED

DEFENSE	+1
MAGIC DEFENSE	+1
EVASION	—
VALUE	+50

WHERE OBTAINED

SOLD	URBETH[B], SPELVIA[B]

FIGHTER GI

BUY	550
SELL	110
DEFENSE	8
MAGIC DEFENSE	3
EVASION	—
MAGIC EVASION	—
EQUIP BONUS	HP/STRENGTH +10%

CHANGES WHEN IMPROVED

DEFENSE	+1
MAGIC DEFENSE	+1
EVASION	—
VALUE	+50

WHERE OBTAINED

SOLD	SPELVIA[A]
SOLD	URBETH[B]

HESTIA'S TUNIC

BUY	1000
SELL	—
DEFENSE	2
MAGIC DEFENSE	2
EVASION	1
MAGIC EVASION	1
EQUIP BONUS	STRENGTH/INTELLECT/SPIRIT +5%

CHANGES WHEN IMPROVED

DEFENSE	+1
MAGIC DEFENSE	+1
EVASION	+1
VALUE	+50

WHERE OBTAINED

MULTIPLAYER SHOP	INVIDIA

ARMOR

HUNTER GARB

BUY	1000
SELL	—
DEFENSE	2
MAGIC DEFENSE	2
EVASION	1
MAGIC EVASION	1
EQUIP BONUS	STRENGTH/INTELLECT/SPIRIT +5%

CHANGES WHEN IMPROVED

DEFENSE	+1
MAGIC DEFENSE	+1
EVASION	+1
VALUE	+50

WHERE OBTAINED

MULTIPLAYER SHOP	ARBOR

MERCHANT TUNIC

BUY	550
SELL	110
DEFENSE	6
MAGIC DEFENSE	5
EVASION	—
MAGIC EVASION	—
EQUIP BONUS	INTELLECT/SPIRIT +10%

CHANGES WHEN IMPROVED

DEFENSE	+1
MAGIC DEFENSE	+1
EVASION	—
VALUE	+50

WHERE OBTAINED

SOLD	ARBOR[A], INVIDIA[A]
SOLD	URBETH[B]

JUSQUA'S COAT

BUY	—
SELL	8
DEFENSE	1
MAGIC DEFENSE	1
EVASION	—
MAGIC EVASION	—
EQUIP BONUS	—

CHANGES WHEN IMPROVED

DEFENSE	+1
MAGIC DEFENSE	+1
EVASION	—
VALUE	+100

WHERE OBTAINED

STARTING GEAR	JUSQUA

MODERN DRESS

BUY	1000
SELL	—
DEFENSE	2
MAGIC DEFENSE	2
EVASION	1
MAGIC EVASION	1
EQUIP BONUS	STRENGTH/INTELLECT/SPIRIT +5%

CHANGES WHEN IMPROVED

DEFENSE	+1
MAGIC DEFENSE	+1
EVASION	+1
VALUE	+50

WHERE OBTAINED

MULTIPLAYER SHOP	SPELVIA

KRINJH'S ROBE

BUY	—
SELL	28
DEFENSE	3
MAGIC DEFENSE	4
EVASION	—
MAGIC EVASION	—
EQUIP BONUS	—

CHANGES WHEN IMPROVED

DEFENSE	+1
MAGIC DEFENSE	+1
EVASION	—
VALUE	+100

WHERE OBTAINED

STARTING GEAR	KRINJH
STOLEN FROM ENEMY	KRINJH

MONK ROBE

BUY	850
SELL	170
DEFENSE	8
MAGIC DEFENSE	9
EVASION	—
MAGIC EVASION	—
EQUIP BONUS	INTELLECT/SPIRIT +10%

CHANGES WHEN IMPROVED

DEFENSE	+1
MAGIC DEFENSE	+1
EVASION	—
VALUE	+50

WHERE OBTAINED

SOLD	LIBERTE TOWN[B]
FOUND IN CHEST	ANIMAL BURROW[B]

MAXIMILLIAN

BUY	1000
SELL	—
DEFENSE	2
MAGIC DEFENSE	2
EVASION	1
MAGIC EVASION	1
EQUIP BONUS	STRENGTH/INTELLECT/SPIRIT +5%

CHANGES WHEN IMPROVED

DEFENSE	+1
MAGIC DEFENSE	+1
EVASION	+1
VALUE	+50

WHERE OBTAINED

MULTIPLAYER SHOP	LIBERTE PORTE

MONKISH GARB

BUY	1000
SELL	—
DEFENSE	2
MAGIC DEFENSE	2
EVASION	1
MAGIC EVASION	1
EQUIP BONUS	STRENGTH/INTELLECT/SPIRIT +5%

CHANGES WHEN IMPROVED

DEFENSE	+1
MAGIC DEFENSE	+1
EVASION	+1
VALUE	+50

WHERE OBTAINED

MULTIPLAYER SHOP	INVIDIA

MUSICIAN ROBES

BUY	—
SELL	170
DEFENSE	9
MAGIC DEFENSE	8
EVASION	—
MAGIC EVASION	—
EQUIP BONUS	SPIRIT +10%, EVADE/MAGIC EVADE +5%

CHANGES WHEN IMPROVED

DEFENSE	+1
MAGIC DEFENSE	+1
EVASION	—
VALUE	+50

WHERE OBTAINED

CHEST	EXTRA DUNGEONS

NINJA UNIFORM

BUY	—
SELL	170
DEFENSE	8
MAGIC DEFENSE	7
EVASION	10
MAGIC EVASION	10
EQUIP BONUS	EVASION +20%

CHANGES WHEN IMPROVED

DEFENSE	+1
MAGIC DEFENSE	+1
EVASION	—
VALUE	—

WHERE OBTAINED

CHEST	EXTRA DUNGEONS

OLD CLOTHES

BUY	—
SELL	—
DEFENSE	1
MAGIC DEFENSE	1
EVASION	—
MAGIC EVASION	—
EQUIP BONUS	—

CHANGES WHEN IMPROVED

DEFENSE	+1
MAGIC DEFENSE	+1
EVASION	—
VALUE	+50

WHERE OBTAINED

[SG]	YUNITA (IN URBETH)

PALADIN ARMOR

BUY	850
SELL	170
DEFENSE	11
MAGIC DEFENSE	6
EVASION	—
MAGIC EVASION	—
EQUIP BONUS	HP +20%

CHANGES WHEN IMPROVED

DEFENSE	+1
MAGIC DEFENSE	+1
EVASION	—
VALUE	+50

WHERE OBTAINED

SOLD	URBETH[B]

PARTY HOST WEAR

BUY	600
SELL	120
DEFENSE	5
MAGIC DEFENSE	7
EVASION	—
MAGIC EVASION	—
EQUIP BONUS	INTELLECT/SPIRIT/EVASION/MAGIC EVASION +5%

CHANGES WHEN IMPROVED

DEFENSE	+1
MAGIC DEFENSE	+1
EVASION	—
VALUE	+50

WHERE OBTAINED

SOLD	URBETH[B], SPELVIA[B]

POET TUNIC

BUY	350
SELL	70
DEFENSE	4
MAGIC DEFENSE	3
EVASION	—
MAGIC EVASION	—
EQUIP BONUS	INTELLECT/SPIRIT +10%

CHANGES WHEN IMPROVED

DEFENSE	+1
MAGIC DEFENSE	+1
EVASION	—
VALUE	+50

WHERE OBTAINED

SOLD	URBETH[A], INVIDIA[A]
SOLD	LIBERTE TOWN[B]

PRIEST'S GOWN

BUY	1000
SELL	—
DEFENSE	2
MAGIC DEFENSE	2
EVASION	1
MAGIC EVASION	1
EQUIP BONUS	STRENGTH/INTELLECT/SPIRIT +5%

CHANGES WHEN IMPROVED

DEFENSE	+1
MAGIC DEFENSE	+1
EVASION	+1
VALUE	+50

WHERE OBTAINED

MULTIPLAYER SHOP	GUERA

RANGER OUTFIT

BUY	380
SELL	76
DEFENSE	5
MAGIC DEFENSE	2
EVASION	5
MAGIC EVASION	1
EQUIP BONUS	STRENGTH/ACCURACY +10%

CHANGES WHEN IMPROVED

DEFENSE	+1
MAGIC DEFENSE	+1
EVASION	—
VALUE	+50

WHERE OBTAINED

SOLD	INVIDIA[A], SPELVIA[A]

ARMOR

RED JACKET

BUY	1000
SELL	—
DEFENSE	2
MAGIC DEFENSE	2
EVASION	1
MAGIC EVASION	1
EQUIP BONUS	STRENGTH/INTELLECT/SPIRIT +5%

CHANGES WHEN IMPROVED

DEFENSE	+1
MAGIC DEFENSE	+1
EVASION	+1
VALUE	+50

WHERE OBTAINED

MULTIPLAYER SHOP	URBETH

ROLAN'S CLOTHES

BUY	—
SELL	60
DEFENSE	8
MAGIC DEFENSE	7
EVASION	—
MAGIC EVASION	—
EQUIP BONUS	—

CHANGES WHEN IMPROVED

DEFENSE	+1
MAGIC DEFENSE	+1
EVASION	—
VALUE	+100

WHERE OBTAINED

STARTING GEAR	ROLAN
STOLEN FROM ENEMY	ROLAN {B}

RED SASH

BUY	1000
SELL	—
DEFENSE	2
MAGIC DEFENSE	2
EVASION	1
MAGIC EVASION	1
EQUIP BONUS	STRENGTH/INTELLECT/SPIRIT +5%

CHANGES WHEN IMPROVED

DEFENSE	+1
MAGIC DEFENSE	+1
EVASION	+1
VALUE	+50

WHERE OBTAINED

MULTIPLAYER SHOP	GUERA

SAGE ROBE

BUY	—
SELL	170
DEFENSE	8
MAGIC DEFENSE	9
EVASION	—
MAGIC EVASION	—
EQUIP BONUS	MAGIC ACCURACY +20%

CHANGES WHEN IMPROVED

DEFENSE	+1
MAGIC DEFENSE	+1
EVASION	—
VALUE	+50

WHERE OBTAINED

CHEST	EXTRA DUNGEONS

REKOTEH'S CLOTHES

BUY	—
SELL	—
DEFENSE	6
MAGIC DEFENSE	4
EVASION	—
MAGIC EVASION	—
EQUIP BONUS	—

CHANGES WHEN IMPROVED

DEFENSE	+1
MAGIC DEFENSE	+1
EVASION	—
VALUE	+100

WHERE OBTAINED

STARTING GEAR	REKOTEH
STOLEN FROM ENEMY	REKOTEH

SALVE-MAKER ROBE

BUY	500
SELL	100
DEFENSE	6
MAGIC DEFENSE	4
EVASION	—
MAGIC EVASION	—
EQUIP BONUS	INTELLECT +10%, EVASION/MAGIC EVASION +5%

CHANGES WHEN IMPROVED

DEFENSE	+1
MAGIC DEFENSE	+1
EVASION	—
VALUE	+50

WHERE OBTAINED

SOLD	ARBOR[A]
SOLD	URBETH[B]

REPLICA PLATE

BUY	1000
SELL	—
DEFENSE	2
MAGIC DEFENSE	2
EVASION	1
MAGIC EVASION	1
EQUIP BONUS	STRENGTH/INTELLECT/SPIRIT +5%

CHANGES WHEN IMPROVED

DEFENSE	+1
MAGIC DEFENSE	+1
EVASION	+1
VALUE	+50

WHERE OBTAINED

MULTIPLAYER SHOP	SPELVIA

SCHOLAR GOWN

BUY	700
SELL	140
DEFENSE	7
MAGIC DEFENSE	7
EVASION	—
MAGIC EVASION	—
EQUIP BONUS	INTELLECT +20%

CHANGES WHEN IMPROVED

DEFENSE	+1
MAGIC DEFENSE	+1
EVASION	—
VALUE	+50

WHERE OBTAINED

SOLD	SPELVIA[A]
SOLD	URBETH[B]

SCRIBE GOWN

BUY	—
SELL	130
DEFENSE	7
MAGIC DEFENSE	6
EVASION	—
MAGIC EVASION	—
EQUIP BONUS	STRENGTH/INTELLECT/SPIRIT +5%

CHANGES WHEN IMPROVED

DEFENSE	+1
MAGIC DEFENSE	+1
EVASION	—
VALUE	+50

WHERE OBTAINED

CHEST	EXTRA DUNGEONS

SEAMSTRESS CLOTHES

BUY	—
SELL	140
DEFENSE	7
MAGIC DEFENSE	7
EVASION	—
MAGIC EVASION	—
EQUIP BONUS	DEFENSE/MAGIC DEFENSE/EVADE/MAGIC EVADE +5%

CHANGES WHEN IMPROVED

DEFENSE	+1
MAGIC DEFENSE	+1
EVASION	—
VALUE	+50

WHERE OBTAINED

CHEST	EXTRA DUNGEONS

SHAMAN ROBE

BUY	850
SELL	170
DEFENSE	8
MAGIC DEFENSE	9
EVASION	—
MAGIC EVASION	—
EQUIP BONUS	MAGIC ACCURACY/INTELLECT +10%

CHANGES WHEN IMPROVED

DEFENSE	+1
MAGIC DEFENSE	+1
EVASION	—
VALUE	+50

WHERE OBTAINED

SOLD	TOWN OF HORNE[B]

SHINOBI GARB

BUY	1000
SELL	—
DEFENSE	2
MAGIC DEFENSE	2
EVASION	1
MAGIC EVASION	1
EQUIP BONUS	STRENGTH/INTELLECT/SPIRIT +5%

CHANGES WHEN IMPROVED

DEFENSE	+1
MAGIC DEFENSE	+1
EVASION	+1
VALUE	+50

WHERE OBTAINED

MULTIPLAYER SHOP	GUERA

SILVER SUIT

BUY	1000
SELL	—
DEFENSE	2
MAGIC DEFENSE	2
EVASION	1
MAGIC EVASION	1
EQUIP BONUS	STRENGTH/INTELLECT/SPIRIT +5%

CHANGES WHEN IMPROVED

DEFENSE	+1
MAGIC DEFENSE	+1
EVASION	+1
VALUE	+50

WHERE OBTAINED

MULTIPLAYER SHOP	URBETH

SPELL FENCER ARMOR

BUY	850
SELL	170
DEFENSE	9
MAGIC DEFENSE	8
EVASION	—
MAGIC EVASION	—
EQUIP BONUS	STRENGTH/INTELLECT +10%

CHANGES WHEN IMPROVED

DEFENSE	+1
MAGIC DEFENSE	+1
EVASION	-
VALUE	+50

WHERE OBTAINED

SOLD	URBETH[B], ARBOR[B]

STEEL ARMOR

BUY	—
SELL	30
DEFENSE	2
MAGIC DEFENSE	1
EVASION	—
MAGIC EVASION	—
EQUIP BONUS	—

CHANGES WHEN IMPROVED

DEFENSE	+1
MAGIC DEFENSE	+1
EVASION	—
VALUE	+50

WHERE OBTAINED

CHEST	WITCH'S MANSION

STORYTELLER ROBE

BUY	—
SELL	90
DEFENSE	5
MAGIC DEFENSE	4
EVASION	—
MAGIC EVASION	—
EQUIP BONUS	DEFENSE +5, MAGIC DEFENSE +4, ALL STATS +5%

CHANGES WHEN IMPROVED

DEFENSE	+1
MAGIC DEFENSE	+1
EVASION	—
VALUE	+50

WHERE OBTAINED

CHEST	EXTRA DUNGEONS

ARMOR

TORTE'S CLOTHES

BUY	—
SELL	28
DEFENSE	4
MAGIC DEFENSE	3
EVASION	—
MAGIC EVASION	—
EQUIP BONUS	—

CHANGES WHEN IMPROVED

DEFENSE	+1
MAGIC DEFENSE	+1
EVASION	—
VALUE	+100

WHERE OBTAINED

STARTING GEAR	TORTE
STOLEN FROM ENEMY	TORTE

WARMAGE ARMOR

BUY	1000
SELL	—
DEFENSE	2
MAGIC DEFENSE	2
EVASION	1
MAGIC EVASION	1
EQUIP BONUS	STRENGTH/INTELLECT/SPIRIT +5%

CHANGES WHEN IMPROVED

DEFENSE	+1
MAGIC DEFENSE	+1
EVASION	+1
VALUE	+50

WHERE OBTAINED

MULTIPLAYER SHOP	TOWN OF HORNE

TRAVELER'S GARB

BUY	150
SELL	30
DEFENSE	2
MAGIC DEFENSE	1
EVASION	—
MAGIC EVASION	—
EQUIP BONUS	STRENGTH/INTELLECT/SPIRIT +5%

CHANGES WHEN IMPROVED

DEFENSE	+1
MAGIC DEFENSE	+1
EVASION	—
VALUE	+50

WHERE OBTAINED

SOLD	GUERA[A]
SOLD	LIBERTE TOWN[A]

WHITE ROBE

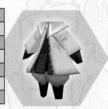

BUY	350
SELL	70
DEFENSE	3
MAGIC DEFENSE	4
EVASION	—
MAGIC EVASION	—
EQUIP BONUS	SPIRIT +20%

CHANGES WHEN IMPROVED

DEFENSE	+1
MAGIC DEFENSE	+1
EVASION	—
VALUE	+50

WHERE OBTAINED

SOLD	LIBERTE TOWN[A], URBETH[A], INVIDIA[A]
SOLD	GUERA[B]

TRYLION'S COAT

BUY	1000
SELL	—
DEFENSE	2
MAGIC DEFENSE	2
EVASION	1
MAGIC EVASION	1
EQUIP BONUS	STRENGTH/INTELLECT/SPIRIT +5%

CHANGES WHEN IMPROVED

DEFENSE	+1
MAGIC DEFENSE	+1
EVASION	+1
VALUE	+50

WHERE OBTAINED

MULTIPLAYER SHOP	URBETH

WORKER'S CLOTHES

BUY	1000
SELL	—
DEFENSE	2
MAGIC DEFENSE	2
EVASION	1
MAGIC EVASION	1
EQUIP BONUS	STRENGTH/INTELLECT/SPIRIT +5%

CHANGES WHEN IMPROVED

DEFENSE	+1
MAGIC DEFENSE	+1
EVASION	+1
VALUE	+50

WHERE OBTAINED

MULTIPLAYER SHOP	URBETH

VERMILLION

BUY	1000
SELL	—
DEFENSE	2
MAGIC DEFENSE	2
EVASION	1
MAGIC EVASION	1
EQUIP BONUS	STRENGTH/INTELLECT/SPIRIT +5%

CHANGES WHEN IMPROVED

DEFENSE	+1
MAGIC DEFENSE	+1
EVASION	+1
VALUE	+50

WHERE OBTAINED

MULTIPLAYER SHOP	ARBOR

YUNITA'S GARB

BUY	—
SELL	8
DEFENSE	1
MAGIC DEFENSE	1
EVASION	—
MAGIC EVASION	—
EQUIP BONUS	—

CHANGES WHEN IMPROVED

DEFENSE	+1
MAGIC DEFENSE	+1
EVASION	—
VALUE	+100

WHERE OBTAINED

STARTING GEAR	YUNITA

SHIELDS

Shields offer a huge boost to your characters' defense. With a few exceptions, Shields provide additional defense and avoidance against regular and magic attacks. As a bonus, there are six shields that nullify a specific elements. If you know an upcoming area is loaded with enemies that deal a certain type of damage, equip the proper shield to reduce the amount of damage that your characters may take.

ANTIMAGE

BUY	100,000
SELL	20,000
DEFENSE	—
MAGIC DEFENSE	5
EVADE	—
MAGIC EVADE	—
NOTE	—

CHANGES WHEN IMPROVED

DEFENSE	—
MAGIC DEFENSE	+2
EVADE	—
VALUE	+100

WHERE OBTAINED

SOLD	MOONSAND RUINS

FLAME SHIELD

BUY	350
SELL	70
DEFENSE	1
MAGIC DEFENSE	1
EVADE	5
MAGIC EVADE	5
NOTE	BLOCKS FIRE (LV. 1)

CHANGES WHEN IMPROVED

DEFENSE	—
MAGIC DEFENSE	—
EVADE	+1
VALUE	+50

WHERE OBTAINED

SOLD	URBETH, SPELVIA[A]

DARKSTEEL SHIELD

BUY	450
SELL	90
DEFENSE	2
MAGIC DEFENSE	2
EVADE	5
MAGIC EVADE	5
NOTE	BLOCKS DARK (LV. 1)

CHANGES WHEN IMPROVED

DEFENSE	—
MAGIC DEFENSE	—
EVADE	+1
VALUE	+50

WHERE OBTAINED

SOLD	URBETH[A], INVIDIA, SPELVIA[A], TOWN OF HORNE (AFTER DEFEAT OF SATAN)

GREAT TREE SHIELD

BUY	280
SELL	56
DEFENSE	2
MAGIC DEFENSE	2
EVADE	8
MAGIC EVADE	8
NOTE	—

CHANGES WHEN IMPROVED

DEFENSE	—
MAGIC DEFENSE	—
EVADE	+1
VALUE	+50

WHERE OBTAINED

SOLD	ARBOR, URBETH[B]

69

 HIDE SHIELD

BUY	100,000
SELL	20,000
DEFENSE	—
MAGIC DEFENSE	—
EVADE	15
MAGIC EVADE	15
NOTE	—

CHANGES WHEN IMPROVED

DEFENSE	—
MAGIC DEFENSE	—
EVADE	+2
VALUE	+100

WHERE OBTAINED

SOLD	MOONSAND RUINS

SHIELD OF LIGHT

BUY	—
SELL	—
DEFENSE	3
MAGIC DEFENSE	3
EVADE	10
MAGIC EVADE	10
NOTE	NULLIFIES AILMENTS

CHANGES WHEN IMPROVED

DEFENSE	+1
MAGIC DEFENSE	+1
EVADE	+1
VALUE	+100

WHERE OBTAINED

FOUND	SPEAK WITH KRINJH AFTER DEFEATING ASMODEUS

HOLY SHIELD

BUY	450
SELL	90
DEFENSE	2
MAGIC DEFENSE	2
EVADE	5
MAGIC EVADE	5
NOTE	BLOCKS LIGHT (LV. 1)

CHANGES WHEN IMPROVED

DEFENSE	—
MAGIC DEFENSE	—
EVADE	+1
VALUE	+50

WHERE OBTAINED

SOLD	LIBERTE TOWN [B], SPELVIA [B]

UNYIELDING SHIELD

BUY	100,000
SELL	20,000
DEFENSE	5
MAGIC DEFENSE	—
EVADE	—
MAGIC EVADE	—
NOTE	—

CHANGES WHEN IMPROVED

DEFENSE	+2
MAGIC DEFENSE	—
EVADE	—
VALUE	+100

WHERE OBTAINED

SOLD	MOONSAND RUINS

ICE SHIELD

BUY	350
SELL	70
DEFENSE	1
MAGIC DEFENSE	1
EVADE	5
MAGIC EVADE	5
NOTE	BLOCKS WATER (LV. 1)

CHANGES WHEN IMPROVED

DEFENSE	—
MAGIC DEFENSE	—
EVADE	+1
VALUE	+50

WHERE OBTAINED

SOLD	LIBERTE TOWN, INVIDIA, SPELVIA[A]

WIND SHIELD

BUY	350
SELL	70
DEFENSE	+1
MAGIC DEFENSE	+1
EVADE	+5
MAGIC EVADE	+5
NOTE	BLOCKS WIND (LV. 1)

CHANGES WHEN IMPROVED

DEFENSE	—
MAGIC DEFENSE	—
EVADE	+1
VALUE	+50

WHERE OBTAINED

SOLD	TOWN OF HORNE[B] (AFTER DEFEAT OF SATAN)

ROCK SHIELD

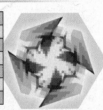

BUY	350
SELL	70
DEFENSE	1
MAGIC DEFENSE	1
EVADE	5
MAGIC EVADE	5
NOTE	BLOCKS EARTH (LV. 1)

CHANGES WHEN IMPROVED

DEFENSE	—
MAGIC DEFENSE	—
EVADE	+1
VALUE	+50

WHERE OBTAINED

SOLD	GUERA, URBETH[A]

WOOD SHIELD

BUY	130
SELL	26
DEFENSE	1
MAGIC DEFENSE	1
EVADE	3
MAGIC EVADE	3
NOTE	—

CHANGES WHEN IMPROVED

DEFENSE	—
MAGIC DEFENSE	—
EVADE	+1
VALUE	+50

WHERE OBTAINED

STARTING GEAR	JUSQUA, YUNITA, AIRE, KRINJH, ROLAN
SOLD	TOWN OF HORNE, URBETH[A]
FOUND IN CHEST	HORNE CASTLE

ACCESSORIES

Use Accessories to fill in the gaps left by the rest of a character's equipment. Need an item that boosts your elemental defense or blocks negative status effects? Try a cape. A powerful new weapon becomes available, but it lacks an elemental componenet to its damage? There's a gauntlet for that. Use the following listing of Accessories to help you round out your party's equipment needs.

APOLLO'S TALISMAN

DESCRIPTION	A TRAVELER'S TALISMAN CRAFTED BY APOLLO. DEFENSE AND MAGIC DEFENSE +5%	HOW OBTAINED	EVENT	OBTAIN FROM APOLLO IN LIBERTE TOWN	BUY	N/A
					SELL	1

BLACK RING

DESCRIPTION	MAGIC DEFENSE +10%	HOW OBTAINED	SOLD	SPELVIA	BUY	500
					SELL	100

BLOODY RING

DESCRIPTION	10% CHANCE OF ABSORBING HP IN A NORMAL ATTACK.	HOW OBTAINED	DROP	VAMPIRE BAT [A]	BUY	N/A
			DROP	BLOOD BAT [B]	SELL	2000

CAPE OF LIGHT

DESCRIPTION	DEFENSE +2, MAGIC DEFENSE +2. BLOCKS ALL ELEMENT ATTACKS (LV.1).	HOW OBTAINED	EVENT	SPEAK WITH THAUZAND AFTER DEFEATING BEELZEBUB	BUY	N/A
					SELL	N/A

CONFUSE CAPE

DESCRIPTION	BLOCKS CONFUSION.	HOW OBTAINED	SOLD	LIBERTE	BUY	250
			SOLD	URBETH	SELL	50

CONFUSE RING

DESCRIPTION	10% CHANCE OF CONFUSING THE FOE IN A NORMAL ATTACK.	HOW OBTAINED	DROP	SUCCUBUS [A]	BUY	N/A
			DROP	SUCCUBUS [B]	SELL	400

COURAGE RING

DESCRIPTION	YOU BECOME PSYCHED UP MORE EASILY.	HOW OBTAINED	SOLD	SPELVIA	BUY	10,000
			DROP	MEDUSA [A]	SELL	2000

CURSE CAPE

DESCRIPTION	BLOCKS CURSES.	HOW OBTAINED	SOLD	SPELVIA	BUY	500
					SELL	100

CURSE RING

DESCRIPTION	10% CHANCE OF INFLICTING A CURSE IN A NORMAL ATTACK.	HOW OBTAINED	STEAL	DOPPELGANGER [AIRE A]	BUY	N/A
			DROP	GHOUL [A]	SELL	400

DARK CAPE

DESCRIPTION	BLOCKS DARK-ELEMENT ATTACKS (LV.1).	HOW OBTAINED	CHEST	TOWER OF THE SKY	BUY	N/A
					SELL	400

DEATH CAPE

DESCRIPTION	BLOCKS SUDDEN DEATH.	HOW OBTAINED	CHEST	SUN TEMPLE	BUY	N/A
					SELL	200

DEATH RING

DESCRIPTION	10% CHANCE OF INFLICTING SUDDEN DEATH IN A NORMAL ATTACK.	HOW OBTAINED	DROP	IKKAKU [A]	BUY	N/A
			DROP	IKKAKU [C]	SELL	2000

DUSK GAUNTLET

DESCRIPTION	ADDS LV.1 DARK-ELEMENT DAMAGE TO WEAPON ATTACKS.	HOW OBTAINED	SOLD	INVIDIA	BUY	500
			DROP	SKELETON [A]	SELL	100

EARTH GAUNTLET

DESCRIPTION	ADDS LV.1 EARTH-ELEMENT DAMAGE TO WEAPON ATTACKS.	HOW OBTAINED	DROP	BIG WORM [A]	BUY	N/A
			DROP	BIG WORM [B]	SELL	100

ELF CAPE

DESCRIPTION	MAGIC EVASION IS DOUBLED.	HOW OBTAINED	CHEST	MT. GULG	BUY	N/A
					SELL	1000

ENERGY SCREEN

DESCRIPTION	GRANTS IMMUNITY FROM PHYSICAL ATTACKS, BUT MAGIC INFLICTS FOUR TIMES THE DAMAGE.	HOW OBTAINED	MULTIPLAYER	INVIDIA	BUY	8000
					SELL	2000

FAIRY CAPE

DESCRIPTION	EVASION RATE IS DOUBLED.	HOW OBTAINED	SOLD	ARBOR	BUY	500
			CHEST	THE GREAT TREE	SELL	100

FLAME CAPE

DESCRIPTION	BLOCKS FIRE-ELEMENT ATTACKS (LV.1).	HOW OBTAINED	CHEST	MT. GULG	BUY	N/A
			DROP	GERI [A]	SELL	400

FLAME GAUNTLET

DESCRIPTION	ADDS LV.1 FIRE-ELEMENT DAMAGE TO WEAPON ATTACKS.	HOW OBTAINED	SOLD	INVIDIA	BUY	500
			DROP	GARGOYLE [A], GERI [A]	SELL	100

FLASH CAPE

DESCRIPTION	BLOCKS BLINDNESS.	HOW OBTAINED	SOLD	URBETH	BUY	250
					SELL	50

FLASH RING

DESCRIPTION	10% CHANCE OF BLINDING THE FOE IN A NORMAL ATTACK.	HOW OBTAINED	SOLD	URBETH	BUY	500
			SOLD	SPELVIA	SELL	100

FORTUNE EGG

DESCRIPTION	DOUBLES NUMBER OF ITEMS DROPPED.	HOW OBTAINED	CHEST	STAR CHAMBER	BUY	3000
			MULTIPLAYER	GUERA	SELL	2000

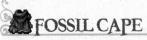
FOSSIL CAPE

DESCRIPTION	BLOCKS PETRIFICATION.	HOW OBTAINED	SOLD	SPELVIA	BUY	500
			SOLD	GUERA	SELL	100

FOSSIL RING

DESCRIPTION	10% CHANCE OF PETRIFYING THE FOE IN A NORMAL ATTACK.	HOW OBTAINED	CHEST	SPELVIA	BUY	N/A
			CHEST	SUN TEMPLE	SELL	400

GALE GAUNTLET

DESCRIPTION	ADDS LV.1 WIND-ELEMENT DAMAGE TO WEAPON ATTACKS.	HOW OBTAINED	DROP	CHIMERA [A]	BUY	N/A
			DROP	FALCON [A]	SELL	100

GEM COLLECTOR

DESCRIPTION	KEEP ALL YOUR GEMS, EVEN AFTER DEATH.	HOW OBTAINED	MULTIPLAYER	URBETH	BUY	4000
					SELL	2000

GIANT'S RING

DESCRIPTION	ATTACK +10%	HOW OBTAINED	SOLD	URBETH	BUY	500
			DROP	BORGBEAR [A]	SELL	100

GLIMMER GAUNTLET

DESCRIPTION	ADDS LV.1 LIGHT-ELEMENT DAMAGE TO WEAPON ATTACKS.	HOW OBTAINED	SOLD	SPELVIA	BUY	500
			DROP	CLOUD PENGUIN [A]	SELL	100

GROWTH EGG

DESCRIPTION	DOUBLES EXPERIENCE POINTS EARNED.	HOW OBTAINED	CHEST	SUN TEMPLE	BUY	3000
			MULTIPLAYER	TOWN OF HORNE	SELL	2000

HERMES SANDALS

DESCRIPTION	ALWAYS ACT FIRST.	HOW OBTAINED	MULTIPLAYER	URBETH	BUY	6000
			MULTIPLAYER	SPELVIA	SELL	2000

HERO'S WILL

DESCRIPTION	IF YOU DIE DURING A BATTLE, YOU WILL HANG ON TO LIFE WITH 1 HP — BUT ONLY ONCE.	HOW OBTAINED	CHEST	STAR CHAMBER	BUY	8000
			MULTIPLAYER	TOWN OF HORNE	SELL	2000

INHERITED RING

DESCRIPTION	A RING INHERITED FROM YOUR FATHER. HP +10	HOW OBTAINED	EVENT	OBTRAIN FROM KUORE IN TOWN OF HORNE	BUY	N/A
					SELL	N/A

INTELLECT RING

DESCRIPTION	BOOSTS INTELLECT BY 10%.	HOW OBTAINED	SOLD	URBETH	BUY	500
			CHEST	ICE CAVERNS	SELL	100

LONE WOLF

DESCRIPTION	DON'T PARTICIPATE IN JOINT ATTACKS.	HOW OBTAINED	DROP	HELLHOUND [A]	BUY	N/A
			DROP	HELLHOUND [B]	SELL	2000

ACCESSORIES

MANA SCREEN

DESCRIPTION	GRANTS IMMUNITY FROM MAGIC, BUT PHYSICAL ATTACKS INFLICT FOUR TIMES THE DAMAGE.	HOW OBTAINED	MULTIPLAYER	ARBOR	BUY	8000
			MULTIPLAYER	INVIDIA	SELL	2000

OLD SHOES

DESCRIPTION	ALWAYS ACT LAST.	HOW OBTAINED	MULTIPLAYER	LIBERTE PORT	BUY	6000
			MULTIPLAYER	ARBOR	SELL	2000

POISON CAPE

DESCRIPTION	BLOCKS POISON.	HOW OBTAINED	SOLD	GUERA	BUY	250
			SOLD	URBETH	SELL	50

POISON RING

DESCRIPTION	10% CHANCE OF POISONING THE FOE IN A NORMAL ATTACK.	HOW OBTAINED	DROP	BASILISK [A]	BUY	N/A
			DROP	COCKATRICE	SELL	400

POWER RING

DESCRIPTION	BOOSTS STRENGTH BY 10%.	HOW OBTAINED	SOLD	GUERA	BUY	500
			SOLD	URBETH	SELL	100

RAINBOW BOOTS

DESCRIPTION	LEGENDARY BOOTS THAT LET YOU WALK ON RAINBOWS! EVASION +5%	HOW OBTAINED	SOLD	LIBERTE TOWN, LIBERTE PORT	BUY	5000
			EVENT	TRADE MYTHRIL TO MYLION IN URBETH.	SELL	1000

RIBBON

DESCRIPTION	BLOCKS ALL AFFLICTIONS.	HOW OBTAINED	CHEST	STAR CHAMBER	BUY	N/A
			STEAL	OGRE BEAR	SELL	2000

SHINE CAPE

DESCRIPTION	BLOCKS LIGHT-ELEMENT ATTACKS (LV.1).	HOW OBTAINED	CHEST	SPELVIA UNDERGROUND	BUY	N/A
			DROP	BEHUGEMORE	SELL	400

SILENCE CAPE

DESCRIPTION	BLOCKS SILENCE.	HOW OBTAINED	SOLD	ARBOR	BUY	250
					SELL	50

SILENCE RING

DESCRIPTION	10% CHANCE OF SILENCING THE FOE IN A NORMAL ATTACK.	HOW OBTAINED	DROP	SILKY [A]	BUY	N/A
			DROP	SILKY [B]	SELL	400

SLEEP CAPE

DESCRIPTION	BLOCKS SLEEP.	HOW OBTAINED	SOLD	ARBOR	BUY	250
					SELL	50

SLEEP RING

DESCRIPTION	10% CHANCE OF PUTTING THE FOE TO SLEEP IN A NORMAL ATTACK.	HOW OBTAINED	DROP	LAMIA [A]	BUY	N/A
			DROP	SCYLLA	SELL	400

SNIPER'S RING

DESCRIPTION	ACCURACY +10%	HOW OBTAINED	SOLD	ARBOR	BUY	500
					SELL	100

SOIL CAPE

DESCRIPTION	BLOCKS EARTH-ELEMENT ATTACKS (LV.1).	HOW OBTAINED	CHEST	TOWER IN THE SKY	BUY	N/A
					SELL	400

SOUL OF THAMASA

DESCRIPTION	MAGIC ATTACK +10%, INTELLECT +5%	HOW OBTAINED	SOLD	SPELVIA	BUY	10,000
			CHEST	TOWN OF HORNE	SELL	2000

SPIRIT RING

DESCRIPTION	BOOSTS SPIRIT BY 10%.	HOW OBTAINED	SOLD	URBETH	BUY	500
			CHEST	FAIRY PATH	SELL	100

SPRING GAUNTLETS

DESCRIPTION	ADDS LV.1 WATER-ELEMENT DAMAGE TO WEAPON ATTACKS.	HOW OBTAINED	CHEST	FAIRY PATH	BUY	N/A
			DROP	ICHTHON [A]	SELL	100

STAR EARRING

DESCRIPTION	MAGIC ATTACK +10%	HOW OBTAINED	SOLD	URBETH	BUY	500
			SOLD	INVIDIA	SELL	100

STREAM CAPE

DESCRIPTION	BLOCKS WATER-ELEMENT ATTACKS.	HOW OBTAINED	CHEST	???	BUY	N/A
			DROP	FREKI [A]	SELL	100

STUN RING

DESCRIPTION	10% CHANCE OF PARALYZING THE FOE IN A NORMAL ATTACK.	HOW OBTAINED	DROP	MANDRAGORA [A]	BUY	N/A
			DROP	MANDRAGORA [B]	SELL	400

STUN CAPE

DESCRIPTION	BLOCKS PARALYSIS.	HOW OBTAINED	SOLD	URBETH	BUY	250
			SOLD	GUERA	SELL	50

TRYLION'S RING

DESCRIPTION	A RING GIVEN TO YOU BY TRYLION. DEFENSE +1, HP +20	HOW OBTAINED	EVENT	SPEAK WITH TRYLION AFTER DEFEATING THE ICE DRAGON.	BUY	N/A
					SELL	N/A

TURTLE SHELL

DESCRIPTION	DEFENSE +10%	HOW OBTAINED	SOLD	URBETH	BUY	500
			CHEST	ICE CAVERNS	SELL	100

WIND CAPE

DESCRIPTION	BLOCKS WIND-ELEMENT ATTACKS (LV.1).	HOW OBTAINED	CHEST	SPELVIA UNDERGROUND	BUY	N/A
			DROP	BEHUGEMORE	SELL	400

MAGIC TOMES

Magic in *Final Fantasy: The 4 Heroes of Light* is divided into three disciplines: Black, Dark, and White. Black Magic deals direct damage to enemies. Dark Magic inflicts a variety of negative status effects. White Magic boosts your party's abilities, restores health, and even returns fallen characters to life. In order to use a spell, a character must have the corresponding Tome in his or her inventory as well as having the magic spell assigned to one of six ability slots.

BLACK MAGIC

BEST BLACK MAGIC CROWNS	BLACK MAGE, SAGE
FIRST TARGET	REAR

Black Magic channels the power of elements to inflict direct damage to enemies, except for Leaf, Leafra, and Leafaga, which inflict non-elemental damage. Both Light (Thunder, Banish) and Water (Water, Blizzard) are represented with two sets of Black Magic spells. The distinctions between spells are subtle, but they do exist. Compared to Banish spells, Thunder spells deal less damage but are executed more quickly. The same is true for Water spells and Blizzard spells. Blizzard spells deal more damage, but take longer to unleash on enemies.

AERO

WIND-ELEMENT ATTACK.	
AP REQUIRED	2
ELEMENT TYPE	AIR LV.1
TARGETS	ONE ENEMY
MAGIC ATTACK	5
TARGET VALUE	5 (5)
ABILITY SPEED	15
COMBINED	YES
IMPLEMENT	YES
DIMINISHED EFFECT	NO

WHERE OBTAINED		
SOLD		TOWN OF HORNE
BUY	500	
SELL	100	

 AERORA

WIND-ELEMENT ATTACK.	
AP REQUIRED	3
ELEMENT TYPE	AIR LV.1
TARGETS	ONE ENEMY
MAGIC ATTACK	12
TARGET VALUE	5 (10)
ABILITY SPEED	10
COMBINED	YES
IMPLEMENT	YES
DIMINISHED EFFECT	NO

WHERE OBTAINED		
SOLD		GUERA
SOLD		TOWN OF HORNE
BUY	1500	
SELL	300	

 AEROGA

WIND-ELEMENT ATTACK.	
AP REQUIRED	4
ELEMENT TYPE	AIR LV.2
TARGETS	ALL ENEMIES
MAGIC ATTACK	15
TARGET VALUE	5 (15)
ABILITY SPEED	5
COMBINED	YES
IMPLEMENT	YES
DIMINISHED EFFECT	YES

WHERE OBTAINED		
SOLD		TOWN OF HORNE[B]
BUY	5000	
SELL	1000	

 BANISH

LIGHT-ELEMENT ATTACK.	
AP REQUIRED	2
ELEMENT TYPE	LIGHT LV.1
TARGETS	ONE ENEMY
MAGIC ATTACK	5
TARGET VALUE	5 (5)
ABILITY SPEED	15
COMBINED	YES
IMPLEMENT	YES
DIMINISHED EFFECT	NO

WHERE OBTAINED		
SOLD		SPELVIA
BUY	500	
SELL	100	

BANISHRA

LIGHT-ELEMENT ATTACK.	
AP REQUIRED	3
ELEMENT TYPE	LIGHT LV.1
TARGETS	ONE ENEMY
MAGIC ATTACK	12
TARGET VALUE	5 (10)
ABILITY SPEED	10
COMBINED	YES
IMPLEMENT	YES
DIMINISHED EFFECT	NO

WHERE OBTAINED		
SOLD		SPELVIA
BUY	1500	
SELL	300	

BANISHGA

LIGHT-ELEMENT ATTACK.	
AP REQUIRED	4
ELEMENT TYPE	LIGHT LV.2
TARGETS	ALL ENEMIES
MAGIC ATTACK	15
TARGET VALUE	5 (15)
ABILITY SPEED	5
COMBINED	YES
IMPLEMENT	YES
DIMINISHED EFFECT	YES

WHERE OBTAINED		
SOLD		SPELVIA
BUY	5000	
SELL	1000	

 BLIZZARD

WATER-ELEMENT ATTACK.

AP REQUIRED	2
ELEMENT TYPE	WATER LV.1
TARGETS	ONE ENEMY
MAGIC ATTACK	8
TARGET VALUE	5 (5)
ABILITY SPEED	10
COMBINED	YES
IMPLEMENT	YES
DIMINISHED EFFECT	NO

WHERE OBTAINED

SOLD		INVIDIA

BUY	500
SELL	100

BLIZZARA

WATER-ELEMENT ATTACK.

AP REQUIRED	3
ELEMENT TYPE	WATER LV.1
TARGETS	ONE ENEMY
MAGIC ATTACK	15
TARGET VALUE	5 (10)
ABILITY SPEED	5
COMBINED	YES
IMPLEMENT	YES
DIMINISHED EFFECT	NO

WHERE OBTAINED

SOLD		INVIDIA

BUY	1500
SELL	300

BLIZZAGA

WATER-ELEMENT ATTACK.

AP REQUIRED	4
ELEMENT TYPE	WATER LV.2
TARGETS	ALL ENEMIES
MAGIC ATTACK	18
TARGET VALUE	5 (15)
ABILITY SPEED	0
COMBINED	YES
IMPLEMENT	YES
DIMINISHED EFFECT	YES

WHERE OBTAINED

SOLD		INVIDIA

BUY	5000
SELL	1000

DARK

DARK-ELEMENT ATTACK.

AP REQUIRED	2
ELEMENT TYPE	DARK LV.1
TARGETS	ONE ENEMY
MAGIC ATTACK	5
TARGET VALUE	5 (5)
ABILITY SPEED	15
COMBINED	YES
IMPLEMENT	YES
DIMINISHED EFFECT	NO

WHERE OBTAINED

SOLD		INVIDIA

BUY	500
SELL	100

DARKRA

DARK-ELEMENT ATTACK.

AP REQUIRED	3
ELEMENT TYPE	DARK LV.1
TARGETS	ONE ENEMY
MAGIC ATTACK	12
TARGET VALUE	5 (10)
ABILITY SPEED	10
COMBINED	YES
IMPLEMENT	YES
DIMINISHED EFFECT	NO

WHERE OBTAINED

SOLD		INVIDIA

BUY	1500
SELL	300

DARKAGA

DARK-ELEMENT ATTACK.

AP REQUIRED	4
ELEMENT TYPE	DARK LV.2
TARGETS	ALL ENEMIES
MAGIC ATTACK	15
TARGET VALUE	5 (15)
ABILITY SPEED	5
COMBINED	YES
IMPLEMENT	YES
DIMINISHED EFFECT	YES

WHERE OBTAINED

SOLD		INVIDIA

BUY	5000
SELL	1000

DESOLATOR

MIGHTY BLACK MAGIC DESTROYS ALL...

AP REQUIRED	5
ELEMENT TYPE	—
TARGETS	ALL ENEMIES
MAGIC ATTACK	30
TARGET VALUE	5 (20)
ABILITY SPEED	5
COMBINED	NO
IMPLEMENT	NO
DIMINISHED EFFECT	NO

WHERE OBTAINED

EVENT	SPEAK WITH KING HORNE AFTER DEFEATING SATAN

BUY	5000
SELL	1000

FIRE

FIRE-ELEMENT ATTACK.

AP REQUIRED	2
ELEMENT TYPE	FIRE LV.1
TARGETS	ONE ENEMY
MAGIC ATTACK	5
TARGET VALUE	5 (5)
ABILITY SPEED	15
COMBINED	YES
IMPLEMENT	YES
DIMINISHED EFFECT	NO

WHERE OBTAINED

SOLD	GUERA
SOLD	LIBERTE TOWN

BUY	500
SELL	50

FIRA

FIRE-ELEMENT ATTACK.

AP REQUIRED	3
ELEMENT TYPE	FIRE LV.1
TARGETS	ONE ENEMY
MAGIC ATTACK	12
TARGET VALUE	5 (10)
ABILITY SPEED	10
COMBINED	YES
IMPLEMENT	YES
DIMINISHED EFFECT	NO

WHERE OBTAINED

SOLD	GUERA
SOLD	TOWN OF URBETH

BUY	1500
SELL	150

FIRAGA

FIRE-ELEMENT ATTACK.

AP REQUIRED	4
ELEMENT TYPE	FIRE LV.2
TARGETS	ALL ENEMIES
MAGIC ATTACK	15
TARGET VALUE	5 (15)
ABILITY SPEED	5
COMBINED	YES
IMPLEMENT	YES
DIMINISHED EFFECT	YES

WHERE OBTAINED

SOLD	TOWN OF URBETH

BUY	5000
SELL	500

 LEAF

NON-ELEMENT ATTACK.

AP REQUIRED	2
ELEMENT TYPE	—
TARGETS	ONE ENEMY
MAGIC ATTACK	5
TARGET VALUE	5 (5)
ABILITY SPEED	15
COMBINED	YES
IMPLEMENT	YES
DIMINISHED EFFECT	NO

WHERE OBTAINED

SOLD		ARBOR

BUY	500
SELL	100

 LEAFRA

NON-ELEMENT ATTACK.

AP REQUIRED	3
ELEMENT TYPE	—
TARGETS	ONE ENEMY
MAGIC ATTACK	12
TARGET VALUE	5 (10)
ABILITY SPEED	10
COMBINED	YES
IMPLEMENT	YES
DIMINISHED EFFECT	NO

WHERE OBTAINED

SOLD		ARBOR

BUY	1500
SELL	150

 LEAFAGA

NON-ELEMENT ATTACK.

AP REQUIRED	4
ELEMENT TYPE	—
TARGETS	ALL ENEMIES
MAGIC ATTACK	15
TARGET VALUE	5 (15)
ABILITY SPEED	5
COMBINED	YES
IMPLEMENT	YES
DIMINISHED EFFECT	YES

WHERE OBTAINED

SOLD		ARBOR

BUY	5000
SELL	1000

 QUAKE

EARTH-ELEMENT ATTACK. DOES NOT WORK ON FLYING ENEMIES.

AP REQUIRED	2
ELEMENT TYPE	EARTH LV.1
TARGETS	ONE ENEMY
MAGIC ATTACK	6
TARGET VALUE	5 (5)
ABILITY SPEED	15
COMBINED	YES
IMPLEMENT	YES
DIMINISHED EFFECT	NO

WHERE OBTAINED

SOLD		GUERA

BUY	500
SELL	50

 QUAKRA

EARTH-ELEMENT ATTACK. DOES NOT WORK ON FLYING ENEMIES.

AP REQUIRED	3
ELEMENT TYPE	EARTH LV.1
TARGETS	ONE ENEMY
MAGIC ATTACK	13
TARGET VALUE	5 (10)
ABILITY SPEED	10
COMBINED	YES
IMPLEMENT	YES
DIMINISHED EFFECT	NO

WHERE OBTAINED

SOLD		GUERA

BUY	1500
SELL	150

 QUAGA

EARTH-ELEMENT ATTACK. DOES NOT WORK ON FLYING ENEMIES.

AP REQUIRED	4
ELEMENT TYPE	EARTH LV.2
TARGETS	ALL ENEMIES
MAGIC ATTACK	16
TARGET VALUE	5 (15)
ABILITY SPEED	5
COMBINED	YES
IMPLEMENT	YES
DIMINISHED EFFECT	YES

WHERE OBTAINED

SOLD		GUERA

BUY	5000
SELL	500

THUNDER

LIGHT-ELEMENT ATTACK.

AP REQUIRED	2
ELEMENT TYPE	LIGHT LV.1
TARGETS	ONE ENEMY
MAGIC ATTACK	3
TARGET VALUE	5 (5)
ABILITY SPEED	20
COMBINED	YES
IMPLEMENT	YES
DIMINISHED EFFECT	NO

WHERE OBTAINED

SOLD		SPELVIA

BUY	500
SELL	100

THUNDARA

LIGHT-ELEMENT ATTACK.

AP REQUIRED	3
ELEMENT TYPE	LIGHT LV.1
TARGETS	ONE ENEMY
MAGIC ATTACK	10
TARGET VALUE	5 (10)
ABILITY SPEED	10
COMBINED	YES
IMPLEMENT	YES
DIMINISHED EFFECT	NO

WHERE OBTAINED

SOLD		SPELVIA

BUY	1500
SELL	300

THUNDAGA

LIGHT-ELEMENT ATTACK.

AP REQUIRED	4
ELEMENT TYPE	LIGHT LV.2
TARGETS	ALL ENEMIES
MAGIC ATTACK	12
TARGET VALUE	5 (15)
ABILITY SPEED	10
COMBINED	YES
IMPLEMENT	YES
DIMINISHED EFFECT	YES

WHERE OBTAINED

SOLD		SPELVIA

BUY	5000
SELL	1000

WATER

WATER-ELEMENT ATTACK.

AP REQUIRED	2
ELEMENT TYPE	WATER LV.1
TARGETS	ONE ENEMY
MAGIC ATTACK	5
TARGET VALUE	5 (5)
ABILITY SPEED	15
COMBINED	YES
IMPLEMENT	YES
DIMINISHED EFFECT	NO

WHERE OBTAINED

SOLD		LIBERTE TOWN
SOLD		TOWN OF URBETH

BUY	500
SELL	50

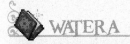 WATERA

WATER-ELEMENT ATTACK.

AP REQUIRED	3
ELEMENT TYPE	WATER LV.1
TARGETS	ONE ENEMY
MAGIC ATTACK	12
TARGET VALUE	5 (10)
ABILITY SPEED	10
COMBINED	YES
IMPLEMENT	YES
DIMINISHED EFFECT	NO

WHERE OBTAINED

SOLD	TOWN OF URBETH
SOLD	SPELVIA

BUY	1500
SELL	150

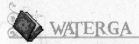 WATERGA

WATER-ELEMENT ATTACK.

AP REQUIRED	4
ELEMENT TYPE	WATER LV.2
TARGETS	ALL ENEMIES
MAGIC ATTACK	15
TARGET VALUE	5 (15)
ABILITY SPEED	5
COMBINED	YES
IMPLEMENT	YES
DIMINISHED EFFECT	YES

WHERE OBTAINED

SOLD	TOWN OF URBETH
SOLD	LIBERTE TOWN

BUY	5000
SELL	500

DARK MAGIC

BEST BLACK MAGIC CROWNS	DARK SHAMAN
FIRST TARGET	REAR

Except for Break and Death, Dark Magic is used to chip away at difficult enemies by inflicting any of a number of negative status ailments on them. Not all enemies are vulnerable to each Dark Magic spell, so it's worthwhile studying the enemy data in this guide to learn which spells to use against each enemy. Most Dark Magic effects are the same as the ones enemies use against the party. Poison and Drain are the only Dark Magic spells that inflict measurable damage. Drain has a Magic Attack value, making it the only Dark Magic spell that scales with a character's gear. Poison ticks off 3% of the afflicted enemy's total health each turn it's in effect. Suppress reduces enemies' statuses, making it easier to damage them as well as making it harder for the enemies to damage your party.

 BREAK

30% CHANCE TO INFLICT PETRIFICATION.

AP REQUIRED	3
TARGETS	ONE ENEMY
MAGIC ATTACK	—
TARGET VALUE	10 (10)
ABILITY SPEED	10
COMBINED	YES
IMPLEMENT	YES

WHERE OBTAINED

SOLD	GUERA
SOLD	TOWN OF URBETH

BUY	2500
SELL	500

DEATH

50% CHANCE TO TAKE A FOE'S LIFE.

AP REQUIRED	4
TARGETS	ONE ENEMY
MAGIC ATTACK	—
TARGET VALUE	15 (15)
ABILITY SPEED	10
COMBINED	YES
IMPLEMENT	YES

WHERE OBTAINED

SOLD	TOWN OF URBETH
CHEST	PIRATE HIDEOUT AFTER OBTAINING MAGIC KEY

BUY	5000
SELL	1000

 CONFUSE

80% CHANCE TO INFLICT CONFUSION.

AP REQUIRED	2
TARGETS	ONE ENEMY
MAGIC ATTACK	—
TARGET VALUE	0 (10)
ABILITY SPEED	15
COMBINED	YES
IMPLEMENT	YES

WHERE OBTAINED

SOLD	GUERA
SOLD	TOWN OF URBETH

BUY	500
SELL	100

DRAIN

ABSORB HP.

AP REQUIRED	2
TARGETS	ONE ENEMY
MAGIC ATTACK	5
TARGET VALUE	0 (10)
ABILITY SPEED	10
COMBINED	YES
IMPLEMENT	YES

WHERE OBTAINED

SOLD	TOWN OF URBETH

BUY	1500
SELL	300

 CURSE

80% CHANCE TO INFLICT A CURSE.

AP REQUIRED	2
TARGETS	ONE ENEMY
MAGIC ATTACK	—
TARGET VALUE	5 (10)
ABILITY SPEED	10
COMBINED	YES
IMPLEMENT	YES

WHERE OBTAINED

SOLD	TOWN OF URBETH

BUY	2000
SELL	400

FLASH

80% CHANCE TO INFLICT BLINDNESS.

AP REQUIRED	2
TARGETS	ONE ENEMY
MAGIC ATTACK	—
TARGET VALUE	5 (10)
ABILITY SPEED	10
COMBINED	YES
IMPLEMENT	YES

WHERE OBTAINED

SOLD	GUERA
SOLD	TOWN OF URBETH

BUY	500
SELL	100

POISON

50% CHANCE TO INFLICT POISON.

AP REQUIRED	2
TARGETS	ONE ENEMY
MAGIC ATTACK	—
TARGET VALUE	0 (10)
ABILITY SPEED	15
COMBINED	YES
IMPLEMENT	YES

WHERE OBTAINED

SOLD	GUERA
SOLD	TOWN OF URBETH

BUY	500
SELL	100

SLEEP

50% TO INFLICT SLEEP.

AP REQUIRED	2
TARGETS	ONE ENEMY
MAGIC ATTACK	—
TARGET VALUE	5 (10)
ABILITY SPEED	15
COMBINED	YES
IMPLEMENT	YES

WHERE OBTAINED

SOLD	GUERA
SOLD	TOWN OF URBETH

BUY	500
SELL	100

SILENCE

50% CHANCE TO INFLICT SILENCE.

AP REQUIRED	2
TARGETS	ONE ENEMY
MAGIC ATTACK	—
TARGET VALUE	10 (10)
ABILITY SPEED	15
COMBINED	YES
IMPLEMENT	YES

WHERE OBTAINED

SOLD	GUERA
SOLD	TOWN OF URBETH

BUY	500
SELL	100

SUPPRESS

80% CHANCE TO LOWER FOE'S STATUS.

AP REQUIRED	2
TARGETS	ONE ENEMY
MAGIC ATTACK	—
TARGET VALUE	5 (10)
ABILITY SPEED	10
COMBINED	YES
IMPLEMENT	YES

WHERE OBTAINED

SOLD	GUERA
SOLD	TOWN OF URBETH

BUY	2000
SELL	400

WHITE MAGIC

BEST WHITE MAGIC CROWNS	WHITE MAGE, SAGE
FIRST TARGET	N/A

White Magic performs three tasks: restore health to allies, boost allies' offensive capabilities, and remove negative status effects from allies. When you obtain Lux, it becomes a must-use spell in every big fight. With Lux, all party members get the benefits of Magick, Berserk, Shell, Regen, and Aura in addition to a 50% boost to their HP. The effects of Lux don't stack with those spells' effects, so don't waste inventory space on those Tomes once you get Lux.

ARISE

COMPLETELY REVIVE. CAN USE FROM THE MENU.

AP REQUIRED	4
TARGETS	ONE ALLY
MAGIC ATTACK	—
TARGET VALUE	10 (10)
ABILITY SPEED	10
COMBINED	NO
IMPLEMENT	NO
DIMINISHED EFFECT	NO

WHERE OBTAINED

SOLD	TOWN OF URBETH

BUY	5000
SELL	1000

AURA

INCREASES STATUS LEVELS BY 10%

AP REQUIRED	3
TARGETS	ONE ALLY
MAGIC ATTACK	—
TARGET VALUE	5 (5)
ABILITY SPEED	30
COMBINED	NO
IMPLEMENT	YES
DIMINISHED EFFECT	NO

WHERE OBTAINED

SOLD	SPELVIA

BUY	2500
SELL	500

BERSERK

INCREASES ATTACK BY 50%.

AP REQUIRED	2
TARGETS	ONE ALLY
MAGIC ATTACK	—
TARGET VALUE	5 (5)
ABILITY SPEED	30
COMBINED	NO
IMPLEMENT	YES
DIMINISHED EFFECT	NO

WHERE OBTAINED

SOLD	GUERA

BUY	1000
SELL	200

CURE

SLIGHT HP RECOVERY. CAN USE FROM THE MENU.

AP REQUIRED	2
TARGETS	ONE ALLY
MAGIC ATTACK	—
TARGET VALUE	5/0
ABILITY SPEED	20
COMBINED	NO
IMPLEMENT	YES
DIMINISHED EFFECT	NO

WHERE OBTAINED

SOLD	GUERA
SOLD	LIBERTE TOWN

BUY	500
SELL	100

 CURA

HP RECOVERY. CAN USE FROM THE MENU.

AP REQUIRED	3
TARGETS	ONE ALLY
MAGIC ATTACK	—
TARGET VALUE	5 (5)
ABILITY SPEED	15
COMBINED	NO
IMPLEMENT	YES
DIMINISHED EFFECT	NO

WHERE OBTAINED

SOLD	GUERA
SOLD	SPELVIA

BUY	1500
SELL	300

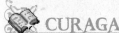 CURAGA

PARTY HP RECOVERY. CAN USE FROM THE MENU.

AP REQUIRED	4
TARGETS	ALL ALLIES
MAGIC ATTACK	—
TARGET VALUE	10 (20)
ABILITY SPEED	20
COMBINED	NO
IMPLEMENT	YES
DIMINISHED EFFECT	YES

WHERE OBTAINED

SOLD	GUERA
SOLD	TOWN OF URBETH

BUY	5000
SELL	1000

 ESUNA

CURE AFFLICTIONS. CAN USE FROM THE MENU.

AP REQUIRED	2
TARGETS	ONE ALLY
MAGIC ATTACK	—
TARGET VALUE	0 (10)
ABILITY SPEED	15
COMBINED	NO
IMPLEMENT	YES
DIMINISHED EFFECT	NO

WHERE OBTAINED

SOLD	GUERA
SOLD	TOWN OF URBETH

BUY	1500
SELL	300

 INVISIBLE

EVASION DOUBLED.

AP REQUIRED	2
TARGETS	ONE ALLY
MAGIC ATTACK	—
TARGET VALUE	0 (5)
ABILITY SPEED	30
COMBINED	NO
IMPLEMENT	YES
DIMINISHED EFFECT	NO

WHERE OBTAINED

SOLD	SPELVIA

BUY	1000
SELL	200

 LUX

MIGHTY WHITE MAGIC STRENGTHENS ALL...

AP REQUIRED	5
TARGETS	ALL ALLIES
MAGIC ATTACK	—
TARGET VALUE	10 (0)
ABILITY SPEED	5
COMBINED	NO
IMPLEMENT	YES
DIMINISHED EFFECT	NO

WHERE OBTAINED

EVENT	SPEAK WITH THE QUEEN IN ARBOR AFTER OBTAINING THE MONK CROWN

BUY	—
SELL	—

 MAGICK

MAGIC ATTACK INCREASED 50%.

AP REQUIRED	2
TARGETS	ONE ALLY
MAGIC ATTACK	—
TARGET VALUE	5 (5)
ABILITY SPEED	30
COMBINED	NO
IMPLEMENT	YES
DIMINISHED EFFECT	NO

WHERE OBTAINED

SOLD	GUERA
SOLD	SPELVIA

BUY	1000
SELL	200

 PROTECT

DEFENSE INCREASED 50%.

AP REQUIRED	2
TARGETS	ONE ALLY
MAGIC ATTACK	—
TARGET VALUE	0 (5)
ABILITY SPEED	30
COMBINED	NO
IMPLEMENT	YES
DIMINISHED EFFECT	NO

WHERE OBTAINED

SOLD	GUERA
SOLD	TOWN OF URBETH

BUY	1000
SELL	200

RAISE

REVIVE FROM DEAD. CAN USE FROM THE MENU.

AP REQUIRED	3
TARGETS	ONE ALLY
MAGIC ATTACK	—
TARGET VALUE	5 (5)
ABILITY SPEED	15
COMBINED	NO
IMPLEMENT	NO
DIMINISHED EFFECT	NO

WHERE OBTAINED

SOLD	GUERA
SOLD	TOWN OF URBETH

BUY	1500
SELL	500

REGEN

RECOVER HEALTH EACH TURN.

AP REQUIRED	3
TARGETS	ONE ALLY
MAGIC ATTACK	—
TARGET VALUE	0 (10)
ABILITY SPEED	30
COMBINED	NO
IMPLEMENT	YES
DIMINISHED EFFECT	NO

WHERE OBTAINED

SOLD	TOWN OF URBETH

BUY	1000
SELL	200

SHELL

MAGIC DEFENSE INCREASED 50%.

AP REQUIRED	2
TARGETS	ONE ALLY
MAGIC ATTACK	—
TARGET VALUE	0 (5)
ABILITY SPEED	30
COMBINED	NO
IMPLEMENT	YES
DIMINISHED EFFECT	NO

WHERE OBTAINED

SOLD	GUERA
SOLD	TOWN OF URBETH

BUY	1000
SELL	200

ITEMS

Items perform a variety of functions, both in and out of battle. Items can be broken down into four types: Attack, Recovery, Utility, and Other.

ATTACK ITEMS

Use Attack Items to exploit elemental weaknesses when Black Magic isn't available. To get the most out of Attack Items, assign one character to be an Alchemist. For more information about Alchemists and Attack Items, turn to the Alchemist page in the Crown section of this guide.

You must be engaged in battle to use any of the following items, and each item targets only a single enemy. Some Attack Items are found for sale around the world, and there's at least one enemy that drops each type of Attack Item. However, the best source for these items is the shop in Urbeth that's unlocked with the Magic Key.

Buy	300
Sell	100

ANTARCTIC WIND

Inflicts Lv.1 water-element damage, equivalent to 50 Magic Attack.

Buy	300
Sell	100

GAIA DRUM

Inflicts Lv.1 earth-element damage, equivalent to 50 Magic Attack. Does not work against flying enemies.

Buy	300
Sell	100

RAVEN'S YAWN

Inflicts Lv.1 wind-element damage, equivalent to 50 Magic Attack.

Buy	300
Sell	100

BOMB FRAGMENT

Inflicts Lv.1 fire-element damage, equivalent to 50 Magic Attack.

Buy	—
Sell	100

GREAT TREE LOG

Inflicts Lv.1 earth-element damage, equivalent to 50 Magic Attack.

Buy	300
Sell	100

ZEUS'S WRATH

Inflicts Lv.1 light-element damage, equivalent to 50 Magic Attack, and paralyzes the foe.

Buy	300
Sell	100

DARK SIGH

Inflicts Lv.1 dark-element damage, equivalent to 50 Magic Attack.

Buy	300
Sell	100

HOLY BREATH

Inflicts Lv.1 light-element damage, equivalent to 50 Magic Attack.

UTILITY ITEMS

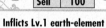

Utility items are usable only from the menu and have no combat function. Torches light up dark dungeons, making navigation much easier. Dragon Wings are a wonderful way to jump back to town if you're stuck somewhere. Use the Hunting Horn to instantly enter a battle anywhere battles are possible (it doesn't work in town, for example). The Hunting Horn can be used as often as you like so long as it is in someone's inventory.

Dragon Wings and Torches are readily available from Item Shops around the world, but the only Hunting Horn you see is from the first trip to the Pirate's Cove.

Buy	60
Sell	20

DRAGON WING

Teleports you back to town, instantly.

Buy	—
Sell	10

HUNTING HORN

Summons monsters to your side.

Buy	10
Sell	3

TORCH

Lights your way in the darkest of dungeons.

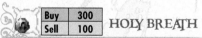

RECOVERY ITEMS

Recovery Items perform the same functions as White Magic, although most of the items have a specific effect they remove instead of being a panacea, like Esuna.

Salve-makers have the most tricks when it comes to recovery items. Dispensary allows Salve-makers to use recovery items without consuming them, and Healthcare applies the effect of the recovery item to everyone in the party. Poison Pill reverses the effect of recovery items, so they cause harm to enemies instead of restoring health. Wayfarers use recovery items most effectively. If a Wayfarer uses an item, it restores twice as much health or AP as it would normally.

The following items may be used in battle or from the menu between battles. These items are readily available from shops around the world, and are dropped by many enemies. Elixir is the one exception. It's only found in treasure chests in the Extra Dungeons.

Buy	20
Sell	7

POTION

Restores 40 HP.

Buy	—
Sell	333,333

ELIXIR

Restores all your HP.

Buy	20
Sell	7

ALARM CLOCK

Wakes you up from any sleep.

Buy	40
Sell	13

HI-POTION

Restores 80 HP.

Buy	1000
Sell	333

ETHER

Restores 3 AP.

Buy	20
Sell	7

ANIMATE TONIC

Cures paralysis.

Buy	400
Sell	133

X-POTION

Restores 160 HP.

Buy	10,000
Sell	3333

HI-ETHER

Restores your AP.

Buy	20
Sell	7

ANTIDOTE

Cures poison.

Buy	50
Sell	17

CROSS

Lifts curses.

Buy	50
Sell	17

GOLD NEEDLE

Cures petrification.

Buy	400
Sell	133

REMEDY

Cures all ailments (except death) and restores 100 HP.

Buy	20
Sell	7

ECHO HERBS

Cures silence.

Buy	100
Sell	33

PHOENIX DOWN

Brings you back from the dead.

Buy	20
Sell	7

TRANQUILIZER

Cures confusion.

Buy	20
Sell	7

EYE DROPS

Cures blindness.

OTHER ITEMS

The items listed here have specific purposes. None of them is usable from the menu or during combat.

 ORIHALCON

Orihalcon comes from the four dragon bosses that appear on the 80th floor of the bonus tower dungeons. Turn it in at the upgrade shop in the town of Urbeth to add 10 levels to the potential upgrades for Armor, Weapons, and Shields.

The upgrade shop stops allowing upgrades at level 99. Sell off any excess Orihalcon for 10,000 gil.

 MUSIC SCORE

The Music Score is available from the Multiplayer Shop in Liberte Port for 2500 points. Buying this item unlocks the Musician Crown. When you're finished with the Music Score, you can sell it for 1667 gil.

 MYTHRIL

Mythril has two uses during the adventure, although one use is optional. In Invidia, you can trade Mythril for a Mythril Hammer. Later, in Urbeth, you can trade Mythril for Rainbow Boots.

The best way to obtain Mythril is to steal it from one of the following enemies: Aspidochelon [A], Rock Golem, or Mythritoise. A few other enemies drop the item, such as Iron Golems and Mimics, but stealing gives a better chance at success.

WORLD MAP

1	NORTH CAVES SOUTH ENTRANCE
2	NORTH CAVES NORTH ENTRANCE
3	WITCH'S MANSION
4	MOONLIGHT TOWER
5	QUICKSAND CASTLE
6	PIRATE HIDEOUT
7	ANIMAL BURROW (LIBERTE ENTRANCE)
8	ANIMAL BURROW (GUERA ENTRANCE)
9	FAIRY PATH (GUERA ENTRANCE)
10	FAIRY PATH (ARBOR ENTRANCE)
11	HUNTING CAVES (LIBERTE ENTRANCE)
12	HUNTING CAVES (URBETH ENTRANCE)

13	ICE CAVERNS ENTRANCE (TO 1F)
14	ICE CAVERNS ENTRANCE (TO B2F)
15	ICE CAVERNS ENTRANCE (TO 1F)
16	ICE CAVERNS ENTRANCE (TO 1F)
17	SUN TEMPLE
18	MT. GULG
19	STAR CHAMBER
20	MOONSAND RUINS
21	HOLY TREE TOWER
22	TRIAL TOWER
23	NAMINGWAY'S CAVE

TOWN OF HORNE & HORNE CASTLE

ENEMIES AROUND HORNE

FALCON [A]

JACK LANTERN [A]

GOBLIN [A]

IMP [A]

LIZARDMAN [A]

INN COSTS 10 GIL

TOWN OF HORNE ITEM SHOP

ITEM	COST	DESCRIPTION
POTION	20 G	PROVIDES A SMALL HP BOOST.
TORCH	10 G	LIGHTS YOUR WAY IN THE DARKEST OF DUNGEONS.
DRAGON WING	60 G	TELEPORTS YOU BACK TO TOWN, INSTANTLY.
STEEL SWORD	200 G	ATTACK +2
HORNE'S BOW	190 G	ATTACK +2
WOOD SHIELD	130 G	DEFENSE +1, MAGIC DEFENSE +1, EVADE/MAGIC EVADE +3

TOWN OF HORNE MULTIPLAYER PRIZES

ITEM	COST	DESCRIPTION
INFERNO	5400	ATTACK +14 (FIRE)
FROST BULL	5160	ATTACK +12 (WATER)
GRAN FISSURE	4080	ATTACK +16 (EARTH)
KRYSTA	5700	ATTACK +15 (WIND)
BLACKSWORD	9600	ATTACK +18 (DARK), INFLICTS SUDDEN DEATH.
FENCER'S GARB	1000	DEFENSE +2, MAGIC DEFENSE +2, STRENGTH/INTELLECT/SPIRIT +5%
WARMAGE ARMOR	1000	DEFENSE +2, MAGIC DEFENSE +2, STRENGTH/INTELLECT/SPIRIT +5%
CEREMONIAL ROBE	1000	DEFENSE +2, MAGIC DEFENSE +2, STRENGTH/INTELLECT/SPIRIT +5%
HERO'S WILL	8000	IF YOU DIE DURING A BATTLE, YOU WILL HANG ON TO LIFE WITH 1 HP — BUT ONLY ONCE.
GROWTH EGG	3000	DOUBLES EXPERIENCE POINTS EARNED.

ITEMS FROM CHESTS

WOOD SHIELD
POTION (X2)

ITEMS FROM PEOPLE

PHOENIX DOWN (X2)
POTION (X2)
STEEL SWORD
100 GIL
INHERITED RING

Rise and Shine

Start your adventure by speaking with Kuore before leaving Brandt's home. Kuore mentioned a trip to the castle, but that can wait until you take care of other business. Chat with the other citizens of Horne as you encounter them, but there are three in particular to seek out. Speak with these individuals before visiting the castle, or they won't hand over their items to Brandt.

Look for a soldier at the south edge of town. Speak with him to obtain a **Phoenix Down**. Speak with the woman in the blue dress outside the Item Shop (it's north of the soldier) for a **Potion**. The man pacing around the Multiplayer building on the north edge of town hands over another **Potion** when you talk to him.

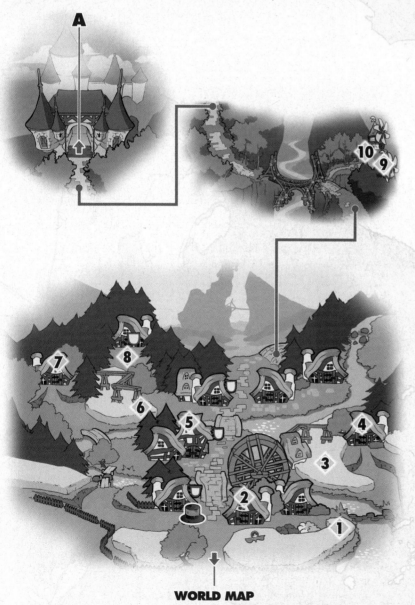

WORLD MAP

8-Item Challenge: Town of Horne

Enter the house in the northeast corner of town. The boy inside the house challenges you to find eight items hidden around town. After completing Item Challenges in each town, stop by the Storage Shop to clear up your party's inventory space.

1. A **Potion** from the fireplace in Brandt's Home

2. A **Potion** from the wheat field near Brandt's home

3. A **Potion** from the wheat field near the river bend

4. A **Potion** under the wooden structure near the Storage Shop

5. A **Dragon Wing** from the blue box inside the home in the northwest corner of town

6. A **Torch** from the Inn's topmost floor

7. A **Dragon Wing** from the barrel inside the house across from the Item Shop

8. A **Potion** from the ledge west of the windmill north of town

	LEGEND	
1	DRAGON WING	
2	POTION	
3	POTION	
4	POTION	
5	TORCH	
6	POTION	
7	DRAGON WING	
8	POTION	
9	POTION	
10	HI-ETHER, X-POTION (REQUIRES MAGIC KEY)	

MAGIC LABORATORY

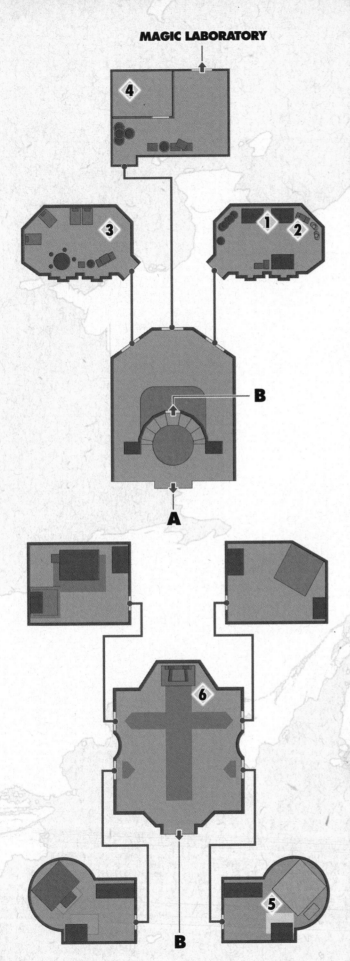

LEGEND

1	WOOD SHIELD
2	POTION
3	POTION
4	SOUL OF THAMASA (REQUIRES MAGIC KEY)
5	PHOENIX DOWN
6	100 GIL

On to Horne Castle

Travel to the castle by heading north from the town of Horne, past the windmills, and across a wooden bridge. The door at the top of the stairs in the middle of the entry room leads to the king's audience chamber.
Speak with King Horne, agree to help, and he hands over a **Steel Sword**. Speak with his minister to earn 100 gil.

Before you leave the audience chamber, go through the southeast door. Speak with the maid inside the room, who provides a **Phoenix Down**. Return to the entry room of the castle, but don't leave just yet. The doors on the north wall lead to a few chests. Beyond the northwest door is a **Potion**, while the northeast door leads to a **Wood Shield** and a **Potion**.

Quick Stops

After speaking with King Horne, stop by the Storage Shop and clear up some of Brandt's inventory space. Keep at least one of everything on hand, and two of each won't hurt you. Go to Brandt's house and speak with Kuore. After she hands over the **Inherited Ring**, it's a good time to save your game with the Adventurer.

The Outside World

Outside the safety of the town of Horne, you must prepare Brandt to face the enemies that pop up in random encounters. Equip the Wood Shield, Steel Sword, and Inherited Ring, then check your inventory for a Torch before you begin the trek to the Northern Cave. Before you enter the cave mouth north of town, seek out random battles and gain a few levels.

Multiplayer Items

Items available with Multiplayer Points are markedly superior to what's available from the regular shops at this early point of the adventure. If you're able to accumulate enough points to obtain these items, you're at a significant advantage. However, since not everyone has access to playing partners, the walkthrough only lists the items and their costs but won't include any of the items as suggested purchases.

NORTH CAVES

ENEMIES IN NORTH CAVES

GOBLIN [A]

JACK LANTERN [A]

BLOOD BAT [A]

MYCONID [A]

LIZARDMAN [A]

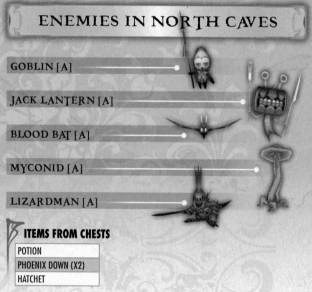

ITEMS FROM CHESTS

POTION
PHOENIX DOWN (X2)
HATCHET

Jusqua

Careful, Brandt! Without magic, you'll never defeat beasts like that.

Upon entering the North Caves, select a Torch from Brandt's inventory to brighten up the area. Collect the items from the nearby chests, then take the stairs down to North Caves B1F. A purple cloud blocks the hallway not far from the staircase. Fortunately, Jusqua appears to help Brandt tackle the creature!

LEGEND

1	POTION
2	PHOENIX DOWN
3	HATCHET
4	PHOENIX DOWN

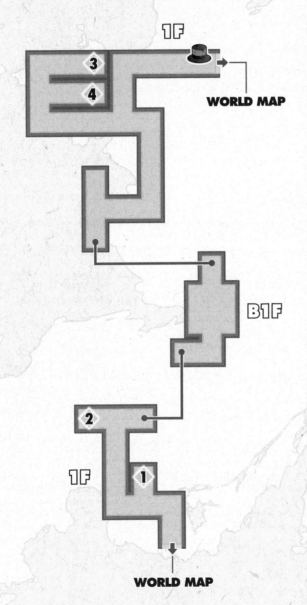

1F

WORLD MAP

B1F

1F

WORLD MAP

Minotaur [B]

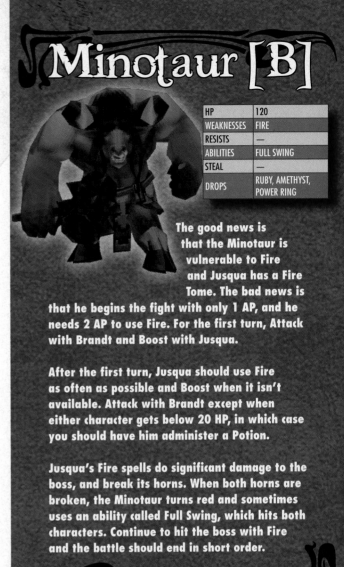

HP	120
WEAKNESSES	FIRE
RESISTS	—
ABILITIES	FULL SWING
STEAL	—
DROPS	RUBY, AMETHYST, POWER RING

The good news is that the Minotaur is vulnerable to Fire and Jusqua has a Fire Tome. The bad news is that he begins the fight with only 1 AP, and he needs 2 AP to use Fire. For the first turn, Attack with Brandt and Boost with Jusqua.

After the first turn, Jusqua should use Fire as often as possible and Boost when it isn't available. Attack with Brandt except when either character gets below 20 HP, in which case you should have him administer a Potion.

Jusqua's Fire spells do significant damage to the boss, and break its horns. When both horns are broken, the Minotaur turns red and sometimes uses an ability called Full Swing, which hits both characters. Continue to hit the boss with Fire and the battle should end in short order.

BOSS

After the battle, Jusqua joins Brandt. Take the stairs up to North Caves 1F North. Grab the contents of the chests on the northwest side of the floor—and save your progress—before leaving the North Caves for the outside world.

Jusqua joins the party!

WITCH'S MANSION

ENEMIES IN WITCH'S MANSION

ORC [A]

COWPEL [A]

GOBLIN [A]

LIZARDMAN [A]

MIMIC

ITEMS FROM CHESTS

CURE TOME
POTION
STEEL ARMOR
PHOENIX DOWN
HORNE'S BOW
DRAGON WING

LEGEND

1	POTION
2	STEEL ARMOR
3	CURE TOME
4	PHOENIX DOWN
5	HORNE'S BOW
6	DRAGON WING

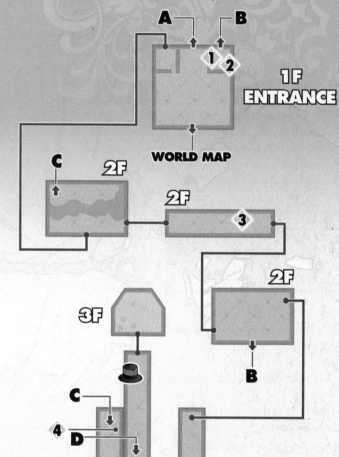

A   B

1   2

**1F
ENTRANCE**

WORLD MAP

C

2F

2F

3

2F

3F

B

C

4

D

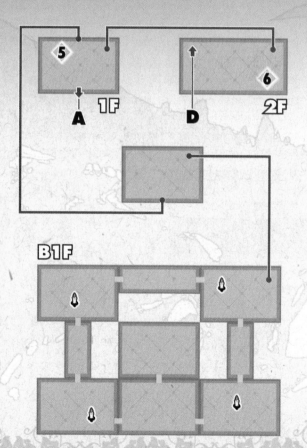

5

A   **1F**

D   **2F**

6

B1F

The Witch's Mansion is a short walk north from the North Cave exit. Once inside, speak with the fallen soldiers and check the central door on the northern wall. It's impossible to open it right now, so go up the west staircase and continue through the door. There's a wide gap in the floor, so your only option is to travel east. Speak with the fallen soldier to learn a bit more about what happened to the soldiers of Horne.

The next room is a narrow corridor. Open the chest near the fallen soldier to pick up a **Cure Tome**. Put it into the inventory of whichever character doesn't have a Cure Tome already, then set it as an ability in the Ability screen.

Maintaining Health between Battles

When there's a single enemy remaining to battle your party, go into Boost mode for all characters. Continue to Boost until everyone is at full AP, although you should use Cure as necessary. When the battle is over, use Cure Tomes to restore everyone to full health.

The next room has a staircase in the northeast corner, but go through the door in the south wall first. It leads back to the first room of the mansion, and two chests. Don't open the lower chest until both characters are in decent health. The chest is actually a creature known as a Mimic. It guards a nice armor upgrade, making the battle worthwhile.

More Party Additions

Return to 2F and take the stairs in the northeast corner. Follow the corridor to another set of stairs, and collect the **Phoenix Down** from the chest before descending. Lighting the candle in the room unlocks the door in the front room, so hurry back in that direction.

When you encounter Yunita under attack in the long corridor, stop to help her! Eliminate the Orc and pair of Goblins that have her trapped. When the enemies are out of the way, she joins the party.

Now the path is clear back to the front room. Go through the previously shut door and claim **Horne's Bow** from the chest on the other side. Go up the next two sets of stairs (don't forget the **Dragon Wing**), then look for the Adventurer at the end of a hallway. Save your progress before going into the next room.

Speak with the prone woman in the middle of the floor. It turns out to be Aire, the missing princess. After Aire joins the party, take a moment to distribute some spells and equipment. Give the Fire Tomes and any weapons that boost Magic Attack to the two characters with the highest Intellect. The other two characters should get the Cure Tomes. If you have any weapons that deal Wind damage, remove them now and use another weapon, such as Horne's Bow. Head back toward the interior of the building, and get ready for a fight!

Greaps [A]

HP	260
WEAKNESSES	FIRE
RESISTS	WIND
ABILITIES	BLAST OF AIR
STEAL	—
DROPS	RUBY, AMETHYST

Greaps is vulnerable to Fire, so the two characters with Fire Tomes should use it every turn, or Boost when it's necessary. The other two characters should attack when possible, and cast Cure when anyone's health drops too low.

On the third turn, Greaps launches into the air. While it is in the air, the boss uses Blast of Air to damage everyone in the party. Take down the boss as quickly as possible! You're only able to heal two characters each turn, but the boss damages everyone! Keep hammering away with Fire, and you should end the battle shortly after Greaps takes to the air.

BOSS

When the fight ends, you're treated to the game's opening credits, and your first Crown: Wayfarer! Before you do anything else, take a moment to chat with the other members

of the party. Also, there's a new option on the character menu: Crown. Use this screen to change everyone into Wayfarers.

A circle appears in the room. Step on it to be teleported down to the base of the castle. From there, enter the North Cave and save your progress.

You now have a choice: If you have a Torch, consider fighting through the Northern Caves to get more items, gems, and experience, or use a Dragon Wing to return instantly to the town of Horne.

Stone Cold Reception

Back in Horne, everyone has been turned into statues! Only the Adventurer seems to be immune among the people in the town. Follow Aire's suggestion and check out the castle.

Aire and Jusqua soon leave the party, but don't worry about losing their equipped items. You'll get a chance to reclaim them!

When you try to check on the king, you encounter an inspection team. Speak with the inspector in the audience chamber. Regardless of your response, your party's roster shrinks by half. Return to the town and speak with the inspector near the Storage Shop for a clue about where to go next. It's time to leave Horne behind and venture out into the world!

MOONLIGHT TOWER

ENEMIES IN MOONLIGHT TOWER

BIG WORM[A]

BASILISK [A]

COWPEL [A]

WIGHT [A]

LEGEND

1	TEMPEST PIKE
2	PHOENIX DOWN
3	RISING SUN
4	1000 GIL

ITEMS FROM CHESTS

TEMPEST PIKE
PHOENIX DOWN
RISING SUN
1000 GIL

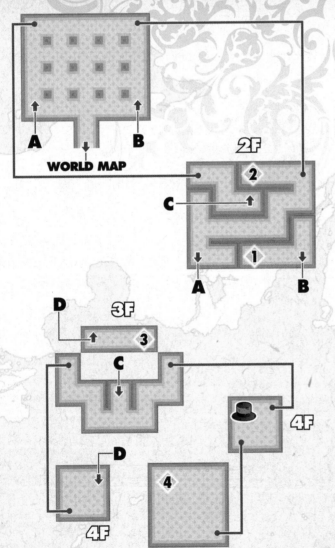

WORLD MAP

2F

A   B

3F

4F

4F

5F

An Unexpected Encounter

From the town of Horne, travel east until you run into the water. Go south around the sea and look for the desert. When it's dark, wander around the desert until you happen upon a man at a campfire. His name is Krinjh, and he joins the party at this point. Krinjh is a Spell Fencer, able to imbue his weapon with Black Magic.

With Krinjh in the party, head to the northeastern edge of the desert, along the seashore where the Moonlight Tower rises up from the sands.

Krinjh

My name is Krinjh, and I am one of the last of the Moon Folk.

Into the Tower

Take the stairs east of the entrance up to 2F and claim the **Tempest Pike** from the nearby chest. Go back down to 1F, then take the stairs in the northeast corner of the room back up to 2F. Grab the **Phoenix Down** from the chest before returning to the first floor. The stairs in the northwest corner eventually lead to the higher floors of Moonlight Tower. Go west initially on the third floor to pick up the **Rising Sun**.

The Adventurer is on 4F, allowing you to save your progress if you wish. On 5F, go to the center structure and interact with it to get the Merkmal. You now have access to a limited World Map. The chest in the northwest corner of the room has **1000 gil**, which will come in handy soon. Exit the tower, pull up the World Map, and head to Guera, which now appears on the map. Travel mainly south and a bit east to reach it.

GUERA

INN COSTS 20 GIL

GUERA ITEM SHOP

ITEM	COST	DESCRIPTION
POTION	20 G	PROVIDES A SMALL HP BOOST.
DRAGON WING	60 G	TELEPORTS YOU BACK TO TOWN, INSTANTLY.
ANTIDOTE	20 G	CURES POISON.
ECHO HERBS	20 G	CURES SILENCE.
ANIMATE TONIC	30 G	CURES PARALYSIS.
EYE DROPS	20 G	CURES BLINDNESS.
TORCH	10 G	LIGHTS YOUR WAY IN THE DARKEST OF DUNGEONS.
ANTARCTIC WIND	300 G	INFLICTS WATER-ELEMENT DAMAGE.

GUERA MAGIC SHOP

ITEM	COST	DESCRIPTION
FIRE TOME	500 G	BLACK MAGIC: FIRE-ELEMENT ATTACK. MAGIC ATTACK: 5 / AP COST: 2
QUAKE TOME	500 G	BLACK MAGIC: EARTH-ELEMENT ATTACK. MAGIC ATTACK: 6 / AP COST: 2
AERO TOME	500 G	BLACK MAGIC: WIND-ELEMENT ATTACK. MAGIC ATTACK: 5 / AP COST: 2
CURE TOME	500 G	WHITE MAGIC: SLIGHT HP RECOVERY. AP COST: 2. CAN USE FROM THE MENU.

GUERA EQUIPMENT SHOP

ITEM	COST	DESCRIPTION
STEEL SWORD	200 G	ATTACK +2
STEEL SPEAR	330 G	ATTACK +3
HORNE'S BOW	190 G	ATTACK +2
WIND BOW	485 G	ATTACK +3 (WIND)
MAGIC STAFF	85 G	ATTACK +1, MAGIC ATTACK +3
ROCK SHIELD	350 G	DEFENSE +1, MAGIC DEFENSE +1, EVADE/MAGIC EVADE +5, BLOCKS EARTH
TRAVELER'S GARB	150 G	DEFENSE +2, MAGIC DEFENSE +1, STRENGTH/INTELLECT/SPIRIT +5%
POWER RING	500 G	BOOSTS STRENGTH BY 10%
POISON CAPE	250 G	BLOCKS POISON.

GUERA MULTIPLAYER PRIZES

ITEM	COST	DESCRIPTION
HERCULES	9000	ATTACK +50
ARES	5130	ATTACK +19
MJOLLNIR	3300	ATTACK +13
AFREET ROBE	1000	DEFENSE +2, MAGIC DEFENSE +2. STRENGTH/INTELLECT/SPIRIT +5%
PRIEST'S GOWN	1000	DEFENSE +2, MAGIC DEFENSE +2. STRENGTH/INTELLECT/SPIRIT +5%
RED SASH	1000	DEFENSE +2, MAGIC DEFENSE +2. STRENGTH/INTELLECT/SPIRIT +5%
SHINOBI GARB	1000	DEFENSE +2, MAGIC DEFENSE +2. STRENGTH/INTELLECT/SPIRIT +5%
HERO'S WILL	8000	IF YOU DIE DURING A BATTLE, YOU WILL HANG ON TO LIFE WITH 1 HP — BUT ONLY ONCE.
FORTUNE EGG	3000	DOUBLES NUMBER OF ITEMS DROPPED.
GROWTH EGG	3000	DOUBLES EXPERIENCE POINTS EARNED.

GUERA CASTLE ENTRANCE

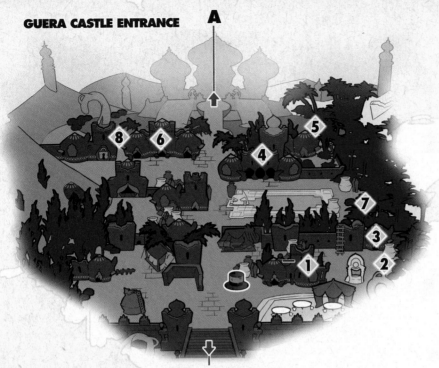

A

EXIT TO WORLD

LEGEND

1	POTION
2	POTION
3	EYE DROPS
4	ANTIDOTE
5	ANTIDOTE
6	POTION
7	ANIMATE TONIC
8	DIRT DIRK

8-Item Challenge: Guera

A boy wearing a red sash in the Inn challenges you to find eight hidden items. Two of the items aren't available during your initial visit to Guera.

1. A **Potion** from the bedstand near the boy

2. A **Potion** from the stand of trees east of the white well

3. **Eye Drops** from the table in the Multiplayer Shop

4. An **Antidote** from the west wardrobe inside the triple archway house

5. An **Antidote** from the tree at the edge of the water behind town

6. A **Potion** from the west bookshelf in the Magic Shop

7. An **Animate Tonic** from behind the Multiplayer Shop (requires animal form)

8. A **Dirt Dirk** from the edge of the water behind the locked building (requires animal form)

A Hidden City

The citizens of Guera are surprised to have visitors, but they don't offer much assistance. The king seems to know something, and he's in the castle north of town.

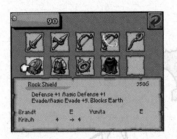

Before you pay him a visit, check out the shops in Guera. Purchase a pair of Rock Shields from the Equipment Shop and equip them on Brandt and Yunita immediately. You could buy many more items here with sufficient gil, but the Rock Shields are the best investment.

Quick Castle Visit

During the daytime, go north of town to visit the castle. The guards there are on alert and they take their jobs seriously. For this visit, follow orders and go directly to meet the king. Use the teleporter pads to reach him.

Agree to help him with his problem, then return to Guera. Rest at the Inn if any of your characters need it. Exit the town and wander in the sands just outside of it until nightfall. If anyone is close to gaining a level, take on a few random encounters, but you must return to Guera before sunrise!

GUERA CASTLE & GUERA CAVERNS

ENEMIES IN GUERA CAVERNS

GOBLIN [A]

BIG WORM [A]

BASILISK [A]

BLOOD BAT [A]

ITEMS FROM CHESTS

TORCH
ETHER
PHOENIX DOWN
WOOD AXE
WATER TOME

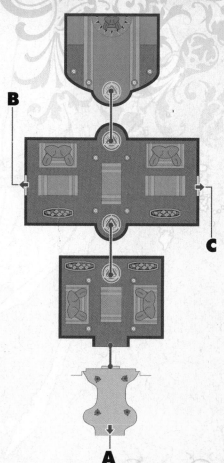

B

C

A

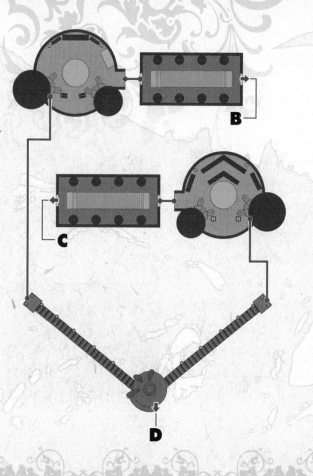

B

C

D

LEGEND

1	TORCH
2	WOOD AXE
3	ETHER
4	WATER TOME
5	PHOENIX DOWN

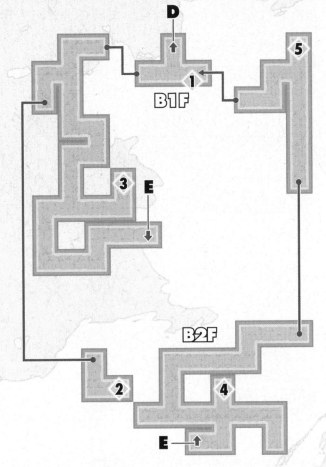

Your first stop should be to grab the **Wood Axe** that's in a chest off the main path. It has a nice attack value, but axes are notoriously inaccurate. You can equip it, but don't expect to hit with it as often. Guera Caverns B2 contains the big prize for the area: a **Water Tome**. Immediately set it as an ability for either Brandt or Yunita. Follow the maps to return to Guera Caverns B1 and claim the **Phoenix Down** from the

chest. There's a quick way to return to the entry area for Guera Caverns near the chest. Just jump down when prompted, then return to Guera Castle.

Back in Guera

Back in town, visit the Storage Shop, drop off unnecessary items (be sure to keep the Water Tome!), and pick up Potions, Phoenix Downs, and a Dragon Wing to replenish any that were used up. Take a set of equipment (armor, shield, and

weapon) that you won't mind losing and stash it in Krinjh's inventory. Exit town and travel roughly north to reach your next destination, Quicksand Castle.

Going Underground

Return to Guera Castle, but do some exploring this time. Speak with the guards and scholars in both wings of the castle, but your destination is one of the doorways (there's one in each wing) that open to a flight of stairs ultimately leading to Guera Caverns. The chest south of the entry point has a Torch, just in case you didn't bring one.

QUICKSAND CASTLE

ENEMIES IN NORTH CAVES

COWPEL [A]

CAIT SITH [A]

BASILISK [A]

WIGHT [A]

CU SITH [A]

ITEMS FROM CHESTS

| BANE KNIFE |
| BLUE SHOT |
| EARTH AXE |
| ETHER |
| PHOENIX DOWN |

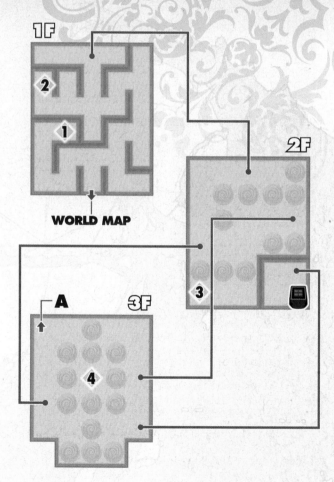

1F

2

1

WORLD MAP

2F

3

A

3F

4

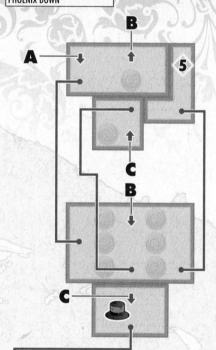

B

A

B

5

C

C

B

C

LEGEND

1	PHOENIX DOWN
2	ETHER
3	BLUE SHOT
4	BANE KNIFE
5	EARTH AXE

Playing in the Sand

Quicksand Castle 1F holds two chests, but no real surprises. Clean out the chests, then take the stairs up to 2F where things get interesting. If the lead character touches the quicksand, the entire party is pulled down to the floor below.

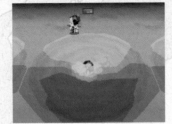

On 2F, go west initially, then south. Ignore the first set of stairs you see. Go to the east staircase and take the stairs there up to 3F. Go directly south

and take the stairs there back to 2F. Inspect the item in the corner and cast a Water spell on it.

Retrace your steps back to 2F, then go to the south end of the room. Where there were three quicksand pits, there are now two with a clear path to a chest that contains a **Blue Shot**. Equip it on Yunita or Brandt—whichever character isn't your primary spell user.

Quicksand Castle Upper Levels

Use the quicksand pit in the middle of 4F to drop back down into the center of 3F's field of quicksand pits. The chest here has a **Bane Knife**. Return to 4F and take the east stairs up to 5F. Drop down through the southeastern quicksand pit to claim the **Earth Axe** in the chest. Use the northernmost quicksand pit to reach the stairs that lead back to 5F. Take the other set of stairs back to 4F and save your game.

> Before you take the staircase beyond the Adventurer, empty Krinjh's inventory of anything that you want to keep. Equip him with a backup set of gear before you take on the boss.

Sand Devil

HP	600
WEAKNESSES	WATER
RESISTS	EARTH
ABILITIES	SANDSTORM
STEAL	—
DROPS	EMERALD, AMETHYST, EARTH SWORD

To deal any significant damage to the boss, you must target it with the Water spell, or an Antarctic Wind. The creature's flowing sand form avoids damage otherwise. Each application of Water or an Antarctic Wind hardens the Sand Devil for 2 turns, so it can take regular physical damage.

The boss's physical attacks have an Earth-element component. Its big ability is Sandstorm, which hits all three characters, deals Earth damage, and often inflicts blindness.

The most important character in this fight is the one who can cast Water during the battle. Always keep that character's AP above 2 so the Water spell is available when it's needed. When the boss falls, do not assign any drops to Krinjh!

BOSS

Two New Crowns

After the battle, and Krinjh's revelation, the crystal appears again and grants two new crowns: Black Mage and White Mage. Step on the purple portal to be transported to the base of Quicksand Castle. Head back to Guera and visit the Storage Shop. You should unload most of your items and spell books here. Yunita and Brandt won't need them for a while, and anything held in the storage shop is made available to everyone.

Any attempts to visit the palace are met with a polite, yet firm, rebuke. Follow the guard's suggestion and stay at the Inn. When Brandt wakes up during the night, step outside the Inn.

LIBERTE TOWN & LIBERTE PORT

INN COSTS 20 GIL

LIBERTE PORT & LIBERTE TOWN (TOP) ITEM SHOP

ITEM	COST	DESCRIPTION
POTION	20 G	PROVIDES A SMALL HP BOOST.
DRAGON WING	60 G	TELEPORTS YOU BACK TO TOWN, INSTANTLY.
TORCH	10 G	LIGHTS YOUR WAY IN THE DARKEST OF DUNGEONS.
TRANQUILIZER	20 G	CURES CONFUSION.
ECHO HERBS	20 G	CURES SILENCE.
FIRE TOME	500 G	BLACK MAGIC: FIRE-ELEMENT ATTACK, MAGIC ATTACK: 5 / AP COST: 2
WATER TOME	500 G	BLACK MAGIC: WATER-ELEMENT ATTACK, MAGIC ATTACK: 5 / AP COST: 2
CURE TOME	500 G	WHITE MAGIC: SLIGHT HP RECOVERY. AP COST 2. CAN USE FROM THE MENU.
CONFUSE CAPE	250 G	BLOCKS CONFUSION.
RAINBOW BOOTS	5000 G	LEGENDARY BOOTS THAT LET YOU WALK ON RAINBOWS!

LIBERTE TOWN ITEM SHOP (LEFT)

ITEM	COST	DESCRIPTION
STEEL SWORD	200 G	ATTACK +2
HORNE'S BOW	190 G	ATTACK +2
MAGIC STAFF	85 G	ATTACK +1, MAGIC ATTACK +3
KNIFE	220 G	ATTACK +2, MAGIC ATTACK +2
FLAME DAGGER	530 G	ATTACK +3, MAGIC ATTACK +3 (FIRE), INFLICTS CONFUSION
HARP	220 G	ATTACK +2, MAGIC ATTACK +2
TRAVELER'S GARB	150 G	DEFENSE +2, MAGIC DEFENSE +1, STRENGTH/INTELLECT/SPIRIT +5%
BLACK ROBE	350 G	DEFENSE +3, MAGIC DEFENSE +4, INTELLECT/MAGIC ATTACK POWER +10%
WHITE ROBE	350 G	DEFENSE +3, MAGIC DEFENSE +4, SPIRIT +20%
ICE SHIELD	350 G	DEFENSE +1, MAGIC DEFENSE +1, EVADE/MAGIC EVADE +5, BLOCKS WATER

LIBERTE PORT MULTIPLAYER PRIZES

ITEM	COST	DESCRIPTION
BOOK OF SECRETS	4860	ATTACK +6, MAGIC ATTACK +10
AVALON SCROLLS	5260	ATTACK +13, MAGIC ATTACK +5
AKASHIC RECORDS	6690	ATTACK +8, MAGIC ATTACK +14
CAT'S TUNIC	1000	DEFENSE +2, MAGIC DEFENSE +2. STRENGTH/INTELLECT/SPIRIT +5%
ANGEL TOGA	1000	DEFENSE +2, MAGIC DEFENSE +2. STRENGTH/INTELLECT/SPIRIT +5%
DANCING WEAR	1000	DEFENSE +2, MAGIC DEFENSE +2. STRENGTH/INTELLECT/SPIRIT +5%
BLUE JACKET	1000	DEFENSE +2, MAGIC DEFENSE +2. STRENGTH/INTELLECT/SPIRIT +5%
MAXIMILLIAN	1000	DEFENSE +2, MAGIC DEFENSE +2. STRENGTH/INTELLECT/SPIRIT +5%
OLD SHOES	6000	ALWAYS ACT LAST.
MUSIC SCORE	2500	FIRST, YOU HAVE TO KNOW HOW TO READ MUSIC...

ENEMIES OUTSIDE LIBERTE

SLIME [A]

GOBLIN [A]

FALCON [A]

LIZARDMAN [A]

ITEMS FROM CHESTS
GIANT'S RING

ITEMS FROM PEOPLE
APOLLO'S TALISMAN

TO LIBERTE PORT

TO LIBERTE TOWN (DAY)
TO ??? (NIGHT)

WORLD MAP

LEGEND

1	POTION
2	GAIA DRUM
3	PHOENIX DOWN
4	DRAGON WING
5	EYE DROPS
6	ECHO HERBS
7	HI-POTION
8	POTION
9	SOUL OF THAMASA, REMEDY, STUNNING HARP (REQUIRES MAGIC KEY)

8-Item Challenge: Liberte

The boy with the blue vest in the Liberte Port Inn challenges you to find eight hidden items.

In Liberte Port

1 A **Potion** on the east wall inside the Storage Shop

2 A **Gaia Drum** behind the Item Shop

3 A **Phoenix Down** near a tree in the southwest corner of town

4 A **Dragon Wing** under the mast of the boat in the northeast corner of town

In Liberte Town

5 **Eye Drops** from the flowers in front of the house east of the bridge to Liberte Port

6 **Echo Herbs** near the bed in the round room on the upper floor of the Inn

7 A **Hi-Potion** under a tree east of Apollo's doorway

8 A **Potion** under a bush on the east side of the king's chamber

Exploring a New Land

When you assume control of Aire, take some time to explore both Liberte Town and Liberte Port. Speak with the citizens, the king, and the pirates on the dock. One of them offers an important clue for later.

The dwelling in the northwest corner of Liberte Town is the home of Apollo, who has a sad tale to tell. Grab the **Giant's Ring** from the chest in the basement, then return to Jusqua who decides to rejoin Aire. With Jusqua in the party, visit the Storage Shop and exchange the pair's equipment for any upgrades left behind by Yunita and Brandt.

In addition, consider selling enough Rubies so you can pick up a White Robe and a Black Robe. These two items offer the highest physical defense, which is necessary for an upcoming boss fight.

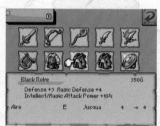

Musician Crown

The Multiplayer Shop in Liberte Port sells an item called Music Score. When you purchase it, you unlock the Musician Crown. It isn't a necessary purchase, but having more Crowns available is never a bad thing!

Random Acts of Violence

The next point of interest is the Pirate Hideout, but don't go there until both characters are at least level 10. Spend some time outside of Liberte trying out your new Crowns. For the upcoming encounter, one character needs to be a White Mage, but you have an option for the other character. Choose a Black Mage, loaded up with all the Black Magic spells, if your best weapon is stacked with Magic Attack power. Go with a Wayfarer if you would rather stick to melee attacks.

Aire makes the better Black Mage, while Jusqua is the better choice for Wayfarer.

It isn't necessary to set someone as a White Mage yet, so while you're engaging in random battles trying to reach level 10, use one Wayfarer and one Black Mage. Once everyone hits level 10, return to Liberte and save your game. Head to the east and look for a cave opening that indicates the Pirate Hideout's location.

The Whirlpool

When you leave town, time starts to flow again. During the night, a Whirlpool appears between Liberte Port and Liberte Town and blocks the path. Stepping

on the whirlpool sends the party to a location known only as ???. It is not a good time to go there at this point because the way inside is blocked.

PIRATE HIDEOUT

ENEMIES IN PIRATE HIDEOUT

- LIZARDMAN [B]
- LIZARDMAN [A]
- SLIME
- METAL FLAN
- BLOOD BAT
- LAMIA
- ASPIDOCHELON

ITEMS FROM CHESTS

300 GIL (X2)	ICEBRAND
500 GIL	OCEAN STAVE
ANTARCTIC WIND	ROCK LANCE
HUNTING HORN	TERRA STAVE

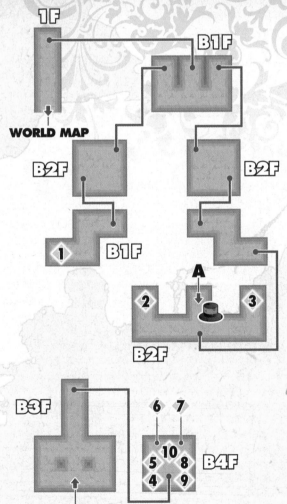

1F

B1F

WORLD MAP

B2F

B2F

B1F

1

A

2   3

B2F

B3F

6   7

5 10 8
4   9

B4F

A

LEGEND

1	300 GIL
2	ROCK LANCE
3	TERRA STAVE
4	500 GIL
5	ICEBRAND
6	500 GIL
7	OCEAN STAVE
8	HUNTING HORN
9	ANTARCTIC WIND

LEGEND

4	FRESH MEAT (AFTER DEFEATING SEADEVIL [A])
5	DANCER CLOTHES (AFTER DEFEATING SEADEVIL [A])
6	1000 GIL (AFTER DEFEATING SEADEVIL [A])
7	MONK'S ROBE (AFTER DEFEATING SEADEVIL [A])
8	DEATH TOME (AFTER DEFEATING SEADEVIL [A])
9	1000 GIL (AFTER DEFEATING SEADEVIL [A])
10	RUSTY COMPASS (AFTER DEFEATING SEADEVIL [A])

Freedom

The sentry who greets the party just inside the Pirate Cave demands a password before he allows anyone to pass. Select "Freedom" and he steps aside.

After claiming the contents of the chests, return to the Adventurer and save your game. At this point (if you haven't already), set either Jusqua or Aire as a White Mage for the upcoming fight. When you're ready, descend the stairs and speak with the pirate captain, who turns out to be another disguised enemy!

It's Not Safe in Here

The pirates have allowed creatures to wander through their hideout. Even though there are people to speak with in the area, expect to run into a bunch of random battles throughout the Pirate Hideout.

The stairs beyond the lookout lead down to Pirate Hideout B1F. Go west first and descend a few flights of stairs until you reach a chest with **300 gil**. Claim the money, return to B1F, and take the east stairs.

When you encounter the Adventurer on B2F, save your game, but don't use the stairs north of him just yet. There are two chests, one each in the eastern and western branches of the room. The pirate standing in front of each chest is actually a Lizardman in disguise. These Lizardmen are tougher than the

ones you fought previously in random encounters. The western chest has a **Rock Lance**, and the eastern chest holds a **Terra Stave**.

Trollud [C]

HP	400
WEAKNESSES	—
RESISTS	—
ABILITIES	BERSERK, WHIRL BLUDGEON
STEAL	—
DROPS	TOPAZ

You may find that the general pattern that this battle follows is to set your White Mage to heal almost every round, while your other character focuses on attacking the Trollud. In the first round, and in any round where the Trollud doesn't deal damage (whether it misses or uses Berserk), the White Mage should use Healthgiver so one Cure spell hits both characters.

The Trollud uses Whirl Bludgeon often, but you should be able to heal through it. However, when the Trollud applies Berserk, which boosts the physical damage dealt, keeping both characters alive becomes a challenge.

This isn't a quick fight because you have only two characters, and one must focus on healing. This is also why one must be a White Mage; any other job runs out of AP too quickly. With patience, you should outlast the Trollud and claim victory.

BOSS

Plunderin' the Spoils

Descend the stairs beyond the boss encounter point. The room is filled with chests and (now freed) hostages. Speak with everyone in the vicinity and collect the spoils from the chest. Inspect the crystal vase in the middle of the room as well.

Further Adventures

Return to Liberte Town during daytime. The next stop is a visit with Apollo, who lives across the bridge that's blocked at night. Talk to Apollo to get **Apollo's Talisman.** Equip it on the character who is lacking an Accessory, and visit the Storage Shop. A Black Mage with a Fire Spell is a big help in the upcoming areas, so switch Aire to a Black Mage if she isn't one already.

When you're satisfied with your characters' setup, go to the coral-covered building where Jusqua and Aire began in Liberte. After a night's rest, Jusua and Aire wake up with full HP and AP.

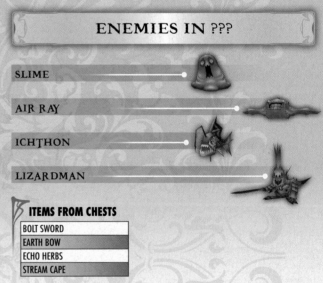

ENEMIES IN ???

- SLIME
- AIR RAY
- ICHTHON
- LIZARDMAN

ITEMS FROM CHESTS

BOLT SWORD
EARTH BOW
ECHO HERBS
STREAM CAPE

A Princess's Vanity

Aire is determined to visit the bottom of the whirlpool, which means some time must be spent outside Liberte until the sun sets. After the sun goes down, return to the town and enter the whirlpool. The area under the whirlpool doesn't have a name, and the green areas on the floor inflict damage to the party when they walk on it.

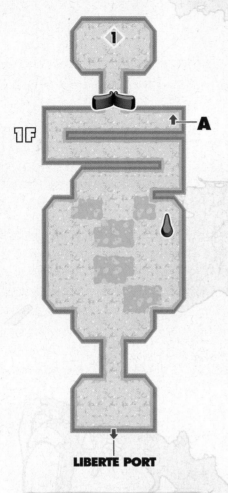

1F

A

LIBERTE PORT

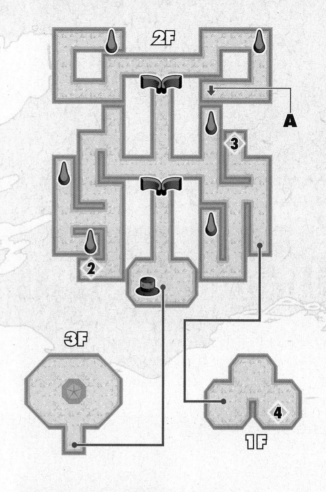

2F

A

3F

1F

LEGEND

1	STREAM CAPE
2	ECHO HERBS
3	EARTH BOW
4	BOLT SWORD

The switch in the northeast corner of the open area on 1F controls the stone doors at the north end of the level. The chest beyond the stone doors contains a **Stream Cape**, but it's guarded by a Mimic. The accessory is a huge help against the upcoming enemies which deal Water-element damage, so it's worth the extra effort to obtain it.

Traversing 2F requires a few long trips to reach the chests scattered around the floor. Trip both switches marked on the maps to open the stone doors.

Stream Cape
Blocks water-element attacks.

Aire obtained an item: Stream Cape!

Pass through the first set of stone doors and go south. Hit all the switches and clean out the chests. Most of the chests yield their items easily, but the chest back on 1F (accessed by the stairs in the southeast corner) is actually a Mimic guarding a **Bolt Sword**.

Jusqua is about to leave the party, but don't worry about removing his good gear. It's a temporary parting, and the upcoming battle is tough enough that both characters need to keep their best gear equipped to survive it.

Once the southern doors swing open, go through them. The Adventurer is there to save your progress before you descend the next flight of stairs. Approaching the chest triggers a disagreement between Aire and Jusqua, but it's quickly interrupted.

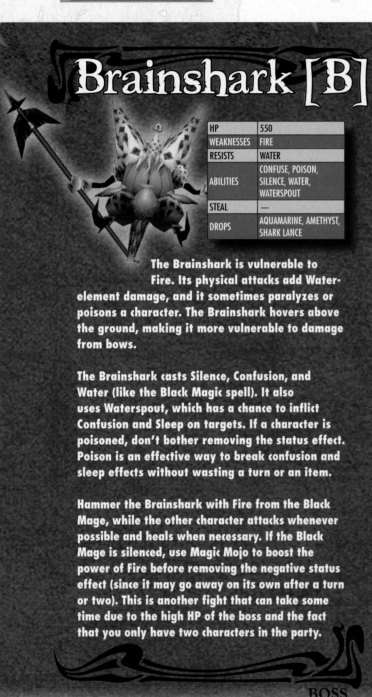

Brainshark [B]

HP	550
WEAKNESSES	FIRE
RESISTS	WATER
ABILITIES	CONFUSE, POISON, SILENCE, WATER, WATERSPOUT
STEAL	—
DROPS	AQUAMARINE, AMETHYST, SHARK LANCE

The Brainshark is vulnerable to Fire. Its physical attacks add Water-element damage, and it sometimes paralyzes or poisons a character. The Brainshark hovers above the ground, making it more vulnerable to damage from bows.

The Brainshark casts Silence, Confusion, and Water (like the Black Magic spell). It also uses Waterspout, which has a chance to inflict Confusion and Sleep on targets. If a character is poisoned, don't bother removing the status effect. Poison is an effective way to break confusion and sleep effects without wasting a turn or an item.

Hammer the Brainshark with Fire from the Black Mage, while the other character attacks whenever possible and heals when necessary. If the Black Mage is silenced, use Magic Mojo to boost the power of Fire before removing the negative status effect (since it may go away on its own after a turn or two). This is another fight that can take some time due to the high HP of the boss and the fact that you only have two characters in the party.

BOSS

A Furry Adventure

After a further disagreement and Jusqua's departure, inspect the treasure chest. Aire is turned into a cat and ends up back in the center of Liberte.

Cross-species Communication

While she's in cat form, Aire is able to speak with the animals around Liberte, including the Adventurer's companion. In fact, speaking with every animal, while in animal form, is an achievement for the game. Don't worry about getting all the animals now as Aire; it's easier to accomplish this feat after you obtain a few special items.

The humans offer different bits of gossip to characters in animal form, including the people who challenge you to find items hidden around town. They offer a hint about the location of one of the hidden items!

Return to the coral-covered house and see what everyone is doing. Lilibelle hands over a map that allows you to see more

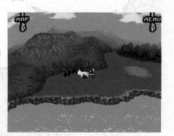

of the World Map and reveals the location of an Animal Burrow. Travel west from Liberte and enter the small stand of trees near the shoreline.

ANIMAL BURROW

WORLD MAP

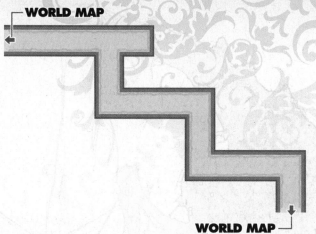

WORLD MAP

The tunnel doesn't have any branches, so just follow it until you encounter a purple cloud. Speak to the floating face (moving past it has the same effect) to begin a fight with an Ogre Bear. There's no actual fight, just one round that doesn't go well.

You obtained the crowns of the Bandit and Bard!

In the aftermath of the ill-fated encounter, Lilibelle hands over **Lilibelle's Wings**, and you get the Bandit and Bard Crowns. Continue through the Animal Burrow; when you hit the desert, go east to Guera.

ENEMIES IN ANIMAL BURROW

IMP [A]

SLIME [A]

GOBLIN [A]

BLOOD BAT [A]

MYCONID [A]

ITEMS FROM PEOPLE

LILIBELLE'S WINGS

GUERA

Aire, in cat form, can collect the final two items from the collection challenge (the **Animate Tonic** and the **Dirt Dirk**) by squeezing through the small doorways cut into the walls of the town. During the night, there's also a new Magic Shop just south of the other Magic Shop (which has three doorways).

GUERA TOWN MAGIC SHOP (OUTDOOR)

ITEM	COST	DESCRIPTION
FIRA TOME	1500 G	BLACK MAGIC: FIRE-ELEMENT ATTACK, MAGIC ATTACK: 12 / AP COST: 3
QUAKRA TOME	1500 G	BLACK MAGIC: EARTH-ELEMENT ATTACK, MAGIC ATTACK: 13 / AP COST: 3
AERORA TOME	1500 G	BLACK MAGIC: WIND-ELEMENT ATTACK, MAGIC ATTACK: 12 / AP COST: 3
CURA TOME	1500 G	WHITE MAGIC: HP RECOVERY. AP COST 3. CAN USE FROM THE MENU.
BERSERK TOME	1000 G	WHITE MAGIC: ATTACK INCREASED 50%. AP COST 2.
PROTECT TOME	1000 G	WHITE MAGIC: DEFENSE INCREASED 50%. AP COST 2.
SHELL TOME	1000 G	WHITE MAGIC: MAGIC DEFENSE INCREASED 50%. AP COST: 2.
MAGICK TOME	1000 G	WHITE MAGIC: MAGIC ATTACK INCREASED 50%. AP COST 2.
RAISE TOME	1500 G	WHITE MAGIC: REVIVE FROM DEAD. AP COST 3. CAN USE FROM THE MENU.

Brandt

I know! I should go to Arbor. They'll be able to help lift the curse from Horne. I'm going there right now!

Brandt appears in front of the Inn only at night. Speak with him to have him rejoin the party. With all the new Crowns available, take some time to set Brandt up with a new Crown and equipment to go with it. Stick a Torch in someone's inventory, then travel north from Guera to a cave entrance in the mountain range. This is the Fairy Path that leads to Arbor.

FAIRY PATH

ENEMIES ON FAIRY PATH

JACK LANTERN [B]

IMP [B]

BLOOD BAT [A]

BATTER FLY [A]

ITEMS FROM CHESTS

SPIRIT RING
SPRING GAUNTLETS

WORLD MAP

1

2

WORLD MAP

LEGEND

| 1 | SPIRIT RING |
| 2 | SPRING GAUNTLETS |

Almost to Arbor

Apparently, the guard posted just inside the path is not a cat lover. He speaks only to Brandt, while giving cat-form Aire the silent treatment. Hurry through the Fairy Path as quickly as possible, but don't miss the **Spirit Ring** and **Spring Gauntlets** from the chests along the way.

After clearing the Fairy Path, head north toward the looming tree in the distance. As Aire and Brandt draw closer to Arbor, an event takes place and the action shifts to Jusqua.

Brandt

Whoa! Wh-what's happening? I...can't...move...

Feline Identification Issues

When you assume control of Jusqua, exit the home and speak with the people around town, and the king (although if you want to skip the story details, you can speak with the cat in the room immediately). Return to Jusqua's temporary home and speak with the cat until it joins the party.

With the cat in tow, visit the king and answer "Yep" to his question. Before you head out, visit the Storage Shop. There's no need to carry Phoenix Downs, but you should grab a Torch, a few Potions, and at least one Antidote. Consider setting Jusqua as a Wayfarer, and enhancing that Crown to level 2. Escape may come in handy with Jusqua traveling alone. When everything is ready, go north from Liberte to a cave entrance cut into the mountains.

HUNTING CAVES

ITEMS FROM CHESTS

ETHER
THUNDER AXE
HI-ETHER

LEGEND

1	ETHER
2	THUNDER AXE
3	HI-ETHER

ENEMIES IN NORTH CAVES

MYCONID [B]

BLOOD BAT [A]

GOBLIN [A]

CHIMERA [A]

HELLHOUND [A]

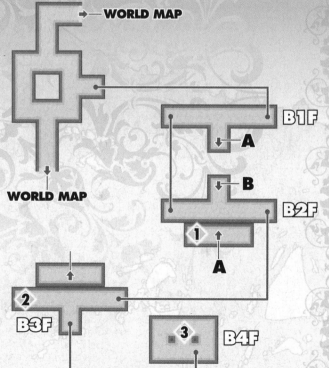

Under the Mountain

It's possible to run directly north and exit the caves without doing anything else. However, you'll miss out on two nice chest items (an **Ether** and a **Thunder Axe**) and a **Hi-Ether** hidden in the bushes on B4F.

Return to the first floor and take the exit to the outside world. Go north to reach your destination: the town of Urbeth.

TOWN OF URBETH

ENEMIES AROUND URBETH

LIZARDMAN [B]

FALCON [A]

SUCCUBUS [A]

HELLHOUND [A]

MYTHRITOISE[A]

GOBLIN [A]

ITEMS FROM CHESTS

RED SHOT

TOWER TO THE SKY (X2)

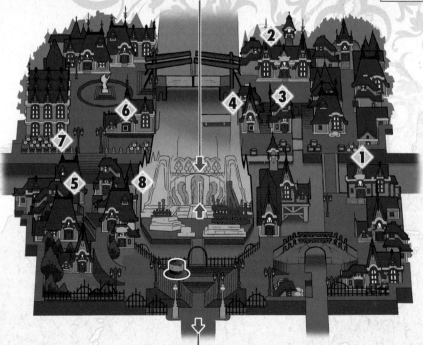

LEGEND

1	HYDRAXE
2	HI-POTION
3	POTION
4	ALARM CLOCK
5	GREAT TREE LOG
6	CROSS
7	HI-POTION
8	ZEUS'S WRATH

WORLD MAP

TOWN OF URBETH ITEM SHOP (BYLION'S SHOP)

ITEM	COST	DESCRIPTION
POTION	20 G	PROVIDES A SMALL HP BOOST.
HI-POTION	40 G	PROVIDES A GOOD HP BOOST.
TORCH	10 G	LIGHTS YOUR WAY IN THE DARKEST OF DUNGEONS.
DRAGON WING	60 G	TELEPORTS YOU BACK TO TOWN, INSTANTLY.
ANTIDOTE	20 G	CURES POISON.
ANIMATE TONIC	30 G	CURES PARALYSIS.
EYE DROPS	20 G	CURES BLINDNESS.
ETHER	1000 G	PROVIDES A SMALL AP BOOST.

TOWN OF URBETH ITEM SHOP (LOWER)

ITEM	COST	DESCRIPTION
POTION	20 G	PROVIDES A SMALL HP BOOST.
HI-POTION	40 G	PROVIDES A GOOD HP BOOST.
ANTIDOTE	20 G	CURES POISON.
GOLD NEEDLE	50 G	CURES PETRIFICATION.
ECHO HERBS	20 G	CURES SILENCE.
ANIMATE TONIC	30 G	CURES PARALYSIS.
EYE DROPS	20 G	CURES BLINDNESS.
ALARM CLOCK	20 G	WAKES YOU UP FROM ANY SLEEP.
CROSS	50 G	LIFTS CURSES.
REMEDY	400 G	CURES ALL AILMENTS (EXCEPT DEATH) AND RESTORES A SMALL AMOUNT OF HP.

TOWN OF URBETH ARMOR SHOP (MYLION'S SHOP)

ITEM	COST	DESCRIPTION
TRAVELER'S GARB	150 G	DEFENSE +2, MAGIC DEFENSE +1, STRENGTH/INTELLECT/SPIRIT +5%
BLACK ROBE	350 G	DEFENSE +3, MAGIC DEFENSE +4, INTELLECT/MAGIC ATTACK POWER +10%
WHITE ROBE	350 G	DEFENSE +3, MAGIC DEFENSE +4, SPIRIT +20%
BANDIT GEAR	350 G	DEFENSE +4, MAGIC DEFENSE +2, ACCURACY +20%
POET TUNIC	350 G	DEFENSE +4, MAGIC DEFENSE +3, INTELLECT/SPIRIT +10%
WOOD SHIELD	130 G	DEFENSE +1, MAGIC DEFENSE +1, EVADE/MAGIC EVADE +3
FLAME SHIELD	350 G	DEFENSE +1, MAGIC DEFENSE +1, EVADE/MAGIC EVADE +5, BLOCKS FIRE
ROCK SHIELD	350 G	DEFENSE +1, MAGIC DEFENSE +1, EVADE/MAGIC EVADE +5, BLOCKS EARTH
DARKSTEEL SHIELD	450 G	DEFENSE +2, MAGIC DEFENSE +2, EVADE/MAGIC EVADE +5, BLOCKS DARK

TOWN OF URBETH ACCESSORY SHOP (TRYLION'S SHOP)

ITEM	COST	DESCRIPTION
POWER RING	500 G	BOOSTS STRENGTH BY 10%
INTELLECT RING	500 G	BOOSTS INTELLECT BY 10%.
SPIRIT RING	500 G	BOOSTS SPIRIT BY 10%.
GIANT'S RING	500 G	ATTACK +10%
STAR EARRING	500 G	MAGIC ATTACK +10%
TURTLE SHELL	500 G	DEFENSE +10%
BLACK RING	500 G	MAGIC DEFENSE +10%
CONFUSE CAPE	250 G	BLOCKS CONFUSION.
POISON CAPE	250 G	BLOCKS POISON.
STUN CAPE	250 G	BLOCKS PARALYSIS.

TOWN OF URBETH WEAPON SHOP (THAUZAND'S SHOP)

ITEM	COST	DESCRIPTION
STEEL SWORD	200 G	ATTACK +2
HATCHET	255 G	ATTACK +3
STEEL SPEAR	330 G	ATTACK +3
KNIFE	220 G	ATTACK +2, MAGIC ATTACK +2
BOLT SWORD	700 G	ATTACK +5 (LIGHT), INFLICTS PARALYSIS
BLUE SHOT	580 G	ATTACK +4 (WATER)
ENCYCLOPEDIA	285 G	ATTACK +3, MAGIC ATTACK +4
CYCLONE STAFF	295 G	ATTACK +1, MAGIC ATTACK +4 (WIND)
BURNING HARP	970 G	ATTACK +7, MAGIC ATTACK +7 (FIRE)
ICE PICK	640 G	ATTACK +4, MAGIC ATTACK +4 (WATER), INFLICTS SLEEP

TOWN OF URBETH MAGIC SHOP

ITEM	COST	DESCRIPTION
FIRE TOME	1500 G	BLACK MAGIC: FIRE-ELEMENT ATTACK, MAGIC ATTACK: 5 / AP COST: 2
FIRA TOME	1500 G	BLACK MAGIC: FIRE-ELEMENT ATTACK, MAGIC ATTACK: 12 / AP COST: 3
FIRAGA TOME	5000 G	BLACK MAGIC: FIRE-ELEMENT ATTACK, MAGIC ATTACK: 15 / AP COST: 4
WATER TOME	500 G	BLACK MAGIC: WATER-ELEMENT ATTACK, MAGIC ATTACK: 5 / AP COST: 2
WATERA TOME	1500 G	BLACK MAGIC: WATER-ELEMENT ATTACK, MAGIC ATTACK: 12 / AP COST: 3
WATERGA TOME	5000 G	BLACK MAGIC: WATER-ELEMENT ATTACK, MAGIC ATTACK: 15 / AP COST: 4
CURE TOME	500 G	WHITE MAGIC: SLIGHT HP RECOVERY. AP COST 2. CAN USE FROM THE MENU.
RAISE TOME	1500 G	WHITE MAGIC: REVIVE FROM DEAD. AP COST 3. CAN USE FROM THE MENU.
SHELL TOME	1000 G	WHITE MAGIC: MAGIC DEFENSE INCREASED 50%. AP COST: 2.
PROTECT TOME	1000 G	WHITE MAGIC: DEFENSE INCREASED 50%. AP COST 2.

TOWN OF URBETH MULTIPLAYER PRIZES

ITEM	COST	DESCRIPTION
MAMMON'S SPEAR	3630	ATTACK +11
GAE BOLG	4290	ATTACK +13
TRIDENT	7200	ATTACK +20
WORKER'S CLOTHES	1000	DEFENSE +2, MAGIC DEFENSE +2. STRENGTH/INTELLECT/SPIRIT +5%
SILVER SUIT	1000	DEFENSE +2, MAGIC DEFENSE +2. STRENGTH/INTELLECT/SPIRIT +5%
RED JACKET	1000	DEFENSE +2, MAGIC DEFENSE +2. STRENGTH/INTELLECT/SPIRIT +5%
TRYLION'S COAT	1000	DEFENSE +2, MAGIC DEFENSE +2. STRENGTH/INTELLECT/SPIRIT +5%
GEM COLLECTOR	4000	KEEP ALL YOUR GEMS, EVEN AFTER DEATH.
FORTUNE EGG	3000	DOUBLES NUMBER OF ITEMS DROPPED.
HERMES SANDALS	6000	ALWAYS ACT FIRST.

Conundrum: Cure Cat's Curse

Urbeth is a center for commerce, ruled by four merchant lords who each hold a quarter of the city. Spend some time exploring the city and chatting with everyone

(one of the town's inhabitants is a bit of a surprise!). The man you need to see, the Sorcerer, locks up his shop at night and is only available during the day. Step outside Urbeth until the sun comes up, then return to the Sorcerer's shop and speak with him inside.

He claims to be able to help, but it will cost 10,000 gil. Fortunately, Urbeth is a town where it's possible to make that much gil in relatively little time while undertaking tasks for the Merchant Lords. The first stop: Trylion's Accessory Shop on the north side of town.

Magic Shop Hours

The Magic Shop vendor leaves his shop during the daytime, so any purchases there must be made at night.

Trylion's Task

While you could complete the Merchant Lord's tasks in any order, the best place to start is Lady Trylion. She requests assistance in selling three rings.

Take the staircase south of the Accessory shop (the narrow staircase between buildings), then enter the west door. Go up the stairs, speak with the woman wearing the dark cloak, and agree to sell her a ring. The second patron is at the end of the dock just west of the house with the first patron. Speak with him and agree to sell him a ring. The final stop is the cloaked man outside the Inn. He's available only during the daytime. After selling all three rings, return to Trylion for 2500 gil.

You obtained three of Trylion's Rings!

That ring is part of Trylion's new collection? Well then there's no way I can refuse—especially not a cute salesperson like yourself!

8-Item Challenge: Town of Urbeth

The boy wearing the blue cape inside the Inn has a hidden treasure challenge.

1. A **Hydraxe** next to a tub inside the Inn, in the second floor's west room

2. A **Hi-Potion** on the east-side shelves in Trylion's Accessory Shop

3. A **Potion** in the set of drawers in the back of the house south of the Accessory Shop

4. An **Alarm Clock** in the box on the dock west of the Accessory Shop

5. A **Great Tree Log** in Bylion's shop, upper level

6. A **Cross** from a barrel inside the building with the bottle and the glass sign

7. A **Hi-Potion** in the window across the alley from the bottle-and-glass-sign building

8. A **Zeus's Wrath** in the water behind the Tower to the Sky

Reinforcements

Bylion

It's playing havoc with our supply chain. Do you fancy going to the Hunting Caves and getting rid of it?

Sure
No

After you complete any task for the Merchant Lords, speak with Yunita to have her join the party. Her starting gear is Old Clothes, but her old equipment is in her inventory.

Mylion's Task

At the Armor shop, speak with Mylion and say "No" when asked about buying something, and "Yeah" when asked about a job. To obtain a Bomb Fragment, set one of your characters as a Bandit and wait for an encounter with a Hellhound. Don't kill the Hellhound until you successfully Steal a Bomb Fragment. Return to Mylion and sell it to him for 2500 gil. Consider combining this task with Bylion's request that sends the party to the Hunting Caves.

Fiery Bow

While you're running errands for the Merchant Lords, or collecting Zeus's Wrath for the item challenge, enter the Tower to the Sky through the back door in the canals. The chest in the area contains a **Red Shot**, which is a nice bow. It isn't necessary to get this item, but picking it up now saves you a return trip later.

Bylion's Task

Pay a visit to Bylion at his Item Shop. When he asks about shopping, reply with "No." His request involves a trip to the Hunting Caves to defeat a Chimera. This Chimera is just south of the entry point to the caves. Interact with the purple cloud to initiate the fight against the creature. It has two actions per turn and is resistant to physical attacks. Stick with Magic attacks to defeat it. Afterward, return to Bylion to claim the 2500 gil.

Thauzand's Task

Speak with Thauzand in the Weapon Shop, and respond "No" when he asks about shopping. After your conversation with Thauzand ends, go down to the counter and speak with the fellow in front of it. Use the counter space he offers to sell items from the Storage Shop (items in characters'

inventories are not available to sell). Thauzand doesn't charge a deposit or take a percentage of your sales, so all the gil earned from sales goes directly to the party's pocket. There's no bonus for selling everything you list, so don't drop prices to try to sell everything!

Follow the game's instructions on how to place and price items. It is important to note that you have a limited number of price tags to distribute between the items for sale. You can price three items (or pairs of items) each at 1000 and 5000 gil, five items (or pairs of items) at 100 or 500 gil, and nine items (or pairs of items) at 50 gil. You can set one item as a Hot Deal to encourage its purchase.

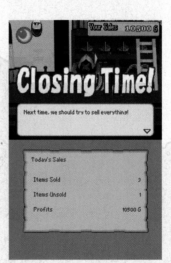

You can sell any number of items, from ten to as few as one. The counter space you get takes one of three configurations: 10 single slots, two double slots (two items sold as a pair) with six single slots, or four double slots with two single slots.

After your first day of sales, the game offers tips on what customers want most. Use these tips to select the types of items to sell. As you build up gil, you can buy additional items from the shops in Urbeth to sell at a better mark-up when they are the "Hot Items" in town. The closer the item's value is to the price you place on it, the better the chance it has to be purchased. Hot Items give you more room to mark up your prices, but don't think a Potion will sell for 500 gold just because it's a Hot Item and you marked it as a Hot Deal!

There's one item that's a consistent seller, and it's one you should stock up on constantly: Ether. Ether is available from Bylion's shop for 1000 gil. Place two Ethers in a paired-up sales slot and price it at 5000 gil, regardless of what's currently hot, and they will sell most of the time. Use the money earned from the previous tasks as seed money and stock up on Ether. Sell a few paired-up Ethers and you should make the 10,000 gil needed for the Sorcerer in no time. Of course, you don't need to stop at 10,000. Continue selling the Hot Items, augmented by the consistent sales of Ethers, and you can outfit everyone in style, fill your Storage Shop with at least one of every type of Spell Tome available in Urbeth, and you should still have plenty of gil left over for future shopping! Whenever you find an item

for sale that isn't in someone's inventory or the Storage Shop, you should buy at least one. Collecting one of every item is an achievement!

Seamstress Crown

If you can sell 20,000 gil worth of items in one day, you get the Seamstress Crown. The only way to earn 20,000 gil is to sell every item you list for sale on a day when there are 10 individual slots.

If you want to get the Crown during your initial visit to Urbeth, wait for spell books to be the hot thing and list spell books at the same price they're selling for at the Magic Shop. However, your best bet is to return to Urbeth at a later point when you have more expensive items that the citizens of Urbeth will snap up, even though you're selling at a loss.

Back to the Sorcerer

After you collect 10,000 gil, return to the Sorcerer (remember, he's only there during the day) and hand over the money. If you haven't done so already, go to the Armor shop and buy two Darksteel Shields. Weapons that deal Light damage have a double benefit in upcoming battles.

There are enemies vulnerable to Light-element damage, and the chance to paralyze enemies can make a tough fight much easier. Equip the shields on both characters, and the Light-element weapon on any melee characters in your party, before you head to the Inn for the night.

During the night, Urbeth is waylaid by groups of monsters. The doors to the Merchant Lords' shops are all blocked by vile creatures! The Armor Shop door is guarded by a Hellhound and a Cowpel. The Accessory Shop door is blocked by a Chimera and a Succubus. A Rock Golem appears in front of Bylion's Item Shop door. Fortunately, the merchants of Urbeth fear a lost sale more than monsters, so every shop remains open after you clear its doorway.

The final stop (it could be your first as well, but it's better to get the experience points from all the encounters) is Thauzand's Weapon Shop. The same Demon guards both doors, and you must defeat it to clear the town of its monster infestation!

When the fight ends, you are rewarded with the Merchant and Salve-maker Crowns. Go inside the Weapon Shop and speak with Thauzand, but stop by the Storage Shop to drop off extra items before you visit the Inn.

Yunita is about to leave the party, but she can keep her equipment if you already built up a good supply of gil. If you haven't, consider spending a few more days selling items at Thauzand's shop.

After staying in the Inn, speak with Thauzand. Head out of town and approach the boat on the beach. Interact with the boat to board it. Remember, it is possible to get into random fights while your party is on the boat. When you want to continue the story, go north along the shore until the screen goes dark.

Demon [B]

HP	500
WEAKNESSES	LIGHT
RESISTS	FIRE, DARK (ABSORBS)
ABILITIES	DARKRA, PROTECT, BLADEBLITZ
STEAL	HI-POTION, ETHER
DROPS	SAPPHIRE, EMERALD

The Demon resists Fire and absorbs Dark, but is vulnerable to Light-based attacks and abilities. Its attacks have a Dark-element component and sometimes can inflict Curse.

Darksteel Shields are a big help against the Demon's attacks, and Darkra, especially when it opens its eye. The Demon's eye opens during the third round of battle, which signifies an increase in the monster's Intellect and damage output when it uses Darkra.

Light-element attacks give a nice boost to your damage output against the boss, and so long as you avoid using Fire and Dark, you should be fine. Don't let any of your party members' HP drop too low before you use Cure, but healing every turn shouldn't be necessary.

BOSS

ARBOR

INN COSTS 100 GIL

ARBOR ITEM SHOP

ITEM	COST	DESCRIPTION
POTION	20 G	PROVIDES A SMALL HP BOOST.
TORCH	10 G	LIGHTS YOUR WAY IN THE DARKEST OF DUNGEONS.
DRAGON WING	60 G	TELEPORTS YOU BACK TO TOWN INSTANTLY.
EYE DROPS	20 G	CURES BLINDNESS.
ANTIDOTE	20 G	CURES POISON.
ECHO HERBS	20 G	CURSE SILENCE.
ALARM CLOCK	20 G	WAKES YOU UP FROM ANY SLEEP.
CURE TOME	500 G	WHITE MAGIC: SLIGHT HP RECOVERY. AP COST 2. CAN USE FROM THE MENU.
RAISE TOME	1500 G	WHITE MAGIC: REVIVE FROM THE DEAD. AP COST 3. CAN USE FROM THE MENU.

ARBOR WEAPON SHOP

ITEM	COST	DESCRIPTION
WOOD LANCE	660 G	ATTACK +6
SACRED TREE STAFF	190 G	ATTTACK +2, MAGIC ATTACK +5
RED SHOT	865 G	ATTACK +7 (FIRE)
RANGER BOW	570 G	ATTACK +6
SUN STILETTO	530 G	ATTACK +3, MAGIC ATTACK +3 (LIGHT), INFLICTS PARALYSIS.
MERCHANT TUNIC	550 G	DEFENSE +6, MAGIC DEFENSE +5, INTELLECT/SPIRIT +10%
SALVE-MAKER ROBE	500 G	DEFENSE +6, MAGIC DEFENSE +4, INTELLECT +10%, EVADE/MAGIC EVADE +5%
GREAT TREE SHIELD	280 G	DEFENSE +2, MAGIC DEFENSE +2, EVADE/MAGIC EVADE +8
SLEEP CAPE	250 G	BLOCKS SLEEP.
SILENCE CAPE	250 G	BLOCKS SILENCE.

ARBOR MULTIPLAYER PRIZES

ITEM	COST	DESCRIPTION
MYTHRIL ROD	5745	ATTACK +5, MAGIC ATTACK +12
SAGE'S STAFF	6750	ATTACK +6, MAGIC ATTACK +14
VERMILLION	1000	DEFENSE +2, MAGIC DEFENSE +2. STRENGTH/INTELLECT/SPIRIT +5%
HUNTER GARB	1000	DEFENSE +2, MAGIC DEFENSE +2. STRENGTH/INTELLECT/SPIRIT +5%
EASTERN GARB	1000	DEFENSE +2, MAGIC DEFENSE +2. STRENGTH/INTELLECT/SPIRIT +5%
DARK ARMOR	1000	DEFENSE +2, MAGIC DEFENSE +2. STRENGTH/INTELLECT/SPIRIT +5%
GARB OF KNOWLEDGE	1000	DEFENSE +2, MAGIC DEFENSE +2. STRENGTH/INTELLECT/SPIRIT +5%
MANA SCREEN	8000	GRANTS IMMUNITY FROM MAGIC, BUT PHYSICAL ATTACKS INFLICT FOUR TIMES THE DAMAGE.
GROWTH EGG	3000	DOUBLES EXPERIENCE POINTS EARNED.
OLD SHOES	6000	ALWAYS ACT LAST.

ENEMIES IN NORTH CAVES

GOBLIN [A]

JACK LANTERN [A]

BLOOD BAT [A]

MYCONID [A]

LIZARDMAN [A]

ITEMS FROM CHESTS

TRANSFORM STAFF

WORLD MAP   A

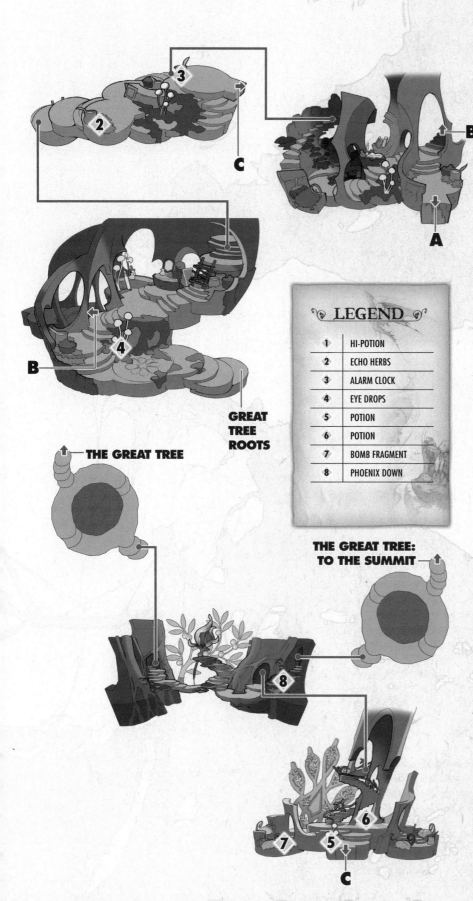

GREAT TREE ROOTS

THE GREAT TREE

THE GREAT TREE: TO THE SUMMIT

LEGEND	
1	HI-POTION
2	ECHO HERBS
3	ALARM CLOCK
4	EYE DROPS
5	POTION
6	POTION
7	BOMB FRAGMENT
8	PHOENIX DOWN

8-Item Challenge: Arbor

The elf outside Arbor challenges you to find eight items, but if Aire speaks with him while in cat form, he offers advice on where to find an item!

1. A **Hi-Potion** from the green, leafy plant behind Brandt

2. **Echo Herbs** from the blue pot across from the Item Shop vendor

3. An **Alarm Clock** from the blue pot above the Item Shop

4. A **Potion** from the skinny blue mushrooms in front of the Multiplayer Shop

5. A **Potion** In the dark baskets behind the Multiplayer Shop

6. A **Bomb Fragment** near the bed in the room southwest of the Multiplayer Shop

7. A **Phoenix Down** in the southeast corner of the queen's chamber

8. **Eye Drops** from the blue mushrooms near the entrance to the Great Tree Roots

Intelligence Gathering

Speak with the inhabitants of Arbor (elf and animal alike) to learn more about the tree city. Your next destination is the Great Tree Roots, but first stop by the shops to pick up upgraded equipment for Aire. Take a Torch, an extra shield, and an accessory as well.

GREAT TREE ROOTS

ENEMIES IN GREAT TREE ROOTS

IMP [B]

MYCONID [B]

JACK LANTERN [B]

MANDRAGORA [A]

BLOOD BAT [A]

ITEMS FROM CHESTS

ANIMAL STAFF
GREAT TREE HARP
PHOENIX DOWN

LEGEND

1	GREAT TREE HARP
2	PHOENIX DOWN
3	ANIMAL STAFF

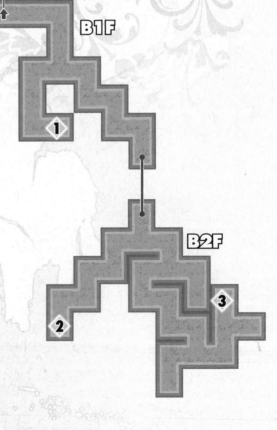

ARBOR

B1F

B2F

Beneath the Great Tree

Shortly after entering the Great Tree Roots, Aire encounters a mouse named Torte. Answer "Yes" to his question and he joins the party. Torte is a Sage, but needs a shield and an accessory to round out his equipment.

Pick up the **Great Tree Harp** from B1F, and the **Phoenix Down** from B2F before claiming the **Animal Staff**. There's

nothing guarding the staff, so you should be in and out of the Great Tree Roots relatively quickly.

Audience with the Queen

Return to the surface and go to plant-Brandt's location. Use the Animal Staff on him to turn him into a dog. Go to the queen's chambers and speak with her. After agreeing to help her, she sends the party to the top of the Great Tree.

THE GREAT TREE

ENEMIES IN THE GREAT TREE

IMP [B]

MYCONID [B]

BATTER FLY [A]

HUGINN [A]

MANDRAGORA [A]

RATTATOX [A]

ITEMS FROM CHESTS

PHOENIX DOWN (X3)	WOOD LANCE
WIND CAPE	ETHER
HI-POTION	FAIRY CAPE

Upward Mobility

Use the west exit from the queen's chambers to reach the path to the top of the Great Tree. Go to the top half of the 1F map first so you can grab the **Phoenix Down**, then get the **Wind Cape** from 2F.

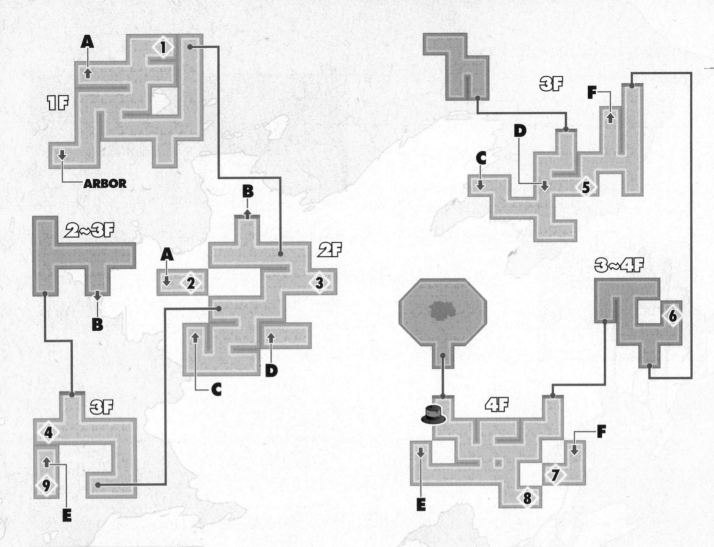

ARBOR

1F · 2~3F · 3F · A · B · 2F · C · D · 3F · 4F · E · F

LEGEND

1	PHOENIX DOWN
2	WIND CAPE
3	WOOD LANCE
4	PHOENIX DOWN
5	HI-POTION
6	ETHER
7	PHOENIX DOWN
8	HI-POTION
9	FAIRY CAPE

Most of the chests are off the direct path to Arbaroc's nest, but you should go out of your way to collect everything. The **Wood Lance** on 2F is guarded by a Mimic, but it's identical to the Mimics faced previously and should be no problem. On 4F, use the southwest corner staircase to reach the **Fairy Cape**.

When you encounter the Adventurer on 4F, equip the Wind Cape on a character who will be able to heal and resurrect allies during battle. Arbaroc deals Wind damage, which the Wind Cape resists. Since this is the first boss with items to steal, consider setting one character as a Bandit. A Bard, using Ditty, could come in handy as well. Arbaroc doesn't have any elemental weaknesses to exploit, so boosting your party's physical attacks should help shorten the fight.

Arbaroc

HP	490
WEAKNESSES	NONE
RESISTS	NONE
ABILITIES	LEAFRA, LEAFAGA, THUNDAGA, AIRSTORM
STEAL	PHOENIX DOWN, WIND CAPE, GALE GAUNTLETS
DROPS	TOPAZ, AMETHYST

Arbaroc acts twice per turn and uses physical attacks, Leafra, and Leafaga. At the start of turn 3, Arbaroc takes to the air and starts using Airstorm and Thundaga.

Since Arbaroc can act twice per round, all three characters could get hit twice in one round of combat. If everyone is low on HP after such a round, forget attacking and focus on keeping the party alive with whatever spells and items are available.

If you're having a hard time keeping characters alive through the fight (Torte's Spell Again ability is nice, but he runs out of AP quickly!), include either a White Mage or a Salve-maker with Healthcare in the party. The fight will last longer, but it's easier to keep everyone in the group alive.

BOSS

Delivering Dark News

After Arbaroc falls, you get the Crowns for Elementalist and Ranger. Step on the purple circle to be sent back to the room with the Great Tree seedling.

You obtained the crowns of the Elementalist and Ranger!

Remove all items from Torte and stick them in the Storage Shop before you speak with the queen! His help was appreciated, but his time in the party is at an end.

Return and speak with the queen again. She changes the Animal Staff into the **Transform Staff**, which allows you to switch characters to their animal forms and back to human at will. Torte parts ways with the group, and then the queen sends the party to the Inn. The next morning, return to the queen. After speaking with her, exit her chamber via the eastern stairs.

Queen Arbor

However, I know someone who does... Rolan, the great hero of Spelvia, might be able to help.

THE GREAT TREE: TO THE SUMMIT

ENEMIES IN THE GREAT TREE: TO THE SUMMIT

IMP [B]

MYCONID [B]

JACK LANTERN [B]

HUGINN [A]

MANDRAGORA [A]

RATTATOX [A]

A Leap of Faith

There's not much to navigating the area. There are no chests to pick up from branching paths, nor are there any bosses to defeat to clear the area. Simply follow the first level to the stairs that lead up to the Summit.

Go as far east and north as possible and look over the edge. Use the Transform Staff to assume animal form and leap over to Spelvia.

Brandt

Wow, check it out! That must be the floating city of Spelvia.

The good news is that Aire makes the jump with ease. The bad news is that Brandt isn't as good a jumper as Aire.

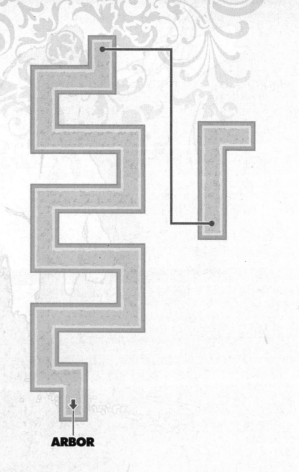

ARBOR

Visit the queen in Arbor, who offers a second route to Spelvia, through Invidia. Stop by the Storage Shop and put the Stun Cape into Brandt's inventory. Brandt makes a good Bandit, and you should strongly consider making him one for the upcoming journey. If you meet up with a Mythritoise, steal Mythril from it because it will be necessary in the near future. Include at least one Black Magic spell among Brandt's abilities, regardless of Brandt's Crown choice. Some enemies have high physical evasion rates. Exit Arbor and go west, then north for a while. It's a long trip to the Ice Caverns.

New Enemies

When Brandt walks over snow-covered terrain, the enemies change to match those found in the Ice Caverns.

ICE CAVERNS

ENEMIES IN THE ICE CAVERNS

LIZARDMAN [B]

YOTON [A]

SILKY [A]

TROLLUD [A]

IKAKKU [A]

BORGBEAR [A]

ITEMS FROM CHESTS
HI-POTION
INTELLECT RING

Melting Ice

The trick to getting around the Ice Caverns is using the candles to melt the walls of ice. Take the first candle south and place it on the holder in the wall. The chest beyond the now-melted wall holds a **Phoenix Down**. Repeat this with the other candle and the north wall. On B1F, you must use four candles to melt through four walls. Brandt can carry only one candle at a time, so be ready for quite a bit of walking back and forth as you penetrate layers of walls.

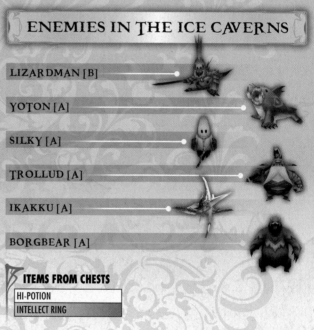

In the next hallway, inspect the small hole in the ground. If you put the Stun Cape in Brandt's inventory, equip it now. Use the Transform Staff to change Brandt into his animal form, then wiggle through this hole.

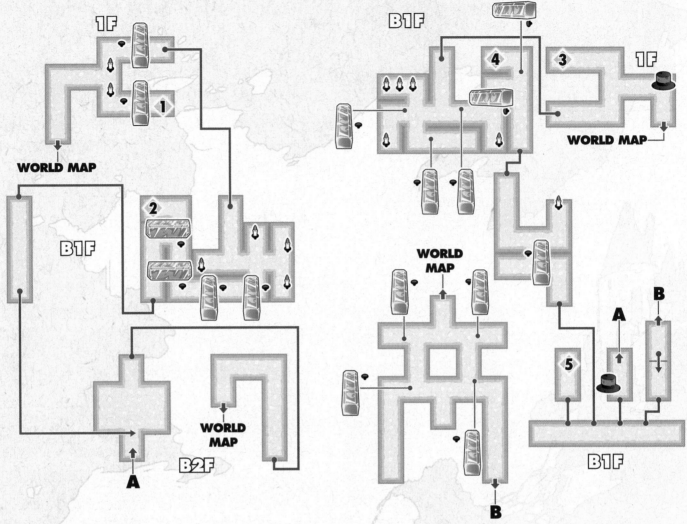

Jusqua at Sea

The scene shifts to Jusqua at sea in the boat that is on loan from Thauzand. Go north, then continue west a bit and aim for the beach on the shoreline. Now, head north to the entrance of the ice cave. Save your progress inside the cave and use the candles to melt the walls to uncover the chest and the way down to the next floor.

In B1F East, you can ignore the empty candle holders that are furthest west and furthest south; they're both dead ends. Get the **Flame Spear** from this floor and the **Darkening Harp** from the next. Ignore the easternmost doorway for now; the path is blocked. Save with the Adventurer, then descend the stairs behind him. In the next room, Jusqua confronts the Sorcerer.

Sorcerer

HP	160
WEAKNESSES	NONE
RESISTS	NONE
ABILITIES	POISON, BLIZZARD, CONFUSE
STEAL	POTION, HI-POTION, X-POTION
DROPS	AQUAMARINE

The Sorcerer uses Confuse, Poison, and Blizzard. If Jusqua is a Black Mage with Mirror, put that ability to work here. Otherwise, just hit the Sorcerer with strong attacks and he shouldn't be too much of a problem.

However, you immediately proceed into a second boss fight after defeating the Sorcerer. Jusqua has no chance to recover HP or AP, so don't end the fight against the Sorcerer if he's low on health or AP.

BOSS

On to Invidia

Follow the path behind the Sorcerer, which leads out of the dungeon. Once Brandt and Jusqua reach the surface, go east to reach Invidia.

Behugemoth [A]

HP	500
WEAKNESSES	NONE
RESISTS	LIGHT
ABILITIES	LIGHTNING BOLT
STEAL	HI-POTION, GLIMMER GAUNTLETS, SHINE CAPE
DROPS	AMETHYST, AQUAMARINE, HI-POTION

At first, the Behugemoth uses regular attacks. When 25% of its life is gone, it changes color and starts to use Lightning Bolt. Lightning Bolt can inflict paralysis, which spells trouble if it afflicts both characters at once.

For the first three turns, the most important thing is to stay alive. Attack if you like, but you should be focused on avoiding damage. After the third turn, there's a break in the fight and Brandt joins the party.

From that point forward, have one character focus on dealing damage to the Behugemoth while the other alternates between attacking the Behugemoth and keeping the party in good shape.

BOSS

127

INVIDIA

SILKY [A]

IKAKKU [A]

YOTON [A]

ITEMS FROM PEOPLE

MYTHRIL HAMMER

INN COSTS 300 GIL

INVIDIA ITEM SHOP (TOP)

ITEM	COST	DESCRIPTION
POTION	20 G	PROVIDES A SMALL HP BOOST.
HI-POTION	40 G	PROVIDES A GOOD HP BOOST.
TORCH	10 G	LIGHTS YOUR WAY IN THE DARKEST OF DUNGEONS.
DRAGON WING	60 G	TELEPORTS YOU BACK TO TOWN, INSTANTLY.
GOLD NEEDLE	50 G	CURES PETRIFICATION.
ANIMATE TONIC	30 G	CURES PARALYSIS.
CROSS	50 G	LIFTS CURSES.
BOMB FRAGMENT	300 G	INFLICTS FIRE-ELEMENT DAMAGE.
DARK TOME	500 G	BLACK MAGIC: DARK-ELEMENT ATTACK. MAGIC ATTACK: 5 / AP COST: 2

INVIDIA WEAPON SHOP

ITEM	COST	DESCRIPTION
FLAME DAGGER	530 G	ATTACK +3, MAGIC ATTACK +3 (FIRE), INFLICTS CONFUSION
ICE PICK	640 G	ATTACK +4, MAGIC ATTACK +4 (WATER), INFLICTS SLEEP
DARKNESS BLADE	1100 G	ATTACK +9 (DARK)
DARKNESS AXE	1135 G	ATTACK +11 (DARK)
RED SHOT	865 G	ATTACK +7 (FIRE)
BLACK BOOK	865 G	ATTACK +7, MAGIC ATTACK +12 (DARK)
WHITE BOOK	675 G	ATTACK +5, MAGIC ATTACK +9 (LIGHT)
INFERNO STAVE	390 G	ATTACK +2, MAGIC ATTACK +5 (FIRE)
DARKNESS STAFF	675 G	ATTACK +5, MAGIC ATTACK +13 (DARK)

INVIDIA ARMOR SHOP

ITEM	COST	DESCRIPTION
BLACK ROBE	350 G	DEFENSE +3, MAGIC DEFENSE +4, INTELLECT/MAGIC ATTACK POWER +10%
WHITE ROBE	350 G	DEFENSE +3, MAGIC DEFENSE +4, SPIRIT +20%
BANDIT GEAR	350 G	DEFENSE +4, MAGIC DEFENSE +2, ACCURACY +20%
POET TUNIC	350 G	DEFENSE +4, MAGIC DEFENSE +3, INTELLECT/SPIRIT +10%
ELEMENTALIST ROBE	550 G	DEFENSE +5, MAGIC DEFENSE +6, MAGIC ACCURACY/ INTELLECT +10%
RANGER OUTFIT	380 G	DEFENSE +5, MAGIC DEFENSE +2, STRENGTH/ACCURACY +10%
MERCHANT TUNIC	550 G	DEFENSE +6, MAGIC DEFENSE +5, INTELLECT/SPIRIT +10%
SALVE-MAKER ROBE	500 G	DEFENSE +6, MAGIC DEFENSE +4, INTELLECT +10%, EVADE/ MAGIC EVADE +5%
DARKSTEEL SHIELD	450 G	DEFENSE +2, MAGIC DEFENSE +2, EVADE/MAGIC EVADE +5, BLOCKS DARK
ICE SHIELD	350 G	DEFENSE +1, MAGIC DEFENSE +1, EVADE/MAGIC EVADE +5, BLOCKS WATER

INVIDIA MULTIPLAYER PRIZES

ITEM	COST	DESCRIPTION
HADES' BOW	6000	ATTACK +10
EXPUNGER	4500	ATTACK +30
FAILNAUGHT	9000	ATTACK +15, MAGIC ATTACK +15
MONKISH GARB	1000	DEFENSE +2, MAGIC DEFENSE +2. STRENGTH/INTELLECT/ SPIRIT +5%
GUNNER'S COAT	1000	DEFENSE +2, MAGIC DEFENSE +2. STRENGTH/INTELLECT/ SPIRIT +5%
CAT'S CLOAK	1000	DEFENSE +2, MAGIC DEFENSE +2. STRENGTH/INTELLECT/ SPIRIT +5%
HESTIA'S TUNIC	1000	DEFENSE +2, MAGIC DEFENSE +2. STRENGTH/INTELLECT/ SPIRIT +5%
MANA SCREEN	8000	GRANTS IMMUNITY FROM MAGIC, BUT PHYSICAL ATTACKS INFLICT FOUR TIMES THE DAMAGE.
ENERGY SCREEN	8000	GRANTS IMMUNITY FROM PHYSICAL ATTACKS, BUT MAGIC INFLICT FOUR TIMES THE DAMAGE.
FORTUNE EGG	3000	DOUBLES NUMBER OF ITEMS DROPPED.

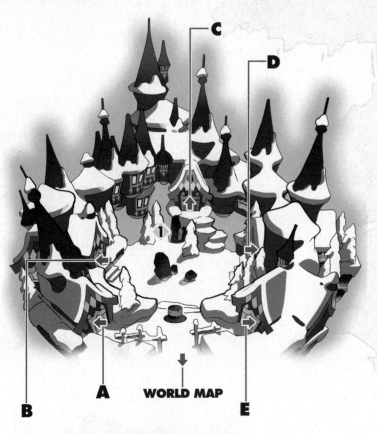

C

D

B

A

WORLD MAP

E

<table>
<thead>
<tr><th colspan="2">LEGEND</th></tr>
</thead>
<tbody>
<tr><td>1</td><td>POTION</td></tr>
<tr><td>2</td><td>POTION</td></tr>
<tr><td>3</td><td>HI-POTION</td></tr>
<tr><td>4</td><td>TRANQUILIZER</td></tr>
<tr><td>5</td><td>ANIMATE TONIC</td></tr>
<tr><td>6</td><td>ANTIDOTE</td></tr>
<tr><td>7</td><td>BOMB FRAGMENT</td></tr>
<tr><td>8</td><td>DARK SIGH</td></tr>
</tbody>
</table>

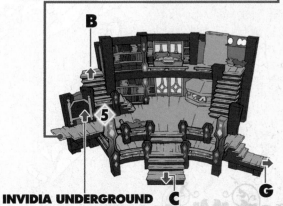

A

F

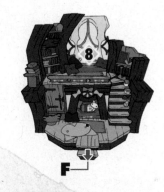

B

G

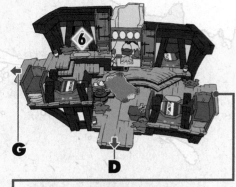

G

D

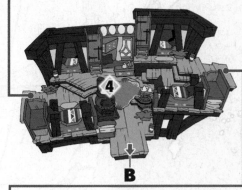

B

INVIDIA UNDERGROUND

C

G

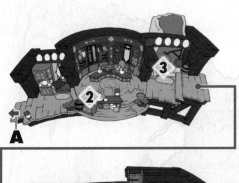

E

8-Item Challenge: Invidia

The boy in the blue coat and black hat near the Armor Shop wants you to find eight items.

1. A **Potion** in the tree north of the Dragon Egg

2. A **Potion** on the table south of the Weapon Shop vendor

3. A **Hi-Potion** in the cooking pot near the Storage Shop

4. A **Tranquilizer** in the pot-belly stove near the Inn

5. An **Animate Tonic** in the bookshelf built into the staircase leading up to Rekoteh

6. An **Antidote** in the bed near the polar bear

7. A **Bomb Fragment** on the green table south of the Item Shop

8. A **Dark Sigh** on the window above Rekoteh

The Mathematics Game

The girl in the red coat near the polar bear has a mathematical game to play. You're given four numbers and must end up with a final value of 10. You can use any of the four basic mathematical operators and two of the provided numbers at a time. You earn points for the total at the end of each mathematical operation, provided that the final result is 10.

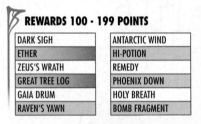

If you don't like the numbers you have, you can pass on them. If you pass when there is a possible way to end up with 10, you're penalized 3 points. If you pass on a set of numbers and there was no way to get them to total 10 (such as getting four number 1s), you're awarded 20 bonus points. Your total score is based on three rounds of four numbers and any adjustments you earned.

REWARDS 50 - 99 POINTS

GOLD NEEDLE	POTION
CROSS	ANIMATE TONIC
TORCH	EYE DROPS
TRANQUILIZER	ALARM CLOCK
ANTIDOTE	ECHO HERBS
DRAGON WING	

REWARDS 100 - 199 POINTS

DARK SIGH	ANTARCTIC WIND
ETHER	HI-POTION
ZEUS'S WRATH	REMEDY
GREAT TREE LOG	PHOENIX DOWN
GAIA DRUM	HOLY BREATH
RAVEN'S YAWN	BOMB FRAGMENT

REWARDS 200 POINTS & UP[1]

X-POTION	HI-ETHER

[1] The first time you score 250 points or more, you unlock the Beastmaster Crown.

To get good scores, you should pass on sets of numbers that have too many low starting values. Even though it costs you a few points, it's worth it to get better starting numbers. To get a good score, here are a few patterns to look for in your starting numbers:

Numbers where two digits are identical, and the other two total 10. For these numbers, the first thing to do is get a result of 10, multiply it by one of the identical numbers, and then divide it by the other.

Numbers where the product of two digits matches the other two digits. For example: 5, 6, 7, 8. 8 times 7 is 56. 56 minus 6 is 50, divided by 5 is 10.

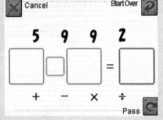

Three matching digits and a 9. Multiply one of the matching numbers by 9, add a second digit, then divide by the last digit to end up with 10.

There are additional sets of numbers that yield good scores, but these are some easy patterns to spot while you're playing. Good luck!

Hi-Ether for Seamstress Crown

While you're in Invidia, play enough of the Mathematics Game to get a good stock of Hi-Ether. You need at least 10 in your Storage Shop, so they can be sold at Thauzand's shop. It's the easiest way to earn the Seamstress Crown.

A New Ally

Take a tour of Invidia's shops, which are all inside. Drop off any excess items at the Storage Shop, and purchase some Ice Shields, as well as any other upgrades you find. Inspect the Dragon Egg in the center of the village, then enter the door directly north of it. Go up to the highest level inside and speak with the girl with

the orange bow in her hair. Her name is Rekoteh and she joins the party. Head outside and inspect the Dragon Egg again.

Cracking the Egg with Mythril

If you have Mythril, put it in someone's inventory, then speak with the Weapon Shop vendor. When he suggests staying overnight at the Inn, take his advice. Return to the Weapon Shop

Whoa, that's Mythril, isn't it? With that I can make you a Mythril Hammer. But it'll take some time, so come back.

vendor to pick up the **Mythril Hammer**. With the Mythril Hammer in anyone's inventory (it doesn't need to be equipped), go to the Dragon Egg and interact with it.

Cracking the Egg with Firaga

If you picked up Firaga in Urbeth, put the Firaga Magic Tome in someone's inventory, then check on the Dragon Egg.

Rekoteh
Wow, that's hot!

Not Cracking Yet

Regardless of the means you used to try to open the Dragon Egg, go through the door directly north of the Dragon Egg. Speak with Rekoteh's father (who happens to be the chief) in

Chief
The Dragon Harp lies somewhere deep in the caverns below the town.

his room. After warning the party about the dangers to come, he hands over a Magic Key. Use the Magic Key to unlock the nearby door, which grants access to Invidia Underground. Grab the Ice Shields from the Storage Shop, if you left them there, before venturing into Invidia Underground.

Help Yunita!

Even if Brandt and Jusqua don't need Mythril, pick one up (or an extra if you used one for the Hammer) and drop it in the Storage Shop. Yunita will need it soon.

INVIDIA UNDERGROUND

ENEMIES IN INVIDIA UNDERGROUND

ORC [B]

COWPEL [B]

WIGHT [B]

SKELETON [A]

ITEMS FROM CHESTS

| BOOK OF SHIVA |
| DRAGON HARP |
| INFERNO STAVE |

LEGEND

| 1 | INFERNO STAVE |
| 2 | BOOK OF SHIVA |

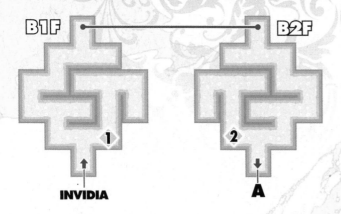

B1F — **1** — INVIDIA

B2F — **2** — A

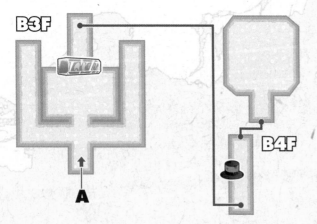

B3F — **A**

B4F

Sound Laid Down by the Underground

The first two basement levels of Invidia Underground are fairly uneventful. Get the **Inferno Stave** from B1, and the **Book of Shiva** from B2.

On B3, things get trickier. There is a puzzle that involves rotating four dragon statues by touching four pedestals. The four dragon statues initially face forward and the goal is to get each dragon statue facing its switch.

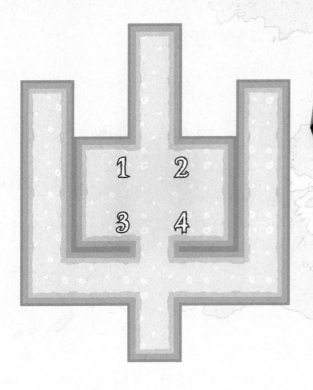

HP	520
WEAKNESSES	FIRE
RESISTS	WATER (ABSORB), WIND, EARTH, LIGHT, DARK
ABILITIES	ICE BREATH
STEAL	POTION, STREAM CAPE
DROPS	AMETHYST, AQUAMARINE

The Ice Dragon acts twice each round, and its physical attacks have a Water-element component. It's considered Level 2 damage, so even with Ice Shields equipped, the party will still feel some pain. The Ice Dragon also uses Ice Breath to hit everyone in the party.

The Ice Dragon resists every Element type, except Fire (to which it's vulnerable) and Water. Don't attack with Water-element spells or weapons, or you'll heal the boss instead of harming it.

As with Arbaroc, if you're having a hard time keeping everyone alive, add a White Mage or a Salve-maker with Healthgiver to the party. You can keep two characters focused on damaging the Ice Dragon (with Fire-element attacks, ideally), but using spells and items to keep everyone alive takes precedence over attacking the boss.

BOSS

Pedestal 1 turns statues 1, 2, and 3—90 degrees clockwise

Pedestal 2 turns statues 1, 2, and 4—90 degrees clockwise

Pedestal 3 turns statues 1, 3, and 4—90 degrees clockwise

Pedestal 4 turns statues 2, 3, and 4—90 degrees clockwise

To get past the statues, follow these steps in order:

1   Turn pedestal 4 once

2   Turn pedestal 3 twice

3   Turn pedestal 1 twice

4   Turn pedestal 3 once

5   Turn pedestal 1 once

6   Turn pedestal 2 once

When the dragon statues all face their pedestals, the ice block at the end of the room vanishes and the party is allowed to pass through. Save your game with the Adventurer, and if you haven't equipped everyone with Ice Shields yet, do it now! The upcoming boss uses Water-based attacks. Also, remove any weapons with Water-element effects that you may have equipped.

When the Ice Dragon is defeated, it leaves behind the **Dragon Harp**. In addition, you obtain the Crowns for the Fighter and Scholar jobs. Return to the surface and visit any necessary shops to bank your items or replenish your inventory.

133

Before you go to the Dragon Egg, remove all of Rekoteh's equipment and put it into the Storage Shop.

Rekoteh
It's working! The egg is beginning to crack!

Go back to the Dragon Egg and interact with it. After the Dragon hatches, interact with it again to travel to Spelvia.

URBETH

URBETH ITEM SHOP

ITEM	COST	DESCRIPTION
BOMB FRAGMENT	300 G	INFLICTS FIRE-ELEMENT DAMAGE.
ANTARCTIC WIND	300 G	INFLICTS WATER-ELEMENT DAMAGE.
GAIA DRUM	300 G	INFLICTS EARTH-ELEMENT DAMAGE.
RAVEN'S YAWN	300 G	INFLICTS WIND-ELEMENT DAMAGE.
ZEUS'S WRATH	300 G	INFLICTS LIGHTNING-ELEMENT DAMAGE AND PARALYZES THE FOE.
DARK SIGH	300 G	INFLICTS DARK-ELEMENT DAMAGE.
HOLY BREATH	300 G	INFLICTS LIGHT-ELEMENT DAMAGE.

ITEMS FROM PEOPLE

POTION
RAINBOW BOOTS
STEEL SWORD (+5)
TRYLION'S RING

When you gain control of Yunita, step outside of the Inn and go west to the locked Item Shop door. The Magic Key allows you access to its inventory.

Take a trip to Thauzand's shop (Bylion and Mylion direct you to him if you try speaking with either of them first) and speak with him. Answer "No" to his question and he hands over a **Steel Sword (+5)**. The Accessory Shop is next. Talk to Trylion and she hands over **Trylion's Ring**. Visit Bylion in his Item Shop and answer "Yes" for a **Potion**.

Mylion at the Armor Shop offers substantial help with the goal of reaching Spelvia. He offers the Rainbow Boots Yunita needs to reach Spelvia in exchange for Mythril. If there's some in the bank already, you're set. If not, wander outside Guera as a Bandit until you can steal some from a Mythritoise. When you have Mythril in your inventory, speak with him again. He trades **Rainbow Boots** for the Mythril. You don't need to equip the Rainbow Boots on Yunita; just leave them in her inventory.

Before going to the Tower of the Sky, it is important to obtain better gear for Yunita. Take a Flame Shield and find the best armor available from either the Storage Shop or the Armor Shop.

You obtained a Steel Sword (+5)!

Mylion
Oh, goodv, that's Mythril, isn't it? Here we go, a deal's a deal...

Inventory Space

If you want to pick up all the items from the Tower of the Sky in one trip, Yunita's inventory needs to be nearly empty. Only carry what's necessary (her equipment, one Magic Tome if you have her set as a spellcaster, and the Rainbow Boots) and a few Potions to restore HP between fights.

TOWER OF THE SKY

ENEMIES IN TOWER OF THE SKY

COWPEL [B]

ORC [B]

LIZARDMAN [B]

HELLHOUND [A]

CHIMERA [A]

ROCK GOLEM [A]

GARGOYLE [A]

SUCCUBUS [A]

ITEMS FROM CHESTS

500 GIL	HI-POTION
CURA TOME	RAISE TOME
DARK CAPE	SOIL CAPE
ETHER	STAR EARRING

TOWN OF URBETH

1F

1

TOWN OF URBETH

2F

3F

2

3

A

B

6

4

4F

A

B

5F

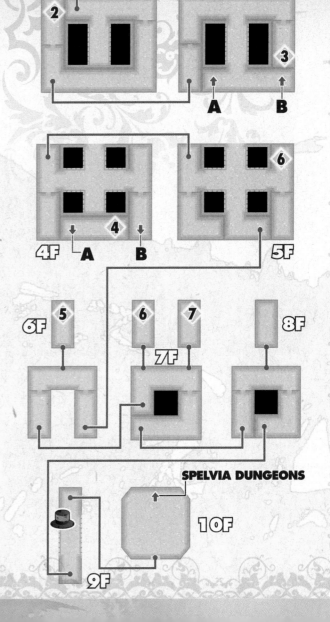

6F

5

6

7

8F

7F

SPELVIA DUNGEONS

10F

9F

Reach for the Sky

Follow the maps for the Tower of the Sky carefully. There are dead ends everywhere, and Yunita is on her own. Every extra step means another chance for a random encounter. If you're having trouble keeping Yunita alive while she's on her own, consider a Crown that offers a self-healing ability, such as a Wayfarer with Recovery. An Elementalist is another good choice because it halves Element-based damage. Not all incoming damage will be Elemental, but any reduction should be a big help.

There is at least one chest per level, including some Accessories such as the **Dark Cape** on 3F, the **Star Earring** on 4F, and the **Soil Cape** on 7F. If you're being choosy about which chests to loot on this trip through the Tower, they are the best ones to target.

Save with the Adventurer, then go up the flight of stairs beyond him to reach the Rainbow Bridge. Walk across the Bridge until you reach Spelvia.

Spelvia Dungeons

ENEMIES IN SPELVIA DUNGEONS

WIGHT [B]

WYVERN [A]

CLOUD PENGUIN [A]

MEDUSA [A]

GOLEM

MIMIC

ITEMS FROM CHESTS

BOOK OF RAMUH
PHOENIX DOWN
SHINE CAPE
SHINING AXE

A Happy Reunion

The pot near the staircase on B4F restores HP at no cost. Go up to 3F and move close to the white cat, which turns out to be Aire, who joins the party.

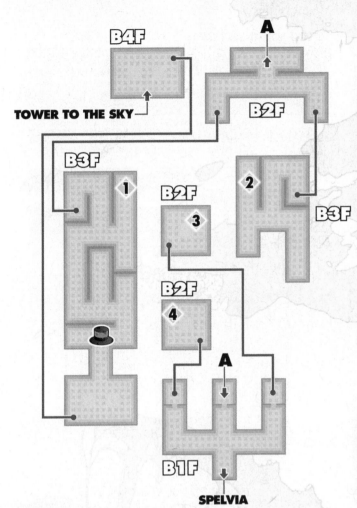

B4F

TOWER TO THE SKY

B3F

1

B2F

3

B2F

4

A

B2F

A

2

B3F

B1F

SPELVIA

LEGEND

1	PHOENIX DOWN
2	SHINING AXE
3	BOOK OF RAMUH
4	SHINE CAPE

Just as with the Tower of the Sky, follow the maps for the Spelvia Dungeons carefully. They are in disrepair and many paths are blocked. Pick up the **Phoenix Down** from the chest on B3F before ascending to B2F, then return to B3F via the eastern stairs to pick up the **Shining Axe**.

When you reach B1F, the staircases to the east and west lead to chests back on B2F. The eastern chest holds a **Book of Ramuh,** while the western chest has a **Shine Cape**. Both chests are guarded by Mimics, which should be fairly easy to dispatch. They're significantly weaker than the randomly encountered enemies in the Spelvia Dungeons.

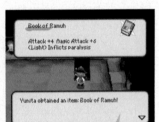

SPELVIA

SPELVIA DUNGEONS

1

A

2

3

ROLAN'S SOUL

ITEMS FROM CHESTS

COURAGE RING

SPELVIA ITEM SHOP

ITEM	COST	DESCRIPTION
POTION	20 G	PROVIDES A SMALL HP BOOST.
HI-POTION	40 G	PROVIDES A GOOD HP BOOST.
REMEDY	400 G	CURES ALL AILMENTS (EXCEPT DEATH) AND RESTORES A SMALL AMOUNT OF HP.
ETHER	1000 G	PROVIDES A SMALL AP BOOST.
BLACK RING	5000 G	MAGIC DEFENSE +10%
FLAME SHIELD	350 G	DEFENSE +1, MAGIC DEFENSE +1, EVADE/MAGIC EVADE +5, BLOCKS: FIRE.
ICE SHIELD	350 G	DEFENSE +1, MAGIC DEFENSE +1, EVADE/MAGIC EVADE +5, BLOCKS: ICE.
DARKSTEEL SHIELD	450 G	DEFENSE +2, MAGIC DEFENSE +2, EVADE/MAGIC EVADE +5, BLOCKS: DARK.
FOSSIL CAPE	500 G	BLOCKS PETRIFICATION.
CURSE CAPE	500 G	BLOCKS CURSES.

SPELVIA WEAPON SHOP

ITEM	COST	DESCRIPTION
SHINING BLADE	900 G	ATTACK +7 (LIGHT)
SHINING AXE	1135 G	ATTACK +11 (LIGHT)
WHITE BOOK	675 G	ATTACK +5, MAGIC ATTACK +9 (LIGHT)
SHINING STAFF	465 G	ATTACK +3, MAGIC ATTACK +7 (LIGHT)
STARDUST BOW	960 G	ATTACK +8 (LIGHT)
SHINING HARP	860 G	ATTACK +6, MAGIC ATTACK +6 (LIGHT)
ELEMENTALIST ROBE	550 G	DEFENSE +5, MAGIC DEFENSE +5, MAGIC ACCURACY/INTELLECT +10%
RANGER OUTFIT	380 G	DEFENSE +5, MAGIC DEFENSE+2, STRENGTH/ACCURACY +10%
FIGHTER GI	550 G	DEFENSE +8, MAGIC DEFENSE +3, HP/STRENGTH +10%
SCHOLAR GOWN	700 G	DEFENSE +7, MAGIC DEFENSE +7, INTELLECT +20%

SPELVIA MAGIC SHOP

ITEM	COST	DESCRIPTION
FIRE TOME	500 G	BLACK MAGIC: FIRE-ELEMENT ATTACK. MAGIC ATTACK: 5 / AP COST: 2
FIRA TOME	1500 G	BLACK MAGIC: FIRE-ELEMENT ATTACK. MAGIC ATTACK: 12 / AP COST: 3
WATER TOME	500 G	BLACK MAGIC: WATER-ELEMENT ATTACK. MAGIC ATTACK: 5 / AP COST: 2
WATERA TOME	1500 G	BLACK MAGIC: FIRE-ELEMENT ATTACK. MAGIC ATTACK: 12 / AP COST: 3
BANISH TOME	500 G	BLACK MAGIC: LIGHT-ELEMENT ATTACK. MAGIC ATTACK: 5 / AP COST: 2
BANISHRA TOME	1500 G	BLACK MAGIC: LIGHT-ELEMENT ATTACK. MAGIC ATTACK: 12 / AP COST: 3
BANISHGA TOME	5000 G	BLACK MAGIC: LIGHT-ELEMENT ATTACK. MAGIC ATTACK: 15 / AP COST: 4
CURE TOME	500 G	WHITE MAGIC: SLIGHT HP RECOVERY. AP COST: 2. CAN USE FROM THE MENU.
CURA TOME	1500 G	WHITE MAGIC: HP RECOVERY. AP COST: 3. CAN USE FROM THE MENU.
RAISE TOME	1500 G	WHITE MAGIC: REVIVE FROM DEAD. AP COST: 3. CAN USE FROM THE MENU.

SPELVIA MULTIPLAYER PRIZES

ITEM	COST	DESCRIPTION
LAMIA'S HARP	6900	ATTACK +12, MAGIC ATTACK +12. INFLICTS PETRIFICATION.
ANGEL HARP	6600	ATTACK +12, MAGIC ATTACK +12. INFLICTS SUDDEN DEATH.
DAVID'S HARP	6000	ATTACK +12, MAGIC ATTACK +12. REDUCES FOE'S STATUS LEVELS.
STILETTO	4680	ATTACK +8, MAGIC ATTACK +4. INFLICTS SILENCE, BLINDNESS.
SASUKE'S KODACHI	4680	ATTACK +8, MAGIC ATTACK +4. INFLICTS CONFUSION, POISON.
MAIN GAUCHE	6180	ATTACK +8, MAGIC ATTACK +4. INFLICTS PARALYSIS, LOWERS STATUS.
TONBERRY KNIFE	7680	ATTACK +8, MAGIC ATTACK +4. INFLICTS SUDDEN DEATH.
MODERN DRESS	1000	DEFENSE +2, MAGIC DEFENSE +2. STRENGTH/INTELLECT/SPIRIT +5%
REPLICA PLATE	1000	DEFENSE +2, MAGIC DEFENSE +2. STRENGTH/INTELLECT/SPIRIT +5%
HERMES SANDALS	6000	ALWAYS ACT FIRST.

8-Item Challenge: Spelvia

The Golem near the Multiplayer vendor challenges you to find eight items.

1. A **Dragon Wing** in the short hall off the west side of Rolan's throne room

2. **Echo Herbs** in the plant located in Rolan's bedroom

3. A **Dark Sigh** in the blue object just outside the doorway to the throne room

4. An **Animate Tonic** in the candles south of the Inn

5. **Indra's Spear** behind the Item Shop

6. A **Holy Breath** at the base of the column north of the Witch of the Sky

7. A **Shining Harp** from behind Mother Dragon's tombstone

8. A **Remedy** from the bushes near the entrance to the Spelvia Dungeons

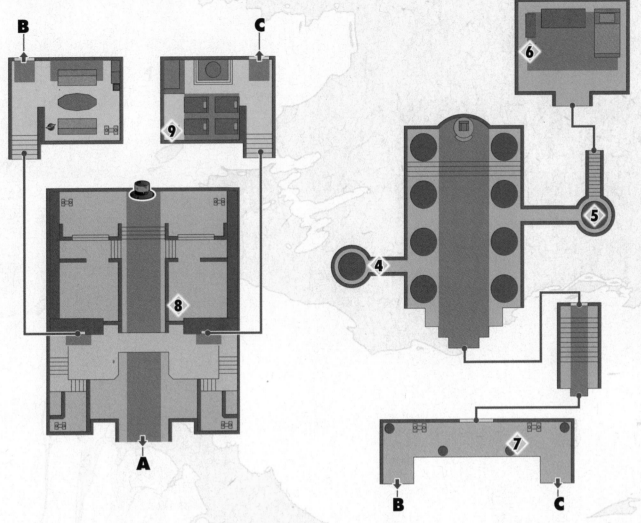

Humans Not Welcome

When Aire and Yunita reach Spelvia, use the Transform Staff to change at least the lead character into animal form. The Golem vendors inside Spelvia will attack if either character speaks with them in human form.

In animal form, explore Spelvia and head for Rolan's throne room. Watch along the east wall for a hallway that leads to a staircase. The chest at the base of the stairway contains the **Courage Ring,** which makes it easier to get Psyched Up.

The golems that maintain this temple have been poisoned by the hate in Rolan's heart. They will attack any human they see.

Talk to Rolan in his throne room, then return to the outdoor area of Spelvia. Look for the Witch of the Sky in the southwest corner of the town. Step into the fountain to enter Rolan's Soul.

Courage Ring

You become psyched up more easily.

Yunita obtained an item: Courage Ring!

Witch of the Sky

If you wish to make his heart free again, then you must enter this, the Fountain of Hope.

ROLAN'S SOUL

ENEMIES IN ROLAN'S SOUL

WIGHT [B]

SILKY [A]

DOPPELGANGER [AIRE A]

DOPPELGANGER [BRANDT A]

DOPPELGANGER [JUSQUA A]

DOPPELGANGER [YUNITA A]

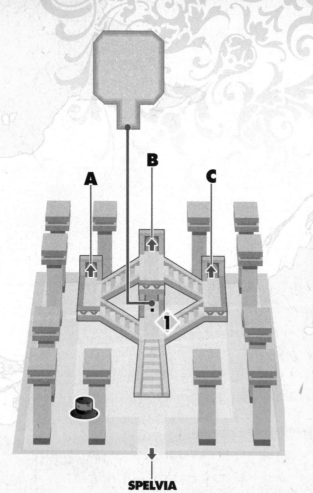

SPELVIA

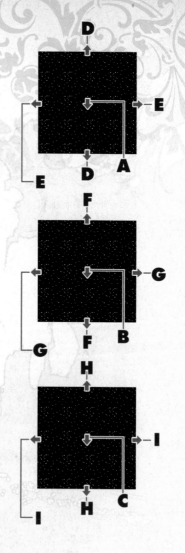

A Shadow of a Hero

Speak with Rolan in the water and he joins the party. Rolan needs a shield and an accessory, so head back to Spelvia to get him some equipment. Rolan can speak with vendors in human form.

Rolan
I am all that is left of Rolan's goodness, a mere shadow of what once was a kind young man. Alone, I am powerless.

Rolan leaves the party immediately after defeating the upcoming bosses, Geri and Freki. The only unique item he carries is his armor, so put that in the Storage Shop and pick up a replacement at the Weapon Shop in Spelvia.

An Elementalist Makes Life Easier

If you haven't added an Elementalist to your party yet, now is the time to start using one. The second-level ability, Mysterio, is the best way to keep everyone alive without carrying every type of shield or cloak that blocks a specific element. Most enemies here, including bosses, have an elemental component to their regular attacks in addition to the big spells that they cast.

The central doorway is blocked by a black cloud. Go through any of the three doors above the main doorway. Each room has a challenge. You must chase the shadow that moves around each time you catch up to it. If you aren't quick enough, you must start over. The pattern never changes in the same room, so you can learn to anticipate where the shadow jumps if you're having trouble completing the challenge.

Catch me if you can! I'm here and there and everywhere—you'll have to move fast if you want to chase me down!

After clearing the three rooms, the way to the main room is open. Beyond the doorway is a battle against a pair of bosses who have opposing weaknesses and resistances to Fire and Water. Before you take them on, set up everyone's equipment to block at least one of those elements, or both if it's possible (combine the effects of shields and capes).

Equip each character with a Flame Shield, and add a Stream Cape (as many as you could collect) to the Accessory slot of any character using a Flame Shield. When everyone is ready to go, return to the door that was previously blocked by the dark cloud. Enter the room and speak with Rolan. As the conversation ends, the fight begins!

WALKTHROUGH

Geri & Freki

HP	450 EACH
WEAKNESSES	FIRE (FREKI), WATER (GERI)
RESISTS	FIRE (GERI), WATER (FREKI)
ABILITIES	(FREKI) MAGICK, BLIZZARD, ICE BREATH. (GERI) BERSERK, FIRE BREATH [B]
STEAL	HI-POTION, X-POTION, BOMB FRAGMENT (FREKI), ANTARCTIC WIND (GERI)
DROPS	(GERI) RUBY, AMETHYST, FLAME GAUNTLETS, FLAME CAPE, (FREKI) LAPIS, AMETHYST, SPRING GAUNTLETS, STREAM CAPE

Freki, the blue one, uses Magick to enhance magic damage output. Geri, the red one, goes Berserk and hits harder with physical attacks. The breath attacks from both enemies hit the entire party and cause serious damage to anyone underprotected from Fire and Water damage.

Even though they appear to be side-by-side, Geri is considered to be in the front row, and Freki in the back row. Keep this in mind when selecting weapons (or avoid selecting either Fire or Water weapons), and especially when using spells. Black Magic always targets the back row first, so stick with Fire spells until Freki is eliminated.

It's vital to maintain Mysterio on the party, especially if you didn't have enough Stream Capes for everyone. The combination of shield, plus cape, plus Mysterio means you should only need to heal the rare physical strikes that the bosses perform. To make it easier on everyone, hit the boss with a Black Magic spell appropriate to its vulnerability, and its status levels will drop for three turns. This does not stack, so you must wait for the first effect to wear off before applying it again.

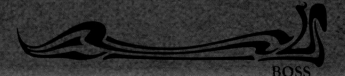

BOSS

142

The Old Gang Back Together

When Aire and Yunita exit Rolan's Soul, the sky goes dark. Go north and speak with Brandt and Jusqua.

After exchanging happy greetings and apologies, the party becomes whole again.

The next task is to face Rolan in his Throne room. First, you need to change everyone's gear so they will be resistant to Dark and Light attacks. Dark resistance is more important, so everyone in the party should get a Darksteel Shield or a Dark Cloak. Light resistance is more of a luxury, so don't worry if no one has it. Forget about using spells to damage Rolan, and try to avoid weapons with Element-based damage. Set your party up for physical damage (include a Bandit so you have a chance to steal the Lightbringer sword)

or use Crowns that boost physical damage output (such as the Bard Crown).

When everyone is prepared, speak with Rolan in his Throne room. If you don't expect a pleasant reception, you won't be disappointed.

Rolan

HP	800
WEAKNESSES	NONE
RESISTS	ALL (ABSORBS DARK)
ABILITIES	DARKAGA, THUNDARA, THUNDAGA
STEAL	X-POTION, LIGHTBRINGER, HOLY BREATH
DROPS	DIAMOND, AMETHYST

Rolan acts twice per round and is highly resistant to all Element-based attacks. In addition to his physical attacks (which include a Lv.1 Dark component), he uses Darkaga, Thundara, and Thundaga.

Paralysis is a concern during the fight, so be ready to remove it from your Elementalist (unless a Stun Cape is available) if Mysterio is about to expire. Having Mysterio active at all times greatly reduces the need for healing. A White Mage or Salve-maker with Healthgiver should be able to handle all the healing solo, but watch out for any time that character gets hit with paralysis.

The party's damage should come from characters like Bandits, Rangers, or Fighters. You don't necessarily need the party to comprise three physical attack Crowns and an Elementalist; you can always use something like a Bard, which makes the physical attack Crowns more effective.

BOSS

After Rolan falls, a few significant things occur. First, he drops Diamonds, the final piece necessary to unlock each Crown's ultimate ability. In addition, you get the Crowns for Party Host and Hero.

You obtained the crowns of the Party Host and Hero!

Rekoteh

Please! My brother can't do it all on his own. Help him to drive back the world of darkness!

The biggest change is waiting outside.

Speak with the Witch of the Sky. She offers a surprising bit of news. Switch to human form and speak with the Dragon. The real adventure is just about to begin!

A Brand New World

The Witch of the Sky's comment about the era being unknown is ominous and something you need to take seriously. The world has changed considerably since everyone left to confront Rolan. When you revisit locations, you should speak with everyone again to get a sense of when you are.

Witch of the Sky

The darkness that poured out of Rolan's soul has warped the entire nature of time and space. Who knows what world, what era this might be?

What Has Changed

The citizens of each town seem to be the same, but they act as though they have no knowledge of the members of the party.

The shops in each town have new items for sale, although some items have carried over from their earlier offerings.

The world map and dungeons are populated with entirely new enemies, or more powerful versions of enemies encountered previously.

Most importantly, many enemies now scale with the level of the party, so you are no longer able to overpower enemies by reaching the highest levels. For more information, check out the Enemy Data section of the guide. The best way to keep characters ahead of the enemy curve is by spending gems to improve gear at the Upgrade Shop.

What Remains the Same

The items in chests you did not loot previously are still in place, and you can collect them when you revisit an area.

The 8-Item Challenges are still active. Anything you found before is gone, but you can still claim the hidden items you missed the first time through an area.

The Multiplayer Shops have the same inventories as before.

Namingway's Hideaway

STATUS   MENU

If you want to customize the names of your spells, visit this out-of-the-way structure north of Horne. Namingway allows you to change the name of any Magic Tome currently in your Storage Shop.

Quick Item Collection

Two key items in your inventory allow you to collect some nice items that were previously locked away. The Dragon allows you to go anywhere in the world in a hurry. You don't even need to worry about random encounters! The Magic Key opens doors that were locked when you visited some areas the first time.

In Horne, the citizens remain petrified, but the Magic Key unlocks the Windmill. Inside, Cid provides some game information including the percentages of chests found and searches performed. The chest on the floor contains an **X-Potion**. The Chest at the top of the stairs contains a **Hi-Ether**. Stop by Horne Castle's dungeon and use the key on the locked cell door. The chest inside holds a **Soul of Thamasa**.

Fly to Liberte Town where another locked door awaits. There are three chests inside the locked building. The items you can now collect are a **Soul of Thamasa**, a **Remedy**, and a **Stunning Harp**.

Continuing the Adventure

You have a few options for where you go next. The following table lists all the destinations you must visit eventually in the order they're presented in this guide. You can tackle them in any order you wish, but you should strongly consider making the Lux Tome your primary acquisition. If you want to follow the storyline, stay in Spelvia and acquire the Paladin Crown first. After you acquire all the items from the table, you can proceed to Horne Castle.

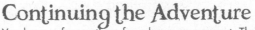

LOCATION	CROWNED UNLOCKED	ITEM EARNED
ARBOR	MONK CROWN	LUX TOME
URBETH	ALCHEMIST CROWN	CAPE OF LIGHT
LIBERTE	DANCER CROWN	RUSTY COMPASS
INVIDIA	SHAMAN CROWN	ARMOR OF LIGHT
SPELVIA	PALADIN CROWN	SWORD OF LIGHT
GUERA	SPELL FENCER CROWN	SHIELD OF LIGHT

ARBOR

INN COSTS 100 GIL

ARBOR ITEM SHOP

ITEM	COST	DESCRIPTION
HI-POTION	40 G	PROVIDES A GOOD HP BOOST.
X-POTION	400 G	PROVIDES A GREAT BIG HP BOOST.
REMEDY	400 G	CURES ALL AILMENTS (EXCEPT DEATH) AND RESTORES A SMALL AMOUNT OF HP.
DRAGON WING	60 G	TELEPORTS YOU BACK TO TOWN, INSTANTLY.
TORCH	10 G	LIGHTS YOUR WAY IN THE DARKEST OF DUNGEONS.
LEAF TOME	500 G	BLACK MAGIC: NON-ELEMENT ATTACK. MAGIC ATTACK: 5 / AP COST: 2.
LEAFRA TOME	1500 G	BLACK MAGIC: NON-ELEMENT ATTACK. MAGIC ATTACK: 12 / AP COST: 3.
LEAFAGA TOME	5000 G	BLACK MAGIC: NON-ELEMENT ATTACK. MAGIC ATTACK: 15 / AP COST: 4.
CURAGA TOME	5000 G	WHITE MAGIC: PARTY HP RECOVERY. AP COST 4. CAN USE FROM THE MENU.
ESUNA TOME	1500 G	WHITE MAGIC: CURE AFFLICTIONS. AP COST: 2. CAN USE FROM MENU.

ARBOR WEAPON SHOP

ITEM	COST	DESCRIPTION
RED SHOT	865 G	ATTACK +7 (FIRE)
WIND BOW	485 G	ATTACK +3 (WIND)
BLUE SHOT	580 G	ATTACK +4 (WATER_
RANGER BOW	570 G	ATTACK +6
BOOK OF DRYAD	475 G	ATTACK +5, MAGIC ATTACK +8
GREAT TREE DAGGER	440 G	ATTACK +4, MAGIC ATTACK +4
GREAT TREE SHIELD	280 G	DEFENSE +2, MAGIC DEFENSE +2, EVADE/MAGIC EVADE +8
SPELL FENCER ARMOR	850 G	DEFENSE +9, MAGIC DEFENSE +8, STRENGTH/INTELLECT +10%
SNIPER'S RING	500 G	ACCURACY +10%
FAIRY CAPE	500 G	EVASION RATE IS DOUBLED.

An Unknown Ally

Speak with the man in front of the Great Tree; his name is given only as "???." To find out where he went, speak with the queen. Follow the unknown man to the Great Tree Roots to see what he is planning.

ENEMIES IN THE GREAT TREE ROOTS

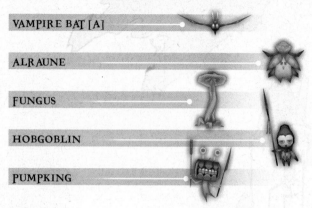

VAMPIRE BAT [A]

ALRAUNE

FUNGUS

HOBGOBLIN

PUMPKING

In the Great Tree Roots, the party meets up with the unknown man again. Agree to team up when he asks, and then he goes off on his own again. Go to B2 where you found the Animal Staff previously. Examine the chest, but let the unknown man open it.

Return to the queen and speak with her. Change into animal form and speak with Torte. When he rushes off to confront Belphegor, prepare for a trip to fiery Mt. Gulg. Equip Fire Shields, weapons that inflict Water damage, and some Water spells. When everyone is ready, fly north to Mt. Gulg.

MT. GULG

ENEMIES IN MT. GULG

VAMPIRE BAT [A]

NUE [A]

MINOTAUR [A]

GARM

RED JELLY

BUFFOHELM

ITEMS FROM CHESTS

FLAMEBLADE	FLAME CAPE
FIRE AXE	ELF CAPE
BURNING HARP	

1F

1 2

WORLD MAP

LEGEND

1	FIRE AXE
2	FLAMEBLADE
3	BURNING HARP
4	FLAME CAPE
5	ELF CAPE

2F

3

A

4

3F

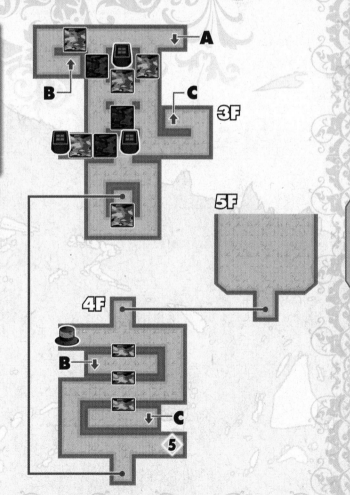

A

B

C

5F

4F

B

C

5

Walking a Fiery Path

Enjoy the easy collection of the contents of two chests on 1F; the real fun begins on the second floor. The fiery spots on the floor cause a great deal of damage with just one quick touch, so the goal is to avoid them completely. On 2F, collect the **Burning Harp** from the chest in the center of the floor. Go to the south switch and activate it. Hitting the switch changes the patches of fire, and the safest path is indicated on the maps. Walk around the south side of the switch to reach the next switch safely. Activate that switch, then go west and north to reach the chest containing the **Flame Cape**. Activate the final switch, and go up the stairs in the northwest corner of the level.

On 3F, hit the switch in the middle of the room, and then the one north of it. Squeeze through the path to reach the final switch (in the nook in the west wall) to clear the path to the southern stairs.

Suddenly, a monster appears!

Carefully navigate 4F's "S"-shaped corridor. The chest near the southern stairs is guarded by a Death Trap, but the **Elf Cape**

inside is worth the battle. Walk up to the Adventurer and save your progress. Go up to the stairs and approach Torte to begin the boss battle.

Belphegor [A] & Cubes

HP	(BELPHEGOR) 2000-2500, (CUBES) 500-625
WEAKNESSES	WATER
RESISTS	ALL (ABSORBS FIRE)
ABILITIES	(BELPHEGOR) FIRAGA, FIRA, CURA, BALLS OF FIRE. (CUBES) FIRAGA, FIRA
STEAL	(BOTH) BOMB FRAGMENT, PHOENIX DOWN, (BELPHEGOR ONLY) FLAME CAPE
DROPS	AMETHYST, DIAMOND

Belphegor is accompanied by three Cubes when the fight begins. The Cubes use Fire-element attacks and sometimes inflict Sleep. Belphegor uses Fire spells, including Balls of Fire, which hits the entire party. They're all resistant to physical damage.

All of these enemies begin with a vulnerability to Water. However, if you hit any of them with a Water-based spell or attack item that does not kill them in one shot, their elemental weakness changes. This also causes the enemies to change which spells they use (from Fira to Watera, for example). The key to this battle is to prepare for Fire-based damage and not to give them the chance to change their elemental affinity.

To boost the party's defense, keep Mysterio active at all times. To keep the fight simple, stick with physical damage boosted by the Water element (either in a character's weapon or by using the Spring Gauntlets). This type of elemental damage doesn't change the enemies' vulnerability, and you won't need to worry about other elemental resistances if you came prepared for Fire-element damage. If you have a Black Mage along, use both Magic Mojo and Spell Focus, then wait for the Elementalist to use both Augment and Amplify before you cast a Water-based spell. Don't use Waterga or Blizzaga because their damage is diminished with each living enemy they hit. Stick with single-target spells to knock off the Cubes one by one.

BOSS

You obtained Lux, the white magic of legend!

After defeating the boss, you obtain the Monk Crown. Use the teleporter to leave Mt. Gulg. Return to Arbor and visit the queen, who hands over the White Magic Lux. Immediately set Lux as someone's ability, and never put it in the Storage Shop. It will be a first-round action for every big fight from this point forward.

TOWN OF URBETH

INN COSTS 50 GIL

TOWN OF URBETH ITEM SHOP (LOWER) (UNCHANGED)

ITEM	COST	DESCRIPTION
POTION	20 G	PROVIDES A SMALL HP BOOST.
HI-POTION	40 G	PROVIDES A GOOD HP BOOST.
ANTIDOTE	20 G	CURES POISON.
GOLD NEEDLE	50 G	CURES PETRIFICATION.
ECHO HERBS	20 G	CURES SILENCE.
ANIMATE TONIC	30 G	CURES PARALYSIS.
EYE DROPS	20 G	CURES BLINDNESS.
ALARM CLOCK	20 G	WAKES YOU UP FROM ANY SLEEP.
CROSS	50 G	LIFTS CURSES.
REMEDY	400 G	CURES ALL AILMENTS (EXCEPT DEATH) AND RESTORES A SMALL AMOUNT OF HP.

TOWN OF URBETH ITEM SHOP (BYLION'S SHOP)

ITEM	COST	DESCRIPTION
POTION	20 G	PROVIDES A SMALL HP BOOST.
HI-POTION	40 G	PROVIDES A GOOD HP BOOST.
X-POTION	400 G	PROVIDES A GREAT BIG HP BOOST.
DRAGON WING	60 G	TELEPORTS YOU BACK TO TOWN, INSTANTLY.
REMEDY	400 G	CURES ALL AILMENTS (EXCEPT DEATH) AND RESTORES A SMALL AMOUNT OF HP.
ETHER	1000 G	PROVIDES A SMALL AP BOOST.
TORCH	10 G	LIGHTS YOUR WAY IN THE DARKEST OF DUNGEONS.

TOWN OF URBETH ARMOR SHOP (MYLION'S SHOP)

ITEM	COST	DESCRIPTION
MERCHANT TUNIC	550 G	DEFENSE +6, MAGIC DEFENSE +5, INTELLECT/SPIRIT +10%
SALVE-MAKER ROBE	500 G	DEFENSE +6, MAGIC DEFENSE +4, INTELLECT +10%, EVADE/MAGIC EVADE +5%
FIGHTER GI	550 G	DEFENSE +8, MAGIC DEFENSE +3, HP/STRENGTH +10%
SCHOLAR GOWN	700 G	DEFENSE +4, MAGIC DEFENSE +7, INTELLECT +20%
PARTY HOST WEAR	600 G	DEFENSE +5, MAGIC DEFENSE +7, INTELLECT/SPIRIT/EVADE/MAGIC EVADE +5%
HERO ARMOR	750 G	DEFENSE +8, MAGIC DEFENSE +7, STRENGTH/INTELLECT/SPIRIT +10%
PALADIN ARMOR	850 G	DEFENSE +11, MAGIC DEFENSE +6, HP +20%
FLAME SHIELD	350 G	DEFENSE +1, MAGIC DEFENSE +1, EVADE/MAGIC EVADE +5%, BLOCKS FIRE
GREAT TREE SHIELD	280 G	DEFENSE +2, MAGIC DEFENSE +2, EVADE/MAGIC EVADE +8

TOWN OF URBETH ACCESSORY SHOP (TRYLION'S SHOP)

ITEM	COST	DESCRIPTION
POWER RING	500 G	BOOSTS STRENGTH BY 10%
INTELLECT RING	500 G	BOOSTS INTELLECT BY 10%.
SPIRIT RING	500 G	BOOSTS SPIRIT BY 10%.
GIANT'S RING	500 G	ATTACK +10%
STAR EARRING	500 G	MAGIC ATTACK +10%
TURTLE SHELL	500 G	DEFENSE +10%
BLACK RING	500 G	MAGIC DEFENSE +10%
POISON CAPE	250 G	BLOCKS POISON.
FLASH CAPE	250 G	BLOCKS BLINDNESS.
CONFUSE CAPE	250 G	BLOCKS CONFUSION.

TOWN OF URBETH WEAPON SHOP (THUZAND'S SHOP)

ITEM	COST	DESCRIPTION
STEEL SWORD	200 G	ATTACK +2
MUTSUNOKAMI	10000 G	ATTACK +13
HATCHET	255 G	ATTACK +3
BOOK OF IFRIT	770 G	ATTACK +6, MAGIC ATTACK +11 (FIRE)
BURNING HARP	970 G	ATTACK +7, MAGIC ATTACK +7 (FIRE)
ENCYCLOPEDIA	285 G	ATTACK +3, MAGIC ATTACK +4
MAGIC STAFF	95 G	ATTACK +1, MAGIC ATTACK +3
STEEL SPEAR	330 G	ATTACK +3
HORNE'S BOW	190 G	ATTACK +2
HARP	220 G	ATTACK +2, MAGIC ATTACK +2

TOWN OF URBETH MAGIC SHOP

ITEM	COST	DESCRIPTION
FIRE TOME	1500 G	BLACK MAGIC: FIRE-ELEMENT ATTACK, MAGIC ATTACK: 5 / AP COST: 2
FIRA TOME	1500 G	BLACK MAGIC: FIRE-ELEMENT ATTACK, MAGIC ATTACK: 12 / AP COST: 3
FIRAGA TOME	5000 G	BLACK MAGIC: FIRE-ELEMENT ATTACK, MAGIC ATTACK: 15 / AP COST: 4
CURE TOME	500 G	WHITE MAGIC: SLIGHT HP RECOVERY. AP COST 2. CAN USE FROM THE MENU.
CURA TOME	1500 G	WHITE MAGIC: HP RECOVERY. AP COST 3. CAN USE FROM THE MENU.
CURAGA TOME	5000 G	WHITE MAGIC: PARTY HP RECOVERY. AP COST 4. CAN USE FROM THE MENU.
REGEN TOME	1000 G	WHITE MAGIC: RECOVER HEALTH EACH TURN. AP COST 3.
ESUNA TOME	1500 G	WHITE MAGIC: CURE AFFLICTIONS. AP COST 2. CAN USE FROM THE MENU.
RAISE TOME	1500 G	WHITE MAGIC: REVIVE FROM DEAD. AP COST 3. CAN USE FROM THE MENU.
ARISE TOME	5000 G	WHITE MAGIC: COMPLETELY REVIVE. AP COST 4. CAN USE FROM THE MENU.

URBETH ITEM SHOP (PREVIOUSLY UNLOCKED WITH MAGIC KEY)

ITEM	COST	DESCRIPTION
DRAIN TOME	1500 G	DARK MAGIC: ABSORB HP. MAGIC ATTACK: 5 / AP COST 2.
CONFUSE TOME	500 G	DARK MAGIC: INFLICT CONFUSION. AP COST 2.
POISON TOME	500 G	DARK MAGIC: INFLICT POISON. AP COST 2.
BREAK TOME	2500 G	DARK MAGIC: INFLICT PETRIFICATION. AP COST 3.
SILENCE TOME	500 G	DARK MAGIC: INFLICT SILENCE. AP COST 2
SUPPRESS TOME	2000 G	DARK MAGIC: LOWER FOES' STATUS. AP COST 2.
FLASH TOME	500 G	DARK MAGIC: INFLICT BLINDNESS. AP COST 2.
CURSE TOME	2000 G	DARK MAGIC: INFLICT A CURSE. AP COST 2.
SLEEP TOME	500 G	DARK MAGIC: INFLICT SLEEP. AP COST 2.
DEATH TOME	5000 G	DARK MAGIC: TAKE A FOE'S LIFE. AP COST 4.

Thauzand's Plight

Fly to Urbeth, then talk to Thauzand at the Weapon Shop. Visit the Apothecary, who has taken up residence in the Sorcerer's former shop. Follow the Apothecary to the Hunting Caves when he departs.

HUNTING CAVES

ENEMIES IN HUNTING CAVES

NUE [A]

VAMPIRE BAT [A]

ORC LORD

FUNGUS

BORGBEAR

Go to the lowest level of the Hunting Caves. Talk to the Apothecary again, resulting in a fight against an Orc Lord. After defeating it, pick up the **Hi-Elixir** it leaves behind.

Return to Urbeth and hand over the Hi-Elixir to Thauzand. Stay at the Inn, then return to the Weapon Shop and talk to Thauzand twice. After he departs, set your party up for upcoming battles, then follow him to the Tower of the Sky.

If you didn't pick up the Leaf spells from Arbor, do so now, especially if you plan on taking a Black Mage. For physical attack Crowns, choose weapons that don't have an elemental component. To boost your defense, take Flame Shields, or equip a Flame Cape.

An accessory that blocks Confuse or Sleep would be a good choice for the character that you've designated for healing.

TOWER OF THE SKY

ENEMIES IN TOWER OF THE SKY

BUFFOHELM [A]

NUE [A]

ARCH DEMON

IRON GOLEM

EVIL KNIGHT

ORC LORD

GARM

LILITH

There are no new tricks, or chests to collect, in the Tower of the Sky. Navigate the maps shown previously to reach the top. When your group arrives, it seems the party may have already started. Approach the group and prepare to face Beelzebub!

Beelzebub [A]

HP	3000-3750
WEAKNESSES	NONE
RESISTS	ALL
ABILITIES	FIRAGA, FIRA, BEZETEOR, FALL OF ANGELS
STEAL	X-POTION
DROPS	AMETHYST, DIAMOND

Beelzebub is resistant to all element-based spell attacks. It acts twice each round, and typically uses Fira or Firaga in most rounds. Its physical attacks inflict a variety of negative status ailments as well.

Every few turns, Beelzebub rises into the air and hovers. At the end of a few turns, it uses Fall of Angels, which deals heavy damage to everyone and may inflict any number of characters with Confusion or Sleep.

The good news is that the newly available Leaf category of Black Magic spells works well here. When Beelzebub rises into the air, you have an opportunity to deal extra damage and interrupt Fall of Angels. Deal sufficient damage to Beelzebub while it is in the air and it crashes to the ground, hurting itself with an ability called Bezeteor. The best way to knock it out of the sky is to use a Black Mage with Magic Mojo and Spell Focus (an Elementalist pitching in with Augment and Amplify helps), but then hold off on casting Leafra until Beelzebub takes to the air. It should come crashing down immediately!

BOSS

After the battle, you obtain the Alchemist Crown. Step on the teleporter to return to the base of the tower. Meet up with Thauzand at the Weapon Shop. He hands over the Cape of Light out of gratitude.

You obtained the Cape of Light!

LIBERTE TOWN

INN COSTS 20 GIL

LIBERTE PORT & LIBERTE TOWN (TOP) ITEM SHOP

ITEM	COST	DESCRIPTION
HI-POTION	40 G	PROVIDES A GOOD HP BOOST.
X-POTION	400 G	PROVIDES A GREAT BIG HP BOOST.
ETHER	1000 G	PROVIDES A SMALL AP BOOST
DRAGON WING	60 G	TELEPORTS YOU BACK TO TOWN, INSTANTLY.
BOMB FRAGMENT	300 G	INFLICTS FIRE-ELEMENT DAMAGE.
TORCH	10 G	LIGHTS YOUR WAY IN THE DARKEST OF DUNGEONS.
WATER TOME	500 G	BLACK MAGIC: WATER-ELEMENT ATTACK, MAGIC ATTACK: 5 / AP COST: 2
WATERA TOME	1500 G	BLACK MAGIC: WATER-ELEMENT ATTACK, MAGIC ATTACK: 12 / AP COST: 3
WATERGA TOME	5000 G	BLACK MAGIC: WATER-ELEMENT ATTACK, MAGIC ATTACK: 15 / AP COST: 4

LIBERTE TOWN ITEM SHOP (LEFT)

ITEM	COST	DESCRIPTION
FIRE AXE	1220 G	ATTACK +12 (FIRE)
BOOK OF SHIVA	675 G	ATTACK +5, MAGIC ATTACK +9 (WATER)
FLAME SPEAR	640 G	ATTACK +4 (WATER)
FLOWING HARP	640 G	ATTACK +4, MAGIC ATTACK +4 (WATER)
BANDIT GEAR	350 G	DEFENSE +4, MAGIC DEFENSE +2, ACCURACY +20%
POET TUNIC	350 G	DEFENSE +4, MAGIC DEFENSE +2, INTELLECT/SPIRIT +10%
MONK ROBE	850 G	DEFENSE +8, MAGIC DEFENSE +9, INTELLECT/SPIRIT +10%
ICE SHIELD	350 G	DEFENSE +1, MAGIC DEFENSE +1, EVADE/MAGIC EVADE +5, BLOCKS WATER
HOLY SHIELD	450 G	DEFENSE +2, MAGIC DEFENSE +2, EVADE/MAGIC EVADE +5, BLOCKS: LIGHT

Liberte's Secret

Speak with the inhabitants of Liberte, and end up at the house next to the coral-covered home where the party stays. Speak with Pione inside, then head to the Animal Burrow.

Pione

I'm looking for something unique and beautiful to set it apart. If you see anything, do let me know!

Unfinished Business

If you haven't done so already, use the Magic Key to unlock the door in Liberte Town. The chests in the house contain a **Soul of Thamasa**, a **Remedy**, and a **Stunning Harp**.

The Multiplayer Shop sells an item called a **Musical Score** that, when purchased, unlocks the Musician Crown. Even if you haven't played any actual multiplayer, you should have accumulated enough points by now to purchase it.

ANIMAL BURROW

ENEMIES IN ANIMAL BURROW

ALRAUNE

ARP

HOBGOBLIN

PUMPKING

RED JELLY

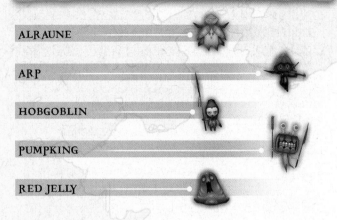

Every character must be in animal form before the party can enter the Animal Burrow. Once inside, look for the fairy caught in a spider web (it's a quicker trip from the Guera side of the tunnel). Agree to help the fairy, then return to Liberte.

Go to Pione's home and speak with him. At the end of the conversation, go to the Inn and rest for the night. The next morning, you find out Pione has been taken to the Pirate Hideout.

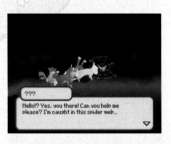

Hello!? Yes, you there! Can you help me please? I'm caught in this spider web...

Pione

Tonight I must put the finishing touches on my work. Come back tomorrow to see the result!

For the upcoming boss fight, take some equipment resistant to Fire, as well as weapons that deal Water damage. However, you should also take weapons and spells that deal other types of damage (or take Leaf spells), since some enemies in the Pirate Hideout are resistant to Water-based damage.

PIRATE HIDEOUT

ENEMIES IN PIRATE HIDEOUT

ARCHELON

DEMON RAY

LIZARDHAWK

OCEANUS

SCYLLA

VAMPIRE BAT

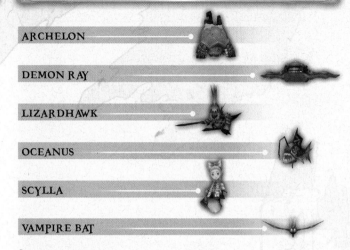

ITEMS FROM CHESTS

1000 GIL (X2)	DEATH TOME
FRESH MEAT	MONK ROBE
DANCER CLOTHES	RUSTY COMPASS

Use the same password as before to enter the Pirate Hideout. There are no new items to collect on the upper levels, so head directly to B3F.

Seadevil [A]

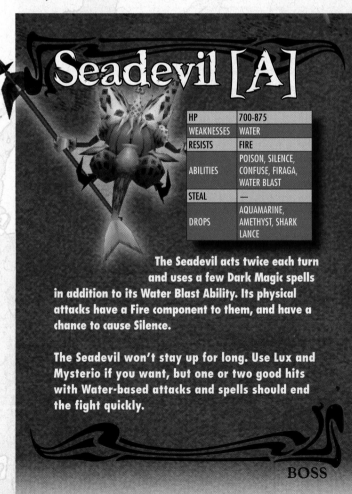

HP	700-875
WEAKNESSES	WATER
RESISTS	FIRE
ABILITIES	POISON, SILENCE, CONFUSE, FIRAGA, WATER BLAST
STEAL	—
DROPS	AQUAMARINE, AMETHYST, SHARK LANCE

The Seadevil acts twice each turn and uses a few Dark Magic spells in addition to its Water Blast Ability. Its physical attacks have a Fire component to them, and have a chance to cause Silence.

The Seadevil won't stay up for long. Use Lux and Mysterio if you want, but one or two good hits with Water-based attacks and spells should end the fight quickly.

BOSS

Now for the Plunder

Speak with Darke, who gives the party access to the pirates' hoard. Go down the stairs and gather the items from the chest. The important item is the **Rusty Compass** from the chest in the center of the room.

Return to Liberte and prepare for the upcoming boss fight. The party must be ready to face Water-based attacks, with a few Light-based attacks mixed in from time to time.

Water-resistance is vital, so Ice Shields or Stream Capes should be standard equipment. Take plenty of Phoenix Downs or spread out Raise Tomes as well. When everyone is ready, visit the museum, which is the first floor of the building with the king. Interact with the item in the center of the room to place the Rusty Compass.

Drake

In one of the boxes we'll find a Rusty Compass. It fits the pedestal in Liberte's Art Museum.

You inserted the Rusty Compass into the slot!

Where's the Driver's Seat?

Liberte Town was built on the back of Cetus. You can only disembark Cetus near a beach. When you board Cetus, you end up at the entrance to Liberte Town. To take control of Cetus, return to the museum and place the Rusty Compass again.

Guide Cetus around the coast, then up the straits near the Pirate Hideout. Look for a dark spot in the middle of the bay. When you reach it, you initiate a fight against Leviathan.

Leviathan [A] & Tentacles

HP	(LEAVIATHAN) 3500-4375, (TENTACLE) 1000-1250
WEAKNESSES	FIRE
RESISTS	EARTH, WATER (ABSORBS)
ABILITIES	WATER, WATERA, THUNDARA, THUNDAGA, CHARGE, TIDAL WAVE
STEAL	PHOENIX DOWN, DEATH RING
DROPS	AMETHYST, DIAMOND

The fight begins with a single tentacle peeking out of the water. When the Tentacle reaches 1% HP, a new tentacle appears. This continues to happen until there are four tentacles visible. When the fourth tentacle is at 1% health, Leviathan's entire body appears and floats above the waves. Leviathan gets one action per turn for each tentacle that appears, and four actions for each turn when its main body is in view.

Leviathan starts using Waterga and Watera often, and mixes in both Thundara and Thundaga (both of which can paralyze). The physical attacks for the tentacles and Leviathan have a Water-element component to their damage. Even worse, Leviathan has a chance to inflict Death with a single blow at any time! When Leviathan pauses in its attacks and starts to Charge, it's about to unleash Tidal Wave, which leaves the party in bad shape should it hit. The good news is that if you can manage to inflict enough damage, Leviathan stops Charging and cancels the Tidal Wave attack.

Anyone assigned to dealing damage should use Fire-based abilities and weapons. Save attacks that deal big chunks of damage (such as a Black Mage using Magic Mojo and Spell Focus, or a Ranger with Smashing Blow) for the rounds when Leviathan starts to Charge. You really don't want to see what Tidal Wave does to an unprotected party!

WALKTHROUGH

BOSS

Defeating Leviathan unlocks the Dancer Crown. There's nothing else to collect here, so you're ready to move to your next challenge.

INVIDIA

INN COSTS 300 GIL

INVIDIA ITEM SHOP (TOP)

ITEM	COST	DESCRIPTION
POTION	20 G	PROVIDES A SMALL HP BOOST.
HI-POTION	40 G	PROVIDES A GOOD HP BOOST.
DRAGON WING	60 G	TELEPORTS YOU BACK TO TOWN, INSTANTLY.
DARK TOME	500 G	BLACK MAGIC: DARK-ELEMENT ATTACK. MAGIC ATTACK : 5 / AP COST: 2.
DARKRA TOME	1500 G	BLACK MAGIC: DARK-ELEMENT ATTACK. MAGIC ATTACK : 12 / AP COST: 3.
DARKAGA TOME	500 G	BLACK MAGIC: DARK-ELEMENT ATTACK. MAGIC ATTACK : 15 / AP COST: 4.
BLIZZARD TOME	500 G	BLACK MAGIC: WATER-ELEMENT ATTACK. MAGIC ATTACK: 5 / AP COST: 2.
BLIZZARA TOME	500 G	BLACK MAGIC: WATER-ELEMENT ATTACK. MAGIC ATTACK: 12 / AP COST: 3.
BLIZZAGA TOME	1500 G	BLACK MAGIC: WATER-ELEMENT ATTACK. MAGIC ATTACK: 15 / AP COST: 4.

INVIDIA WEAPON SHOP

ITEM	COST	DESCRIPTION
DARKNESS BLADE	1100 G	ATTACK +9 (DARK)
FIRE AXE	1220 G	ATTACK +12 (FIRE)
BOOK OF IFRIT	770 G	ATTACK +6, MAGIC ATTACK +11 (FIRE)
INFERNO STAVE	390 G	ATTACK +2, MAGIC ATTACK +5 (FIRE)
EVIL LANCE	2070 G	ATTACK +17 (DARK)
BLOODY BOW	865 G	ATTACK +7 (DARK)
BURNING HARP	970 G	ATTACK +7, MAGIC ATTACK +7 (FIRE)
DARKENING HARP	860 G	ATTACK +6, MAGIC ATTACK +6 (DARK)
OCEAN STAVE	295 G	ATTACK +1, MAGIC ATTACK +3 (WATER)
DARKNESS STAFF	675 G	ATTACK +5, MAGIC ATTACK +13 (DARK)

INVIDIA ARMOR SHOP

ITEM	COST	DESCRIPTION
FIGHTER GI	550 G	DEFENSE +8, MAGIC DEFENSE +3, HP/STRENGTH +10%
SCHOLAR GOWN	700 G	DEFENSE +7, MAGIC DEFENSE +7, INTELLECT +20%
ALCHEMIST GOWN	850 G	DEFENSE +9, MAGIC DEFENSE +8, DEFENSE/MAGIC DEFENSE/ ACCURACY/MAGIC ACCURACY +5%
STAR EARRING	500 G	MAGIC ATTACK +10%
ICE SHIELD	350 G	DEFENSE +1, MAGIC DEFENSE +1, EVADE/MAGIC EVADE +5. BLOCKS WATER
DARKSTEEL SHIELD	450 G	DEFENSE +2, MAGIC DEFENSE +2, EVADE/MAGIC EVADE +5. BLOCKS DARK
FLAME GAUNTLET	500 G	ADDS FIRE-ELEMENT DAMAGE TO WEAPON ATTACKS.
DUSK GAUNTLET	500 G	ADDS DARK-ELEMENT DAMAGE TO WEAPON ATTACKS.

The Land of Ice and Snow

Speak with Invidia's chief in the main hall. Afterward, step outside and speak with Rekoteh. If you aren't sure where to go next, speak with the advisor on the walkway above the chief. Before you head to the Invidia Underground, prepare for the upcoming battles by equipping Water-resistant gear and Fire-enhanced weapons. Load up offensive magic-users with Fire-based spells and you should be ready to go.

INVIDIA UNDERGROUND

ENEMIES IN INVIDIA UNDERGROUND

GHOUL [A]

TROLLUD ZOMBIE

GORGON

LILITH

NIDHOGG

SHADE TROLLUD

SCYLLA

On B3, to get past the ice barrier, each dragon statue must be set to face a certain direction. To solve the puzzle, turn the bottom-right pedestal three times, the bottom-left pedestal two times, and the upper-left pedestal one time. Save your game, then continue to the next room. Check the treasure chest to start a battle.

Ice Dragon

HP	1200-1500
WEAKNESSES	FIRE
RESISTS	WATER (ABSORBS), WIND, EARTH, LIGHT, DARK
ABILITIES	ICE BREATH [B]
STEAL	POTION, STREAM CAPE, X-POTION
DROPS	AMETHYST, AQUAMARINE

The Ice Dragon acts twice per turn, and often uses Ice Breath to hit everyone in the party. The Dragon is vulnerable to Fire, absorbs Water, and resists everything else.

Hit the Ice Dragon with Fira, or weapons with Fire-boosted damage, until it drops. With Mysterio active, and Ice Shields or Stream Capes equipped, no one should take much damage during this brief battle.

BOSS

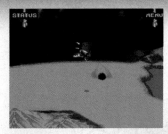

After the battle, you obtain the Dragon's Mark. Return to Invida and speak with Rekoteh. Follow Rekoteh when she hurries away, then talk to her father, the chief. When Rekoteh runs off again, follow her up to her room and speak with her for a bit more information. Head outside, summon the dragon, and fly to the Sun Temple, which is just south of Invida.

Sun Temple

ITEMS FROM CHESTS

GROWTH EGG
FOSSIL RING
DEATH CAPE

ENEMIES IN SUN TEMPLE

- SHADE TROLLUD
- TROLLUD ZOMBIE
- GHOUL
- GORGON
- NIDHOGG
- SCYLLA
- LILITH
- DEATH TRAP

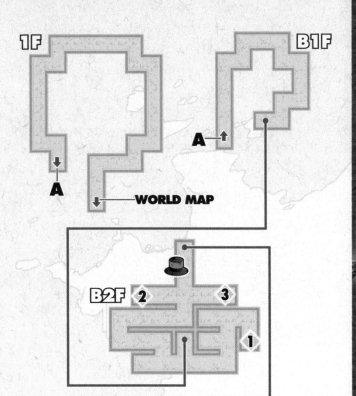

1F **B1F**

A

WORLD MAP

B2F 2 3

1

B3F

LEGEND

1	GROWTH EGG
2	FOSSIL RING
3	DEATH CAPE

Bringing the Heat

Approach the wall, then select "Yes" when prompted to hold the Dragon's Mark over the carving. The first two floors are long hallways with no points of interest. B2F has three chests in

addition to the Adventurer. The southeastern chest is a Death Trap, and holds a **Growth Egg**. Grab the other items, save your game, and move on to B3F to face Mammon.

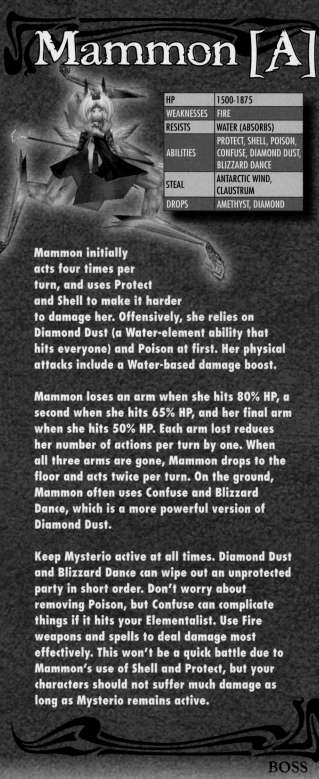

Mammon [A]

HP	1500-1875
WEAKNESSES	FIRE
RESISTS	WATER (ABSORBS)
ABILITIES	PROTECT, SHELL, POISON, CONFUSE, DIAMOND DUST, BLIZZARD DANCE
STEAL	ANTARCTIC WIND, CLAUSTRUM
DROPS	AMETHYST, DIAMOND

Mammon initially acts four times per turn, and uses Protect and Shell to make it harder to damage her. Offensively, she relies on Diamond Dust (a Water-element ability that hits everyone) and Poison at first. Her physical attacks include a Water-based damage boost.

Mammon loses an arm when she hits 80% HP, a second when she hits 65% HP, and her final arm when she hits 50% HP. Each arm lost reduces her number of actions per turn by one. When all three arms are gone, Mammon drops to the floor and acts twice per turn. On the ground, Mammon often uses Confuse and Blizzard Dance, which is a more powerful version of Diamond Dust.

Keep Mysterio active at all times. Diamond Dust and Blizzard Dance can wipe out an unprotected party in short order. Don't worry about removing Poison, but Confuse can complicate things if it hits your Elementalist. Use Fire weapons and spells to deal damage most effectively. This won't be a quick battle due to Mammon's use of Shell and Protect, but your characters should not suffer much damage as long as Mysterio remains active.

BOSS

The Shaman Crown is the reward for defeating Mammon. Use the teleporter that appears to return to the outside world. Talk to the chief twice to receive the **Armor of Light**.

Spelvia

No Charge to Stay at Inn

SPELVIA ITEM SHOP

ITEM	COST	DESCRIPTION
POTION	20 G	PROVIDES A SMALL HP BOOST.
HI-POTION	40 G	PROVIDES A GOOD HP BOOST.
REMEDY	400 G	CURES ALL AILMENTS (EXCEPT DEATH) AND RESTORES A SMALL AMOUNT OF HP.
ETHER	1000 G	PROVIDES A SMALL AP BOOST.
SOUL OF THAMASA	10000 G	MAGIC ATTACK +10, MAGIC ACCURACY +10%, INTELLECT +5
GLIMMER GAUNTLET	500 G	ADDS LIGHT-ELEMENT DAMAGE TO WEAPON ATTACKS
COURAGE RING	10000 G	YOU BECOME PSYCHED UP MORE EASILY.
FOSSIL CAPE	500 G	BLOCKS PETRIFICATION.
CURSE CAPE	500 G	BLOCKS CURSES.

SPELVIA WEAPON SHOP

ITEM	COST	DESCRIPTION
HOLY KNIFE	1080 G	ATTACK +8, MAGIC ATTACK +8 (LIGHT). REDUCES FOE'S STATUS LEVELS
BOLT BOW	960 G	ATTACK +8 (LIGHT)
SHINING BLADE	900 G	ATTACK +7 (LIGHT)
SHINING AXE	1135 G	ATTACK +11 (LIGHT)
WHITE BOOK	675 G	ATTACK +5, MAGIC ATTACK +9 (LIGHT)
SHINING STAFF	465 G	ATTACK +3, MAGIC ATTACK +7 (LIGHT)
PARTY HOST WEAR	600 G	DEFENSE +5, MAGIC DEFENSE +7, INTELLECT/SPIRIT/EVADE/MAGIC EVADE +5%
HERO ARMOR	750 G	DEFENSE +6, MAGIC DEFENSE+7, STRENGTH/INTELLECT/SPIRIT +10%
DANCER CLOTHES	735 G	DEFENSE +7, MAGIC DEFENSE +6, EVADE/SPIRIT +10%
HOLY SHIELD	450 G	DEFENSE +2, MAGIC DEFENSE +2, EVADE/MAGIC EVADE +5. BLOCKS LIGHT

SPELVIA MAGIC SHOP

ITEM	COST	DESCRIPTION
THUNDER TOME	500 G	BLACK MAGIC: LIGHT-ELEMENT ATTACK. MAGIC ATTACK: 5 / AP COST: 2
THUNDARA TOME	1500 G	BLACK MAGIC: LIGHT-ELEMENT ATTACK. MAGIC ATTACK: 10 / AP COST: 3
THUNDAGA TOME	5000 G	BLACK MAGIC: LIGHT-ELEMENT ATTACK. MAGIC ATTACK: 12 / AP COST: 4
BANISH TOME	500 G	BLACK MAGIC: LIGHT-ELEMENT ATTACK. MAGIC ATTACK: 5 / AP COST: 2
BANISHRA TOME	1500 G	BLACK MAGIC: LIGHT-ELEMENT ATTACK. MAGIC ATTACK: 12 / AP COST: 3
BANISHGA TOME	5000 G	BLACK MAGIC: LIGHT-ELEMENT ATTACK. MAGIC ATTACK: 15 / AP COST: 4
INVISIBLE TOME	1000 G	WHITE MAGIC: EVASION DOUBLED. AP COST: 2
AURA TOME	2500 G	WHITE MAGIC: INCREASE STATUS LEVELS BY 10%. AP COST: 3
MAGICK TOME	1000 G	WHITE MAGIC: MAGIC ATTACK INCREASED BY 50%. AP COST: 2

Light and Dark Dance

Fly to Spelvia and do some exploring. Don't forget to change into animal form if you want to speak with any of the Golem vendors or the innkeeper. To find Rolan, you must venture to the lowest floor of Spelvia Dungeon.

Spelvia Dungeon

Enemies in Spelvia Dungeon

- GHOUL [A]
- NIDHOGG
- GOLEM
- GORGON
- KAISER PENGUIN

It's a relatively quick trip unless you need to pick up any chests that you may have skipped earlier. Head down to B4F. Rolan is not far from the pot that restores HP. He doesn't have much to say, so return to the surface of Spelvia.

The next destination is Rolan's Soul, but first you need to get ready for the upcoming battles. Equip everyone with a Darksteel Shield or a Dark Cape. Equip items with Light-enhanced dam-

Rolan
I won't open my heart to anyone. Not any more!

age, or fill your ability slots with Banish- or Thunder-type spells. When everyone is set, head to Rolan's Soul.

ROLAN'S SOUL

ENEMIES IN ROLAN'S SOUL

DOPPELGANGER [AIRE B]

DOPPELGANGER [BRANDT B]

DOPPELGANGER [JUSQUA B]

DOPPELGANGER [YUNITA B]

GHOUL [A]

ARCH DEMON

Speak with Rolan on the main staircase, then enter each of the doors on the nearby platforms. There's an Arch Demon behind each door, but you may need to do some hunting in the area to turn up each one.

The Arch Demons each have 1000 HP and act twice per round of combat. They have two Dark-based abilities that hit everyone in the party: World of Darkness (which also inflicts multiple negative status ailments) and Bladeblitz. They're vulnerable to

Light, and Dark attacks heal them.

As you eliminate the Arch Demons, Rolan reveals more and more of the root of his inner anguish. When the last Arch Demon falls, check on Rolan and he bolts through the main doors. Don't follow him immediately. In terms of resistances and weaknesses, the next boss is the opposite of the Arch Demons you faced, so run out to Spelvia and change up your gear (don't forget to change to animal form first).

Switch out Darksteel Shields for Holy Shields, and equip a Wind Cape on your designated healer. Add Dark-element spells and weapons to your inventory, but don't equip them yet. There's a possibility of a random encounter before you reach the boss, and the party will not be set up properly to face any other enemies in Rolan's Soul.

Switch weapons and spells right after you pass through the main doorways and see the boss, Lucifer.

Lucifer [A]

HP	2000-2500
WEAKNESSES	DARK
RESISTS	LIGHT
ABILITIES	THUNDARA, THUNDAGA, AEROGA, JUDGEMENT BOLT, CURA
STEAL	HOLY BREATH, LIGHTBRINGER
DROPS	AMETHYST, DIAMOND

Lucifer acts twice per round, is vulnerable to Dark, and is healed by Light-based damage. When attacking the party, Lucifer uses Thundara, Thundaga, and Aeroga in addition to his Light-enhanced melee attacks.

After three turns, Lucifer takes to air and uses Judgement Bolt to remove everyone's AP. It doesn't inflict any damage, but it prevents everyone in your party from performing any action.

If possible, try to take Lucifer out before he takes to the air. Judgement Bolt is a pain to work around because it cancels whatever actions you try to take. Hit him hard with Dark-elemental attacks and spells right from the start and you should be able to make this a quick fight. If you have Lux, it goes a long way toward keeping party members healthy through the phases of the fight when Lucifer is flying. At least with Lux active, you're able to get in some healing between rounds!

BOSS

158

You obtained the Sword of Light!

After defeating Lucifer, you obtain the Paladin Crown. Even better, the Golems of Spelvia are no longer angry at humans, so there's no need to change to animal form to shop. Talk to Rolan, who is back in his throne room, to receive the **Sword of Light**.

GUERA

INN COSTS 20 GIL

GUERA ITEM SHOP

ITEM	COST	DESCRIPTION
HI-POTION	40 G	PROVIDES A GOOD HP BOOST.
X-POTION	400 G	PROVIDES A GREAT BIG HP BOOST.
ETHER	1000 G	PROVIDES A SMALL AP BOOST.
REMEDY	400 G	CURES ALL AILMENTS (EXCEPT DEATH) AND RESTORES A SMALL AMOUNT OF HP.
DRAGON WING	60 G	TELEPORTS YOU BACK TO TOWN, INSTANTLY.
TORCH	10 G	LIGHTS YOUR WAY IN THE DARKEST OF DUNGEONS.
POISON CAPE	250 G	BLOCKS POISON.
FOSSIL CAPE	500 G	BLOCKS PETRIFICATION.
STUN CAPE	250 G	BLOCKS PARALYSIS.

GUERA EQUIPMENT SHOP

ITEM	COST	DESCRIPTION
WIND FOIL	500 G	ATTACK +3 (WIND)
BOOK OF SYLPH	865 G	ATTACK +7, MAGIC ATTACK +13 (WIND)
BOOK OF TITAN	380 G	ATTACK +4, MAGIC ATTACK +7 (EARTH)
ROCK SHIELD	350 G	DEFENSE +1, MAGIC DEFENSE +1, EVADE/MAGIC EVADE +5, BLOCKS EARTH
BLACK ROBE	350 G	DEFENSE +3, MAGIC DEFENSE +4, INTELLECT/MAGIC ATTACK +10%
WHITE ROBE	350 G	DEFENSE +3, MAGIC DEFENSE +4, SPIRIT +20%
SPELL FENCER ARMOR	850 G	DEFENSE +9, MAGIC DEFENSE +8, STRENGTH/INTELLECT +10%
HERO ARMOR	750 G	DEFENSE +8, MAGIC DEFENSE +7, STRENGTH/INTELLECT/SPIRIT +10%

GUERA MAGIC SHOP

ITEM	COST	DESCRIPTION
BERSERK TOME	1000 G	WHITE MAGIC: ATTACK INCREASED 50%. AP COST 2.
PROTECT TOME	1000 G	WHITE MAGIC: DEFENSE INCREASED 50%. AP COST 2.
MAGICK TOME	1000 G	WHITE MAGIC: MAGIC ATTACK INCREASED 50%. AP COST 2.
SHELL TOME	1000 G	WHITE MAGIC: MAGIC DEFENSE INCREASED 50%. AP COST: 2.
CONFUSE TOME	500 G	DARK MAGIC: INFLICT CONFUSION. AP COST 2
POISON TOME	500 G	DARK MAGIC: INFLICT POISON. AP COST 2.
BREAK TOME	2500 G	DARK MAGIC: INFLICT PETRIFICATION. AP COST 3.
SILENCE TOME	500 G	DARK MAGIC: INFLICT SILENCE. AP COST 2.
FLASH TOME	500 G	DARK MAGIC: INFLICT BLINDNESS. AP COST 2.
SLEEP TOME	500 G	DARK MAGIC: INFLICT SLEEP. AP COST 2.

GEURA TOWN MAGIC SHOP (OUTDOORS)

ITEM	COST	DESCRIPTION
QUAKE TOME	500 G	BLACK MAGIC: EARTH-ELEMENT ATTACK, MAGIC ATTACK: 12 / AP COST: 3
QUAKRA TOME	1500 G	BLACK MAGIC: EARTH-ELEMENT ATTACK, MAGIC ATTACK: 13 / AP COST: 3
QUAGA TOME	5000 G	BLACK MAGIC: EARTH-ELEMENT ATTACK, MAGIC ATTACK: 16 / AP COST: 4
PROTECT TOME	1000 G	WHITE MAGIC: DEFENSE INCREASED 50%. AP COST: 2.
SHELL TOME	1000 G	WHITE MAGIC: MAGIC DEFENSE INCREASED 50%. AP COST: 2.
CURE TOME	500 G	WHITE MAGIC: SLIGHT HP RECOVERY. AP COST 2. CAN USE FROM THE MENU.
CURA TOME	1500 G	WHITE MAGIC: HP RECOVERY. AP COST 3. CAN USE FROM THE MENU.
CURAGA TOME	5000 G	WHITE MAGIC: PARTY HP RECOVERY. AP COST 4. CAN USE FROM THE MENU.
ESUNA TOME	1500 G	WHITE MAGIC: CURE AFFLICTIONS. AP COST 2. CAN USE FROM THE MENU.
RAISE TOME	1500 G	WHITE MAGIC: REVIVE FROM DEAD. AP COST 3. CAN USE FROM THE MENU.

A Cruel Deception

Fly to Guera and head up to the palace. The king is still in his throne room, but he doesn't remember the party. The conversation is cut short by Krinjh's appearance. When Krinjh departs, follow him to Moonlight Tower.

King Guera
Ah, you bring a seedling of the Great Tree. Well done, Krinjh, well done!

MOONLIGHT TOWER

ENEMIES IN MOONLIGHT TOWER

GHOUL [A]

COCKARICE

PUMPKING

WYORM

BUFFOHELM

You must ascend to Moonlight Tower 5F, where Krinjh is under attack. Dispatch the pair of Trollud Zombies and the Ghoul. Your next destination is Quicksand Castle, but first you need to prepare for the final confrontation inside it.

Incoming Earth damage is your main concern, but the party will likely get hit with Fire and Wind as well. There is also a host of negative status effects to worry about. An Elementalist is a key asset in the battle, as is a good supply of Remedy items. Go with Water-element weapons and Magic Tomes for dealing damage.

QUICKSAND CASTLE

ENEMIES IN QUICKSAND CASTLE

- GHOUL [A]
- BULLKING
- NEKO NATTER
- COCKATRICE
- MINOTAUR
- WYORM

With nothing new to collect, take the shortest route down to 6F. Approach the king to interrupt his conversation with Ariadne. He turns his attention to the party and a quick fight begins. This isn't a true battle, since it lasts three turns at the most. During the battle, King Guera uses Quakra and Firaga, and acts twice each turn. He has between 400 and 500 HP, and it's possible to steal a Potion, Hi-Potion, or X-Potion from him. Don't burn up too much AP against the king, as the next battle begins before the party gets a chance to rest. After three turns (or after you defeat the king in battle), the scene shifts. Agree to use the Merkmal's Shine and the real battle starts.

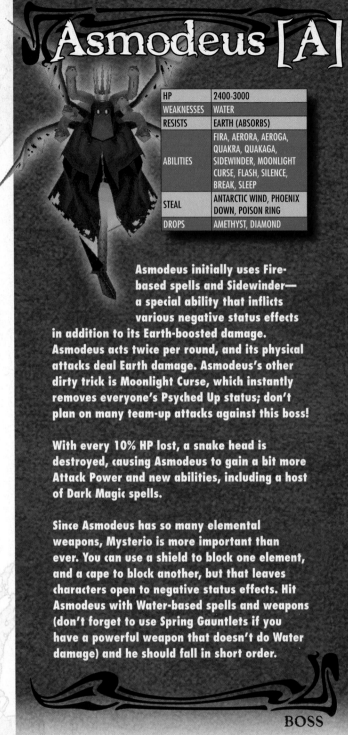

Asmodeus [A]

HP	2400-3000
WEAKNESSES	WATER
RESISTS	EARTH (ABSORBS)
ABILITIES	FIRA, AERORA, AEROGA, QUAKRA, QUAKAGA, SIDEWINDER, MOONLIGHT CURSE, FLASH, SILENCE, BREAK, SLEEP
STEAL	ANTARCTIC WIND, PHOENIX DOWN, POISON RING
DROPS	AMETHYST, DIAMOND

Asmodeus initially uses Fire-based spells and Sidewinder—a special ability that inflicts various negative status effects in addition to its Earth-boosted damage. Asmodeus acts twice per round, and its physical attacks deal Earth damage. Asmodeus's other dirty trick is Moonlight Curse, which instantly removes everyone's Psyched Up status; don't plan on many team-up attacks against this boss!

With every 10% HP lost, a snake head is destroyed, causing Asmodeus to gain a bit more Attack Power and new abilities, including a host of Dark Magic spells.

Since Asmodeus has so many elemental weapons, Mysterio is more important than ever. You can use a shield to block one element, and a cape to block another, but that leaves characters open to negative status effects. Hit Asmodeus with Water-based spells and weapons (don't forget to use Spring Gauntlets if you have a powerful weapon that doesn't do Water damage) and he should fall in short order.

BOSS

When Asmodeus falls, you're given the Spell Fencer Crown. When you regain control of the party, speak with Krinjh to obtain the **Shield of Light**. Step on the purple portal to return to the surface.

You obtained the Shield of Light!

TOWN OF HORNE

INN COSTS 10 GIL

TOWN OF HORNE ITEM SHOP

ITEM	COST	DESCRIPTION
STORMAXE	1220 G	ATTACK +12 (WIND)
BOOK OF SYLPH	865 G	ATTACK +7, MAGIC ATTACK +13 (WIND)
BOOK OF RAMUH	580 G	ATTACK +4, MAGIC ATTACK +6 (LIGHT). INFLICTS PARALYSIS.
WOOD SHIELD	130 G	DEFENSE +1, MAGIC DEFENSE +1, EVADE/MAGIC EVADE +3
TRAVELER'S GARB	150 G	DEFENSE +2, MAGIC DEFENSE +1, STRENGTH/INTELLECT/SPIRIT +5%
SHAMAN ROBE	850 G	DEFENSE +8, MAGIC DEFENSE +9, MAGIC ACCURACY/INTELLECT +10%
REMEDY	400 G	CURES ALL AILMENTS (EXCEPT DEATH) AND RESTORES A SMALL AMOUNT OF HP.
HI-POTION	40 G	PROVIDES A GOOD HP BOOST.
DRAGON WING	60 G	TELEPORTS YOU BACK TO TOWN, INSTANTLY.
TORCH	10 G	LIGHTS YOUR WAY IN THE DARKEST OF DUNGEONS.

Before you defeat all the demons and collect the Cape of Light, Shield of Light, Sword of Light, Armor of Light, Rusty Compass,

and Lux Tome, all you can do in Horne is pick up the items locked up in the windmill and the castle's dungeon. However, once you've obtained all the items on that list, the citizens of Horne are freed from the curse that turned them all to stone.

Go to the castle and talk to its inhabitants to get a sense of current events. Head down to the dungeon to find that the door near the locked cell is finally unguarded. Go through the door to reach the Magic Laboratory.

The only required activity at this point is to head down to B1F and spy on the king and the minister as they converse in the octagonal room just beyond the Adventurer's location. If you want to take the time now to explore the dungeon and collect the items inside, flip ahead a few pages to see the list of items and their locations on the maps. None of the items is necessary to face the upcoming bosses and you must fully explore the Magic Laboratory soon enough.

Before you head out, outfit everyone with shields or accessories that block Dark damage. Everyone should have Light-element weapons and spells. There's actually a warm-up fight before the main encounter. The first boss uses Light and Wind attacks and is vulnerable to Fire. However, it shouldn't be much of a fight, so taking a second set of gear to deal with this threat is optional.

WITCH'S MANSION

ENEMIES IN WITCH'S MANSION

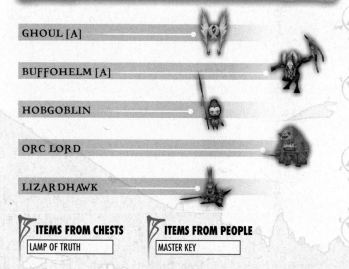

GHOUL [A]

BUFFOHELM [A]

HOBGOBLIN

ORC LORD

LIZARDHAWK

ITEMS FROM CHESTS
LAMP OF TRUTH

ITEMS FROM PEOPLE
MASTER KEY

To reach the Witch, you must retrace the steps you took the first time you visited the Witch's Mansion: Go up to 2F and light the

candle to unlock the door in the mansion's first room. Go through that door to confront the Witch, who turns into Greaps!

Greaps [B]

HP	800-1000
WEAKNESSES	FIRE
RESISTS	WIND
ABILITIES	THUNDARA, AEROGA, CURA
STEAL	—
DROPS	RUBY, AMETHYST

Greaps acts twice each turn, and favors using spells over its Wind-element-enhanced physical attacks. Aeroga is the greater threat because it strikes everyone in the party, but so long as the party's equipment has been kept up-to-date, neither Aeroga nor Thundara should cause much damage.

Hitting Greaps with Fire damage is ideal, but hardly necessary. Nearly 1000 HP seems like a big number to get through, but Greaps has much lower stats than other bosses you have fought recently. Keep everyone alive and attacking, and the fight should end quickly.

BOSS

When the battle ends, you obtain the **Master Key**. Go to the locked door on 1F and open it with the Master Key. Speak to the paintings inside for clues on how to solve the puzzle.

The solution to the puzzle is to go to the southeastern room and light the candle. Move north and light the candle in the northeastern room. Go west into the next room and light that candle. Go south to the southwestern room and light the candle within. At this point you receive a message about a door opening if you did this correctly. Go through the door north of the four lit candles in the center room. Outfit your characters with the proper gear (Dark-resistant), then check the chest in the newly opened room to start the battle.

Extra Dungeons Now Available

Scattered throughout the world are four towers that have been inaccessible due to the locks on their doors. The Master Key unlocks the doors and grants you access to their secrets. For more information on these towers, turn to the "Extra Dungeons" section of the guide.

Doppelganger [Aire C]

Doppelganger [Brandt C]

HP	390-488
WEAKNESSES	LIGHT
RESISTS	DARK
ABILITIES	(AIRE) CURA, CURAGA, SLEEP, SILENCE, FLASH. (BRANDT) CURA, BERSERK. (JUSQUA) DARKRA, DARKAGA. (YUNITA) CURA
STEAL	HI-POTION, PHOENIX DOWN, CURSE RING
DROPS	AMETHYST, CROSS, CURSED BLADE

HP 478-588

Doppelganger [Jusqua C]

HP 440-550

Doppelganger [Yunita C]

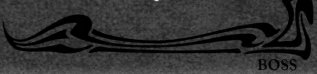

These powerful opponents are the biggest test of your abilities to date. They use a variety of spells from all the schools of magic. Their physical attacks are enhanced by Dark-element damage and have a chance to inflict Curse with each successful attack. They each perform two actions in every round of combat. (Just wait until you feel Doppelganger Brandt use Berserk and follow it up immediately with an attack. Ouch!) In short, this fight can end before the first round of combat is over, leaving you looking at the Game Over screen.

HP 410-513

Dark resistance is vital for this battle. Darksteel Shields (plus a Dark Cape for your designated healer) reduce incoming damage considerably. Lux and Mysterio are necessities. Use both abilities during the first round, keep Mysterio active, and consider reapplying Lux when any character is killed and subsequently resurrected.

Inflict as much Light-based damage as you can, but you may be hard-pressed to keep everyone healed. The Doppelganger HP pool may not seem like much compared to other bosses you have faced leading up to them, but Aire and Brandt are quick to use Cura when it's necessary. Try to use abilities that boost attacks (Ditty, Magic Mojo, Amplify, etc.) so your designated attack characters can take down a target with one hit without a chance for healing.

BOSS

At the end of the battle, you obtain the **Lamp of Truth**. Take your prize and return to the Magic Laboratory under Horne Castle.

WALKTHROUGH

163

MAGIC LABORATORY

ENEMIES IN NORTH CAVES

- GHOUL [A]
- BUFFOHELM [A]
- HOBGOBLIN
- ORC LORD
- ARCH DEMON
- LIZARDHAWK

ITEMS FROM CHESTS

BLACK BOOK	EVIL LANCE
DARKAGA TOME	STAR EARRING
DARKNESS STAFF	

ITEMS FROM PEOPLE

DESOLATOR TOME

LEGEND

1	DARKNESS STAFF
2	EVIL LANCE
3	DARKAGA TOME
4	BLACK BOOK
5	STAR EARRING

A

1F

HORNE CASTLE

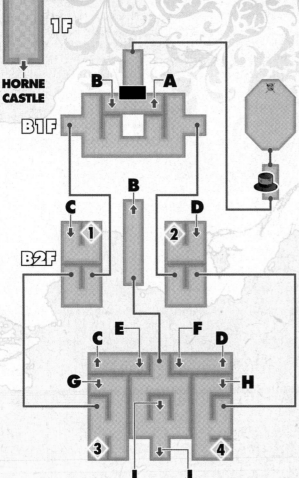

B1F

B2F

3 **4**

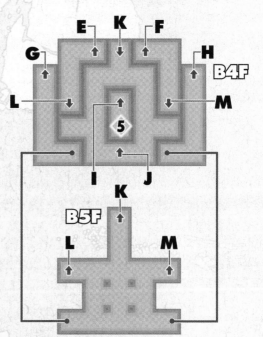

B4F

B5F

Born Under a Baaa-ad Sign

Retrace your steps to the place where you watched the king and his minster previously. Unfortunately, a magical door was erected while the party was at the Witch's Mansion. The sheep statue on B5F provides a reminder of the importance of what

you learned of Horne's sheep previously at the windmill. Head down to B5F (collect the items if you haven't already) and interact with the statue.

The first thing to do on B5F is to take the northern stairs to reach a pair of chests a few levels higher. The northwestern stairs lead to a **Darkness Staff,** while a trip up the northeastern stairs yields an **Evil Lance**.

To unlock the door decorated with sheep, you must ascend the southern stairs (it doesn't matter which side) on B5F to reach the smaller sheep statues on B1F. Touch the sheep in the following order: southeast, northwest, northeast, southwest.

After the door opens, return to B5F using the opposite stairs you used before (if you need to collect the chest on the way back down). The gear used in the battle against the Doppelgangers should work well against the upcoming boss, so if you never made changes, the party should still be set up properly. Return to the large room where you observed the minister and king plotting, and speak with the king to start the next fight.

Satan

HP	3000-3750
WEAKNESSES	LIGHT
RESISTS	DARK (ABSORBS)
ABILITIES	ARCANE FOCUS, DARKRA, DARKAGA, CURA
STEAL	X-POTION, PHOENIX DOWN, DARKBRINGER
DROPS	AMETHYST, DIAMOND

Four arms for Satan means four actions per round of combat. His physical attacks (expect to see at least two of these each round) are boosted by Level 2 Dark-element damage, making Dark-element resistance vital to surviving this battle. Arcane Focus hits the entire party and is Satan's only attack that doesn't deal Dark-element damage.

There are two system messages to watch for during this battle. When Satan assumes Demon Lord stance, he's immune to physical attacks for a few rounds. When Demon God stance is active, Magic attacks inflict no damage. Pay close attention to these stance changes! Don't waste any charged-up attacks because you were impatient or inattentive.

Beyond the stances, there isn't much to this fight beyond using Lux during the first turn (and reapplying it if anyone is killed and resurrected during the battle), keeping Mysterio active, and keeping everyone alive so they can whittle away the boss's HP with Light-element attacks and spells. With at least 3000 HP and random immunity to different types of attacks at different times, don't expect a short fight.

BOSS

On to the Star Chamber

After defeating the boss, you obtain the Dark Fencer Crown. Use the teleporter to return to the dungeon of Castle Horne. Visit the queen's chambers off the throne room and speak with the king. He hands over the **Desolator Tome**, a powerful Black Magic spell.

Stop by the Town of Horne Item Shop, which has some new items for sale. The items for sale previously are now available from the woman behind the counter, and she has added a Wind Shield to her inventory. When you're finished checking out Horne, travel to Spelvia and speak with Rolan.

You obtained the crown of the Dark Fencer!

TOWN OF HORNE ITEM SHOP

ITEM	COST	DESCRIPTION
CYCLONE STAFF	295 G	ATTACK +1, MAGIC ATTACK +4 (WIND)
TEMPEST PIKE	530 G	ATTACK +3 (WIND)
DARKSTEEL SHIELD	450 G	DEFENSE +2, MAGIC DEFENSE +2, EVADE/MAGIC EVADE +5. BLOCKS DARK.
DARK FENCER ARMOR	850 G	DEFENSE +10, MAGIC DEFENSE +7, ATTACK POWER/ STRENGTH +10%
AERO TOME	500 G	BLACK MAGIC: WIND-ELEMENT ATTACK. MAGIC ATTACK: 5/ AP COST: 2.
AERORA TOME	1500 G	BLACK MAGIC: WIND-ELEMENT ATTACK. MAGIC ATTACK: 12/ AP COST: 3.
AEROGA TOME	5000 G	BLACK MAGIC: WIND-ELEMENT ATTACK. MAGIC ATTACK: 5/ AP COST: 2.
SHELL TOME	1000 G	WHITE MAGIC: MAGIC DEFENSE INCREASED 50% / AP COST: 2.
PROTECT TOME	1000 G	WHITE MAGIC: DEFENSE INCREASED 50%. AP COST: 2.
ETHER	1000 G	PROVIDES A SMALL AP BOOST.

Choices, Choices

If you like, you can pick up the final four Crowns (Ninja, Sage, Scribe, and Storyteller) from the Extra Dungeons before you head down to the bosses in the Star Chamber. The downside to this plan is that you gain levels, which means the final boss becomes more difficult when you face him at higher levels. The only way to survive the battle is to use gems to boost armor, weapons, and shields. If you want to visit the Extra Dungeons first, consider spending time in Urbeth to build up your gil account. There are items for sale in each dungeon that are incredibly expensive!

You could always complete the Star Chamber first, then visit the Extra Dungeons because the game allows you to continue to play even after you defeat the final boss. The downside is that you won't have access to the final four Crowns for the Star Chamber.

STAR CHAMBER

ITEMS FROM CHESTS

PHOENIX DOWN	HERO'S WILL
RIBBON	HI-ETHER
FRESH MEAT	KIKU-ICHIMONJI
ETHER	X-POTION
FORTUNE EGG	

LEGEND

1	PHOENIX DOWN
2	FRESH MEAT
3	RIBBON
4	ETHER
5	KIKU-ICHIMONJI
6	HERO'S WILL
7	HI-ETHER
8	FORTUNE EGG
9	X-POTION

1F

WORLD MAP

B1F

BELPHEGOR

A

ASMODEUS

B3F

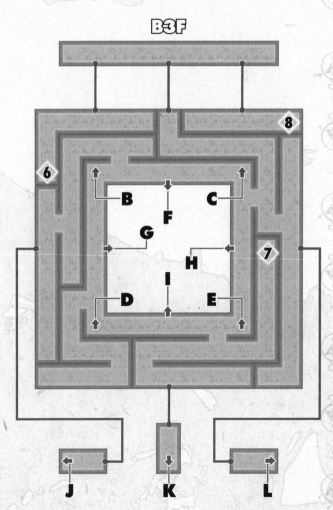

LEVIATHAN

B2F

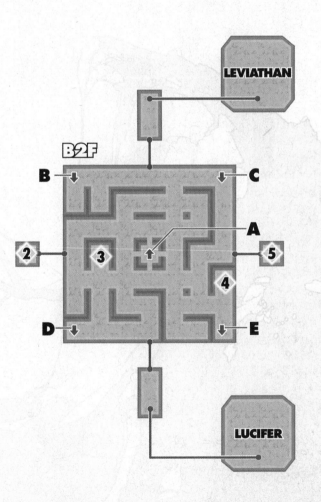

LUCIFER

SATAN   MAMMON   BEELZEBUB

J   K   L

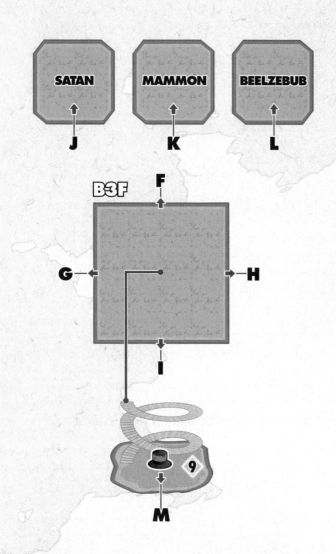

B3F

F

G   H

I

9

M

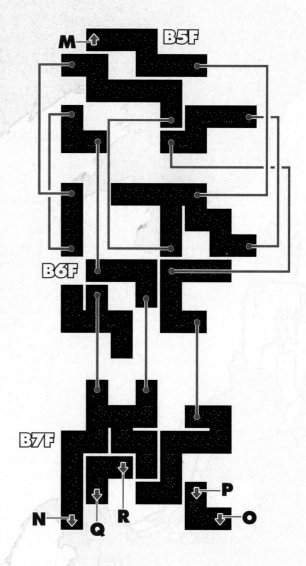

B5F

M

B6F

B7F

N   Q   R   P   O

ENEMIES IN STAR CHAMBER

METAL FLAN [B]

DOPPELGANGER [AIRE A]

DOPPELGANGER [BRANDT A]

DOPPELGANGER [JUSQUA A]

DOPPELGANGER [YUNITA A]

GHOUL [A]

SEA DEVIL [A]

BUFFOHELM [A]

MINOTAUR [A]

WRAITH

ARCH DEMON

IRON GOLEM

VAMPIRE BAT

TROLLUD ZOMBIE

NIDHOGG

BEHEMOTH

BULLKING

EVIL KNIGHT

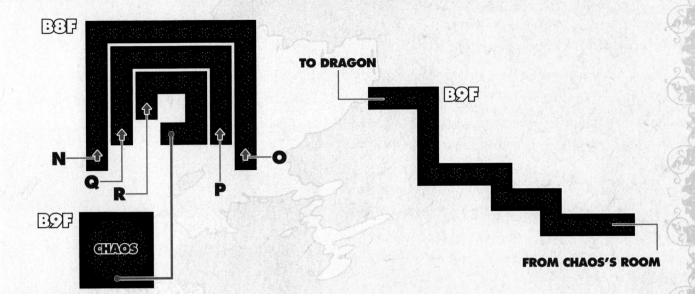

B8F

N

Q

R

P

O

B9F

CHAOS

TO DRAGON

B9F

FROM CHAOS'S ROOM

What's in Store in the Star Chamber

Before you depart for the Star Chamber, here are a few things you should know:

1. There are eight bosses waiting for you inside.

2. There is no set order for facing the bosses. You can skip everything and face the final boss immediately.

3. You lose access to every Crown while inside the Star Chamber until you unlock them by defeating the first seven bosses.

4. Defeating each boss unlocks four Crowns (except for the first boss, which only unlocks three). The Crowns are unlocked in a set order (starting with Wayfarer and ending with Storyteller, assuming you have obtained that crown) and aren't assigned to specific bosses.

5. You can collect every chest inside the Star Chamber without triggering a single boss fight. However, you may not want to try to collect every chest before gaining access to at least the first set of Crowns, because the enemies inside are brutal.

6. The first seven bosses you face in the Star Chamber are powered-up versions of bosses you faced before. The strategies are similar to what was presented the first time you faced them. Crown-specific mentions will be reduced in the strategy, since you may not have access to certain Crowns—depending on when you decide to face a given boss.

7. Take a Torch or two. The Star Chamber is dark!

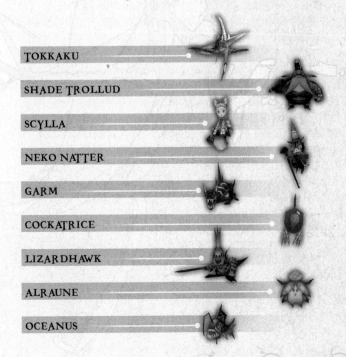

TOKKAKU

SHADE TROLLUD

SCYLLA

NEKO NATTER

GARM

COCKATRICE

LIZARDHAWK

ALRAUNE

OCEANUS

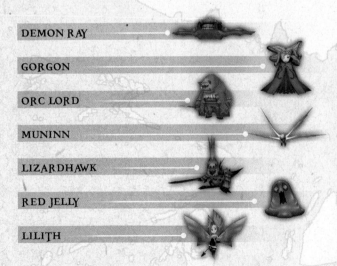

DEMON RAY

GORGON

ORC LORD

MUNINN

LIZARDHAWK

RED JELLY

LILITH

Freelance Assignment

For your first trip to the Star Chamber, Lux takes on an even bigger significance to the party. Your characters are limited to the weapons and Magic Tomes they carry (no access to Crowns means that there is no access to extra abilities), so they need every bit of help they can get. Regardless of the boss you choose to face first, apply Lux immediately in that fight and keep it active!

To reach the Star Chamber, fly to Cetus's location and guide him south of Urbeth to a dark blue bubble that appears in the water. Upon entering the dungeon, everyone is turned into a Freelancer, and the party is locked out of every other Crown. While you could skip to any boss, you should strongly consider tackling Belphegor first. Belphegor doesn't have many tricks, as long as you are patient with the fight, and you don't need to travel far from the entrance to initiate the battle.

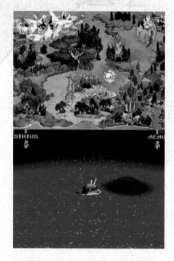 

Asmodeus is also near the entrance to the Star Chamber, but since Asmodeus uses so many different elements, you may want to consider skipping this boss until you have an Elementalist in the party. Lucifer, one level lower, is a good candidate for an early fight due to its mere two actions per turn.

Belphegor [B] & Cubes

HP	(BELPHEGOR) 3400-4250, (CUBES) 1200-1500
WEAKNESSES	WATER
RESISTS	ALL (ABSORBS FIRE)
ABILITIES	(BELPHEGOR) FIRAGA, FIRA, CURA, BALLS OF FIRE. (CUBES) FIRAGA, FIRA
STEAL	(BOTH) BOMB FRAGMENT, (BELPHEGOR ONLY) PHOENIX DOWN, FLAME CAPE
DROPS	AMETHYST, DIAMOND

Belphegor is accompanied by three cubes when the fight begins. The Cubes use Fire-element attacks and sometimes inflict Sleep. Belphegor uses Fire spells, including Balls of Fire, which hits the entire party. They are all resistant to physical damage.

All four enemies begin with a vulnerability to Water. However, if you hit any of them with a Water-based spell or attack item that does not kill them in one shot, it changes their elemental weakness. This also causes the enemies to change which spells they use (from Fira to Watera, for example). The key to this battle is to prepare your characters to resist Fire-based damage and don't give Belphegor and the Cubes the chance to change their elemental affinity.

To keep the fight simple, stick with Desoloator and physical damage boosted with Water-element attacks (either in a character's weapon or using the Spring Gauntlets). This type of elemental damage doesn't change the enemies' vulnerability, and you won't need to worry about other elemental resistances if you came prepared for Fire-element damage.

BOSS

Asmodeus [B]

HP	3500-4375
WEAKNESSES	WATER
RESISTS	EARTH (ABSORBS)
ABILITIES	FIRA, AERORA, AEROGA, QUAKRA, QUAKAGA, SIDEWINDER, MOONLIGHT CURSE, FLASH, SILENCE, BREAK, SLEEP
STEAL	HI-POTION
DROPS	AMETHYST, DIAMOND

Asmodeus initially uses Fire-based spells and Sidewinder—a special ability that inflicts various negative status effects in addition to its Earth-boosted damage. Asmodeus acts four times per round, and its physical attacks also deal Earth damage. Asmodeus's other dirty trick is Moonlight Curse, which instantly removes everyone's Psyched Up status; don't plan on many team-up attacks against this boss!

With every 10% HP lost, a snake head is destroyed, causing Asmodeus to gain a bit more Attack Power and new abilities, including a host of Dark Magic spells. When all the snake heads are destroyed, Asmodeus is limited to two actions per turn.

Be sure to hit Asmodeus with Water-based spells and weapons (don't forget to use Spring Gauntlets if you have a powerful weapon that doesn't do Water damage) and he should fall in short order.

BOSS

There are two bosses on B2F: Lucifer to the south, and Leviathan to the north. B2F is also loaded with chests. Go west from the stairs that lead down from B1F for a **Ribbon**, and farther west to get **Fresh Meat**. Heading east from the stairs leads to an **Ether**, and then a Death Trap guarding a **Kiku-ichimonji**.

Room for Improvement

If you find it difficult to defeat the bosses because they are taking your characters down with one or two hits, consider spending some gems to upgrade your party's gear in Urbeth. It is important to note that these enemies scale with the level of your party, but the party's equipment does not. Upgrade Armor first, because you get the most benefit from it.

Leviathan [B]

HP	(LEAVIATHAN) 4400-5500
WEAKNESSES	FIRE
RESISTS	EARTH, WATER (REFLECTS)
ABILITIES	WATERA, THUNDARA, THUNDAGA, CHARGE, TIDAL WAVE
STEAL	HI-POTION
DROPS	AMETHYST, DIAMOND

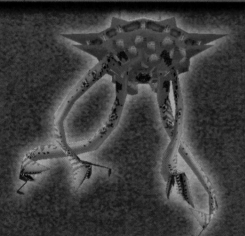

This time around, Leviathan is in full view from the start of the fight. It acts four times each turn, and its physical attacks retain the chance to instantly kill a character with one hit. When Leviathan pauses in its attacks and starts to Charge, it's about to unleash Tidal Wave, which leaves the party in bad shape if it hits. Performing Charge also significantly reduces the amount of damage Leviathan takes.

The good news is that if you can manage to inflict enough damage to Leviathan before it charges four times, you can stop Tidal Wave from happening. Tidal Wave actually happens after the fifth charge, but they're consecutive actions, so you must stop Leviathan during the same round as the fourth charge.

The other bit of good news is that if you have enough resistance to Water damage, Tidal Wave's effectiveness is reduced significantly. The combination of an Ice Shield and a Stream Cape is enough to blunt Tidal Wave's damage. You just need to be ready to revive the inadequately equipped characters right after Tidal Wave hits!

BOSS

Lucifer [B]

HP	3600-4500
WEAKNESSES	DARK
RESISTS	LIGHT (ABSORBS)
ABILITIES	THUNDARA, THUNDAGA, AEROGA, JUDGEMENT BOLT, CURA
STEAL	HI-POTION, LIGHTBRINGER
DROPS	AMETHYST, DIAMOND

Lucifer acts twice per round, is vulnerable to Dark, and is healed by Light-based attacks. When attacking the party, Lucifer uses Thundara, Thundaga, and Aeroga in addition to his Light-enhanced melee attacks that inflict a few negative status effects.

After three turns, Lucifer takes to the air and uses Judgement Bolt to remove everyone's AP. It doesn't inflict any damage, but it stops everyone in your party from performing any action.

Hit Lucifer hard with Dark-elemental attacks and spells right from the start. If you have Lux, it goes a long way toward keeping the party healthy through the phases of the fight when Lucifer is flying.

BOSS

The three bosses on B3F are Satan to the west, Mammon in the south, and Beelzebub to the east.

The items collected from chests on this floor are two odd Accessories (**Fortune Egg** and **Hero's Will**) and a **Hi-Ether**.

Satan [B]

HP	3700-4625
WEAKNESSES	LIGHT
RESISTS	DARK (ABSORBS)
ABILITIES	ARCANE FOCUS, DARKRA, DARKAGA, CURA
STEAL	HI-POTION, DARKBRINGER
DROPS	AMETHYST, DIAMOND

Four arms for Satan means four actions per round of combat. His physical attacks (expect to see at least two of these each round) are boosted by Level 2 Dark-element damage, making Dark-element resistance vital to surviving this battle. Arcane Focus hits the entire party and now deals Dark-element damage.

There are two system messages to watch for during this battle. When Satan assumes Demon Lord stance, he's immune to physical attacks for a few rounds. When Demon God stance is active, Magic attacks inflict no damage. Pay close attention to these stance changes! Don't waste any charged-up attacks because you were impatient or inattentive.

Besides the stances, there isn't much to this fight beyond using Lux during the first turn (and reapplying it if anyone is killed and resurrected during the battle), keeping Mysterio active and keeping everyone alive so they can whittle away the boss's HP with Light-element attacks and spells.

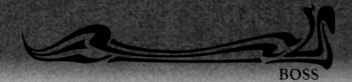

BOSS

Mammon [B]

HP	3200-4250
WEAKNESSES	FIRE
RESISTS	WATER (ABSORBS)
ABILITIES	PROTECT, SHELL, POISON, CONFUSE, DIAMOND DUST, BLIZZARD DANCE
STEAL	HI-POTION, MAMMON'S SPEAR
DROPS	AMETHYST, DIAMOND

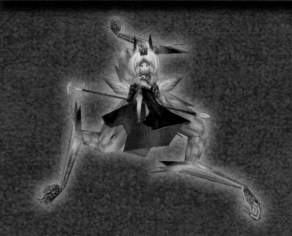

Mammon initially acts four times per turn, and uses Protect and Shell to make it harder to damage her. Offensively, she relies on Diamond Dust (a Water-element ability that hits everyone) and Poison at first. Her physical attacks include a Water-based damage boost.

Mammon loses an arm when she hits 90% HP, a second when she hits 80% HP, and her final arm when she hits 70% HP. Each arm lost reduces her number of actions per turn by one. When all three arms are gone, Mammon drops to the floor and acts twice each turn. On the ground, Mammon often uses Confuse and Blizzard Dance, which is a more powerful version of Diamond Dust.

It is important to keep Mysterio active at all times. Diamond Dust and Blizzard Dance can wipe out an unprotected party in short order. Don't worry about removing Poison, but Confuse can complicate things if it hits your Elementalist. Use Fire weapons and spells to deal damage most effectively. This won't be a quick battle due to Mammon's use of Shell and Protect, but your characters shouldn't suffer much damage as long as Mysterio remains active.

BOSS

Beelzebub [B]

HP	4200-5250
WEAKNESSES	NONE
RESISTS	ALL
ABILITIES	FIRAGA, FIRA, BEZETEOR, FALL OF ANGELS
STEAL	HI-POTION, NECRONOMICON
DROPS	AMETHYST, DIAMOND

Beelzebub is resistant to all element-based spells and attacks. It acts four times each round, and typically uses Fira or Firaga in most rounds. Its physical attacks inflict a variety of negative status ailments as well.

Every few turns, Beelzebub rises into the air and hovers. At the end of a few more turns, it uses Fall of Angels, which deals heavy damage to everyone and may inflict any number of characters with Confuse or Sleep. Deal sufficient damage to Beelzebub while it's in the air and it crashes to the ground, hurting itself with an ability called Bezeteor.

The key to this battle is boosting the party's physical defense or reducing Beelzebub's attack power. That means including either a Scholar (Quell) or Bard (Motet) in the party. If you want to include a spellcaster in the group that tackles Beelzebub, use the Leaf category of spells, Desolator, or a Black Mage with Magic Might.

BOSS

After clearing these seven bosses, you again have access to every Crown unlocked up to this point. There's only one obstacle remaining between the world and peace: The three forms of Chaos. To reach Chaos's chamber, carefully follow the maps with the starry background. There are no chests to collect during this last stretch, so stick to the path that leads to Chaos.

Setting Up Your Party's Offense

When it comes to the "best way" to attack Chaos, there are no right or wrong answers. Chaos has equal resistance to all types of damage. Use the Crowns you like, equip weapons, distribute Magic Tomes, and assign abilities based on your experiences thus far in the game. Just remember that at least one character needs to be responsible for keeping the others alive, and an Elementalist in the party makes the healer's life much easier!

Chaos (1st form)

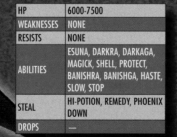

HP	6000-7500
WEAKNESSES	NONE
RESISTS	NONE
ABILITIES	ESUNA, DARKRA, DARKAGA, MAGICK, SHELL, PROTECT, BANISHRA, BANISHGA, HASTE, SLOW, STOP
STEAL	HI-POTION, REMEDY, PHOENIX DOWN
DROPS	—

Don't let the top hat and cloak fool you. Chaos is no gentleman! Chaos gets two actions each turn and uses a variety of Black and White Magic spells. Watch out for Haste, Slow, and especially Stop—which keeps one character from taking any action for a few turns.

Mysterio is a big help with all the incoming elemental damage, and you could even use Mirror with a Black Mage in the party (just be careful with healing spells if it's active), since Chaos isn't immune to any type of damage.

The most important thing to remember about this fight is that the character responsible for Lux needs to end this fight with at least four AP. When you defeat this initial form of Chaos, you are awarded experience points and you are able to view the post-battle screen, but the party begins the next battle without an opportunity to restore HP or AP.

BOSS

Chaos (2nd form)

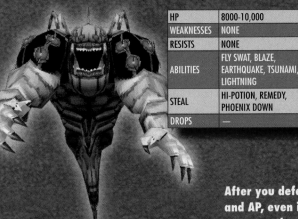

HP	8000-10,000
WEAKNESSES	NONE
RESISTS	NONE
ABILITIES	FLY SWAT, BLAZE, EARTHQUAKE, TSUNAMI, LIGHTNING
STEAL	HI-POTION, REMEDY, PHOENIX DOWN
DROPS	—

The second form of Chaos also gets two actions per turn, but initially sticks to physical attacks and the Fly Swat ability. Fly Swat is the bane of any party that enters this fight with low health.

At the start of this battle, Boost until Lux is applied and everyone in the group is back up to full HP. Even Mysterio can wait in this fight—until Chaos hits 75% health, no incoming damage has an elemental aspect to it. Once Chaos starts using its other abilities, however, Mysterio is a necessity.

After you defeat this form of Chaos, everyone in the party is restored to full HP and AP, even if they were dead when battle ended. One more form to go until you save the world!

BOSS

Chaos (final form), Left Arm, Right Arm

HP	(CHAOS) 9999-12,498, (EACH ARM) 4000-5000
WEAKNESSES	NONE
RESISTS	NONE
ABILITIES	(CHAOS) BIG BANG, BANISHRA, DARKRA, DARKGA, TSUNAMI, EARTHQUAKE, BLACK HOLE, CURA, BLAZE (RIGHT ARM) HURL, (LEFT ARM) CURAGA, CURSE, HASTE, SLOW, STOP, FLASH, CONFUSE, POISON, DEATH
STEAL	HI-POTION, REMEDY, PHOENIX DOWN
DROPS	—

This stage of the fight begins with Chaos watching from the sidelines as the party takes on its Left Arm and Right Arm. Each Arm acts once per round of battle. The Left Arm has a host of abilities, but nothing you haven't encountered already. The Right Arm only has one ability (which it mixes in with physical attacks), but it's brutal. Hurl turns one character into a missile that's aimed at another character. Both characters involved in the attack lose a good chunk of their HP, but at least the attack's animation is fun to watch.

When both Arms have been defeated, Chaos enters the fray. Most of its abilities are carry-overs from the previous form of Chaos, but Big Bang and Black Hole are both new. Big Bang is exactly what it sounds like: a gigantic explosion that hits the entire party with non-elemental magic damage. Two of these in the same turn could end the battle, so it's vital to keep everyone at maximum HP as much as possible. Think of Black Hole as an eraser. The character hit by Black Hole is removed from the fight for four turns. There's nothing you can do to bring back that character, so you'll need a back-up plan for healing if your designated healer is the one targeted.

BOSS

Congratulations! There's Still More to Do

After defeating the final form of Chaos, run to the exit and fly out. Enjoy the ending! Save after watching everything and you can continue your game to complete some of the tasks necessary to unlock all the images on the loading screen. For a full list of these tasks, check out the end of the Game Basics section.

EXTRAS
Extending Your Adventure

There's much more to this game than just the storyline adventure. The following section details the other goals you can accomplish while playing *Final Fantasy: The 4 Heroes of Light*. Whether you tackle the following tasks before or after you defeat the final boss of the adventure is completely up to you.

Unlocking the Load Screen Images

To unlock the final seven images on the loading screen, you must accomplish the following tasks (each of these tasks unlocks one image):

- Have 9,999,999 gil on hand
- Clear all Extra Dungeons
- Have every Crown at Level 3
- Strengthen any armor, shield, or weapon to +99
- Open 100% of treasure chests
- Obtain one of every item
- While in animal form, speak to every animal

Most of these are accomplished with a significant investment of time to gather sufficient resources. The best way to earn gil is to spend time at Thauzand's storefront mini-game. After you unlock the on-hand gil image, start spending the gil in the Extra Dungeons to help with the "Obtain one of every item" challenge. Extra Dungeons are also the only way to pick up enough Diamonds to complete the Level 3 Crown challenge. Strengthening any armor, shield or weapon to level +99 while spending gems on Crowns at the same time calls for a significant number of gems. Stick a Merchant (or a Storyteller with the Finder or Keeper ability) in your party to collect gems faster.

Difficult to Acquire Items

Many items are fairly easy to collect. Anything for sale after the encounter with Rolan in Rolan's Soul remains available for purchase indefinitely. Except for the items in the Pirate's Hideout, items from chests never change and don't go away; you can collect them at any point. Multiplayer Shop inventory remains static for the entire adventure. For the following items, you have a relatively small window of opportunity to obtain them. For the items that are obtained from a boss, if you don't get the item in question (whether it's a Steal or Drop item), you must start from your last save and try the boss fight again.

ITEMS OBTAINED FROM PEOPLE DURING THE ADVENTURE

- Inherited Ring from Kuore in Horne
- Apollo's Talisman from Apollo in Liberte
- Mythril Hammer from the Weapon Shop vendor in Invidia

ITEMS AVAILABLE FOR SALE ONLY BEFORE DEFEATING ROLAN IN ROLAN'S SOUL

- Elementalist Robe in Invidia or Spelvia
- Ranger Outfit in Invidia or Spelvia
- Traveler's Garb in Horne or Guera
- Black Ring in Spelvia
- Silence Cape in Arbor
- Flame Dagger in Liberte or Invidia

ITEMS UNIQUE TO BOSSES

ITEM	BOSS
EARTH SWORD	DROP FROM FIRST VERSION OF SAND DEVIL
LIGHTBRINGER	STEAL FROM EITHER VERSION OF ROLAN OR LUCIFER
CLAUSTRUM	STEAL FROM THE FIRST VERSION OF MAMMON
DARKBRINGER	STEAL FROM EITHER VERSION OF SATAN
ADVENTURER'S GARB	DROP/STEAL FROM ADVENTURER

CHESTS IN EXTRA DUNGEONS

The items from the chests on floors 70 and 90 in the Extra Dungeons are unique to those chests. These chests reappear every time you restart an Extra Dungeon, and the item found inside changes. The full list of potential items is included in the Extra Dungeons section of the guide.

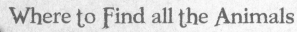

Where to Find all the Animals

Many animals change locations depending on the time of day, but they remain in those two spots throughout the adventure. However, there's one animal you must get before you first visit Spelvia. Rekoteh's cat in Invidia vanishes after you leave for Spelvia, so talk to the kitty before you depart in search of Rolan.

It isn't necessary to speak with Faithful Fox every time you encounter him. Speaking with him once is enough.

TOWN OF HORNE	LOCATION (DAY)	LOCATION (NIGHT)
SHEEP A	NEAR THE WINDMILL	CAN'T SPEAK WITH IT
SHEEP B	NEAR THE WINDMILL	CAN'T SPEAK WITH IT
DOG	WEST OF THE ITEM SHOP	INSIDE A HOME

GUERA	LOCATION (DAY)	LOCATION (NIGHT)
PIG A	NORTHWEST OF THE ITEM SHOP	NORTHWEST OF THE ITEM SHOP
PIG B	BEHIND THE LOCKED DOOR (NEED MAGIC KEY)	NOT FOUND
PIG C	NEAR THE MAGIC SHOP WITH THREE DOORS	NEAR THE MAGIC SHOP WITH THREE DOORS
CAT A	BEHIND THE LOCKED DOOR (NEED MAGIC KEY)	NOT FOUND
CAT B	BEHIND THE LOCKED DOOR (NEED MAGIC KEY)	NOT FOUND
CAT C	NEAR THE WELL EAST OF THE ENTRANCE	NEAR THE LAKE IN THE NORTHWEST PART OF TOWN
CAT D	ON THE WALL ABOVE THE MULTIPLAYER SHOP	NOT FOUND
GULL	BEHIND THE LOCKED DOOR (NEED MAGIC KEY)	NOT FOUND

LIBERTE	LOCATION (DAY)	LOCATION (NIGHT)
GULL A	NEAR THE ENTRANCE TO LIBERTE TOWN	NEAR THE INN IN LIBERTE TOWN
GULL B	NEAR THE MYSTERIOUS TOWER IN LIBERTE TOWN	NEAR THE MYSTERIOUS TOWER IN LIBERTE TOWN
GULL C	NEAR THE BOAT ON THE NORTH SIDE OF LIBERTE PORT	NEAR THE BOAT ON THE NORTH SIDE OF LIBERTE PORT
GULL D	SOUTH OF THE ITEM SHOP IN LIBERTE PORT	NEAR THE INN IN LIBERTE PORT
CAT A	NEAR THE CORAL-COVERED HOUSE IN LIBERTE TOWN	NOT FOUND
CAT B	HOUSE EAST OF THE INN IN LIBERTE TOWN	NOT FOUND

TOWN OF URBETH	LOCATION (DAY)	LOCATION (NIGHT)
DOG A	BETWEEN THE HOMES SOUTH OF THE ACCESSORY SHOP	NEAR THE BAR
DOG B	IN THE ALLEY NEAR THE SORCERER'S SHOP	NEAR THE ARMOR SHOP
DOG C	IN FRONT OF THE MULTIPLAYER SHOP	IN FRONT OF THE MULTIPLAYER SHOP
DOG D	INSIDE THE EASTERN HOUSE, SOUTH OF THE ACCESSORY SHOP	INSIDE THE EASTERN HOUSE, SOUTH OF THE ACCESSORY SHOP

ARBOR	LOCATION
FERRET A	NEAR THE ENTRANCE TO THE WORLD MAP
FERRET B	NEAR THE ITEM SHOP
FERRET C	NEAR THE MULTIPLAYER SHOP
FERRET D	NEAR THE GREAT TREE SAPLING EAST OF THE QUEEN'S ROOM

INVIDIA	LOCATION
POLAR BEAR A	CENTER COURTYARD OF THE EXTERIOR PART OF TOWN
POLAR BEAR B	NEAR THE GIRL WITH THE MATH GAME
CAT	IN REKOTEH'S ROOM BEFORE THE TRIP TO SPELVIA. AFTER THE WORLD CHANGES, THE CAT IS GONE.

SPELVIA	LOCATION
GOAT A	SOUTHWEST CORNER OF THE EXTERIOR AREA
GOAT B	OUTSIDE THE DOUBLE DOORS LEADING TO THE THRONE ROOM
GOAT C	WEST OF THE DOUBLE DOORS LEADING TO THE THRONE ROOM
GOAT D	IN THE HALLWAY LEADING TO THE THRONE ROOM

Battling the Ogre Bear

The Ogre Bear that guards the Animal Path remains in place after Aire and Lilibelle's first encounter, so you are free to return to face it at any point. Facing the creature is the only way to get an additional Ribbon, and you must use Steal to get it.

If you want to defeat the Ogre Bear, get an Energy Screen and prepare for an all-out physical battle. The Ogre Bear has no evasion, so stick with powerful melee attacks to take it down. There's no other reward for defeating the Ogre Bear, so enjoy your victory over the beast!

Extra Dungeons

The Extra Dungeons in *Final Fantasy: the 4 Heroes of Light* are available once you obtain the Master Key after defeating Greaps in the Magic Laboratory under Horne Castle. The Extra Dungeons are the four towers scattered around the world map. Each is assigned a level of difficulty, from 1 to 4.

EXTRAS

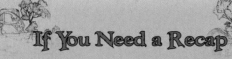
Speak with the hooded man that appears in front of each tower for an explanation of how the towers work. After you start the dungeon, speak with the same man to get a progress report and an option to restart the tower.

FLOOR	EVENT
FLOOR 10	BOSS FIGHT
FLOOR 20	PORTAL TO SURFACE
FLOOR 30	BOSS FIGHT
FLOOR 40	VENDOR
FLOOR 50	BOSS FIGHT
FLOOR 60	PORTAL TO SURFACE
FLOOR 70	CHEST CONTAINING ARMOR
FLOOR 80	FIGHT A DRAGON AND OBTAIN ORIHALCON
FLOOR 90	CHEST CONTAINING A WEAPON
FLOOR 100	FINAL BOSS FIGHT

All four towers work in a similar fashion. When you begin exploring, your goal is to find the staircase on each floor that leads up to the next level. There are no downward stairs in the Extra Dungeons, leaving you with two voluntary options to return to the world map. One is a portal that becomes available on every tenth floor. Your progress in the tower is saved automatically (you still need to save your game's progress). The other option for returning to the World Map is through the use of a Dragon Wing. The Dragon Wing allows

But if your whole party dies or you use a Dragon Wing, your progress won't be saved. Best be careful!

you to exit at any point, but you aren't credited for any floors you cleared beyond the last multiple-of-ten floor (10, 20, 30, etc.).

The items found in the chests on Levels 70 and 90 are randomly determined from the following lists.

Level 70 (Armor)	Level 90 (Weapon)
Musician's Robe	Apollo's Harp
Storyteller Robe	Artemis Bow
Scribe Gown	Excalibur
Beastmaster Coat	Giant's Toothpick
Sage Robe	Zodiac Spear
Ninja Robe	Great Wizard Stave
Seamstress Clothes	Necronomicon
	Wizard's Axe

What's Waiting Inside

The first eight floors have relatively simple layouts. The stairs that lead upward are placed randomly on each floor. The ninth floor has a much larger, more intricate layout that requires a bit more exploration before you discover the staircase to the tenth floor. The tenth floor has a special event, and an exit portal back to the World Map. This pattern repeats for subsequent sets of 10 floors, meaning floors 11 through 18 are relatively simple to navigate, floor 19 is tougher, and floor 20 has something different waiting for you. All four Extra Dungeons follow the same pattern.

Additional Chests

While you're exploring the rest of the dungeon, look for treasure chests beyond the ones that appear on Level 70 and Level 90. Most of the items from these chests are common restorative items, such as Potions. However, you could get lucky and obtain an Elixir. These chests are the only sources of Elixirs, which make the Salve-maker Crown really shine.

Obtaining Orihalcon

Whoa! That's Orihalcon, isn't it!? With that I could make your equipment even stronger yet!

The boss on Level 80 in each tower is a dragon. When you defeat the dragon, your spoil is a lump of Orihalcon. These dragons are the only source of Orihalcon, the element needed by the Upgrade shop in the Town of Urbeth to improve the party's weapons, armor, and shields.

Why Reset Dungeons?

Why would you need to reset the dungeons after claiming the Crowns held by the final boss in each? The first reason is to get enough Orihalcon to unlock the potential to raise your equipment at the Upgrade shop to +99. You won't get enough Orihalcon with just one trip through each dungeon.

Secondly, there are eight pieces of armor and eight weapons available from the chests on Levels 70 and 90. Even if you were fortunate and picked up a different item from each tower, you'd need to visit each tower twice before you had everything available.

Additionally, the bosses in the Extra Dungeons are the only farmable source of Diamonds, which are necessary to upgrade weapons, armor, and shields beyond +77.

Save After Each Boss

There's no penalty for exiting the tower after defeating a boss. Get in the habit of taking down one boss and exiting the tower to save your progress. While you're out, take the opportunity to scout out the next boss and set your party up with the proper offensive and defensive equipment. When you return to the tower, you'll pick up one floor above the last boss you took down successfully.

Moonsand Ruins

The reward for defeating the boss on Level 100 is the Ninja Crown.

From Horne, fly north over the Witch's Mansion until a tower appears on the map. This is the Moonsand Ruins, which has a difficulty level of 1.

This is a rather strange tower. It is built so that its floors change every time you enter it.

Luckily, your progress will be saved each time you manage to clear ten floors. You can also leave the tower then.

LEVEL 40 ITEMS FOR SALE

ITEM	COST	DESCRIPTION
X-POTION	400 G	PROVIDES A GREAT BIG HP BOOST.
PHOENIX DOWN	100 G	BRINGS YOU BACK FROM THE DEAD.
HI-ETHER	10,000 G	RESTORES YOUR AP.
GUGNIR	65,000 G	ATTACK +21
UNYIELDING SHIELD	100,000 G	DEFENSE +5
ANTIMAGE	100,000 G	MAGIC DEFENSE +5
HIDE SHIELD	100,000 G	EVADE/MAGIC EVADE +15

ENEMIES IN MOONSAND RUINS

JACK LANTERN [C]

DOPPELGANGER [AIRE C]

DOPPELGANGER [JUSQUA C]

DOPPELGANGER [BRANDT C]

DOPPELGANGER [YUNITA C]

IMP [C]

AIR RAY [B]

ASPIDOCHELON [B]

HELLHOUND [B]

ICHTHON [B]

MEDUSA [B]

VAMPIRE BAT [B]

DEMON [A]

NUE [A]

ARP

BULLKING

GIANT MOTH

KAISER PENGUIN

LILITH

NEKO NATTER

LEVEL 10

Behugemoth [B]

The Behugemoth acts three times per round of combat. While its two abilities deal Light damage, the Behugemoth isn't resistant to any element. When the Behugemonth's health drops below 50%, watch out for more Lightning Bolt attacks. The Behugemoth has multiple ways to paralyze your characters, so be ready to remove each negative status effect.

HP	2000-2500
WEAKNESSES	—
RESISTS	—
ABILITIES	LIGHTNING BOLT, THUNDARA
STEAL	HI-POTION, X-POTION
DROPS	AMETHYST

Demon Lord

What sets the Demon Lord apart from other enemies that share a similar character model is its weakness. Normally, when you encounter demons, they're vulnerable to Light-based attacks, but the Demon Lord stands up to Light damage just fine; it's Water damage that it has trouble handling. Set up the party to face Dark-element damage because the Demon Lord's abilities inflict it, and its melee attacks include Dark damage as well as a chance to curse its target.

HP	2500-3125
WEAKNESSES	WATER
RESISTS	LIGHT, DARK (ABSORBS)
ABILITIES	BLADEBLITZ, WORLD OF DARKNESS
STEAL	HI-POTION, X-POTION
DROPS	AMETHYST, DIAMOND

Sand Devil

The Sand Devil acts twice in each round, dishing out Earth-element damage with its abilities and its regular attacks. Even worse, a successful hit carries a 5% chance to petrify its target! At 50% HP, the Sand Devil relies on Sandstorm for most of its actions.

HP	3000-3759
WEAKNESSES	WATER
RESISTS	FIRE, EARTH
ABILITIES	SANDSTORM, QUAKRA
STEAL	—
DROPS	DIAMOND

Bahumut

Bahumut acts twice in each round of combat, and enjoys bathing the party in Fire Breath. Leave the Light-based weapons and spells behind for this fight, but beyond that, anything goes. If you're doing the extra dungeons in order, this is your first taste of Orihalcon. Take it to Urbeth as soon as you finish this fight!

HP	5000-6250
WEAKNESSES	—
RESISTS	LIGHT (ABSORBS)
ABILITIES	FIRE BREATH, CURA, BANISHGA, FLASH
STEAL	—
DROPS	ORIHALCON

Krinjh

This formidable former ally is all that stands between you and the Ninja Crown. Krinjh takes three actions per turn and is difficult to hit with melee attacks. He isn't shy about using Silence, so if you brought any spell casters, they'll need some immunity to it or you'll spend as many rounds restoring their ability to cast spells asactually casting them. His attacks deal Earth damage and sometimes Blind on a successful hit.

HP	8000-10,000
WEAKNESSES	WIND
RESISTS	EARTH
ABILITIES	QUAGA, WATERA, CURA, SILENCE
STEAL	POTION, KRINJH'S ROBE, HOLY BREATH
DROPS	DIAMOND, KRINJH'S ROBE

Krinjh is a big step up even from the other bosses in the Moonsand Ruins, so don't get discouraged if you fall to him a few times. If the fight becomes frustrating, spend some time upgrading armor and weapons in Urbeth. Krinjh hits hard, and the party will need all the protection they can get.

EXTRAS

Holy Tree Tower

The reward for defeating the boss on Level 100 is the Sage Crown.

To reach the Holy Tree Tower, you must use Cetus. Guide Cetus south of Invidia and west of Arbor to a small island shaped like the letter "C." The cave mouth that sticks up in the center of the island is the entrance to the Holy Tree Tower, which has a difficulty level of 2.

LEVEL 40 ITEMS FOR SALE

ITEM	COST	DESCRIPTION
X-POTION	400 G	PROVIDES A GREAT BIG HP BOOST.
PHOENIX DOWN	100 G	BRINGS YOU BACK FROM THE DEAD.
HI-ETHER	10,000 G	RESTORES YOUR AP.
MOONRING BLADE	22,000 G	ATTACK +10, MAGIC ATTACK +10, INFLICTS SUDDEN DEATH.
KOGA SHURIKEN	28,000 G	ATTACK +15, INFLICTS CONFUSION, BLINDNESS.
GUAN YU'S PIKE	55,000 G	ATTACK +18

ENEMIES IN HOLY TREE TOWER

IKKAKU [C]

COWPEL [C]

WIGHT [C]

CAIT SITH [B]

CHIMERA [B]

CLOUD PENGUIN [B]

CU SITH [B]

GREAPS [B]

GHOUL [A]

LAMIA [B]

SILKY [B]

SLIME [B]

BRAINSHARK [A]

WRAITH [A]

ARCH DEMON

COCKATRICE

GORGON

DEMON RAY

VULTURE

MUNIN

Seadevil [B]

LEVEL 10

HP	3000-3750
WEAKNESSES	FIRE
RESISTS	WATER (ABSORBS)
ABILITIES	WATERSPRAY, SILENCE, CONFUSE, POISON
STEAL	HI-POTION, X-POTION
DROPS	AMETHYST

The Seadevil takes three actions per turn; its melee swings deal Water damage and have a chance to inflict Silence or Curse (or both) on a successful attack. Waterspray hits everyone and inflicts a few negative status effects as well. Be prepared to take Water damage, and remove the myriad afflictions the Seadevil uses, and you should do fine.

Nue [B] and Wraith [B]

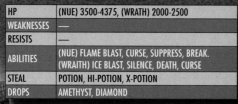

HP	(NUE) 3500-4375, (WRATH) 2000-2500
WEAKNESSES	—
RESISTS	—
ABILITIES	(NUE) FLAME BLAST, CURSE, SUPPRESS, BREAK. (WRAITH) ICE BLAST, SILENCE, DEATH, CURSE
STEAL	POTION, HI-POTION, X-POTION
DROPS	AMETHYST, DIAMOND

This is the first (but not the last) time you face two improved versions of previously encountered enemies in one encounter in the extra dungeons. The Nue enjoys three actions per turn, while the Wraith gets two.

The Nue's attacks sometimes inflict Poison, but they do not include elemental damage. When it hits 50% HP, expect to see more Flame Blasts, and watch out for Break to be mixed in with its attacks.

The Wraith is tough to catch with physical attacks, so take it down with spells. Its attacks sometimes Curse its target. When the Wraith hits 50% HP, it leans more on Ice Blast and Silence, drops the use of Curse and Suppress, and adds Death to its rotation.

Goblin Lord

HP	3500-4375
WEAKNESSES	—
RESISTS	—
ABILITIES	GOBLIN STRIKE, LEAFRA
STEAL	POTION, HI-POTION, X-POTION
DROPS	DIAMOND

If you took every Goblin and Hobgoblin you faced during the adventure and combined them into one creature to fight, that battle still wouldn't be as tough as the one here against the Goblin Lord. With no weaknesses to exploit, you must take down the Goblin Lord with your best abilities and spells.

Handling Leafra isn't a big deal, but this guy's version of Goblin Strike is nasty. At 50% HP, expect to see Goblin Strike taking up most of the Goblin Lord's two actions per turn. If you have problems handling the Goblin Lord, put a Bard or Scholar in the party. They're designed to deal with enemies that focus on dealing melee damage.

Red Dragon

HP	5000-6250
WEAKNESSES	—
RESISTS	FIRE (ABSORBS)
ABILITIES	FIRE BREATH, CURA
STEAL	—
DROPS	ORIHALCON

When an enemy has a single ability, you can be sure that it will be used often. Sure, the Red Dragon has Cura, but you won't see it used until it reaches 25% HP or so. The Red Dragon splits its two actions per turn between melee attacks (which deal Level 2 Fire damage) and Fire Breath, but the more damage it takes, the more often you'll see Fire Breath. Prepare your party to face Fire damage. It's all the Red Dragon uses throughout the entire fight.

Torte

HP	8000-10,000
WEAKNESSES	WIND
RESISTS	EARTH
ABILITIES	SHELL, LEAFRA, LEAFGA, MAGICK, CURA
STEAL	POTION, TORTE'S CLOTHES, HOLY BREATH
DROPS	DIAMOND, TORTE'S CLOTHES

Torte rarely uses any of his three actions per turn for melee attacks. Instead, he relies on Leaf spells (boosted by Magick) for damage. It's really too bad, because his melee attacks sometimes Silence and are boosted with additional Wind damage.

Surprisingly, Torte is one of the easiest boss fights in the game. He's vulnerable to Wind, the same element that fuels Leafra and Leafga, and these are the spells he uses most often. All you really need to do is take a Black Mage and use Mirror. Heal the party after Torte's rare melee attacks and you should be fine.

Mysterious Tower

The reward for defeating the boss on Level 100 is the Storyteller Crown.

The entrance for the Mysterious Tower is in Liberte Town. By the time you get access to the dungeon, Liberte Town is located on Cetus's back, wherever you left him parked on the World Map.

Luckily, your progress will be saved each time you manage to clear ten floors. You can also leave the lighthouse then.

LEVEL 40 ITEMS FOR SALE

ITEM	COST	DESCRIPTION
X-POTION	400	PROVIDES A GREAT BIG HP BOOST.
PHOENIX DOWN	100	BRINGS YOU BACK FROM THE DEAD.
HI-ETHER	10000	RESTORES YOUR AP.
MURAMASA	9000	ATTACK +14, REDUCES FOE'S STATUS LEVELS.
FUMA SHURIKEN	28000	ATTACK +15, INFLICTS POISON, PARALYSIS.
SHIRANUI	50000	ATTACK +20, EVADE +20%

ENEMIES IN MYSTERIOUS TOWER

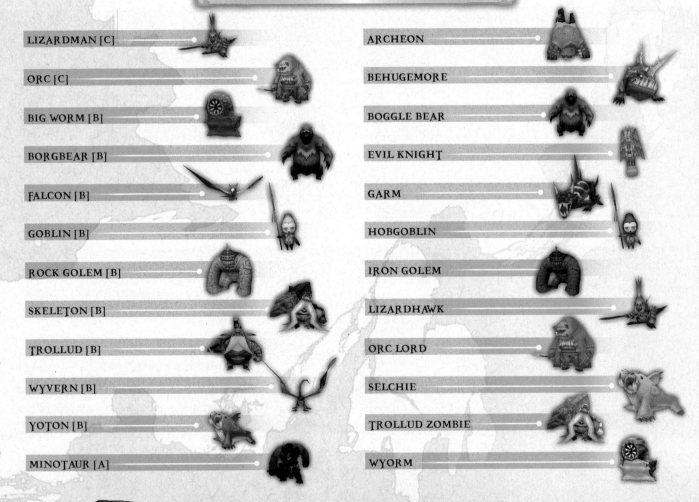

LIZARDMAN [C]

ORC [C]

BIG WORM [B]

BORGBEAR [B]

FALCON [B]

GOBLIN [B]

ROCK GOLEM [B]

SKELETON [B]

TROLLUD [B]

WYVERN [B]

YOTON [B]

MINOTAUR [A]

ARCHEON

BEHUGEMORE

BOGGLE BEAR

EVIL KNIGHT

GARM

HOBGOBLIN

IRON GOLEM

LIZARDHAWK

ORC LORD

SELCHIE

TROLLUD ZOMBIE

WYORM

Minotaur [C]

LEVEL 10

HP	3500-4375
WEAKNESSES	WIND
RESISTS	EARTH
ABILITIES	FULL SWING
STEAL	HI-POTION, X-POTION
DROPS	AMETHYST

The Minotaur spends many of its three actions per turn using Full Swing to clobber the entire party in one attack. All its attacks (including Full Swing) deal Earth damage, so proper equipment helps to blunt incoming damage. When the Minotaur hits 50% HP, expect to see more of its actions spent using Full Swing.

Mythril Golem

HP	4500-5625
WEAKNESSES	—
RESISTS	EARTH (REFLECTS)
ABILITIES	WHIRL BLUDGEON
STEAL	MYTHRIL
DROPS	AMETHYST, DIAMOND

The Mythril Golem starts out using Whirl Bludgeon often and relies on it more and more as its HP drops closer to 0. With three actions each turn, just expect at least one of them to be Whirl Bludgeon. Its attacks deal Earth damage, so you should stick with the equipment you used to take down the Minotaur. However, you're better off using spells to take down the Mythril Golem. Its defense against physical attacks is incredibly high and there are no elemental weaknesses to exploit.

Geri [B] & Freki[B]

HP	(EACH) 3500-4375
WEAKNESSES	(GERI) WATER, (FREKI) FIRE
RESISTS	(GERI) FIRE, (FREKI) WATER
ABILITIES	(GERI) FIRE BREATH, BERSERK (FREKI) ICE BREATH, MAGICK
STEAL	(BOTH) HI-POTION, X-POTION, (GERI) BOMB FRAGMENT, (FREKI)ANTARCTIC WIND
DROPS	DIAMOND

This encounter with Geri and Freki is nearly identical to the fight against them in Rolan's Soul. They're more powerful and each acts twice per round, but everything else remains the same. Combine shields and cloaks with Mysterio to stand up to their powerful elemental attacks. Hit them with the proper element or use non-elemental spells like Leafga, Magic Might, and Desolator.

Dragon

HP	5200-6500
WEAKNESSES	—
RESISTS	FIRE, WATER, WIND, EARTH
ABILITIES	FIRE BREATH
STEAL	—
DROPS	ORIHALCON

The Dragon has more actions per turn (two) than special abilities (one). Be prepared to deal with Fire-based damage, because it uses Fire Breath often throughout the fight. Stick with Light, Dark, or non-elemental weapons and spells to damage this boss. You don't need to worry about any negative status effects, so doubling up on Fire protection with shields and cloaks is a solid strategy.

Rolan & Rekoteh

HP	(ROLAN) 8500-10,625, (REKOTEH) 6500-8125
WEAKNESSES	(ROLAN) —, (REKOTEH) FIRE
RESISTS	(ROLAN) LIGHT, (REKOTEH) WATER
ABILITIES	(ROLAN) THUNDARA, THUNDAGA, CURA, DARKRA, DARKGA (REKOTEH) THUNDAGA, CURA, BLIZZARA, BLIZZAGA, SILENCE, SHELL, PROTECT
STEAL	(BOTH) POTION, HOLY BREATH, (ROLAN) ROLAN'S CLOTHES, (REKOTEH) REKOTEH'S CLOTHES
DROPS	(BOTH) DIAMOND, (ROLAN) ROLAN'S CLOTHES, REKOTEH'S CLOTHES

These siblings each get two actions per turn and have a variety of Black Magic at their disposal. An Elementalist is vital for this fight because it's impossible to be prepared for all the elemental damage types that these two can bring to the battle. If you want maximum protection, go with Water (Rekoteh's attacks) and Light (Rolan's attacks), and just heal through Rolan's occasional Dark spells.

If you have problems with this battle, go after Rekoteh first. Her use of Shell and Protect, combined with her proclivity to heal, extend the fight considerably. She's considered to be in the back row for this fight, so use weapons that target the back row first combined with Fire spells to take her down.

Trial Tower

The reward for defeating the boss on Level 100 is the Scribe Crown.

From the town of Urbeth, fly north and slightly east. There's a peninsula that sticks into the water in the area, and the tower is there.

ENEMIES IN TRIAL TOWER

- IKKAKU [C]
- LIZARDMAN [C]
- MYCONID [C]
- ORC [C]
- AIR RAY [B]
- BASILISK [B]
- BATTER FLY [B]
- GARGOYLE [B]
- BLOOD BAT [B]
- HELLHOUND [B]
- HUGINN [B]
- LAMIA [B]
- MANDRAGORA [B]
- MEDUSA [B]
- RATTATOX [B]
- ROCK GOLEM [B]
- SKELETON [B]
- SUCCUBUS [B]
- TROLLUD [B]

- WYVERN [B]
- BRAINSHARK [A]
- BUFFOHELM [A]
- DEMON [A]
- VAMPIRE BAT [A]
- CARBUNCLE
- SHADE TROLLUD
- SCYLLA
- OCEANUS
- TOKKAKU
- NIDHOGG
- ALRAUNE
- PUMPKING
- FUNGUS
- RED JELLY

LEVEL 40 ITEMS FOR SALE

ITEM	COST	DESCRIPTION
X-POTION	400	PROVIDES A GREAT BIG HP BOOST.
PHOENIX DOWN	100	BRINGS YOU BACK FROM THE DEAD.
HI-ETHER	10,000	RESTORES YOUR AP.
KUNAI	20,000	ATTACK +10
OBORO	50,000	ATTACK +20, EVADE +20%
GIANT NEEDLE	25,000	ATTACK +17

LEVEL 10

Demon Prince

HP	4300-5375
WEAKNESSES	WATER
RESISTS	—
ABILITIES	BLADEBLITZ, WORLD OF DARKNESS, FIRA, FIRAGA
STEAL	HI-POTION, X-POTION
DROPS	AMETHYST

The Demon Prince uses its three actions per turn to hit the party with either Fire damage (two spells) or Dark damage (from Bladeblitz, World of Dark, or its melee attacks). Watch out for a variety of negative status ailments. Melee swings can Curse or Blind, while World of Dark has a chance to inflict anything.

Buffohelm & Ghoul

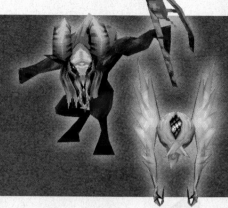

HP	(BUFFOHELM) 4000-5000, (GHOUL) 3500-4375
WEAKNESSES	(BUFFOHELM) FIRE, (GHOUL) —
RESISTS	(BOTH) —
ABILITIES	(BUFFOHELM) CURSE, SILENCE, BREAK, POISON, FLASH, FIRAGA (GHOUL) DARKRA, DARKGA, SILENCE, DEATH, CURSE
STEAL	POTION, HI-POTION, X-POTION
DROPS	AMETHYST, DIAMOND

Both enemies act twice per round of combat and use a variety of Black Magic spells. The Buffohelm's melee attacks have a chance to inflict Curse or Silence, while the Ghoul's attacks can Poison or reduce the target's stats.

Greaps

HP	5500-6875
WEAKNESSES	—
RESISTS	WIND, EARTH
ABILITIES	AEROGA, THUNDRA, CURA
STEAL	HI-POTION, X-POTION
DROPS	DIAMOND

Greaps acts three times each turn and favors Aeroga as its primary attack. Greaps mixes in Thundara, but you're likely to see Aeroga far more often. Its melee attacks deal Wind-aided damage and can either silence its target or put the target to sleep. Greaps is completely immune to both Wind and Earth attacks, so remove any spells or weapons with those elements before you take it on.

Black Dragon

HP	6500-8125
WEAKNESSES	—
RESISTS	DARK
ABILITIES	DARK BREATH, DARKGA, SUPPRESS, CURA
STEAL	—
DROPS	ORIHALCON

All of the Black Dragon's attacks that deal damage have a Dark-element component to them, while the Black Dragon is immune to Dark damage entirely. You don't have any weaknesses to exploit in this fight, but if you're looking for an edge, the Black Dragon's magic defense is slightly lower than its physical defense, so go after it with spells that don't inflict Dark damage.

Adventurer & Faithful Fox

HP	(ADVENTURER) 9000-11,250 (FAITHFUL FOX) 5000-6250
WEAKNESSES	—
RESISTS	(ADVENTURER) — (FAITHFUL FOX) FIRE
ABILITIES	(ADVENTURER) BERSERK, PROTECT, SUPPRESS, CURA, CURAGA (FAITHFUL FOX) MAGICK, PROTECT, SHELL, BERSERK, CURSE, DEATH, BREAK, CONFUSE, FLASH, POISON, SILENCE, FIRA, CURA, CURAGA
STEAL	(BOTH) POTION, (ADVENTURER) ADVENTURER'S GARB, HOLY BREATH (FAITHFUL FOX) HI-POTION, RAVEN'S YAWN
DROPS	(BOTH) DIAMOND, (ADVENTURER) ADVENTURER'S GARB (FAITHFUL FOX) PHOENIX DOWN, X-POTION

Both the Adventurer and the Faithful Fox act twice per turn, but they perform completely different functions. The Faithful Fox focuses on support abilities and hitting the party with negative status effects. The Adventurer spends his actions trying to annihilate individual party members with Berserk-enhanced melee attacks that can Silence or Poison when they land. The Faithful Fox's attacks actually deal Fire damage and include a possibility of Paralysis or Confusion on a successful attack, but lucky for you, the vulpine enemy rarely chooses to do this.

There's not much in the way of elemental damage to avoid, but the Adventurer is a nightmare if you don't do something to blunt his attacks. Bring a Bard (for Motet and Fugue) and Scholar (for Quell) or, better yet, bring both. Take down the Faithful Fox first, as it spends as much time boosting and healing the Adventurer as it does trying to drive you crazy by throwing almost every Dark Magic spell possible at your party.

CHIMERA [A]

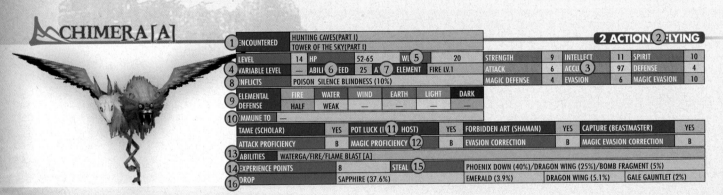

2 ACTION ②**FLYING**

1	ENCOUNTERED	HUNTING CAVES(PART I)												
		TOWER OF THE SKY(PART I)												
	LEVEL	14	HP	52-65	WL⑤	20		STRENGTH	9	INTELLECT	11	SPIRIT	10
4	VARIABLE LEVEL	—	ABILI ⑥ EED	25	A ⑦	ELEMENT	FIRE LV.1	ATTACK	6	ACCU ③	97	DEFENSE	4
8	INFLICTS	POISON SILENCE BLINDNESS (10%)						MAGIC DEFENSE	4	EVASION	6	MAGIC EVASION	10

9 ELEMENTAL DEFENSE	FIRE	WATER	WIND	EARTH	LIGHT	DARK
	HALF	WEAK	—	—	—	—

10 IMMUNE TO	—					
TAME (SCHOLAR)	YES	POT LUCK (I⑪ HOST)	YES	FORBIDDEN ART (SHAMAN)	YES	CAPTURE (BEASTMASTER)	YES
ATTACK PROFICIENCY	B	MAGIC PROFICIENCY ⑫	B	EVASION CORRECTION	B	MAGIC EVASION CORRECTION	B

13	ABILITIES	WATERGA/FIRE/FLAME BLAST [A]			
14	EXPERIENCE POINTS	8	STEAL ⑮	PHOENIX DOWN (40%)/DRAGON WING (25%)/BOMB FRAGMENT (5%)	
16	DROP	SAPPHIRE (37.6%)	EMERALD (3.9%)	DRAGON WING (5.1%)	GALE GAUNTLET (2%)

ENEMY DATA

①ENCOUNTERED	The primary locations where you encounter each enemy. Part I means the encounter takes place before defeating Rolan in Rolan's Soul. Part II means everything that follows.
②# ACTIONS, FLYING	If an enemy has multiple actions per round of combat, or is a flying enemy, the information appears here. Flying enemies are immune to the Quake line of spells, but take more damage from certain types of weapons.
③ENEMY STATS	They have the same effect for enemies as they do for the characters you control during the adventure.
④VARIABLE LEVEL	A YES indicates the creature has a Variable Level. See next page for more information.
⑤WEIGHT	Used in battle calculations. See Game Basics for more information.
⑥ABILITY SPEED	The speed of the enemy's melee attack.
⑦ATTACK ELEMENT	If an enemy has element-based damage added to its regular damage, the information is given here.
⑧INFLICTS	The negative status ailments the enemy's melee attack may inflict, and the percentage chance of application on a successful attack.
⑨ELEMENTAL DEFENSE	The enemy's resistance to the six elements. The possible values are: Half (takes half damage); Weak (takes extra damage); No Effect (takes no damage); Absorbs (Damage amount heals instead of hurts); or Reflects (spell effect hits caster instead of enemy).
⑩IMMUNE TO	The creature is immune to any negative status effect that appears here.
⑪TAME, POT LUCK, FORBIDDEN ART, CAPTURE	If the value is YES, the creature is vulnerable to these Crown-specific abilities.
⑫ATTACK PROFICIENCY, MAGIC PROFICIENCY, EVASION CORRECTION, MAGIC EVASION CORRECTION	These values have two functions. First, they are used in combat situations as described in the Game Basics. Second, they are used in the calcultions for Variable Level enemies on the oppsoite page.
⑬ABILITIES	A list of the abilities available to the enemy. Details about each ability are provided on the following pages.
⑭EXPERIENCE POINTS	The possible rewards.
⑮STEAL	The items obtained through the use of various Bandit abilities. Each enemy encountered carries only one of the items.
⑯DROP	Each enemy drops up to four potential items or gems when defeated. The percentages indicate the likelihood of each item dropping at the end of battle.

Enemies that Scale with the Party's Level

In the first part of the adventure, battles are generally easier when your party's levels are higher than those of the enemies they face. However, after defeating Rolan in Spelvia, there are many monsters whose levels and stats increase in relation to the party's average level.

MONSTER ABILITY LEVEL REVISER

Any enemy with a "yes" next to "Variable Level" scales with the party's level. (If the party's average level is lower than that of the monster, there is no change.) Its HP, Strength, Intellect, Spirit, Attack, Magic Defense, Hit Rate, and Evade stats change based on the following formulae. There's no way to see enemy data in the game; you must refer to this section of the guide.

MINIMUM HP	Enemy HP base value + [(Party average level – Enemy base level) x 2]
MAXIMUM HP	Minimum HP x 1.25
STRENGTH	Enemy Strength base value + (Party average level – Enemy base level) x (1-(2 + Enemy Physical Attack reviser) divided by10))
INTELLECT	Enemy Intellect base value + (Party average level – Enemy base level) x (1-(2 + Enemy Attack Magic reviser) divided by10))
SPIRIT	Enemy Spirit base value + (Party averge level – Enemy level) x (1-(2 + Enemy Magic Evade reviser) divided by10))
ATTACK	Enemy Attack base value + (3 + (Party average level – Enemy level) x (Enemy Strength base value divided by 24))
MAGIC DEFENSE	Enemy Magic Defense base value + 2 + (Party average level – Enemy level) x (Enemy Spirit base divided by100)
HIT RATE	Enemy Hit Rate base value + 95 + (Party average level – Enemy level divided by10)
EVADE	Enemy Evade base + (Party average level – Enemy level divided by10) x (5 – Enemy Evade reviser)

A Little Random

For every creature (even those with static levels), HP could be any number in the range between the Minimum HP and the Maximum HP.

When adjusted with the following formulae, Strength, Intelligence, Spirit, and Evade are also random to a degree.

THE ENEMIES MET IN BATTLE

The following pages provide greater detail for all the enemies and bosses encountered in *Final Fantasy: The 4 Heroes of Light*. Many enemy abilities are the same spells available to your party, but the abilities unique to the creatures in *Final Fantasy: The 4 Heroes of Light* are summarized in the following table.

ENEMY ABILITIES

ABILITY NAME	ELEMENTAL COMPONENT	TARGET	POWER	ACCURACY	ABILITY SPEED	DIMINISHED EFFECT	DESCRIPTION
AIR STORM	WIND LV.1	ENTIRE PARTY	7	98	20	—	WIND-ELEMENT ATTACK
ARCANE FORCE	—	ENTIRE PARTY	15	300	10	—	NON-ELEMENTAL DAMAGE ATTACK, 30% CHANCE TO INFLICT STATUS DOWN ON TARGET
BLADEBLITZ	DARK LV.2	ENTIRE PARTY	6	95	5	YES	DARK-ELEMENT ATTACK
BALL OF FIRE	FIRE LV.2	ENTIRE PARTY	17	95	10	YES	FIRE-ELEMENT ATTACK
BEZETEOR	—	SELF	0	200	1	—	FALLS TO THE GROUND AND TAKES ADDITIONAL DAMAGE
BIG BANG	—	ENTIRE PARTY	20	150	1	—	NON-ELEMENTAL DAMAGE ATTACK
BLACK HOLE	—	ONE TARGET	0	95	1	—	REMOVES TARGET FROM BATTLE FOR 4 TURNS
BLAST OF AIR	WIND LV.1	ENTIRE PARTY	6	95	20	YES	WIND-ELEMENT ATTACK
BLAZE	FIRE LV.2	ENTIRE PARTY	18	150	10	—	FIRE-ELEMENT MAGIC ATTACK, 10% TO CONFUSE TARGET
BLIZZARD DANCE	WATER LV.2	ENTIRE PARTY	12	95	20	—	WATER-ELEMENT MAGIC ATTACK
BLOODFEAST	—	ONE TARGET	2	95	5	—	NON-ELEMENTAL DAMAGE ATTACK, RESTORES SOME HP
CHARGE	WATER/LIGHT LV.1	SELF	0	100	100	—	PREPARING TO USE TIDAL WAVE
DARK BLAST	DARK LV.1	ONE TARGET	8	98	10	—	DARK-ELEMENT MAGIC ATTACK, 50% TO INFLICT CURSE ON TARGET
DARK BREATH	DARK LV.1	ENTIRE PARTY	15	100	10	—	DARK-ELEMENT MAGIC ATTACK
DIAMOND DUST	WATER LV.2	ENTIRE PARTY	9	95	20	—	WATER-ELEMENT MAGIC ATTACK
DIVE	—	ONE TARGET	2	95	10	—	NON-ELEMENTAL DAMAGE ATTACK
EARTH BLAST	EARTH LV.1	ONE TARGET	2	98	10	—	EARTH-ELEMENT MAGIC ATTACK
EARTHQUAKE	EARTH LV.2	ENTIRE PARTY	18	150	5	—	EARTH-ELEMENT ATTACK, 10% CHANCE TO BLIND TARGET
ENTICE [A]	—	ONE TARGET	5	95	10	—	CONFUSE TARGET
ENTICE [B]	—	ONE TARGET	3	95	10	—	CONFUSE TARGET
FALL OF ANGELS	—	ENTIRE PARTY	112	200	1	—	PHYSICAL DAMAGE ATTACK, 5% OF INFLICTING NEGATIVE STATUS EFFECT
FIRE BREATH [A]	FIRE LV.1	ENTIRE PARTY	3	98	10	YES	FIRE-ELEMENT MAGIC ATTACK
FIRE BREATH [B]	FIRE LV.1	ENTIRE PARTY	11	95	10	YES	FIRE-ELEMENT MAGIC ATTACK
FIRE BREATH [C]	FIRE LV.1	ENTIRE PARTY	11	100	10	—	FIRE-ELEMENT MAGIC ATTACK
FLAME BLAST [A]	FIRE LV.1	ONE TARGET	5	98	10	—	FIRE-ELEMENT MAGIC ATTACK
FLAME BLAST [B]	FIRE LV.1	ENTIRE PARTY	4	98	10	—	FIRE-ELEMENT MAGIC ATTACK
FLUTTER EFFECT	WATER LV.1	ONE TARGET	5	98	10	—	WATER-ELEMENT MAGIC ATTACK, CHANCE TO CONFUSE TARGET
FLY SWAT	—	ENTIRE PARTY	50	50	5	YES	NON-ELEMENTAL DAMAGE ATTACK
FULL SWING	—	ENTIRE PARTY	5	70	5	YES	NON-ELEMENTAL AND PHYSICAL DAMAGE ATTACK
GOBLIN STRIKE	—	ONE TARGET	2	95	5	—	NON-ELEMENTAL DAMAGE ATTACK
HASTE	—	SELF	0	100	30	—	INCREASES ACTION SPEED
HURL	—	ONE TARGET	8	95	5	—	NON-ELEMENTAL AND PHYSICAL DAMAGE ATTACK
ICE BLAST	DARK LV.1	ENTIRE PARTY	8	98	10	—	DARK-ELEMENT ATTACK
ICE BREATH	WATER LV.1	ENTIRE PARTY	11	95	10	YES	WATER-ELEMENT ATTACK
IMPALE	EARTH LV.1	ONE TARGET	3	98	5	—	EARTH-ELEMENT ATTACK

ABILITY NAME	ELEMENTAL COMPONENT	TARGET	POWER	ACCURACY	ABILITY SPEED	DIMINISHED EFFECT	DESCRIPTION
IRON BLAST	—	ENTIRE PARTY	0	95	10	—	RAISES DEFENSE
JUDGMENT BOLT	—	ENTIRE PARTY	5	200	10	—	REDUCES TARGET'S AP TO 0
LIGHTNING	LIGHT LV.2	ENTIRE PARTY	18	150	20	—	LIGHT-ELEMENT ATTACK, 10% CHANCE TO PARALYZE TARGET
LIGHTNING BOLT [A]	LIGHT LV.1	ONE TARGET	7	95	10	—	LIGHT-ELEMENT MAGIC ATTACK, 60% TO PARALYZE TARGET
LIGHTNING BOLT [B]	LIGHT LV.1	ENTIRE PARTY	7	98	10	YES	LIGHT-ELEMENT MAGIC ATTACK
LIGHTNING BOLT [C]	WATER/LIGHT LV.1	ENTIRE PARTY	8	98	10	YES	LIGHT- AND WATER-ELEMENT MAGIC ATTACK
LIGHTNING BOLT [D]	LIGHT LV.1	ENTIRE PARTY	8	98	10	YES	LIGHT-ELEMENT MAGIC ATTACK, 50% CHANCE TO PARALYZE TARGET
MARKING	—	ONE TARGET	2	95	10	—	INFLICTS STATUS DOWN ON TARGET
MASH	WATER LV.1	ONE TARGET	4	95	5	—	WATER-ELEMENT AND PHYSICAL DAMAGE ATTACK
MERGE	—	ONE TARGET	0	95	5	—	UNITE WITH ANOTHER SLIME; HP, STRENGTH, AND INTELLECT ARE COMBINED
MIGHTY SLAP	WATER LV.1	ONE TARGET	8	95	5	—	WATER-ELEMENT AND PHYSICAL DAMAGE ATTACK
MOONLIGHT CURSE	—	ENTIRE PARTY	0	100	20	—	REDUCES TARGET'S PSYCHE UP LEVEL BY 100
ORC STRIKE	—	ONE TARGET	4	80	5	—	PHYSICAL DAMAGE ATTACK
PERFORMANCE	WIND LV.1	ENTIRE PARTY	0	50	10	—	WIND-ELEMENT ATTACK, 55% CHANCE TO PUT TARGET TO SLEEP
PETRIFY	—	ONE TARGET	3	95	10	—	CHANCE TO TURN TARGET INTO STONE
SANDSTORM	EARTH LV.1	ENTIRE PARTY	8	95	20	YES	EARTH-ELEMENT ATTACK, 50% CHANCE TO BLIND TARGET
SCREAM	—	ENTIRE PARTY	4	95	10	—	MAGIC DAMAGE ATTACK, 15% OF INSTANT DEATH
SIDEWINDER	EARTH LV.2	ENTIRE PARTY	26	95	10	YES	EARTH-ELEMENT ATTACK, 15% CHANCE OF INFLICTING NEGATIVE STATUS EFFECT
SLASH'N'DASH	—	ONE TARGET	4	80	5	—	PHYSICAL DAMAGE ATTACK
SLOW	—	ONE TARGET	0	100	30	—	SLOWS TARGET
SPORE	—	ENTIRE PARTY	0	95	10	—	NON-ELEMENTAL DAMAGE MAGIC ATTACK, 55% CHANCE TO POISON TARGET
STOP	—	ONE TARGET	0	100	30	—	RENDERS TARGET UNABLE TO ACT
TIDAL WAVE	WATER LV.2	ENTIRE PARTY	500	200	10	—	WATER-ELEMENT ATTACK
TSUNAMI	WATER LV.2	ENTIRE PARTY	18	150	15	—	WATER-ELEMENT MAGIC ATTACK, 10% TO POISON TARGET
UNBREAKABLE	—	SELF	3	95	200	—	BECOMES IMMUNE TO PHYSICAL ATTACKS
VITRIOL	—	ONE TARGET	3	95	10	—	INFLICTS STATUS DOWN ON TARGET
WALLOP	—	ONE TARGET	3	95	5	—	PHYSICAL DAMAGE ATTACK
WATER BLAST	WATER LV.1	ENTIRE PARTY	2	95	10	—	WATER-ELEMENT MAGIC ATTACK, 25% TO INFLICT POISON ON TARGET
WATERSPRAY	WATER LV.1	ENTIRE PARTY	6	95	20	YES	WATER-ELEMENT MAGIC ATTACK, 33% CHANCE TO INFLICT SILENCE, SLEEP, PARALYSIS, POISON, AND CONFUSION ON TARGET
WHIRL BLUDGEON [A]	—	ONE TARGET	4	95	5	—	NON-ELEMENTAL AND PHYSICAL DAMAGE ATTACK
WHIRL BLUDGEON [B]	—	ENTIRE PARTY	3	95	5	—	NON-ELEMENTAL AND PHYSICAL DAMAGE ATTACK
WHIRL BLUDGEON [C]	—	ENTIRE PARTY	4	95	5	—	NON-ELEMENTAL AND PHYSICAL DAMAGE ATTACK
WHIRL BLUDGEON [D]	—	ENTIRE PARTY	6	80	10	YES	NON-ELEMENTAL AND PHYSICAL DAMAGE ATTACK
WOOD BLAST	—	ONE TARGET	3	98	10	—	NON-ELEMENTAL DAMAGE ATTACK
WORLD OF DARK	DARK LV.2	ENTIRE PARTY	8	98	10	YES	DARK-ELEMENT MAGIC ATTACK, 50% TO SILENCE OR CURSE TARGET

AIR RAY [A]

ENCOUNTERED	AT SEA (PART I)				FLYING		
	??? (PART I)						
LEVEL	11	HP	45-56	WEIGHT	—		
VARIABLE LEVEL	—	ABILITY SPEED	30	ATTACK ELEMENT	WATER LV.1		
INFLICTS	SILENCE (10%)						

STRENGTH	9	INTELLECT	8	SPIRIT	8
ATTACK	5	ACCURACY	97	DEFENSE	2
MAGIC DEFENSE	4	EVASION	4	MAGIC EVASION	10

ELEMENTAL DEFENSE	FIRE	WATER	WIND	EARTH	LIGHT	DARK
	WEAK	NO EFFECT	—	—	—	

IMMUNE TO	—

TAME (SCHOLAR)	YES	POT LUCK (PARTY HOST)	YES	FORBIDDEN ART (SHAMAN)	YES	CAPTURE (BEASTMASTER)	YES
ATTACK PROFICIENCY	B	MAGIC PROFICIENCY	B	EVASION CORRECTION	B	MAGIC EVASION CORRECTION	B
ABILITIES	SILENCE/LIGHTNING BOLT [C]						
EXPERIENCE POINTS	7	STEAL		PHOENIX DOWN (40%)/SLEEP RING (25%)/ANTARCTIC WIND (5%)			
DROP	TOPAZ (37.6%)			SAPPHIRE (3.9%)	PHOENIX DOWN (10.2%)	ECHO HERBS (5.1%)	

AIR RAY [B]

ENCOUNTERED	MOONSAND RUINS (PART II)				2 ACTIONS, FLYING		
	TRIAL TOWER						
LEVEL	50	HP	380-475	WEIGHT	30		
VARIABLE LEVEL	YES	ABILITY SPEED	60	ATTACK ELEMENT	WATER LV.1		
INFLICTS	SILENCE (10%)						

STRENGTH	25	INTELLECT	128	SPIRIT	40
ATTACK	32	ACCURACY	150	DEFENSE	11
MAGIC DEFENSE	17	EVASION	5	MAGIC EVASION	10

ELEMENTAL DEFENSE	FIRE	WATER	WIND	EARTH	LIGHT	DARK
	—	NO EFFECT	—	WEAK	—	—

IMMUNE TO	CURSE

TAME (SCHOLAR)	YES	POT LUCK (PARTY HOST)	YES	FORBIDDEN ART (SHAMAN)	YES	CAPTURE (BEASTMASTER)	YES
ATTACK PROFICIENCY	A	MAGIC PROFICIENCY	A	EVASION CORRECTION	A	MAGIC EVASION CORRECTION	A
ABILITIES	SILENCE/LIGHTNING BOLT [C]						
EXPERIENCE POINTS	100	STEAL		POTION (40%)/HI-POTION (25%)/ANTARCTIC WIND (5%)			
DROP	TOPAZ (37.6%)			PHOENIX DOWN (7.8%)	ECHO HERBS (3.9%)	—	

ALRAUNE

ENCOUNTERED	ARBOR SOUTH AREA(PART II)						
	GREAT TREE ROOTS(PART II)						
LEVEL	25	HP	125-156	WEIGHT	—		
VARIABLE LEVEL	YES	ABILITY SPEED	30	ATTACK ELEMENT	EARTH LV.1		
INFLICTS	—						

STRENGTH	12	INTELLECT	19	SPIRIT	18
ATTACK	6	ACCURACY	3	DEFENSE	4
MAGIC DEFENSE	6	EVASION	5	MAGIC EVASION	7

ELEMENTAL DEFENSE	FIRE	WATER	WIND	EARTH	LIGHT	DARK
	—	—	—	HALF	—	—

IMMUNE TO	—

TAME (SCHOLAR)	YES	POT LUCK (PARTY HOST)	YES	FORBIDDEN ART (SHAMAN)	YES	CAPTURE (BEASTMASTER)	YES
ATTACK PROFICIENCY	B	MAGIC PROFICIENCY	B	EVASION CORRECTION	B	MAGIC EVASION CORRECTION	B
ABILITIES	CURAGA/SCREAM/SLEEP/POISON						
EXPERIENCE POINTS	14	STEAL		PHOENIX DOWN (40%)/X-POTION (25%)/GREAT TREE LOG (5%)			
DROP	SAPPHIRE (37.6%)			AQUAMARINE (3.9%)	HI-POTION (10.2%)	STUN RING (5.1%)	

ARCH DEMON

ENCOUNTERED	ROLAN'S SOUL(PART II)				2 ACTIONS		
	TOWER OF THE SKY(PART II)						
LEVEL	30	HP	1000	WEIGHT	10		
VARIABLE LEVEL	YES	ABILITY SPEED	50	ATTACK ELEMENT	DARK LV.1		
INFLICTS	CURSE (13%)						

STRENGTH	13	INTELLECT	30	SPIRIT	25
ATTACK	10	ACCURACY	5	DEFENSE	10
MAGIC DEFENSE	12	EVASION	12	MAGIC EVASION	10

ELEMENTAL DEFENSE	FIRE	WATER	WIND	EARTH	LIGHT	DARK
	—	—	—	—	WEAK	ABSORBS

IMMUNE TO	PETRIFY / CURSE / DEATH

TAME (SCHOLAR)	YES	POT LUCK (PARTY HOST)	YES	FORBIDDEN ART (SHAMAN)	YES	CAPTURE (BEASTMASTER)	YES
ATTACK PROFICIENCY	A	MAGIC PROFICIENCY	A	EVASION CORRECTION	B	MAGIC EVASION CORRECTION	B
ABILITIES	BLADEBLITZ/WORLD OF DARK						
EXPERIENCE POINTS	16	STEAL		X-POTION (40%)/ETHER (25%)			
DROP	AQUAMARINE (37.6%)			AQUAMARINE (7.8%)	X-POTION (3.9%)	—	

ARCHELON

ENCOUNTERED	LIBERTE AREA(PART II)						
	PIRATE HIDEOUT(PART II)						
LEVEL	25	HP	135-169	WEIGHT	—		
VARIABLE LEVEL	YES	ABILITY SPEED	5	ATTACK ELEMENT	EARTH LV.1		
INFLICTS	—						

STRENGTH	11	INTELLECT	8	SPIRIT	20
ATTACK	7	ACCURACY	5	DEFENSE	9
MAGIC DEFENSE	10	EVASION	1	MAGIC EVASION	10

ELEMENTAL DEFENSE	FIRE	WATER	WIND	EARTH	LIGHT	DARK
	—	—	—	HALF	—	—

IMMUNE TO	—

TAME (SCHOLAR)	YES	POT LUCK (PARTY HOST)	YES	FORBIDDEN ART (SHAMAN)	YES	CAPTURE (BEASTMASTER)	YES
ATTACK PROFICIENCY	B	MAGIC PROFICIENCY	B	EVASION CORRECTION	C	MAGIC EVASION CORRECTION	A
ABILITIES	UNBREAKABLE						
EXPERIENCE POINTS	14	STEAL		HI-POTION (40%)/TURTLE SHELL (25%)/ANTARCTIC WIND (5%)			
DROP	TOPAZ (37.6%)			TOPAZ (3.9%)	TURTLE SHELL (10.2%)	PHOENIX DOWN (5.1%)	

ARP

											FLYING
ENCOUNTERED	ARBOR SOUTH AREA(PART II)										
	ANIMAL BURROW(PART II)										
LEVEL	25	HP	119-149	WEIGHT	—	STRENGTH	10	INTELLECT	15	SPIRIT	16
VARIABLE LEVEL	YES	ABILITY SPEED	40	ATTACK ELEMENT	—	ATTACK	5	ACCURACY	3	DEFENSE	3
INFLICTS	PARALYSIS (10%)					MAGIC DEFENSE	6	EVASION	5	MAGIC EVASION	6

ELEMENTAL DEFENSE	FIRE	WATER	WIND	EARTH	LIGHT	DARK
	—	—	—	—	—	—

IMMUNE TO	—

TAME (SCHOLAR)	YES	POT LUCK (PARTY HOST)	YES	FORBIDDEN ART (SHAMAN)	YES	CAPTURE (BEASTMASTER)	YES
ATTACK PROFICIENCY	B	MAGIC PROFICIENCY	A	EVASION CORRECTION	B	MAGIC EVASION CORRECTION	B

ABILITIES	PERFORMANCE			
EXPERIENCE POINTS	14	STEAL	ETHER (40%)/WHISPERING HARP (25%)/RAVEN'S YAWN (5%)	
DROP	RUBY (37.6%)	EMERALD (3.9%)	QUAKING HARP (10.2%)	GALE GAUNTLET (5.1%)

ASPIDOCHELON [A]

ENCOUNTERED	LIBERTE AREA (PART I)										
	PIRATE HIDEOUT (PART I)										
LEVEL	9	HP	49-61	WEIGHT	—	STRENGTH	6	INTELLECT	8	SPIRIT	6
VARIABLE LEVEL	—	ABILITY SPEED	10	ATTACK ELEMENT	WATER LV.1	ATTACK	4	ACCURACY	97	DEFENSE	5
INFLICTS	—					MAGIC DEFENSE	2	EVASION	0	MAGIC EVASION	10

ELEMENTAL DEFENSE	FIRE	WATER	WIND	EARTH	LIGHT	DARK
	—	—	—	—	—	—

IMMUNE TO	—

TAME (SCHOLAR)	YES	POT LUCK (PARTY HOST)	YES	FORBIDDEN ART (SHAMAN)	YES	CAPTURE (BEASTMASTER)	YES
ATTACK PROFICIENCY	B	MAGIC PROFICIENCY	B	EVASION CORRECTION	C	MAGIC EVASION CORRECTION	B

ABILITIES	UNBREAKABLE			
EXPERIENCE POINTS	6	STEAL	TURTLE SHELL (40%)/HI-POTION (25%)/MYTHRIL (5%)	
DROP	TOPAZ (37.6%)	TOPAZ (3.9%)	PHOENIX DOWN (2%)	TURTLE SHELL (5.1%)

ASPIDOCHELON [B]

											2 ACTIONS
ENCOUNTERED	MOONSAND RUINS (PART II)										
LEVEL	50	HP	368-460	WEIGHT	30	STRENGTH	22	INTELLECT	8	SPIRIT	94
VARIABLE LEVEL	YES	ABILITY SPEED	60	ATTACK ELEMENT	WATER LV.1	ATTACK	28	ACCURACY	150	DEFENSE	56
INFLICTS	—					MAGIC DEFENSE	12	EVASION	1	MAGIC EVASION	47

ELEMENTAL DEFENSE	FIRE	WATER	WIND	EARTH	LIGHT	DARK
	—	NO EFFECT	—	WEAK	—	—

IMMUNE TO	CURSE

TAME (SCHOLAR)	YES	POT LUCK (PARTY HOST)	YES	FORBIDDEN ART (SHAMAN)	YES	CAPTURE (BEASTMASTER)	YES
ATTACK PROFICIENCY	A	MAGIC PROFICIENCY	A	EVASION CORRECTION	A	MAGIC EVASION CORRECTION	A

ABILITIES	UNBREAKABLE			
EXPERIENCE POINTS	100	STEAL	TURTLE SHELL (40%)/HI-POTION (25%)/ANTARCTIC WIND (5%)	
DROP	TOPAZ (37.6%)	POTION (7.8%)	—	TURTLE SHELL (2%)

ENEMY DATA

197

BASILISK [A]

ENCOUNTERED	GUERA AREA (PART I)						
	MOONLIGHT TOWER (PART I)						

LEVEL	10	HP	42-53	WEIGHT	—	STRENGTH	7	INTELLECT	7	SPIRIT	6
VARIABLE LEVEL	—	ABILITY SPEED	30	ATTACK ELEMENT	EARTH LV.1	ATTACK	3	ACCURACY	97	DEFENSE	2
INFLICTS	—					MAGIC DEFENSE	4	EVASION	3	MAGIC EVASION	10

ELEMENTAL DEFENSE	FIRE	WATER	WIND	EARTH	LIGHT	DARK
	WEAK	HALF	—	—	—	—

IMMUNE TO	—

TAME (SCHOLAR)	YES	POT LUCK (PARTY HOST)	YES	FORBIDDEN ART (SHAMAN)	YES	CAPTURE (BEASTMASTER)	YES
ATTACK PROFICIENCY	C	MAGIC PROFICIENCY	B	EVASION CORRECTION	C	MAGIC EVASION CORRECTION	B

ABILITIES	POISON		
EXPERIENCE POINTS	6	STEAL	POTION (40%)/HI-POTION (25%)/GAIA DRUM (5%)
DROP	EMERALD (37.6%)	RUBY (3.9%)	PHOENIX DOWN (5.1%) / POISON RING (2%)

BASILISK [B]

2 ACTIONS, FLYING

ENCOUNTERED	TRIAL TOWER (PART II)

LEVEL	90	HP	850-1063	WEIGHT	30	STRENGTH	73	INTELLECT	124	SPIRIT	14
VARIABLE LEVEL	YES	ABILITY SPEED	60	ATTACK ELEMENT	EARTH LV.1	ATTACK	54	ACCURACY	150	DEFENSE	36
INFLICTS	—					MAGIC DEFENSE	37	EVASION	5	MAGIC EVASION	7

ELEMENTAL DEFENSE	FIRE	WATER	WIND	EARTH	LIGHT	DARK
	—	—	WEAK	NO EFFECT	—	—

IMMUNE TO	CURSE

TAME (SCHOLAR)	YES	POT LUCK (PARTY HOST)	YES	FORBIDDEN ART (SHAMAN)	YES	CAPTURE (BEASTMASTER)	YES
ATTACK PROFICIENCY	A	MAGIC PROFICIENCY	A	EVASION CORRECTION	A	MAGIC EVASION CORRECTION	A

ABILITIES	POISON		
EXPERIENCE POINTS	100	STEAL	POTION (40%)/HI-POTION (25%)/GAIA DRUM (5%)
DROP	EMERALD (37.6%)	ANTIDOTE (7.8%)	— / POISON RING (2%)

BATTERFLY [A]

FLYING

ENCOUNTERED	ARBOR SOUTH AREA (PART I)						
	FAIRY PATH (PART I)						

LEVEL	13	HP	47-59	WEIGHT	—	STRENGTH	9	INTELLECT	12	SPIRIT	9
VARIABLE LEVEL	—	ABILITY SPEED	30	ATTACK ELEMENT		ATTACK	5	ACCURACY	97	DEFENSE	1
INFLICTS	BLINDNESS (10%)					MAGIC DEFENSE	7	EVASION	7	MAGIC EVASION	10

ELEMENTAL DEFENSE	FIRE	WATER	WIND	EARTH	LIGHT	DARK
	WEAK	—	—	—	—	—

IMMUNE TO	—

TAME (SCHOLAR)	YES	POT LUCK (PARTY HOST)	YES	FORBIDDEN ART (SHAMAN)	YES	CAPTURE (BEASTMASTER)	YES
ATTACK PROFICIENCY	C	MAGIC PROFICIENCY	B	EVASION CORRECTION	A	MAGIC EVASION CORRECTION	B

ABILITIES	SLEEP/FLUTTER EFFECT			
EXPERIENCE POINTS	8	STEAL	HI-POTION (40%)/PHOENIX DOWN (25%)/GREAT TREE LOG (5%)	
DROP	LAPIS (37.6%)	TOPAZ (3.9%)	ALARM CLOCK (10.2%)	FLASH RING (2%)

BATTERFLY [B]

FLYING

ENCOUNTERED	TRIAL TOWER (PART II)

LEVEL	90	HP	824-1030	WEIGHT	—	STRENGTH	65	INTELLECT	92	SPIRIT	72
VARIABLE LEVEL	YES	ABILITY SPEED	60	ATTACK ELEMENT	—	ATTACK	53	ACCURACY	150	DEFENSE	26
INFLICTS	BLINDNESS (15%)					MAGIC DEFENSE	36	EVASION	5	MAGIC EVASION	36

ELEMENTAL DEFENSE	FIRE	WATER	WIND	EARTH	LIGHT	DARK
	WEAK	—	—	NO EFFECT	—	—

IMMUNE TO	CURSE

TAME (SCHOLAR)	YES	POT LUCK (PARTY HOST)	YES	FORBIDDEN ART (SHAMAN)	YES	CAPTURE (BEASTMASTER)	YES
ATTACK PROFICIENCY	A	MAGIC PROFICIENCY	A	EVASION CORRECTION	A	MAGIC EVASION CORRECTION	A

ABILITIES	SLEEP/FLUTTER EFFECT		
EXPERIENCE POINTS	100	STEAL	POTION (40%)/HI-POTION (25%)/GREAT TREE LOG (5%)
DROP	SAPPHIRE (37.6%)	ALARM CLOCK (7.8%)	— / FLASH RING (2%)

BEHUGEMORE

2 ACTIONS

ENCOUNTERED	STAR CHAMBER (PART II)						
	ICE CAVERNS (PART II)						

LEVEL	30	HP	800-1000	WEIGHT	10	STRENGTH	11	INTELLECT	5	SPIRIT	5
VARIABLE LEVEL	YES	ABILITY SPEED	30	ATTACK ELEMENT	LIGHT LV.1	ATTACK	8	ACCURACY	5	DEFENSE	8
INFLICTS	CONFUSION (25%)					MAGIC DEFENSE	8	EVASION	12	MAGIC EVASION	2

ELEMENTAL DEFENSE	FIRE	WATER	WIND	EARTH	LIGHT	DARK
	—	—	—	—	HALF	—

IMMUNE TO	—

TAME (SCHOLAR)	YES	POT LUCK (PARTY HOST)	YES	FORBIDDEN ART (SHAMAN)	YES	CAPTURE (BEASTMASTER)	YES
ATTACK PROFICIENCY	A	MAGIC PROFICIENCY	B	EVASION CORRECTION	B	MAGIC EVASION CORRECTION	B

ABILITIES	LIGHTNING BOLT [D]			
EXPERIENCE POINTS	930	STEAL	HI-POTION (40%)/GLIMMER GAUNTLET (25%)/SHINE CAPE (5%)	
DROP	AQUAMARINE (37.6%)	HI-POTION (7.8%)	SHINE CAPE (3.9%)	AMETHYST (5.1%)

BIG WORM [A]

ENCOUNTERED	GUERA AREA (PART I) MOONLIGHT TOWER(PART I)							
LEVEL	9	HP	45-56	WEIGHT	—	STRENGTH	8	INTELLECT 5 SPIRIT 6
VARIABLE LEVEL	—	ABILITY SPEED	10	ATTACK ELEMENT	EARTH LV.1	ATTACK	3	ACCURACY 97 DEFENSE 3
INFLICTS	—					MAGIC DEFENSE	2	EVASION 4 MAGIC EVASION 10

ELEMENTAL DEFENSE	FIRE	WATER	WIND	EARTH	LIGHT	DARK
	—	—	WEAK	NO EFFECT	—	—

IMMUNE TO	—

TAME (SCHOLAR)	YES	POT LUCK (PARTY HOST)	YES	FORBIDDEN ART (SHAMAN)	YES	CAPTURE (BEASTMASTER)	YES
ATTACK PROFICIENCY	B	MAGIC PROFICIENCY	C	EVASION CORRECTION	B	MAGIC EVASION CORRECTION	C

ABILITIES	—			
EXPERIENCE POINTS	6	STEAL	POTION (40%)/HI-POTION (25%)/GAIA DRUM (5%)	
DROP	EMERALD (37.6%)	EMERALD (3.9%)	ANTIDOTE (10.2%)	EARTH GAUNTLET (5.1%)

BIG WORM [B]

2 ACTIONS

ENCOUNTERED	MYSTERIOUS TOWER (PART II)							
LEVEL	70	HP	630-788	WEIGHT	60	STRENGTH	39	INTELLECT 11 SPIRIT 10
VARIABLE LEVEL	YES	ABILITY SPEED	100	ATTACK ELEMENT	EARTH LV.1	ATTACK	38	ACCURACY 150 DEFENSE 29
INFLICTS	—					MAGIC DEFENSE	23	EVASION 5 MAGIC EVASION 5

ELEMENTAL DEFENSE	FIRE	WATER	WIND	EARTH	LIGHT	DARK
	—	—	WEAK	NO EFFECT	—	—

IMMUNE TO	CURSE

TAME (SCHOLAR)	YES	POT LUCK (PARTY HOST)	YES	FORBIDDEN ART (SHAMAN)	YES	CAPTURE (BEASTMASTER)	YES
ATTACK PROFICIENCY	A	MAGIC PROFICIENCY	A	EVASION CORRECTION	A	MAGIC EVASION CORRECTION	A

ABILITIES	VITRIOL			
EXPERIENCE POINTS	100	STEAL	POTION (40%)/HI-POTION (25%)/GAIA DRUM (5%)	
DROP	EMERALD (37.6%)	ANTIDOTE (7.8%)	—	EARTH GAUNTLET (2%)

BLOOD BAT [A]

FLYING

ENCOUNTERED	NORTHERN CAVES(PART I) GUERA CAVERNS(PART I)							
LEVEL	2	HP	4-5	WEIGHT	—	STRENGTH	2	INTELLECT 2 SPIRIT 2
VARIABLE LEVEL	—	ABILITY SPEED	25	ATTACK ELEMENT	—	ATTACK	2	ACCURACY 96 DEFENSE 1
INFLICTS	—					MAGIC DEFENSE	2	EVASION 2 MAGIC EVASION 2

ELEMENTAL DEFENSE	FIRE	WATER	WIND	EARTH	LIGHT	DARK
	—	—	—	—	—	—

IMMUNE TO	—

TAME (SCHOLAR)	YES	POT LUCK (PARTY HOST)	YES	FORBIDDEN ART (SHAMAN)	YES	CAPTURE (BEASTMASTER)	YES
ATTACK PROFICIENCY	B	MAGIC PROFICIENCY	B	EVASION CORRECTION	B	MAGIC EVASION CORRECTION	B

ABILITIES	BLOODFEAST			
EXPERIENCE POINTS	1	STEAL	POTION (40%)/HI-POTION (25%)/RAVEN'S YAWN (5%)	
DROP	RUBY (37.6%)	EMERALD (3.9%)	HI-POTION (5.1%)	BLOODY RING (0.8%)

BLOOD BAT [B]

FLYING

ENCOUNTERED	TRIAL TOWER (PART II)							
LEVEL	90	HP	760-950	WEIGHT	—	STRENGTH	65	INTELLECT 100 SPIRIT 12
VARIABLE LEVEL	YES	ABILITY SPEED	60	ATTACK ELEMENT	—	ATTACK	52	ACCURACY 150 DEFENSE 36
INFLICTS	—					MAGIC DEFENSE	32	EVASION 2 MAGIC EVASION 2

ELEMENTAL DEFENSE	FIRE	WATER	WIND	EARTH	LIGHT	DARK
	—	—	—	NO EFFECT	—	—

IMMUNE TO	CURSE

TAME (SCHOLAR)	YES	POT LUCK (PARTY HOST)	YES	FORBIDDEN ART (SHAMAN)	YES	CAPTURE (BEASTMASTER)	YES
ATTACK PROFICIENCY	A	MAGIC PROFICIENCY	A	EVASION CORRECTION	A	MAGIC EVASION CORRECTION	A

ABILITIES	BLOODFEAST			
EXPERIENCE POINTS	100	STEAL	POTION (40%)/HI-POTION (25%)/RAVEN'S YAWN (5%)	
DROP	RUBY (37.6%)	POTION (7.8%)	BLOODY RING (1.2%)	EMERALD (1.2%)

BOGGLE BEAR

ENCOUNTERED	ARBOR NORTH AREA (PART II) FAIRY PATH(PART II)							
LEVEL	25	HP	134-168	WEIGHT	—	STRENGTH	14	INTELLECT 18 SPIRIT 18
VARIABLE LEVEL	YES	ABILITY SPEED	40	ATTACK ELEMENT	—	ATTACK	8	ACCURACY 5 DEFENSE 5
INFLICTS	—					MAGIC DEFENSE	7	EVASION 5 MAGIC EVASION 7

ELEMENTAL DEFENSE	FIRE	WATER	WIND	EARTH	LIGHT	DARK
	—	—	—	—	—	—

IMMUNE TO	—

TAME (SCHOLAR)	YES	POT LUCK (PARTY HOST)	YES	FORBIDDEN ART (SHAMAN)	YES	CAPTURE (BEASTMASTER)	YES
ATTACK PROFICIENCY	B	MAGIC PROFICIENCY	B	EVASION CORRECTION	B	MAGIC EVASION CORRECTION	B

ABILITIES	WHIRL BLUDGEON [C]			
EXPERIENCE POINTS	14	STEAL	HI-POTION (40%)/X-POTION (25%)/DARK SIGH (5%)	
DROP	AQUAMARINE (37.6%)	TOPAZ (3.9%)	—	—

BORGBEAR [A]

ENCOUNTERED	ARBOR NORTH AREA(PART I) ICE CAVERNS(PART I)								
LEVEL	22	HP	61-76	WEIGHT	—	STRENGTH	11	INTELLECT	10	SPIRIT	13
VARIABLE LEVEL	—	ABILITY SPEED	30	ATTACK ELEMENT	—	ATTACK	7	ACCURACY	98	DEFENSE	6
INFLICTS	—					MAGIC DEFENSE	4	EVASION	9	MAGIC EVASION	4

ELEMENTAL DEFENSE	FIRE	WATER	WIND	EARTH	LIGHT	DARK
	—	—	—	—	WEAK	—

IMMUNE TO	—

TAME (SCHOLAR)	YES	POT LUCK (PARTY HOST)	YES	FORBIDDEN ART (SHAMAN)	YES	CAPTURE (BEASTMASTER)	YES
ATTACK PROFICIENCY	B	MAGIC PROFICIENCY	C	EVASION CORRECTION	B	MAGIC EVASION CORRECTION	C

ABILITIES	WHIRL BLUDGEON [C]		
EXPERIENCE POINTS	12	STEAL	HI-POTION (40%)/DARK SIGH (25%)/GIANT'S RING (5%)
DROP	AQUAMARINE (37.6%)	TOPAZ (3.9%)	PHOENIX DOWN (5.1%)	GIANT'S RING (2%)

BORGBEAR [B]

2 ACTIONS

ENCOUNTERED	MYSTERIOUS TOWER (PART II)								
LEVEL	70	HP	688-860	WEIGHT	60	STRENGTH	42	INTELLECT	34	SPIRIT	56
VARIABLE LEVEL	YES	ABILITY SPEED	100	ATTACK ELEMENT	—	ATTACK	49	ACCURACY	150	DEFENSE	28
INFLICTS	—					MAGIC DEFENSE	26	EVASION	0	MAGIC EVASION	28

ELEMENTAL DEFENSE	FIRE	WATER	WIND	EARTH	LIGHT	DARK
	—	—	—	—	WEAK	—

IMMUNE TO	CURSE

TAME (SCHOLAR)	YES	POT LUCK (PARTY HOST)	YES	FORBIDDEN ART (SHAMAN)	YES	CAPTURE (BEASTMASTER)	YES
ATTACK PROFICIENCY	A	MAGIC PROFICIENCY	A	EVASION CORRECTION	A	MAGIC EVASION CORRECTION	A

ABILITIES	WHIRL BLUDGEON [C]		
EXPERIENCE POINTS	100	STEAL	POTION (40%)/HI-POTION (25%)/DARK SIGH (5%)
DROP	SAPPHIRE (37.6%)	HI-POTION (7.8%)	—	BLOODY BOW (2%)

BRAINSHARK [A]

ENCOUNTERED	HOLY TREE TOWER(PART II) TRIAL TOWER(PART II)								
LEVEL	90	HP	1600-2000	WEIGHT	30	STRENGTH	78	INTELLECT	255	SPIRIT	56
VARIABLE LEVEL	YES	ABILITY SPEED	60	ATTACK ELEMENT	FIRE LV.1	ATTACK	53	ACCURACY	150	DEFENSE	38
INFLICTS	POISON, CURSE (50%)					MAGIC DEFENSE	50	EVASION	2	MAGIC EVASION	28

ELEMENTAL DEFENSE	FIRE	WATER	WIND	EARTH	LIGHT	DARK
	ABSORBS	WEAK	—	—	—	—

IMMUNE TO	PETRIFY / CURSE / DEATH

TAME (SCHOLAR)	YES	POT LUCK (PARTY HOST)	YES	FORBIDDEN ART (SHAMAN)	—	CAPTURE (BEASTMASTER)	—
ATTACK PROFICIENCY	A	MAGIC PROFICIENCY	A	EVASION CORRECTION	A	MAGIC EVASION CORRECTION	A

ABILITIES	WATERSPRAY			
EXPERIENCE POINTS	100	STEAL	—	
DROP	AQUAMARINE (100%)	AMETHYST (100%)	AMETHYST (100%)	SHARK LANCE (2%)

BUFFOHELM [A]

ENCOUNTERED	GUERA AREA (PART II) MT. GULG(PART II)								
LEVEL	25	HP	131-164	WEIGHT	—	STRENGTH	11	INTELLECT	28	SPIRIT	15
VARIABLE LEVEL	YES	ABILITY SPEED	30	ATTACK ELEMENT	FIRE LV.1	ATTACK	6	ACCURACY	3	DEFENSE	4
INFLICTS	SILENCE (10%)					MAGIC DEFENSE	8	EVASION	5	MAGIC EVASION	6

ELEMENTAL DEFENSE	FIRE	WATER	WIND	EARTH	LIGHT	DARK
	HALF	—	—	—	—	—

IMMUNE TO	

TAME (SCHOLAR)	YES	POT LUCK (PARTY HOST)	YES	FORBIDDEN ART (SHAMAN)	YES	CAPTURE (BEASTMASTER)	YES
ATTACK PROFICIENCY	B	MAGIC PROFICIENCY	A	EVASION CORRECTION	B	MAGIC EVASION CORRECTION	A

ABILITIES	FIRA/FLAME BLAST [B]			
EXPERIENCE POINTS	14	STEAL	INFERNO STAVE (40%)/PHOENIX DOWN (25%)/RAVEN'S YAWN (5%)	
DROP	RUBY (37.6%)	LAPIS (3.9%)	ECHO HERBS (10.2%)	MAGIC STAFF (5.1%)

BULLKING

ENCOUNTERED	QUICKSAND CASTLE(PART II) STAR CHAMBER(PART II)								
LEVEL	25	HP	132-165	WEIGHT	—	STRENGTH	14	INTELLECT	12	SPIRIT	15
VARIABLE LEVEL	YES	ABILITY SPEED	30	ATTACK ELEMENT	LIGHT LV.1	ATTACK	7	ACCURACY	5	DEFENSE	8
INFLICTS	—					MAGIC DEFENSE	5	EVASION	5	MAGIC EVASION	6

ELEMENTAL DEFENSE	FIRE	WATER	WIND	EARTH	LIGHT	DARK
	—	—	—	—	HALF	WEAK

IMMUNE TO	

TAME (SCHOLAR)	YES	POT LUCK (PARTY HOST)	YES	FORBIDDEN ART (SHAMAN)	YES	CAPTURE (BEASTMASTER)	YES
ATTACK PROFICIENCY	B	MAGIC PROFICIENCY	A	EVASION CORRECTION	B	MAGIC EVASION CORRECTION	B

ABILITIES	MARKING			
EXPERIENCE POINTS	14	STEAL	HI-POTION (40%)/REMEDY (25%)/GAIA DRUM (5%)	
DROP	EMERALD (37.6%)	TOPAZ (3.9%)	PHOENIX DOWN (10.2%)	HI-POTION (5.1%)

CAIT SITH [A]

ENCOUNTERED	QUICKSAND CASTLE (PART I)								
LEVEL	12	HP	53-66	WEIGHT	—	STRENGTH	8	INTELLECT	11	SPIRIT	9
VARIABLE LEVEL	—	ABILITY SPEED	45	ATTACK ELEMENT		ATTACK	3	ACCURACY	97	DEFENSE	2
INFLICTS	SLEEP (12%)					MAGIC DEFENSE	4	EVASION	10	MAGIC EVASION	10

ELEMENTAL DEFENSE	FIRE	WATER	WIND	EARTH	LIGHT	DARK
	—	WEAK	—	—	—	—

IMMUNE TO	

TAME (SCHOLAR)	YES	POT LUCK (PARTY HOST)	YES	FORBIDDEN ART (SHAMAN)	YES	CAPTURE (BEASTMASTER)	YES
ATTACK PROFICIENCY	C	MAGIC PROFICIENCY	B	EVASION CORRECTION	B	MAGIC EVASION CORRECTION	B

ABILITIES	WATERGA/EARTH BLAST/PROTECT/POISON			
EXPERIENCE POINTS	7	STEAL	HI-POTION (40%)/PHOENIX DOWN (25%)/GAIA DRUM (5%)	
DROP	EMERALD (37.6%)	TOPAZ (3.9%)	PHOENIX DOWN (10.2%)	TERRA STAVE (5.1%)

CAIT SITH [B]

ENCOUNTERED	HOLY TREE TOWER (PART II)								
LEVEL	60	HP	414-518	WEIGHT	30	STRENGTH	22	INTELLECT	130	SPIRIT	50
VARIABLE LEVEL	YES	ABILITY SPEED	80	ATTACK ELEMENT	—	ATTACK	25	ACCURACY	150	DEFENSE	20
INFLICTS	SLEEP (12%)					MAGIC DEFENSE	19	EVASION	10	MAGIC EVASION	25

ELEMENTAL DEFENSE	FIRE	WATER	WIND	EARTH	LIGHT	DARK
	—	—	—	NO EFFECT	—	—

IMMUNE TO	CURSE

TAME (SCHOLAR)	YES	POT LUCK (PARTY HOST)	YES	FORBIDDEN ART (SHAMAN)	YES	CAPTURE (BEASTMASTER)	YES
ATTACK PROFICIENCY	A	MAGIC PROFICIENCY	A	EVASION CORRECTION	A	MAGIC EVASION CORRECTION	A

ABILITIES	WATERGA/EARTH BLAST/PROTECT/POISON			
EXPERIENCE POINTS	100	STEAL	POTION (40%)/HI-POTION (25%)/GAIA DRUM (5%)	
DROP	EMERALD (37.6%)	PHOENIX DOWN (7.8%)	EYE DROPS (3.9%)	TERRA STAVE (2%)

CARBUNCLE

ENCOUNTERED	GREAT TREE(PART II) GREAT TREE: TO THE SUMMIT					FLYING		
LEVEL	25	HP	124-155	WEIGHT	—	STRENGTH	13	INTELLECT 22	SPIRIT 18
VARIABLE LEVEL	YES	ABILITY SPEED 60		ATTACK ELEMENT	LIGHT LV.1	ATTACK	6	ACCURACY 3	DEFENSE 5
INFLICTS	—					MAGIC DEFENSE	10	EVASION 5	MAGIC EVASION 7

ELEMENTAL DEFENSE	FIRE	WATER	WIND	EARTH	LIGHT	DARK
	WEAK	—	—	—	NO EFFECT	—

IMMUNE TO —

TAME (SCHOLAR)	YES	POT LUCK (PARTY HOST)	YES	FORBIDDEN ART (SHAMAN)	YES	CAPTURE (BEASTMASTER)	YES
ATTACK PROFICIENCY	B	MAGIC PROFICIENCY	A	EVASION CORRECTION	B	MAGIC EVASION CORRECTION	B

ABILITIES WOOD BLAST/CURE/SILENCE/SLEEP/PROTECT

EXPERIENCE POINTS	14	STEAL	X-POTION (40%)/GREAT TREE SWORD (25%)/GREAT TREE LOG (5%)		
DROP	SAPPHIRE (37.6%)		TOPAZ (3.9%)	HI-POTION (10.2%)	WIND DAGGER (5.1%)

CHIMERA [A]

ENCOUNTERED	HUNTING CAVES(PART I) TOWER OF THE SKY(PART I)					2 ACTIONS, FLYING		
LEVEL	14	HP	52-65	WEIGHT	20	STRENGTH	9	INTELLECT 11	SPIRIT 10
VARIABLE LEVEL	—	ABILITY SPEED 25		ATTACK ELEMENT	FIRE LV.1	ATTACK	6	ACCURACY 97	DEFENSE 4
INFLICTS	POISON SILENCE BLINDNESS (10%)					MAGIC DEFENSE	4	EVASION 6	MAGIC EVASION 10

ELEMENTAL DEFENSE	FIRE	WATER	WIND	EARTH	LIGHT	DARK
	HALF	WEAK	—	—	—	—

IMMUNE TO —

TAME (SCHOLAR)	YES	POT LUCK (PARTY HOST)	YES	FORBIDDEN ART (SHAMAN)	YES	CAPTURE (BEASTMASTER)	YES
ATTACK PROFICIENCY	B	MAGIC PROFICIENCY	B	EVASION CORRECTION	B	MAGIC EVASION CORRECTION	B

ABILITIES WATERGA/FIRE/FLAME BLAST [A]

EXPERIENCE POINTS	8	STEAL	PHOENIX DOWN (40%)/DRAGON WING (25%)/BOMB FRAGMENT (5%)		
DROP	SAPPHIRE (37.6%)		EMERALD (3.9%)	DRAGON WING (5.1%)	GALE GAUNTLET (2%)

CHIMERA [B]

ENCOUNTERED	HOLY TREE TOWER (PART II)					2 ACTIONS, FLYING		
LEVEL	60	HP	420-525	WEIGHT	30	STRENGTH	24	INTELLECT 103	SPIRIT 48
VARIABLE LEVEL	YES	ABILITY SPEED 80		ATTACK ELEMENT	FIRE LV.1	ATTACK	32	ACCURACY 150	DEFENSE 20
INFLICTS	POISON SILENCE BLINDNESS (10%)					MAGIC DEFENSE	18	EVASION 1	MAGIC EVASION 24

ELEMENTAL DEFENSE	FIRE	WATER	WIND	EARTH	LIGHT	DARK
	HALF	WEAK	—	NO EFFECT	—	—

IMMUNE TO CURSE

TAME (SCHOLAR)	YES	POT LUCK (PARTY HOST)	YES	FORBIDDEN ART (SHAMAN)	YES	CAPTURE (BEASTMASTER)	YES
ATTACK PROFICIENCY	A	MAGIC PROFICIENCY	A	EVASION CORRECTION	A	MAGIC EVASION CORRECTION	A

ABILITIES CURSE/QUAKRA/FIRA/FLAME BLAST [A]

EXPERIENCE POINTS	100	STEAL	POTION (40%)/DRAGON WING (25%)/BOMB FRAGMENT (5%)		
DROP	LAPIS (37.6%)		BOMB FRAGMENT (7.8%)	DRAGON WING (3.9%)	RED SHOT (2%)

CLOUD PENGUIN [A]

ENCOUNTERED	SPELVIA DUNGEONS(PART I)					FLYING		
LEVEL	20	HP	68-85	WEIGHT	—	STRENGTH	10	INTELLECT 14	SPIRIT 16
VARIABLE LEVEL	—	ABILITY SPEED 30		ATTACK ELEMENT	—	ATTACK	7	ACCURACY 98	DEFENSE 3
INFLICTS	SILENCE (10%)					MAGIC DEFENSE	5	EVASION 70	MAGIC EVASION 8

ELEMENTAL DEFENSE	FIRE	WATER	WIND	EARTH	LIGHT	DARK
	—	WEAK	—	—	—	WEAK

IMMUNE TO —

TAME (SCHOLAR)	YES	POT LUCK (PARTY HOST)	YES	FORBIDDEN ART (SHAMAN)	YES	CAPTURE (BEASTMASTER)	YES
ATTACK PROFICIENCY	B	MAGIC PROFICIENCY	A	EVASION CORRECTION	A	MAGIC EVASION CORRECTION	A

ABILITIES BLIZZARD/LIGHTNING BOLT [B]

EXPERIENCE POINTS	11	STEAL	POTION (40%)/HI-POTION (25%)/HOLY BREATH (5%)		
DROP	AQUAMARINE (37.6%)		RUBY (3.9%)	PHOENIX DOWN (5.1%)	GLIMMER GAUNTLET (2%)

CLOUD PENGUIN [B]

ENCOUNTERED	HOLY TREE TOWER (PART II)					2 ACTIONS, FLYING		
LEVEL	60	HP	412-515	WEIGHT	30	STRENGTH	22	INTELLECT 106	SPIRIT 48
VARIABLE LEVEL	YES	ABILITY SPEED 80		ATTACK ELEMENT	LIGHT LV.1	ATTACK	36	ACCURACY 150	DEFENSE 19
INFLICTS	SILENCE (15%)					MAGIC DEFENSE	17	EVASION 3	MAGIC EVASION 24

ELEMENTAL DEFENSE	FIRE	WATER	WIND	EARTH	LIGHT	DARK
	—	WEAK	—	NO EFFECT	—	—

IMMUNE TO CURSE

TAME (SCHOLAR)	YES	POT LUCK (PARTY HOST)	YES	FORBIDDEN ART (SHAMAN)	YES	CAPTURE (BEASTMASTER)	YES
ATTACK PROFICIENCY	A	MAGIC PROFICIENCY	A	EVASION CORRECTION	A	MAGIC EVASION CORRECTION	A

ABILITIES BLIZZARD/LIGHTNING BOLT [B]

EXPERIENCE POINTS	100	STEAL	POTION (40%)/HI-POTION (25%)/HOLY BREATH (5%)		
DROP	AMETHYST (37.6%)		HI-POTION (7.8%)	—	GLIMMER GAUNTLET (2%)

COCKATRICE

FLYING

ENCOUNTERED	MOONLIGHT TOWER(PART II) QUICKSAND CASTLE(PART II)								
LEVEL	25	HP	130-163	WEIGHT	—	STRENGTH	11	INTELLECT	14	SPIRIT	14
VARIABLE LEVEL	YES	ABILITY SPEED	30	ATTACK ELEMENT	—	ATTACK	6	ACCURACY	3	DEFENSE	4
INFLICTS		POISON (10%)				MAGIC DEFENSE	6	EVASION	5	MAGIC EVASION	6

ELEMENTAL DEFENSE	FIRE	WATER	WIND	EARTH	LIGHT	DARK
	HALF	WEAK	—	—	—	—

IMMUNE TO —

TAME (SCHOLAR)	YES	POT LUCK (PARTY HOST)	YES	FORBIDDEN ART (SHAMAN)	YES	CAPTURE (BEASTMASTER)	YES
ATTACK PROFICIENCY	B	MAGIC PROFICIENCY	A	EVASION CORRECTION	B	MAGIC EVASION CORRECTION	B

ABILITIES	PETRIFY				
EXPERIENCE POINTS	14	STEAL	GOLD NEEDLE (40%)/X-POTION (25%)/GAIA DRUM (5%)		
DROP	EMERALD (37.6%)		TOPAZ (3.9%)	GOLD NEEDLE (10.2%)	POISON RING (5.1%)

COWPEL [A]

ENCOUNTERED	GUERA AREA (PART I) WITCH'S MANSION(PART I)								
LEVEL	5	HP	10-13	WEIGHT	—	STRENGTH	3	INTELLECT	2	SPIRIT	2
VARIABLE LEVEL		ABILITY SPEED	40	ATTACK ELEMENT	—	ATTACK	3	ACCURACY	97	DEFENSE	1
INFLICTS		—				MAGIC DEFENSE	5	EVASION	3	MAGIC EVASION	10

ELEMENTAL DEFENSE	FIRE	WATER	WIND	EARTH	LIGHT	DARK
	—	—	—	WEAK	—	—

IMMUNE TO —

TAME (SCHOLAR)	YES	POT LUCK (PARTY HOST)	YES	FORBIDDEN ART (SHAMAN)	YES	CAPTURE (BEASTMASTER)	YES
ATTACK PROFICIENCY	C	MAGIC PROFICIENCY	B	EVASION CORRECTION	C	MAGIC EVASION CORRECTION	B

ABILITIES	FIRE/FLAME BLAST [B]				
EXPERIENCE POINTS	4	STEAL	PHOENIX DOWN (40%)/ETHER (25%)/RAVEN'S YAWN (5%)		
DROP	RUBY (37.6%)		LAPIS (3.9%)	PHOENIX DOWN (10.2%)	MAGIC STAFF (5.1%)

COWPEL [B]

ENCOUNTERED	INVIDIA UNDERGROUND(PART I) TOWER OF THE SKY(PART I)								
LEVEL	5	HP	50-63	WEIGHT	—	STRENGTH	6	INTELLECT	15	SPIRIT	8
VARIABLE LEVEL		ABILITY SPEED	30	ATTACK ELEMENT	WIND LV.1	ATTACK	4	ACCURACY	98	DEFENSE	2
INFLICTS		—				MAGIC DEFENSE	8	EVASION	3	MAGIC EVASION	3

ELEMENTAL DEFENSE	FIRE	WATER	WIND	EARTH	LIGHT	DARK
	—	—	HALF	—	—	—

IMMUNE TO —

TAME (SCHOLAR)	YES	POT LUCK (PARTY HOST)	YES	FORBIDDEN ART (SHAMAN)	YES	CAPTURE (BEASTMASTER)	YES
ATTACK PROFICIENCY	C	MAGIC PROFICIENCY	B	EVASION CORRECTION	C	MAGIC EVASION CORRECTION	B

ABILITIES	FIRA/FLAME BLAST [B]				
EXPERIENCE POINTS	7	STEAL	OCEAN STAVE (40%)/X-POTION (25%)/BOMB FRAGMENT (5%)		
DROP	SAPPHIRE (37.6%)		AQUAMARINE (10.2%)	PHOENIX DOWN (7.8%)	MAGIC STAFF (3.9%)

COWPEL [C]

2 ACTIONS

ENCOUNTERED	HOLY TREE TOWER (PART II)								
LEVEL	60	HP	368-460	WEIGHT	30	STRENGTH	27	INTELLECT	120	SPIRIT	35
VARIABLE LEVEL	YES	ABILITY SPEED	80	ATTACK ELEMENT	—	ATTACK	25	ACCURACY	150	DEFENSE	21
INFLICTS		—				MAGIC DEFENSE	16	EVASION	3	MAGIC EVASION	18

ELEMENTAL DEFENSE	FIRE	WATER	WIND	EARTH	LIGHT	DARK
	—	—	—	—	—	—

IMMUNE TO CURSE

TAME (SCHOLAR)	YES	POT LUCK (PARTY HOST)	YES	FORBIDDEN ART (SHAMAN)	YES	CAPTURE (BEASTMASTER)	YES
ATTACK PROFICIENCY		MAGIC PROFICIENCY		EVASION CORRECTION		MAGIC EVASION CORRECTION	

ABILITIES	FIRA/FLAME BLAST [B]				
EXPERIENCE POINTS	100	STEAL	POTION (40%)/HI-POTION (25%)/RAVEN'S YAWN (5%)		
DROP	RUBY (37.6%)		POTION (7.8%)	PHOENIX DOWN (3.9%)	MAGIC STAFF (2%)

CU SITH [A]

FLYING

ENCOUNTERED	QUICKSAND CASTLE (PART I)								
LEVEL	12	HP	62-78	WEIGHT	—	STRENGTH	9	INTELLECT	9	SPIRIT	9
VARIABLE LEVEL		ABILITY SPEED	35	ATTACK ELEMENT	—	ATTACK	4	ACCURACY	97	DEFENSE	3
INFLICTS		—				MAGIC DEFENSE	2	EVASION	3	MAGIC EVASION	10

ELEMENTAL DEFENSE	FIRE	WATER	WIND	EARTH	LIGHT	DARK
	—	—	WEAK	—	—	—

IMMUNE TO —

TAME (SCHOLAR)	YES	POT LUCK (PARTY HOST)	YES	FORBIDDEN ART (SHAMAN)	YES	CAPTURE (BEASTMASTER)	YES
ATTACK PROFICIENCY	B	MAGIC PROFICIENCY	C	EVASION CORRECTION	B	MAGIC EVASION CORRECTION	C

ABILITIES	MARKING				
EXPERIENCE POINTS	7	STEAL	HI-POTION (40%)/ETHER (25%)/GAIA DRUM (5%)		
DROP	EMERALD (37.6%)		AQUAMARINE (3.9%)	ANTIDOTE (10.2%)	EYE DROPS (5.1%)

CU SITH [B]

2 ACTIONS, FLYING

ENCOUNTERED	HOLY TREE TOWER (PART II)								
LEVEL	60	HP	434-543		WEIGHT	30	STRENGTH	25	INTELLECT	12	SPIRIT	55

STRENGTH	25	INTELLECT	12	SPIRIT	55
ATTACK	32	ACCURACY	150	DEFENSE	23
MAGIC DEFENSE	18	EVASION	3	MAGIC EVASION	28

LEVEL	60	HP	434-543	WEIGHT	30
VARIABLE LEVEL	YES	ABILITY SPEED	80	ATTACK ELEMENT	—
INFLICTS	—				

ELEMENTAL DEFENSE	FIRE	WATER	WIND	EARTH	LIGHT	DARK
	—	—	—	NO EFFECT	—	—

IMMUNE TO	CURSE

TAME (SCHOLAR)	YES	POT LUCK (PARTY HOST)	YES	FORBIDDEN ART (SHAMAN)	YES	CAPTURE (BEASTMASTER)	YES
ATTACK PROFICIENCY	A	MAGIC PROFICIENCY	A	EVASION CORRECTION	A	MAGIC EVASION CORRECTION	A

ABILITIES	MARKING			
EXPERIENCE POINTS	100	STEAL	POTION (40%)/HI-POTION (25%)/GAIA DRUM (5%)	
DROP	EMERALD (37.6%)	ANTIDOTE (7.8%)	EYE DROPS (3.9%)	—

DEATH TRAP

ENCOUNTERED	MT. GULG (PART II)
	STAR CHAMBER (PART II)

STRENGTH	10	INTELLECT	18	SPIRIT	18
ATTACK	8	ACCURACY	5	DEFENSE	8
MAGIC DEFENSE	5	EVASION	0	MAGIC EVASION	7

LEVEL	25	HP	130-150	WEIGHT	—
VARIABLE LEVEL	YES	ABILITY SPEED	10	ATTACK ELEMENT	—
INFLICTS	—				

ELEMENTAL DEFENSE	FIRE	WATER	WIND	EARTH	LIGHT	DARK
	—	—	—	—	—	—

IMMUNE TO	PETRIFY / CURSE / DEATH

TAME (SCHOLAR)	YES	POT LUCK (PARTY HOST)	YES	FORBIDDEN ART (SHAMAN)	YES	CAPTURE (BEASTMASTER)	YES
ATTACK PROFICIENCY	B	MAGIC PROFICIENCY	B	EVASION CORRECTION	B	MAGIC EVASION CORRECTION	B

ABILITIES	WALLOP			
EXPERIENCE POINTS	14	STEAL	HI-POTION (40%)/PHOENIX DOWN (25%)/X-POTION (5%)	
DROP	EMERALD (37.6%)	LAPIS (3.9%)	AQUAMARINE (15.7%)	MYTHRIL (5.1%)

DEMON

2 ACTIONS

ENCOUNTERED	MOONSAND RUINS (PART II)
	TRIAL TOWER (PART II)

STRENGTH	32	INTELLECT	102	SPIRIT	28
ATTACK	32	ACCURACY	150	DEFENSE	19
MAGIC DEFENSE	18	EVASION	0	MAGIC EVASION	14

LEVEL	90	HP	3500-4375	WEIGHT	30
VARIABLE LEVEL	YES	ABILITY SPEED	60	ATTACK ELEMENT	DARK LV.1
INFLICTS	CURSE (13%)			

ELEMENTAL DEFENSE	FIRE	WATER	WIND	EARTH	LIGHT	DARK
	HALF	—	—	—	WEAK	NO EFFECT

IMMUNE TO	PETRIFY / CURSE / DEATH

TAME (SCHOLAR)	YES	POT LUCK (PARTY HOST)	YES	FORBIDDEN ART (SHAMAN)	—	CAPTURE (BEASTMASTER)	—
ATTACK PROFICIENCY	A	MAGIC PROFICIENCY	A	EVASION CORRECTION	A	MAGIC EVASION CORRECTION	A

ABILITIES	BLADEBLITZ/WORLD OF DARK			
EXPERIENCE POINTS	100	STEAL	HI-POTION (40%)/X-POTION (25%)/X-POTION (5%)	
DROP	EMERALD (9.8%)	ALARM CLOCK (7.8%)	—	—

DEMON RAY

FLYING

ENCOUNTERED	PIRATE HIDEOUT (PART II)
	STAR CHAMBER (PART II)

STRENGTH	14	INTELLECT	20	SPIRIT	18
ATTACK	7	ACCURACY	3	DEFENSE	4
MAGIC DEFENSE	7	EVASION	5	MAGIC EVASION	7

LEVEL	25	HP	134-168	WEIGHT	—
VARIABLE LEVEL	YES	ABILITY SPEED	50	ATTACK ELEMENT	DARK LV.1
INFLICTS	—			

ELEMENTAL DEFENSE	FIRE	WATER	WIND	EARTH	LIGHT	DARK
	—	—	—	—	—	HALF

IMMUNE TO	

TAME (SCHOLAR)	YES	POT LUCK (PARTY HOST)	YES	FORBIDDEN ART (SHAMAN)	YES	CAPTURE (BEASTMASTER)	YES
ATTACK PROFICIENCY	B	MAGIC PROFICIENCY	A	EVASION CORRECTION	B	MAGIC EVASION CORRECTION	B

ABILITIES	SILENCE/LIGHTNING BOLT [C]			
EXPERIENCE POINTS	14	STEAL	ECHO HERBS (40%)/HI-POTION (25%)/ANTARCTIC WIND (5%)	
DROP	TOPAZ (37.6%)	EMERALD (3.9%)	HI-POTION (10.2%)	ETHER (5.1%)

DOPPELGANGER [AIRE A]

ENCOUNTERED	ROLAN'S SOUL (PART I)
	STAR CHAMBER (PART II)

STRENGTH	12	INTELLECT	10	SPIRIT	16
ATTACK	8	ACCURACY	98	DEFENSE	3
MAGIC DEFENSE	6	EVASION	9	MAGIC EVASION	6

LEVEL	23	HP	60-75	WEIGHT	—
VARIABLE LEVEL	—	ABILITY SPEED	55	ATTACK ELEMENT	DARK LV.1
INFLICTS	CURSE, STATUS DOWN (15%)			

ELEMENTAL DEFENSE	FIRE	WATER	WIND	EARTH	LIGHT	DARK
	—	—	—	—	WEAK	NO EFFECT

IMMUNE TO	

TAME (SCHOLAR)	YES	POT LUCK (PARTY HOST)	YES	FORBIDDEN ART (SHAMAN)	YES	CAPTURE (BEASTMASTER)	—
ATTACK PROFICIENCY	B	MAGIC PROFICIENCY	B	EVASION CORRECTION	B	MAGIC EVASION CORRECTION	B

ABILITIES	CURAGA/CURA/SILENCE/SLEEP/FLASH			
EXPERIENCE POINTS	12	STEAL	CURSED BLADE (40%)/HOLY BREATH (25%)/CURSE RING (5%)	
DROP	AQUAMARINE (37.6%)	EMERALD (3.9%)	CROSS (10.2%)	CURSED BLADE (5.1%)

DOPPELGANGER [AIRE B]

ENCOUNTERED	ROLAN'S SOUL(PART II)								
LEVEL	25	HP	177-221	WEIGHT	—	STRENGTH	12	INTELLECT	24	SPIRIT	20
VARIABLE LEVEL	YES	ABILITY SPEED	60	ATTACK ELEMENT	DARK LV.1	ATTACK	8	ACCURACY	5	DEFENSE	6
INFLICTS	CURSE, STATUS DOWN (15%)					MAGIC DEFENSE	10	EVASION	13	MAGIC EVASION	10

ELEMENTAL DEFENSE	FIRE	WATER	WIND	EARTH	LIGHT	DARK
	—	—	—	—	WEAK	NO EFFECT

IMMUNE TO	CURSE

TAME (SCHOLAR)	YES	POT LUCK (PARTY HOST)	YES	FORBIDDEN ART (SHAMAN)	YES	CAPTURE (BEASTMASTER)	—
ATTACK PROFICIENCY	A	MAGIC PROFICIENCY	A	EVASION CORRECTION	A	MAGIC EVASION CORRECTION	A
ABILITIES	CURAGA/CURA/SILENCE/SLEEP/FLASH						
EXPERIENCE POINTS	14	STEAL		PHOENIX DOWN (25%)/HOLY BREATH (5%)			
DROP	AQUAMARINE (37.6%)		CROSS (7.8%)	CURSED BLADE (7.8%)	CURSE RING (2%)		

DOPPELGANGER [BRANDT A]

ENCOUNTERED	ROLAN'S SOUL(PART I) STAR CHAMBER(PART II)								
LEVEL	23	HP	60-75	WEIGHT	—	STRENGTH	12	INTELLECT	10	SPIRIT	16
VARIABLE LEVEL	—	ABILITY SPEED	55	ATTACK ELEMENT	DARK LV.1	ATTACK	8	ACCURACY	98	DEFENSE	5
INFLICTS	CURSE, STATUS DOWN (15%)					MAGIC DEFENSE	4	EVASION	9	MAGIC EVASION	6

ELEMENTAL DEFENSE	FIRE	WATER	WIND	EARTH	LIGHT	DARK
	—	—	—	—	WEAK	NO EFFECT

IMMUNE TO	—

TAME (SCHOLAR)	YES	POT LUCK (PARTY HOST)	YES	FORBIDDEN ART (SHAMAN)	YES	CAPTURE (BEASTMASTER)	—
ATTACK PROFICIENCY	B	MAGIC PROFICIENCY	B	EVASION CORRECTION	B	MAGIC EVASION CORRECTION	B
ABILITIES	CURA/BERSERK						
EXPERIENCE POINTS	12	STEAL		ICE PICK (40%)/HOLY BREATH (25%)/CURSE RING (5%)			
DROP	AQUAMARINE (37.6%)		RUBY (3.9%)	CROSS (10.2%)	CURSED BLADE (5.1%)		

DOPPELGANGER [BRANDT B]

ENCOUNTERED	ROLAN'S SOUL(PART II)								
LEVEL	25	HP	192-240	WEIGHT	—	STRENGTH	16	INTELLECT	20	SPIRIT	20
VARIABLE LEVEL	YES	ABILITY SPEED	60	ATTACK ELEMENT	DARK LV.1	ATTACK	8	ACCURACY	5	DEFENSE	6
INFLICTS	CURSE, STATUS DOWN (15%)					MAGIC DEFENSE	4	EVASION	50	MAGIC EVASION	10

ELEMENTAL DEFENSE	FIRE	WATER	WIND	EARTH	LIGHT	DARK
	—	—	—	—	WEAK	NO EFFECT

IMMUNE TO	CURSE

TAME (SCHOLAR)	YES	POT LUCK (PARTY HOST)	YES	FORBIDDEN ART (SHAMAN)	YES	CAPTURE (BEASTMASTER)	—
ATTACK PROFICIENCY	A	MAGIC PROFICIENCY	A	EVASION CORRECTION	A	MAGIC EVASION CORRECTION	A
ABILITIES	CURA/BERSERK						
EXPERIENCE POINTS	14	STEAL		PHOENIX DOWN (25%)/HOLY BREATH (5%)			
DROP	AQUAMARINE (37.6%)		CROSS (7.8%)	ICE PICK (7.8%)	CURSE RING (2%)		

DOPPELGANGER [JUSQUA A]

ENCOUNTERED	ROLAN'S SOUL(PART I) STAR CHAMBER(PART II)								
LEVEL	23	HP	60-75	WEIGHT	—	STRENGTH	12	INTELLECT	10	SPIRIT	16
VARIABLE LEVEL	—	ABILITY SPEED	55	ATTACK ELEMENT	DARK LV.1	ATTACK	8	ACCURACY	98	DEFENSE	5
INFLICTS	CURSE, STATUS DOWN (15%)					MAGIC DEFENSE	4	EVASION	9	MAGIC EVASION	6

ELEMENTAL DEFENSE	FIRE	WATER	WIND	EARTH	LIGHT	DARK
	—	—	—	—	WEAK	NO EFFECT

IMMUNE TO	—

TAME (SCHOLAR)	YES	POT LUCK (PARTY HOST)	YES	FORBIDDEN ART (SHAMAN)	YES	CAPTURE (BEASTMASTER)	—
ATTACK PROFICIENCY	B	MAGIC PROFICIENCY	B	EVASION CORRECTION	B	MAGIC EVASION CORRECTION	B
ABILITIES	DARKAGA/DARKRA						
EXPERIENCE POINTS	12	STEAL		HOLY KNIFE (40%)/HOLY BREATH (25%)/CURSE RING (5%)			
DROP	AQUAMARINE (37.6%)		SAPPHIRE (3.9%)	CROSS (10.2%)	CURSED BLADE (5.1%)		

DOPPELGANGER [JUSQUA B]

ENCOUNTERED	ROLAN'S SOUL(PART II)								
LEVEL	25	HP	187-234	WEIGHT	—	STRENGTH	15	INTELLECT	10	SPIRIT	16
VARIABLE LEVEL	YES	ABILITY SPEED	60	ATTACK ELEMENT	DARK LV.1	ATTACK	8	ACCURACY	5	DEFENSE	6
INFLICTS	CURSE, STATUS DOWN (15%)					MAGIC DEFENSE	10	EVASION	13	MAGIC EVASION	10

ELEMENTAL DEFENSE	FIRE	WATER	WIND	EARTH	LIGHT	DARK
	—	—	—	—	WEAK	NO EFFECT

IMMUNE TO	CURSE

TAME (SCHOLAR)	YES	POT LUCK (PARTY HOST)	YES	FORBIDDEN ART (SHAMAN)	YES	CAPTURE (BEASTMASTER)	—
ATTACK PROFICIENCY	A	MAGIC PROFICIENCY	A	EVASION CORRECTION	A	MAGIC EVASION CORRECTION	A
ABILITIES	DARKAGA/DARKRA						
EXPERIENCE POINTS	14	STEAL		PHOENIX DOWN (25%)/HOLY BREATH (5%)			
DROP	AQUAMARINE (37.6%)		CROSS (7.8%)	HOLY KNIFE (7.8%)	CURSE RING (2%)		

DOPPELGANGER [YUNITA A]

ENCOUNTERED	ROLAN'S SOUL(PART I) STAR CHAMBER(PART II)							
LEVEL	23	HP	60-75	WEIGHT	—	STRENGTH	12	INTELLECT	10	SPIRIT	16
VARIABLE LEVEL	—	ABILITY SPEED	55	ATTACK ELEMENT	DARK LV.1	ATTACK	8	ACCURACY	98	DEFENSE	3
INFLICTS	CURSE, STATUS DOWN (15%)					MAGIC DEFENSE	6	EVASION	9	MAGIC EVASION	6

ELEMENTAL DEFENSE	FIRE	WATER	WIND	EARTH	LIGHT	DARK
	—	—	—	—	WEAK	NO EFFECT

IMMUNE TO —

TAME (SCHOLAR)	YES	POT LUCK (PARTY HOST)	YES	FORBIDDEN ART (SHAMAN)	YES	CAPTURE (BEASTMASTER)	—
ATTACK PROFICIENCY	B	MAGIC PROFICIENCY	B	EVASION CORRECTION	B	MAGIC EVASION CORRECTION	B

ABILITIES CURA

EXPERIENCE POINTS	12	STEAL	FLAME DAGGER (40%)/HOLY BREATH (25%)/CURSE RING (5%)
DROP	AQUAMARINE (37.6%)	LAPIS (3.9%)	CROSS (10.2%)	CURSED BLADE (5.1%)

DOPPELGANGER [YUNITA B]

ENCOUNTERED	ROLAN'S SOUL(PART II)							
LEVEL	25	HP	185-231	WEIGHT	—	STRENGTH	14	INTELLECT	21	SPIRIT	22
VARIABLE LEVEL	YES	ABILITY SPEED	60	ATTACK ELEMENT	DARK LV.1	ATTACK	8	ACCURACY	5	DEFENSE	10
INFLICTS	CURSE, STATUS DOWN (15%)					MAGIC DEFENSE	4	EVASION	13	MAGIC EVASION	11

ELEMENTAL DEFENSE	FIRE	WATER	WIND	EARTH	LIGHT	DARK
	—	—	—	—	WEAK	NO EFFECT

IMMUNE TO CURSE

TAME (SCHOLAR)	YES	POT LUCK (PARTY HOST)	YES	FORBIDDEN ART (SHAMAN)	YES	CAPTURE (BEASTMASTER)	—
ATTACK PROFICIENCY	A	MAGIC PROFICIENCY	A	EVASION CORRECTION	A	MAGIC EVASION CORRECTION	A

ABILITIES CURA

EXPERIENCE POINTS	12	STEAL	FLAME DAGGER (40%)/HOLY BREATH (25%)/CURSE RING (5%)
DROP	AQUAMARINE (37.6%)	LAPIS (3.9%)	CROSS (10.2%)	CURSED BLADE (5.1%)

EVIL KNIGHT

FLYING

ENCOUNTERED	TOWER OF THE SKY(PART II) STAR CHAMBER(PART II)							
LEVEL	25	HP	138-173	WEIGHT	—	STRENGTH	13	INTELLECT	18	SPIRIT	18
VARIABLE LEVEL	YES	ABILITY SPEED	35	ATTACK ELEMENT	EARTH LV.2	ATTACK	6	ACCURACY	3	DEFENSE	5
INFLICTS	—					MAGIC DEFENSE	10	EVASION	5	MAGIC EVASION	7

ELEMENTAL DEFENSE	FIRE	WATER	WIND	EARTH	LIGHT	DARK
	—	WEAK	—	ABSORBS	—	—

IMMUNE TO —

TAME (SCHOLAR)	YES	POT LUCK (PARTY HOST)	YES	FORBIDDEN ART (SHAMAN)	YES	CAPTURE (BEASTMASTER)	YES
ATTACK PROFICIENCY		MAGIC PROFICIENCY		EVASION CORRECTION		MAGIC EVASION CORRECTION	

ABILITIES SHELL/IRON BLAST

EXPERIENCE POINTS	14	STEAL	HI-POTION (40%)/PHOENIX DOWN (25%)/BOMB FRAGMENT (5%)
DROP	LAPIS (37.6%)	AQUAMARINE (3.9%)	HI-POTION (10.2%)	PHOENIX DOWN (5.1%)

FALCON [A]

FLYING

ENCOUNTERED	HORNE AREA (PART I) LIBERTE AREA (PART II)							
LEVEL	3	HP	5-6	WEIGHT	—	STRENGTH	2	INTELLECT	3	SPIRIT	3
VARIABLE LEVEL	—	ABILITY SPEED	30	ATTACK ELEMENT		ATTACK	3	ACCURACY	96	DEFENSE	2
INFLICTS	—					MAGIC DEFENSE	3	EVASION	2	MAGIC EVASION	2

ELEMENTAL DEFENSE	FIRE	WATER	WIND	EARTH	LIGHT	DARK
	—	—	WEAK	—	—	—

IMMUNE TO —

TAME (SCHOLAR)	YES	POT LUCK (PARTY HOST)	YES	FORBIDDEN ART (SHAMAN)	YES	CAPTURE (BEASTMASTER)	YES
ATTACK PROFICIENCY	B	MAGIC PROFICIENCY	C	EVASION CORRECTION	B	MAGIC EVASION CORRECTION	C

ABILITIES DIVE

EXPERIENCE POINTS	3	STEAL	POTION (40%)/PHOENIX DOWN (25%)/RAVEN'S YAWN (5%)
DROP	RUBY (37.6%)	TOPAZ (3.9%)	PHOENIX DOWN (5.1%)	GALE GAUNTLET (2%)

FALCON [B]

2 ACTIONS, FLYING

ENCOUNTERED	MYSTERIOUS TOWER (PART II)							
LEVEL	70	HP	482-603	WEIGHT	60	STRENGTH	34	INTELLECT	23	SPIRIT	33
VARIABLE LEVEL	YES	ABILITY SPEED	100	ATTACK ELEMENT		ATTACK	33	ACCURACY	150	DEFENSE	22
INFLICTS	—					MAGIC DEFENSE	21	EVASION	2	MAGIC EVASION	2

ELEMENTAL DEFENSE	FIRE	WATER	WIND	EARTH	LIGHT	DARK
	—	—	WEAK	NO EFFECT	—	—

IMMUNE TO CURSE

TAME (SCHOLAR)	YES	POT LUCK (PARTY HOST)	YES	FORBIDDEN ART (SHAMAN)	YES	CAPTURE (BEASTMASTER)	YES
ATTACK PROFICIENCY	A	MAGIC PROFICIENCY	A	EVASION CORRECTION	A	MAGIC EVASION CORRECTION	A

ABILITIES DIVE

EXPERIENCE POINTS	100	STEAL	POTION (40%)/HI-POTION (25%)/RAVEN'S YAWN (5%)
DROP	RUBY (37.6%)	POTION (7.8%)	—	GALE GAUNTLET (2%)

FUNGUS

ENCOUNTERED	GREAT TREE ROOTS(PART II)									
	HUNTING CAVES(PART II)									

LEVEL	25	HP		122-153	WEIGHT	—	STRENGTH	13	INTELLECT	18	SPIRIT	18
VARIABLE LEVEL	YES	ABILITY SPEED	30	ATTACK ELEMENT	EARTH LV.1		ATTACK	7	ACCURACY	3	DEFENSE	3
INFLICTS	—						MAGIC DEFENSE	6	EVASION	5	MAGIC EVASION	7

ELEMENTAL DEFENSE	FIRE	WATER	WIND	EARTH	LIGHT	DARK
	—	—		HALF		

IMMUNE TO	—

TAME (SCHOLAR)	YES	POT LUCK (PARTY HOST)	YES	FORBIDDEN ART (SHAMAN)	YES	CAPTURE (BEASTMASTER)	YES
ATTACK PROFICIENCY	B	MAGIC PROFICIENCY	B	EVASION CORRECTION	B	MAGIC EVASION CORRECTION	B

ABILITIES	SPORE			
EXPERIENCE POINTS	14	STEAL	ANTIDOTE (40%)/X-POTION (25%)/GREAT TREE LOG (5%)		
DROP	SAPPHIRE (37.6%)		EMERALD (3.9%)	ANTIDOTE (10.2%)	GREAT TREE SWORD (5.1%)

GARGOYLE [A]

ENCOUNTERED	TOWER OF THE SKY(PART I)								FLYING	

LEVEL	17	HP		50-63	WEIGHT	—	STRENGTH	8	INTELLECT	12	SPIRIT	14
VARIABLE LEVEL	—	ABILITY SPEED	25	ATTACK ELEMENT	EARTH LV.1		ATTACK	6	ACCURACY	98	DEFENSE	3
INFLICTS	—						MAGIC DEFENSE	7	EVASION	7	MAGIC EVASION	10

ELEMENTAL DEFENSE	FIRE	WATER	WIND	EARTH	LIGHT	DARK
	—	—	WEAK	NO EFFECT		

IMMUNE TO	—

TAME (SCHOLAR)	YES	POT LUCK (PARTY HOST)	YES	FORBIDDEN ART (SHAMAN)	YES	CAPTURE (BEASTMASTER)	YES
ATTACK PROFICIENCY	B	MAGIC PROFICIENCY	B	EVASION CORRECTION	B	MAGIC EVASION CORRECTION	A

ABILITIES	SHELL/IRON BLAST			
EXPERIENCE POINTS	10	STEAL	HI-POTION (40%)/GAIA DRUM (25%)/BOMB FRAGMENT (5%)		
DROP	SAPPHIRE (37.6%)		AQUAMARINE (3.9%)	HI-POTION (10.2%)	FLAME GAUNTLETS (5.1%)

GARGOYLE [B]

ENCOUNTERED	TRIAL TOWER (PART II)							2 ACTIONS, FLYING	

LEVEL	90	HP		846-1058	WEIGHT	30	STRENGTH	81	INTELLECT	91	SPIRIT	72
VARIABLE LEVEL	YES	ABILITY SPEED	60	ATTACK ELEMENT	EARTH LV.1		ATTACK	57	ACCURACY	150	DEFENSE	50
INFLICTS	—						MAGIC DEFENSE	38	EVASION	5	MAGIC EVASION	36

ELEMENTAL DEFENSE	FIRE	WATER	WIND	EARTH	LIGHT	DARK
	—	—	WEAK	NO EFFECT		

IMMUNE TO	CURSE

TAME (SCHOLAR)	YES	POT LUCK (PARTY HOST)	YES	FORBIDDEN ART (SHAMAN)	YES	CAPTURE (BEASTMASTER)	YES
ATTACK PROFICIENCY	A	MAGIC PROFICIENCY	A	EVASION CORRECTION	A	MAGIC EVASION CORRECTION	A

ABILITIES	SHELL/IRON BLAST			
EXPERIENCE POINTS	100	STEAL	POTION (40%)/HI-POTION (25%)/BOMB FRAGMENT (5%)		
DROP	LAPIS (37.6%)		HI-POTION (7.8%)	—	FLAME GAUNTLET (2%)

GARM

ENCOUNTERED	URBETH AREA (PART II)										
	MT. GULG(PART II)										

LEVEL	25	HP		134-168	WEIGHT	—	STRENGTH	13	INTELLECT	20	SPIRIT	18
VARIABLE LEVEL	YES	ABILITY SPEED	50	ATTACK ELEMENT	FIRE LV.1		ATTACK	7	ACCURACY	5	DEFENSE	4
INFLICTS	—						MAGIC DEFENSE	6	EVASION	5	MAGIC EVASION	7

ELEMENTAL DEFENSE	FIRE	WATER	WIND	EARTH	LIGHT	DARK
	—	—	—	—		

IMMUNE TO	—

TAME (SCHOLAR)	YES	POT LUCK (PARTY HOST)	YES	FORBIDDEN ART (SHAMAN)	YES	CAPTURE (BEASTMASTER)	YES
ATTACK PROFICIENCY	B	MAGIC PROFICIENCY	A	EVASION CORRECTION	B	MAGIC EVASION CORRECTION	B

ABILITIES	FIRE BREATH [A]			
EXPERIENCE POINTS	14	STEAL	BOMB FRAGMENT (40%)/HI-POTION (25%)/ETHER (5%)		
DROP	LAPIS (37.6%)		RUBY (3.9%)	BOMB FRAGMENT (5.1%)	LONE WOLF (2%)

GHOUL [A]

ENCOUNTERED	INVIDIA AREA (PART II)								FLYING	
	SPELVIA DUNGEONS(PART II)									

LEVEL	25	HP		133-166	WEIGHT	—	STRENGTH	11	INTELLECT	16	SPIRIT	18
VARIABLE LEVEL	YES	ABILITY SPEED	40	ATTACK ELEMENT	DARK LV.1		ATTACK	7	ACCURACY	3	DEFENSE	6
INFLICTS	—						MAGIC DEFENSE	6	EVASION	5	MAGIC EVASION	7

ELEMENTAL DEFENSE	FIRE	WATER	WIND	EARTH	LIGHT	DARK
	—	—	—	—	WEAK	HALF

IMMUNE TO	—

TAME (SCHOLAR)	YES	POT LUCK (PARTY HOST)	YES	FORBIDDEN ART (SHAMAN)	YES	CAPTURE (BEASTMASTER)	YES
ATTACK PROFICIENCY	B	MAGIC PROFICIENCY	A	EVASION CORRECTION	B	MAGIC EVASION CORRECTION	B

ABILITIES	FLASH/DARK BLAST			
EXPERIENCE POINTS	14	STEAL	HI-POTION (40%)/PHOENIX DOWN (25%)/GAIA DRUM (5%)		
DROP	EMERALD (37.6%)		TOPAZ (3.9%)	HI-POTION (10.2%)	CURSE RING (5.1%)

GIANT MOTH

ENCOUNTERED	ARBOR SOUTH AREA (PART II) GREAT TREE(PART II)								
LEVEL	25	HP	118-148	WEIGHT	—	STRENGTH	12	INTELLECT	18	SPIRIT	18
VARIABLE LEVEL	YES	ABILITY SPEED	55	ATTACK ELEMENT	—	ATTACK	6	ACCURACY	3	DEFENSE	4
INFLICTS	—					MAGIC DEFENSE	6	EVASION	5	MAGIC EVASION	7

ELEMENTAL DEFENSE	FIRE	WATER	WIND	EARTH	LIGHT	DARK
	WEAK	—	—	—	—	—

IMMUNE TO	—

TAME (SCHOLAR)	YES	POT LUCK (PARTY HOST)	YES	FORBIDDEN ART (SHAMAN)	YES	CAPTURE (BEASTMASTER)	YES
ATTACK PROFICIENCY	B	MAGIC PROFICIENCY	B	EVASION CORRECTION	B	MAGIC EVASION CORRECTION	B

ABILITIES	SLEEP/FLUTTER EFFECT			
EXPERIENCE POINTS	14	STEAL	ANTIDOTE (40%)/EYE DROPS (25%)/GREAT TREE LOG (5%)	
DROP	SAPPHIRE (37.6%)	SAPPHIRE (3.9%)	HI-POTION (10.2%)	FLASH RING (5.1%)

GOBLIN [A]

ENCOUNTERED	HORNE AREA (PART I) NORTHERN CAVES(PART I)								
LEVEL	3	HP	5-6	WEIGHT	—	STRENGTH	2	INTELLECT	2	SPIRIT	2
VARIABLE LEVEL	—	ABILITY SPEED	25	ATTACK ELEMENT	—	ATTACK	2	ACCURACY	96	DEFENSE	1
INFLICTS	—					MAGIC DEFENSE	3	EVASION	2	MAGIC EVASION	2

ELEMENTAL DEFENSE	FIRE	WATER	WIND	EARTH	LIGHT	DARK
	—	—	—	—	—	—

IMMUNE TO	—

TAME (SCHOLAR)	YES	POT LUCK (PARTY HOST)	YES	FORBIDDEN ART (SHAMAN)	YES	CAPTURE (BEASTMASTER)	YES
ATTACK PROFICIENCY	B	MAGIC PROFICIENCY	B	EVASION CORRECTION	B	MAGIC EVASION CORRECTION	C

ABILITIES	GOBLIN STRIKE			
EXPERIENCE POINTS	2	STEAL	STEEL SPEAR (40%)/HI-POTION (25%)/RAVEN'S YAWN (5%)	
DROP	RUBY (37.6%)	TOPAZ (3.9%)	HI-POTION (5.1%)	—

GOBLIN [B]

ENCOUNTERED	MYSTERIOUS TOWER (PART II)								
LEVEL	70	HP	492-615	WEIGHT	—	STRENGTH	36	INTELLECT	28	SPIRIT	56
VARIABLE LEVEL	YES	ABILITY SPEED	100	ATTACK ELEMENT	—	ATTACK	37	ACCURACY	150	DEFENSE	23
INFLICTS	—					MAGIC DEFENSE	21	EVASION	2	MAGIC EVASION	2

ELEMENTAL DEFENSE	FIRE	WATER	WIND	EARTH	LIGHT	DARK
	—	—	—	—	—	—

IMMUNE TO	CURSE

TAME (SCHOLAR)	YES	POT LUCK (PARTY HOST)	YES	FORBIDDEN ART (SHAMAN)	YES	CAPTURE (BEASTMASTER)	YES
ATTACK PROFICIENCY	A	MAGIC PROFICIENCY	A	EVASION CORRECTION	A	MAGIC EVASION CORRECTION	A

ABILITIES	GOBLIN STRIKE			
EXPERIENCE POINTS	100	STEAL	POTION (40%)/HI-POTION (25%)/RAVEN'S YAWN (5%)	
DROP	RUBY (37.6%)	POTION (7.8%)	—	TEMPEST PIKE (2%)

GOLEM

ENCOUNTERED	SPELVIA DUNGEONS(PART I) SPELVIA DUNGEONS(PART II)								
LEVEL	20	HP	70-88	WEIGHT	—	STRENGTH	10	INTELLECT	10	SPIRIT	10
VARIABLE LEVEL	—	ABILITY SPEED	50	ATTACK ELEMENT	—	ATTACK	9	ACCURACY	97	DEFENSE	3
INFLICTS	—					MAGIC DEFENSE	5	EVASION	7	MAGIC EVASION	5

ELEMENTAL DEFENSE	FIRE	WATER	WIND	EARTH	LIGHT	DARK
	—	—	—	—	—	—

IMMUNE TO	ALL

TAME (SCHOLAR)	YES	POT LUCK (PARTY HOST)	YES	FORBIDDEN ART (SHAMAN)	YES	CAPTURE (BEASTMASTER)	—
ATTACK PROFICIENCY	B	MAGIC PROFICIENCY	B	EVASION CORRECTION	B	MAGIC EVASION CORRECTION	B

ABILITIES	—			
EXPERIENCE POINTS	11	STEAL	—	
DROP	—			

GORGON

ENCOUNTERED	SPELVIA DUNGEONS(PART II) INVIDIA UNDERGROUND(PART II)								
LEVEL	25	HP	126-158	WEIGHT	—	STRENGTH	13	INTELLECT	22	SPIRIT	16
VARIABLE LEVEL	YES	ABILITY SPEED	40	ATTACK ELEMENT	—	ATTACK	6	ACCURACY	3	DEFENSE	8
INFLICTS	CONFUSION (13%)					MAGIC DEFENSE	10	EVASION	5	MAGIC EVASION	6

ELEMENTAL DEFENSE	FIRE	WATER	WIND	EARTH	LIGHT	DARK
	—	—	—	—	—	—

IMMUNE TO	PETRIFY

TAME (SCHOLAR)	YES	POT LUCK (PARTY HOST)	YES	FORBIDDEN ART (SHAMAN)	YES	CAPTURE (BEASTMASTER)	YES
ATTACK PROFICIENCY	B	MAGIC PROFICIENCY	B	EVASION CORRECTION	B	MAGIC EVASION CORRECTION	B

ABILITIES	PETRIFY			
EXPERIENCE POINTS	14	STEAL	GOLD NEEDLE (40%)/FOSSIL CAPE (25%)/HOLY BREATH (5%)	
DROP	AQUAMARINE (37.6%)	SAPPHIRE (3.9%)	HI-POTION (5.1%)	COURAGE RING (2%)

HELLHOUND [A]

ENCOUNTERED	URBETH AREA (PART I)								
	HUNTING CAVES (PART I)								

LEVEL	13	HP	51-64	WEIGHT	—	STRENGTH	10	INTELLECT	10	SPIRIT	8
VARIABLE LEVEL	—	ABILITY SPEED	30	ATTACK ELEMENT	FIRE LV.1	ATTACK	7	ACCURACY	97	DEFENSE	4
INFLICTS						MAGIC DEFENSE	4	EVASION	7	MAGIC EVASION	10

ELEMENTAL DEFENSE	FIRE	WATER	WIND	EARTH	LIGHT	DARK
	HALF	WEAK	—	—	—	—

IMMUNE TO	—

TAME (SCHOLAR)	YES	POT LUCK (PARTY HOST)	YES	FORBIDDEN ART (SHAMAN)	YES	CAPTURE (BEASTMASTER)	YES
ATTACK PROFICIENCY	B	MAGIC PROFICIENCY	B	EVASION CORRECTION	A	MAGIC EVASION CORRECTION	C

ABILITIES	FIRE BREATH [A]			
EXPERIENCE POINTS	8	STEAL	BOMB FRAGMENT (40%)/HI-POTION (25%)/BOMB FRAGMENT (5%)	
DROP	SAPPHIRE (37.6%)	RUBY (3.9%)	BOMB FRAGMENT (5.1%)	LONE WOLF (2%)

HELLHOUND [B]

2 ACTIONS

ENCOUNTERED	MOONSAND RUINS (PART II)								
	TRIAL TOWER (PART II)								

LEVEL	50	HP	400-500	WEIGHT	30	STRENGTH	25	INTELLECT	95	SPIRIT	40
VARIABLE LEVEL	YES	ABILITY SPEED	60	ATTACK ELEMENT	FIRE LV.1	ATTACK	32	ACCURACY	150	DEFENSE	19
INFLICTS						MAGIC DEFENSE	18	EVASION	5	MAGIC EVASION	20

ELEMENTAL DEFENSE	FIRE	WATER	WIND	EARTH	LIGHT	DARK
	HALF	WEAK	—	—	—	—

IMMUNE TO	CURSE

TAME (SCHOLAR)	YES	POT LUCK (PARTY HOST)	YES	FORBIDDEN ART (SHAMAN)	YES	CAPTURE (BEASTMASTER)	YES
ATTACK PROFICIENCY	A	MAGIC PROFICIENCY	A	EVASION CORRECTION	A	MAGIC EVASION CORRECTION	A

ABILITIES	FIRE BREATH [A]			
EXPERIENCE POINTS	100	STEAL	POTION (40%)/HI-POTION (25%)/BOMB FRAGMENT (5%)	
DROP	LAPIS (37.6%)	BOMB FRAGMENT (7.8%)	ECHO HERBS (3.9%)	LONE WOLF (2%)

HOBGOBLIN

ENCOUNTERED	ARBOR SOUTH AREA (PART II)								
	GREAT TREE ROOTS (PART II)								

LEVEL	25	HP	122-153	WEIGHT	—	STRENGTH	11	INTELLECT	18	SPIRIT	18
VARIABLE LEVEL	YES	ABILITY SPEED	50	ATTACK ELEMENT	—	ATTACK	7	ACCURACY	5	DEFENSE	5
INFLICTS						MAGIC DEFENSE	4	EVASION	5	MAGIC EVASION	7

ELEMENTAL DEFENSE	FIRE	WATER	WIND	EARTH	LIGHT	DARK
	—	—	—	—	—	—

IMMUNE TO	—

TAME (SCHOLAR)	YES	POT LUCK (PARTY HOST)	YES	FORBIDDEN ART (SHAMAN)	YES	CAPTURE (BEASTMASTER)	YES
ATTACK PROFICIENCY		MAGIC PROFICIENCY		EVASION CORRECTION		MAGIC EVASION CORRECTION	

ABILITIES	GOBLIN STRIKE			
EXPERIENCE POINTS	14	STEAL	ROCK LANCE (40%)/WOOD LANCE (25%)/GREAT TREE LOG (5%)	
DROP	SAPPHIRE (37.6%)	LAPIS (3.9%)	HI-POTION (10.2%)	TEMPEST PIKE (5.1%)

HUGIN [A]

FLYING

ENCOUNTERED	GREAT TREE (PART I)								
	GREAT TREE TO THE SUMMIT (PART I)								

LEVEL	14	HP	47-59	WEIGHT	—	STRENGTH	9	INTELLECT	13	SPIRIT	10
VARIABLE LEVEL	—	ABILITY SPEED	30	ATTACK ELEMENT	—	ATTACK	5	ACCURACY	97	DEFENSE	1
INFLICTS	SLEEP (10%)					MAGIC DEFENSE	9	EVASION	6	MAGIC EVASION	10

ELEMENTAL DEFENSE	FIRE	WATER	WIND	EARTH	LIGHT	DARK
	—	—	WEAK	—	—	—

IMMUNE TO	—

TAME (SCHOLAR)	YES	POT LUCK (PARTY HOST)	YES	FORBIDDEN ART (SHAMAN)	YES	CAPTURE (BEASTMASTER)	YES
ATTACK PROFICIENCY	B	MAGIC PROFICIENCY	B	EVASION CORRECTION	B	MAGIC EVASION CORRECTION	B

ABILITIES	WOOD BLAST/SILENCE/FLASH			
EXPERIENCE POINTS	8	STEAL	POTION (40%)/HI-POTION (25%)/GREAT TREE LOG (5%)	
DROP	LAPIS (37.6%)	AQUAMARINE (3.9%)	EYE DROPS (10.2%)	PHOENIX DOWN (5.1%)

HUGIN [B]

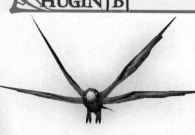

FLYING

ENCOUNTERED	TRIAL TOWER (PART II)								

LEVEL	90	HP	852-1065	WEIGHT	—	STRENGTH	81	INTELLECT	191	SPIRIT	72
VARIABLE LEVEL	YES	ABILITY SPEED	60	ATTACK ELEMENT	—	ATTACK	52	ACCURACY	150	DEFENSE	36
INFLICTS	SLEEP (15%)					MAGIC DEFENSE	37	EVASION	25	MAGIC EVASION	36

ELEMENTAL DEFENSE	FIRE	WATER	WIND	EARTH	LIGHT	DARK
	—	—	WEAK	NO EFFECT	—	—

IMMUNE TO	CURSE

TAME (SCHOLAR)	YES	POT LUCK (PARTY HOST)	YES	FORBIDDEN ART (SHAMAN)	YES	CAPTURE (BEASTMASTER)	YES
ATTACK PROFICIENCY	A	MAGIC PROFICIENCY	A	EVASION CORRECTION	A	MAGIC EVASION CORRECTION	A

ABILITIES	WOOD BLAST/SILENCE/FLASH			
EXPERIENCE POINTS	100	STEAL	POTION (40%)/HI-POTION (25%)/GREAT TREE LOG (5%)	
DROP	SAPPHIRE (37.6%)	EYE DROPS (7.8%)	—	—

ICHTHON [A]

FLYING

ENCOUNTERED	SEA (PART I)
	??? (PART I)

LEVEL	9	HP	35-44	WEIGHT	—		STRENGTH	8	INTELLECT	6	SPIRIT	6
VARIABLE LEVEL	—	ABILITY SPEED	30	ATTACK ELEMENT	WATER LV.1		ATTACK	5	ACCURACY	97	DEFENSE	2
INFLICTS							MAGIC DEFENSE	4	EVASION	4	MAGIC EVASION	10

ELEMENTAL DEFENSE	FIRE	WATER	WIND	EARTH	LIGHT	DARK
	WEAK	NO EFFECT	—	—	—	—

IMMUNE TO —

TAME (SCHOLAR)	YES	POT LUCK (PARTY HOST)	YES	FORBIDDEN ART (SHAMAN)	YES	CAPTURE (BEASTMASTER)	YES
ATTACK PROFICIENCY	B	MAGIC PROFICIENCY	B	EVASION CORRECTION	B	MAGIC EVASION CORRECTION	B

ABILITIES —

EXPERIENCE POINTS	6	STEAL	ANTIDOTE (40%)/ECHO HERBS (25%)/ANTARCTIC WIND (5%)		
DROP	TOPAZ (37.6%)		AQUAMARINE (3.9%)	PHOENIX DOWN (5.1%)	SPRING GAUNTLETS (2%)

ICHTHON [B]

FLYING

ENCOUNTERED	MOONSAND RUINS (PART II)

LEVEL	50	HP	260-325	WEIGHT	—		STRENGTH	21	INTELLECT	130	SPIRIT	40
VARIABLE LEVEL	YES	ABILITY SPEED	60	ATTACK ELEMENT	WATER LV.1		ATTACK	22	ACCURACY	150	DEFENSE	7
INFLICTS							MAGIC DEFENSE	8	EVASION	7	MAGIC EVASION	10

ELEMENTAL DEFENSE	FIRE	WATER	WIND	EARTH	LIGHT	DARK
	—	NO EFFECT	—	WEAK	—	—

IMMUNE TO CURSE

TAME (SCHOLAR)	YES	POT LUCK (PARTY HOST)	YES	FORBIDDEN ART (SHAMAN)	YES	CAPTURE (BEASTMASTER)	YES
ATTACK PROFICIENCY	A	MAGIC PROFICIENCY	A	EVASION CORRECTION	A	MAGIC EVASION CORRECTION	A

ABILITIES WATER BLAST

EXPERIENCE POINTS	100	STEAL	POTION (40%)/HI-POTION (25%)/ANTARCTIC WIND (5%)		
DROP	TOPAZ (37.6%)		POTION (7.8%)	PHOENIX DOWN (3.9%)	SPRING GAUNTLETS (2%)

IKKAKU [A]

FLYING

ENCOUNTERED	INVIDIA AREA (PART I)
	ICE CAVERNS (PART I)

LEVEL	23	HP	65-81	WEIGHT	—		STRENGTH	10	INTELLECT	12	SPIRIT	16
VARIABLE LEVEL	—	ABILITY SPEED	30	ATTACK ELEMENT	WATER LV.1		ATTACK	5	ACCURACY	98	DEFENSE	3
INFLICTS	PARALYSIS (13%)						MAGIC DEFENSE	7	EVASION	9	MAGIC EVASION	6

ELEMENTAL DEFENSE	FIRE	WATER	WIND	EARTH	LIGHT	DARK
	WEAK	HALF	—	—	—	WEAK

IMMUNE TO —

TAME (SCHOLAR)	YES	POT LUCK (PARTY HOST)	YES	FORBIDDEN ART (SHAMAN)	YES	CAPTURE (BEASTMASTER)	YES
ATTACK PROFICIENCY	A	MAGIC PROFICIENCY	B	EVASION CORRECTION	B	MAGIC EVASION CORRECTION	B

ABILITIES LIGHTNING BOLT [A]

EXPERIENCE POINTS	13	STEAL	ANIMATE TONIC (40%)/HI-POTION (25%)/DARK SIGH (5%)		
DROP	AQUAMARINE (37.6%)		SAPPHIRE (3.9%)	PHOENIX DOWN (5.1%)	DEATH RING (1.2%)

IKKAKU [B]

FLYING

ENCOUNTERED	SEA (PART I)

LEVEL	23	HP	75-94	WEIGHT	—		STRENGTH	10	INTELLECT	16	SPIRIT	16
VARIABLE LEVEL	—	ABILITY SPEED	40	ATTACK ELEMENT	DARK LV.1		ATTACK	7	ACCURACY	99	DEFENSE	2
INFLICTS							MAGIC DEFENSE	5	EVASION	9	MAGIC EVASION	6

ELEMENTAL DEFENSE	FIRE	WATER	WIND	EARTH	LIGHT	DARK
	—	—	—	NO EFFECT	WEAK	HALF

IMMUNE TO —

TAME (SCHOLAR)	YES	POT LUCK (PARTY HOST)	YES	FORBIDDEN ART (SHAMAN)	YES	CAPTURE (BEASTMASTER)	YES
ATTACK PROFICIENCY	A	MAGIC PROFICIENCY	B	EVASION CORRECTION	B	MAGIC EVASION CORRECTION	B

ABILITIES LIGHTNING BOLT [A]

EXPERIENCE POINTS	13	STEAL	HI-POTION (40%)/X-POTION (25%)/HOLY BREATH (5%)		
DROP	TOPAZ (37.6%)		SAPPHIRE (10.2%)	POTION (7.8%)	DEATH RING (1.2%)

IKKAKU [C]

2 ACTIONS, FLYING

ENCOUNTERED	HOLY TREE TOWER (PART II)
	TRIAL TOWER (PART II)

LEVEL	60	HP	416-520	WEIGHT	30		STRENGTH	22	INTELLECT	108	SPIRIT	48
VARIABLE LEVEL	YES	ABILITY SPEED	80	ATTACK ELEMENT	WATER LV.1		ATTACK	28	ACCURACY	150	DEFENSE	20
INFLICTS	PARALYSIS (13%)						MAGIC DEFENSE	14	EVASION	3	MAGIC EVASION	24

ELEMENTAL DEFENSE	FIRE	WATER	WIND	EARTH	LIGHT	DARK
	—	HALF	—	WEAK	—	—

IMMUNE TO CURSE

TAME (SCHOLAR)	YES	POT LUCK (PARTY HOST)	YES	FORBIDDEN ART (SHAMAN)	YES	CAPTURE (BEASTMASTER)	YES
ATTACK PROFICIENCY	A	MAGIC PROFICIENCY	A	EVASION CORRECTION	A	MAGIC EVASION CORRECTION	A

ABILITIES LIGHTNING BOLT [A]

EXPERIENCE POINTS	100	STEAL	POTION (40%)/HI-POTION (25%)/DARK SIGH (5%)		
DROP	TOPAZ (37.6%)		ANIMATE TONIC (7.8%)	PHOENIX DOWN (3.9%)	DEATH RING (2%)

IMP [A]

ENCOUNTERED	HORNE AREA (PART I) ANIMAL BURROW(PART I)							FLYING	
LEVEL	1	HP	5-6	WEIGHT	—	STRENGTH	1	INTELLECT	1	SPIRIT	1
VARIABLE LEVEL	—	ABILITY SPEED	35	ATTACK ELEMENT	WIND LV.1	ATTACK	2	ACCURACY	96	DEFENSE	1
INFLICTS	—					MAGIC DEFENSE	1	EVASION	1	MAGIC EVASION	10

ELEMENTAL DEFENSE	FIRE	WATER	WIND	EARTH	LIGHT	DARK
	—	—	—	—	—	

IMMUNE TO	—

TAME (SCHOLAR)	YES	POT LUCK (PARTY HOST)	YES	FORBIDDEN ART (SHAMAN)	YES	CAPTURE (BEASTMASTER)	YES
ATTACK PROFICIENCY	C	MAGIC PROFICIENCY	B	EVASION CORRECTION	C	MAGIC EVASION CORRECTION	B
ABILITIES							
EXPERIENCE POINTS	1	STEAL		POTION (40%)/HI-POTION (25%)/RAVEN'S YAWN (5%)			
DROP	RUBY (37.6%)		EMERALD (3.9%)		POTION (10.2%)		HARP (5.1%)

IMP [B]

ENCOUNTERED	ARBOR SOUTH AREA (PART I) FAIRY PATH(PART I)							FLYING	
LEVEL	1	HP	40-50	WEIGHT	—	STRENGTH	6	INTELLECT	6	SPIRIT	3
VARIABLE LEVEL	—	ABILITY SPEED	45	ATTACK ELEMENT	WIND LV.1	ATTACK	6	ACCURACY	98	DEFENSE	2
INFLICTS	—					MAGIC DEFENSE	5	EVASION	1	MAGIC EVASION	1

ELEMENTAL DEFENSE	FIRE	WATER	WIND	EARTH	LIGHT	DARK
	—	—	HALF	HALF	—	

IMMUNE TO	—

TAME (SCHOLAR)	YES	POT LUCK (PARTY HOST)	YES	FORBIDDEN ART (SHAMAN)	YES	CAPTURE (BEASTMASTER)	YES
ATTACK PROFICIENCY	C	MAGIC PROFICIENCY	B	EVASION CORRECTION	C	MAGIC EVASION CORRECTION	B
ABILITIES	PERFORMANCE						
EXPERIENCE POINTS	6	STEAL		WHISPERING HARP (40%)/X-POTION (25%)/GAIA DRUM (5%)			
DROP	LAPIS (37.6%)		SAPPHIRE (10.2%)		POTION (7.8%)		HARP (3.9%)

IMP [C]

ENCOUNTERED	MOONSAND RUINS (PART II)							FLYING	
LEVEL	50	HP	252-315	WEIGHT	—	STRENGTH	20	INTELLECT	15	SPIRIT	16
VARIABLE LEVEL	YES	ABILITY SPEED	60	ATTACK ELEMENT	WIND LV.1	ATTACK	20	ACCURACY	150	DEFENSE	5
INFLICTS	—					MAGIC DEFENSE	7	EVASION	1	MAGIC EVASION	8

ELEMENTAL DEFENSE	FIRE	WATER	WIND	EARTH	LIGHT	DARK
	—	—	HALF	NO EFFECT	—	

IMMUNE TO	SLEEP /CURSE

TAME (SCHOLAR)	YES	POT LUCK (PARTY HOST)	YES	FORBIDDEN ART (SHAMAN)	YES	CAPTURE (BEASTMASTER)	YES
ATTACK PROFICIENCY	A	MAGIC PROFICIENCY	A	EVASION CORRECTION	A	MAGIC EVASION CORRECTION	A
ABILITIES	PERFORMANCE						
EXPERIENCE POINTS	100	STEAL		POTION (40%)/HI-POTION (25%)/RAVEN'S YAWN (5%)			
DROP	RUBY (37.6%)		POTION (7.8%)		—		HARP (2%)

IRON GOLEM

ENCOUNTERED	TOWER OF THE SKY(PART II) STAR CHAMBER(PART II)								
LEVEL	25	HP	145-181	WEIGHT	—	STRENGTH	15	INTELLECT	18	SPIRIT	18
VARIABLE LEVEL	YES	ABILITY SPEED	5	ATTACK ELEMENT	EARTH LV.2	ATTACK	8	ACCURACY	5	DEFENSE	10
INFLICTS	—					MAGIC DEFENSE	6	EVASION	0	MAGIC EVASION	7

ELEMENTAL DEFENSE	FIRE	WATER	WIND	EARTH	LIGHT	DARK
	—	WEAK	—	REFLECT	—	

IMMUNE TO	—

TAME (SCHOLAR)	YES	POT LUCK (PARTY HOST)	YES	FORBIDDEN ART (SHAMAN)	YES	CAPTURE (BEASTMASTER)	YES
ATTACK PROFICIENCY	A	MAGIC PROFICIENCY	B	EVASION CORRECTION	C	MAGIC EVASION CORRECTION	B
ABILITIES	WHIRL BLUDGEON [B]						
EXPERIENCE POINTS	14	STEAL		HI-POTION (40%)/GIANT'S RING (25%)/BOMB FRAGMENT (5%)			
DROP	LAPIS (37.6%)		EMERALD (3.9%)		MYTHRIL (5.1%)		EARTH AXE (5.1%)

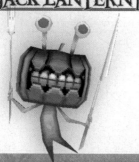

JACK LANTERN [A]

ENCOUNTERED	HORNE AREA (PART I) NORTHERN CAVES(PART I)								
LEVEL	2	HP	6-8	WEIGHT	—	STRENGTH	2	INTELLECT	1	SPIRIT	1
VARIABLE LEVEL	—	ABILITY SPEED	30	ATTACK ELEMENT	WIND LV.1	ATTACK	2	ACCURACY	96	DEFENSE	1
INFLICTS	—					MAGIC DEFENSE	4	EVASION	1	MAGIC EVASION	10

ELEMENTAL DEFENSE	FIRE	WATER	WIND	EARTH	LIGHT	DARK
	—	—	HALF	—	—	

IMMUNE TO	—

TAME (SCHOLAR)	YES	POT LUCK (PARTY HOST)	YES	FORBIDDEN ART (SHAMAN)	YES	CAPTURE (BEASTMASTER)	YES
ATTACK PROFICIENCY	B	MAGIC PROFICIENCY	C	EVASION CORRECTION	B	MAGIC EVASION CORRECTION	C
ABILITIES	IMPALE						
EXPERIENCE POINTS	2	STEAL		POTION (40%)/HI-POTION (25%)/RAVEN'S YAWN (5%)			
DROP	RUBY (37.6%)		SAPPHIRE (3.9%)		POTION (10.2%)		—

JACK LANTERN [B]

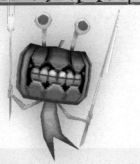

ENCOUNTERED	ARBOR NORTH AREA(PART I) FAIRY PATH(PART I)									
LEVEL	2	HP	43-54	WEIGHT	—	STRENGTH	7	INTELLECT	3	SPIRIT	3
VARIABLE LEVEL	—	ABILITY SPEED	40	ATTACK ELEMENT	WIND LV.1	ATTACK	6	ACCURACY	98	DEFENSE	2
INFLICTS	—					MAGIC DEFENSE	7	EVASION	1	MAGIC EVASION	1

ELEMENTAL DEFENSE	FIRE	WATER	WIND	EARTH	LIGHT	DARK
	—	—	HALF	—	—	—

IMMUNE TO	—

TAME (SCHOLAR)	YES	POT LUCK (PARTY HOST)	YES	FORBIDDEN ART (SHAMAN)	YES	CAPTURE (BEASTMASTER)	YES
ATTACK PROFICIENCY	B	MAGIC PROFICIENCY	C	EVASION CORRECTION	B	MAGIC EVASION CORRECTION	C

ABILITIES	IMPALE		
EXPERIENCE POINTS	8	STEAL	HI-POTION (40%)/X-POTION (25%)/GAIA DRUM (5%)
DROP	LAPIS (37.6%)		SAPPHIRE (10.2%)	POTION (7.8%)	—

JACK LANTERN [C]

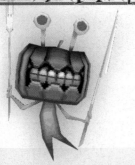

2 ACTIONS

ENCOUNTERED	MOONSAND RUINS (PART II)									
LEVEL	50	HP	268-335	WEIGHT	30	STRENGTH	24	INTELLECT	15	SPIRIT	15
VARIABLE LEVEL	YES	ABILITY SPEED	60	ATTACK ELEMENT	WIND LV.1	ATTACK	24	ACCURACY	150	DEFENSE	8
INFLICTS	—					MAGIC DEFENSE	7	EVASION	5	MAGIC EVASION	8

ELEMENTAL DEFENSE	FIRE	WATER	WIND	EARTH	LIGHT	DARK
	—	—	HALF	—	—	—

IMMUNE TO	CURSE

TAME (SCHOLAR)	YES	POT LUCK (PARTY HOST)	YES	FORBIDDEN ART (SHAMAN)	YES	CAPTURE (BEASTMASTER)	YES
ATTACK PROFICIENCY	A	MAGIC PROFICIENCY	A	EVASION CORRECTION	A	MAGIC EVASION CORRECTION	A

ABILITIES	IMPALE		
EXPERIENCE POINTS	100	STEAL	POTION (40%)/HI-POTION (25%)/RAVEN'S YAWN (5%)
DROP	RUBY (37.6%)		POTION (7.8%)	—	—

KAISER PENGUIN

FLYING

ENCOUNTERED	SPELVIA DUNGEONS(PART II) MOONSAND RUINS(PART II)									
LEVEL	25	HP	132-165	WEIGHT	—	STRENGTH	11	INTELLECT	24	SPIRIT	18
VARIABLE LEVEL	YES	ABILITY SPEED	40	ATTACK ELEMENT	LIGHT LV.1	ATTACK	6	ACCURACY	3	DEFENSE	4
INFLICTS	—					MAGIC DEFENSE	6	EVASION	5	MAGIC EVASION	7

ELEMENTAL DEFENSE	FIRE	WATER	WIND	EARTH	LIGHT	DARK
	—	—	WEAK	—	HALF	—

IMMUNE TO	—

TAME (SCHOLAR)	YES	POT LUCK (PARTY HOST)	YES	FORBIDDEN ART (SHAMAN)	YES	CAPTURE (BEASTMASTER)	YES
ATTACK PROFICIENCY	B	MAGIC PROFICIENCY	A	EVASION CORRECTION	B	MAGIC EVASION CORRECTION	B

ABILITIES	BLIZZARA/LIGHTNING BOLT [B]			
EXPERIENCE POINTS	14	STEAL	HI-POTION (40%)/X-POTION (25%)/DARK SIGH (5%)	
DROP	AQUAMARINE (37.6%)	EMERALD (3.9%)	HI-POTION (10.2%)	GLIMMER GAUNTLET (5.1%)

LAMIA [A]

ENCOUNTERED	PIRATE HIDEOUT(PART I)									
LEVEL	10	HP	42-53	WEIGHT	—	STRENGTH	7	INTELLECT	7	SPIRIT	7
VARIABLE LEVEL	—	ABILITY SPEED	50	ATTACK ELEMENT	—	ATTACK	5	ACCURACY	97	DEFENSE	2
INFLICTS	—					MAGIC DEFENSE	5	EVASION	4	MAGIC EVASION	10

ELEMENTAL DEFENSE	FIRE	WATER	WIND	EARTH	LIGHT	DARK
	—	—	—	—	—	—

IMMUNE TO	—

TAME (SCHOLAR)	YES	POT LUCK (PARTY HOST)	YES	FORBIDDEN ART (SHAMAN)	YES	CAPTURE (BEASTMASTER)	YES
ATTACK PROFICIENCY	B	MAGIC PROFICIENCY	B	EVASION CORRECTION	B	MAGIC EVASION CORRECTION	B

ABILITIES	DRAIN/ENTICE [B]			
EXPERIENCE POINTS	6	STEAL	PHOENIX DOWN (40%)/SLEEP RING (25%)/ANTARCTIC WIND (5%)	
DROP	TOPAZ (37.6%)	RUBY (3.9%)	PHOENIX DOWN (10.2%)	SLEEP RING (5.1%)

LAMIA [B]

2 ACTIONS

ENCOUNTERED	HOLY TREE TOWER(PART II) TRIAL TOWER(PART II)									
LEVEL	60	HP	390-488	WEIGHT	30	STRENGTH	22	INTELLECT	94	SPIRIT	48
VARIABLE LEVEL	YES	ABILITY SPEED	80	ATTACK ELEMENT	—	ATTACK	28	ACCURACY	150	DEFENSE	20
INFLICTS	—					MAGIC DEFENSE	17	EVASION	5	MAGIC EVASION	24

ELEMENTAL DEFENSE	FIRE	WATER	WIND	EARTH	LIGHT	DARK
	—	—	—	—	—	—

IMMUNE TO	CURSE

TAME (SCHOLAR)	YES	POT LUCK (PARTY HOST)	YES	FORBIDDEN ART (SHAMAN)	YES	CAPTURE (BEASTMASTER)	YES
ATTACK PROFICIENCY	A	MAGIC PROFICIENCY	A	EVASION CORRECTION	A	MAGIC EVASION CORRECTION	A

ABILITIES	DRAIN/ENTICE [B]		
EXPERIENCE POINTS	100	STEAL	PHOENIX DOWN (40%)/HI-POTION (25%)/ANTARCTIC WIND (5%)
DROP	TOPAZ (37.6%)		PHOENIX DOWN (7.8%)	—	—

LILITH

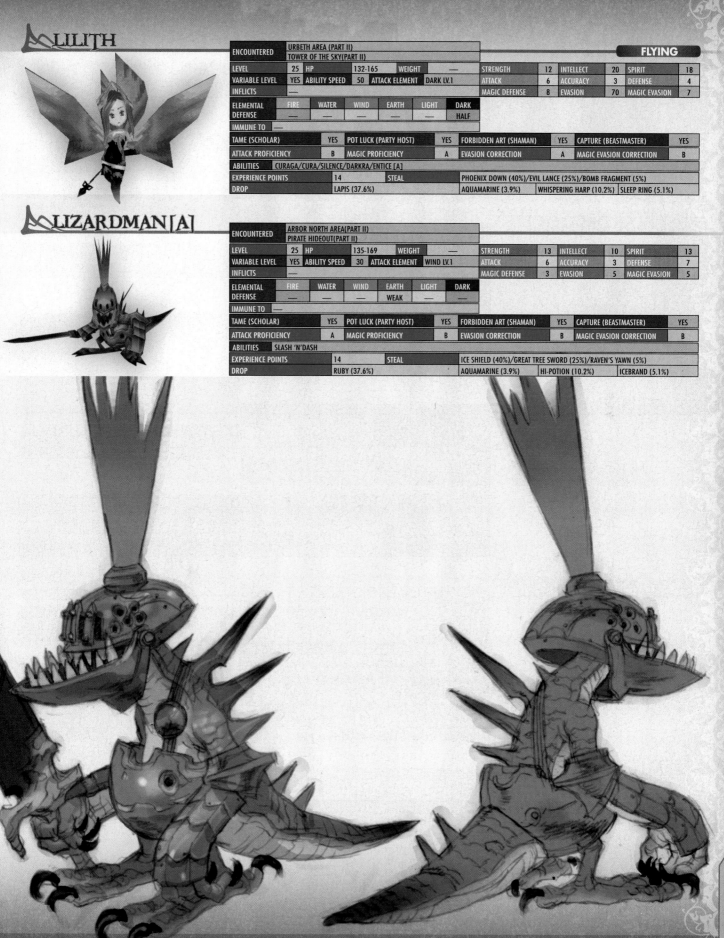

ENCOUNTERED	URBETH AREA (PART II)								
	TOWER OF THE SKY (PART II)							FLYING	

LEVEL	25	HP	132-165	WEIGHT	—		STRENGTH	12	INTELLECT	20	SPIRIT	18
VARIABLE LEVEL	YES	ABILITY SPEED	50	ATTACK ELEMENT	DARK LV.1		ATTACK	6	ACCURACY	3	DEFENSE	4
INFLICTS	—						MAGIC DEFENSE	8	EVASION	70	MAGIC EVASION	7

ELEMENTAL DEFENSE	FIRE	WATER	WIND	EARTH	LIGHT	DARK
	—	—	—	—	—	HALF

IMMUNE TO	—

TAME (SCHOLAR)	YES	POT LUCK (PARTY HOST)	YES	FORBIDDEN ART (SHAMAN)	YES	CAPTURE (BEASTMASTER)	YES
ATTACK PROFICIENCY	B	MAGIC PROFICIENCY	A	EVASION CORRECTION	A	MAGIC EVASION CORRECTION	B

ABILITIES	CURAGA/CURA/SILENCE/DARKRA/ENTICE [A]			
EXPERIENCE POINTS	14	STEAL	PHOENIX DOWN (40%)/EVIL LANCE (25%)/BOMB FRAGMENT (5%)	
DROP	LAPIS (37.6%)	AQUAMARINE (3.9%)	WHISPERING HARP (10.2%)	SLEEP RING (5.1%)

LIZARDMAN [A]

ENCOUNTERED	ARBOR NORTH AREA (PART II)
	PIRATE HIDEOUT (PART II)

LEVEL	25	HP	135-169	WEIGHT	—		STRENGTH	13	INTELLECT	10	SPIRIT	13
VARIABLE LEVEL	YES	ABILITY SPEED	30	ATTACK ELEMENT	WIND LV.1		ATTACK	6	ACCURACY	3	DEFENSE	7
INFLICTS	—						MAGIC DEFENSE	3	EVASION	5	MAGIC EVASION	5

ELEMENTAL DEFENSE	FIRE	WATER	WIND	EARTH	LIGHT	DARK
	—	—	—	WEAK	—	—

IMMUNE TO	—

TAME (SCHOLAR)	YES	POT LUCK (PARTY HOST)	YES	FORBIDDEN ART (SHAMAN)	YES	CAPTURE (BEASTMASTER)	YES
ATTACK PROFICIENCY	A	MAGIC PROFICIENCY	B	EVASION CORRECTION	B	MAGIC EVASION CORRECTION	B

ABILITIES	SLASH 'N' DASH			
EXPERIENCE POINTS	14	STEAL	ICE SHIELD (40%)/GREAT TREE SWORD (25%)/RAVEN'S YAWN (5%)	
DROP	RUBY (37.6%)	AQUAMARINE (3.9%)	HI-POTION (10.2%)	ICEBRAND (5.1%)

LIZARDMAN [B]

ENCOUNTERED	URBETH AREA (PART I) PIRATE HIDEOUT(PART I)							
LEVEL	3	HP	55-69	WEIGHT	—	STRENGTH	6	INTELLECT	4	SPIRIT	4

LEVEL	3	HP	55-69	WEIGHT	—		STRENGTH	6	INTELLECT	4	SPIRIT	4
VARIABLE LEVEL	—	ABILITY SPEED	30	ATTACK ELEMENT	WIND LV.1		ATTACK	6	ACCURACY	98	DEFENSE	5
INFLICTS	—						MAGIC DEFENSE	4	EVASION	1	MAGIC EVASION	1

ELEMENTAL DEFENSE	FIRE	WATER	WIND	EARTH	LIGHT	DARK
	—	—	—	WEAK	HALF	—

IMMUNE TO —

TAME (SCHOLAR)	YES	POT LUCK (PARTY HOST)	YES	FORBIDDEN ART (SHAMAN)	YES	CAPTURE (BEASTMASTER)	YES
ATTACK PROFICIENCY	B	MAGIC PROFICIENCY	C	EVASION CORRECTION	B	MAGIC EVASION CORRECTION	C

ABILITIES: SLASH 'N' DASH

EXPERIENCE POINTS	8	STEAL	WIND FOIL (40%)/X-POTION (25%)/ANTARCTIC WIND (5%)		
DROP	SAPPHIRE (37.6%)	AQUAMARINE (10.2%)	POTION (7.8%)	—	

LIZARDMAN [C]

2 ACTIONS

ENCOUNTERED	MYSTERIOUS LIGHTHOUSE(PART II) TRIAL TOWER(PART II)

LEVEL	70	HP	535-669	WEIGHT	60		STRENGTH	38	INTELLECT	10	SPIRIT	13
VARIABLE LEVEL	YES	ABILITY SPEED	100	ATTACK ELEMENT	WIND LV.1		ATTACK	43	ACCURACY	150	DEFENSE	28
INFLICTS	—						MAGIC DEFENSE	24	EVASION	5	MAGIC EVASION	7

ELEMENTAL DEFENSE	FIRE	WATER	WIND	EARTH	LIGHT	DARK
	—	—	HALF	—	—	—

IMMUNE TO CURSE

TAME (SCHOLAR)	YES	POT LUCK (PARTY HOST)	YES	FORBIDDEN ART (SHAMAN)	YES	CAPTURE (BEASTMASTER)	YES
ATTACK PROFICIENCY	A	MAGIC PROFICIENCY	A	EVASION CORRECTION	A	MAGIC EVASION CORRECTION	A

ABILITIES: SLASH 'N' DASH

EXPERIENCE POINTS	100	STEAL	POTION (40%)/HI-POTION (25%)/RAVEN'S YAWN (5%)		
DROP	RUBY (37.6%)	POTION (7.8%)	—	WIND FOIL (2%)	

MANDRAGORA [A]

ENCOUNTERED	ARBOR SOUTH AREA (PART I) GREAT TREE ROOTS(PART I)

LEVEL	12	HP	48-60	WEIGHT	—		STRENGTH	8	INTELLECT	11	SPIRIT	8
VARIABLE LEVEL	—	ABILITY SPEED	35	ATTACK ELEMENT	EARTH LV.1		ATTACK	4	ACCURACY	97	DEFENSE	1
INFLICTS	—						MAGIC DEFENSE	7	EVASION	5	MAGIC EVASION	10

ELEMENTAL DEFENSE	FIRE	WATER	WIND	EARTH	LIGHT	DARK
	WEAK	—	—	HALF	—	—

IMMUNE TO —

TAME (SCHOLAR)	YES	POT LUCK (PARTY HOST)	YES	FORBIDDEN ART (SHAMAN)	YES	CAPTURE (BEASTMASTER)	YES
ATTACK PROFICIENCY	C	MAGIC PROFICIENCY	B	EVASION CORRECTION	B	MAGIC EVASION CORRECTION	B

ABILITIES: CURE/SLEEP/POISON

EXPERIENCE POINTS	7	STEAL	POTION (40%)/HI-POTION (25%)/GREAT TREE LOG (5%)		
DROP	LAPIS (37.6%)	EMERALD (3.9%)	PHOENIX DOWN (5.1%)	STUN RING (2%)	

MANDRAGORA [B]

2 ACTIONS

ENCOUNTERED	TRIAL TOWER(PART II)

LEVEL	90	HP	880-1100	WEIGHT	30		STRENGTH	65	INTELLECT	99	SPIRIT	72
VARIABLE LEVEL	YES	ABILITY SPEED	60	ATTACK ELEMENT			ATTACK	58	ACCURACY	150	DEFENSE	30
INFLICTS	PARALYSIS (10%)						MAGIC DEFENSE	36	EVASION	5	MAGIC EVASION	36

ELEMENTAL DEFENSE	FIRE	WATER	WIND	EARTH	LIGHT	DARK
	WEAK	—	—	—	—	—

IMMUNE TO CURSE

TAME (SCHOLAR)	YES	POT LUCK (PARTY HOST)	YES	FORBIDDEN ART (SHAMAN)	YES	CAPTURE (BEASTMASTER)	YES
ATTACK PROFICIENCY	A	MAGIC PROFICIENCY	A	EVASION CORRECTION	A	MAGIC EVASION CORRECTION	A

ABILITIES: CURE/SLEEP/POISON

EXPERIENCE POINTS	100	STEAL	POTION (40%)/HI-POTION (25%)/GREAT TREE LOG (5%)		
DROP	SAPPHIRE (37.6%)	HI-POTION (7.8%)	—	STUN RING (2%)	

MEDUSA [A]

ENCOUNTERED	SPELVIA DUNGEONS(PART I)

LEVEL	22	HP	69-86	WEIGHT	—		STRENGTH	10	INTELLECT	18	SPIRIT	10
VARIABLE LEVEL	—	ABILITY SPEED	55	ATTACK ELEMENT	—		ATTACK	6	ACCURACY	97	DEFENSE	3
INFLICTS	CONFUSION (13%)						MAGIC DEFENSE	5	EVASION	9	MAGIC EVASION	4

ELEMENTAL DEFENSE	FIRE	WATER	WIND	EARTH	LIGHT	DARK
	—	—	—	—	—	—

IMMUNE TO PETRIFY

TAME (SCHOLAR)	YES	POT LUCK (PARTY HOST)	YES	FORBIDDEN ART (SHAMAN)	YES	CAPTURE (BEASTMASTER)	YES
ATTACK PROFICIENCY	B	MAGIC PROFICIENCY	B	EVASION CORRECTION	B	MAGIC EVASION CORRECTION	B

ABILITIES: PETRIFY

EXPERIENCE POINTS	12	STEAL	GOLD NEEDLE (40%)/X-POTION (25%)/HOLY BREATH (5%)		
DROP	AQUAMARINE (37.6%)	GOLD NEEDLE (3.9%)	HI-POTION (5.1%)	COURAGE RING (2%)	

MEDUSA [B]

ENCOUNTERED	MOONSAND RUINS (PART II)
	TRIAL TOWER (PART II)

LEVEL	50	HP	380-475	WEIGHT	30	STRENGTH	23	INTELLECT	94	SPIRIT	16
VARIABLE LEVEL	YES	ABILITY SPEED	60	ATTACK ELEMENT	—	ATTACK	25	ACCURACY	150	DEFENSE	18
INFLICTS	CONFUSION (13%)					MAGIC DEFENSE	20	EVASION	5	MAGIC EVASION	8

ELEMENTAL DEFENSE	FIRE	WATER	WIND	EARTH	LIGHT	DARK
	—	—	—	—	—	—

IMMUNE TO	PETRIFY/CURSE

TAME (SCHOLAR)	YES	POT LUCK (PARTY HOST)	YES	FORBIDDEN ART (SHAMAN)	YES	CAPTURE (BEASTMASTER)	YES
ATTACK PROFICIENCY	A	MAGIC PROFICIENCY	A	EVASION CORRECTION	A	MAGIC EVASION CORRECTION	A

ABILITIES	PETRIFY			
EXPERIENCE POINTS	100	STEAL	GOLD NEEDLE (40%)/X-POTION (25%)/HOLY BREATH (5%)	
DROP	AMETHYST (37.6%)	GOLD NEEDLE (7.8%)	HI-POTION (3.9%)	COURAGE RING (2%)

METAL FLAN [A]

ENCOUNTERED	ANYWHERE

LEVEL	2	HP	8-10	WEIGHT	—	STRENGTH	2	INTELLECT	1	SPIRIT	2
VARIABLE LEVEL	—	ABILITY SPEED	200	ATTACK ELEMENT	—	ATTACK	3	ACCURACY	96	DEFENSE	12
INFLICTS	—					MAGIC DEFENSE	20	EVASION	70	MAGIC EVASION	20

ELEMENTAL DEFENSE	FIRE	WATER	WIND	EARTH	LIGHT	DARK
	HALF	HALF	HALF	HALF	HALF	HALF

IMMUNE TO	ALL

TAME (SCHOLAR)	YES	POT LUCK (PARTY HOST)	YES	FORBIDDEN ART (SHAMAN)	YES	CAPTURE (BEASTMASTER)	YES
ATTACK PROFICIENCY	B	MAGIC PROFICIENCY	B	EVASION CORRECTION	A	MAGIC EVASION CORRECTION	B

ABILITIES	MERGE		
EXPERIENCE POINTS	40	STEAL	HI-POTION (40%)/ETHER (25%)/DARK SIGH (5%)
DROP	AMETHYST (100%)	—	—	—

METAL FLAN [B]

ENCOUNTERED	STAR CHAMBER (PART II)

LEVEL	25	HP	120-150	WEIGHT	—	STRENGTH	7	INTELLECT	28	SPIRIT	20
VARIABLE LEVEL	YES	ABILITY SPEED	200	ATTACK ELEMENT	—	ATTACK	5	ACCURACY	5	DEFENSE	13
INFLICTS	—					MAGIC DEFENSE	25	EVASION	60	MAGIC EVASION	20

ELEMENTAL DEFENSE	FIRE	WATER	WIND	EARTH	LIGHT	DARK
	HALF	HALF	HALF	HALF	HALF	HALF

IMMUNE TO	ALL

TAME (SCHOLAR)	YES	POT LUCK (PARTY HOST)	YES	FORBIDDEN ART (SHAMAN)	YES	CAPTURE (BEASTMASTER)	YES
ATTACK PROFICIENCY	A	MAGIC PROFICIENCY	A	EVASION CORRECTION	A	MAGIC EVASION CORRECTION	A

ABILITIES	MERGE		
EXPERIENCE POINTS	120	STEAL	POTION (40%)/HI-POTION (25%)/DARK SIGH (5%)
DROP	AMETHYST (100%)	—	—	—

MIMIC [A]

ENCOUNTERED	???
	SPELVIA DUNGEONS

LEVEL	5	HP	25-31	WEIGHT	—	STRENGTH	4	INTELLECT	4	SPIRIT	4
VARIABLE LEVEL	YES	ABILITY SPEED	5	ATTACK ELEMENT	—	ATTACK	3	ACCURACY	5	DEFENSE	2
INFLICTS	—					MAGIC DEFENSE	3	EVASION	0	MAGIC EVASION	4

ELEMENTAL DEFENSE	FIRE	WATER	WIND	EARTH	LIGHT	DARK
	—	—	—	—	—	—

IMMUNE TO	

TAME (SCHOLAR)	YES	POT LUCK (PARTY HOST)	YES	FORBIDDEN ART (SHAMAN)	YES	CAPTURE (BEASTMASTER)	YES
ATTACK PROFICIENCY	B	MAGIC PROFICIENCY	B	EVASION CORRECTION	B	MAGIC EVASION CORRECTION	B

ABILITIES	WALLOP			
EXPERIENCE POINTS	4	STEAL	POTION (40%)/HI-POTION (25%)/RAVEN'S YAWN (5%)	
DROP	RUBY (37.6%)	SAPPHIRE (3.9%)	POTION (10.2%)	MYTHRIL (5.1%)

MIMIC [B]

ENCOUNTERED	EXTRA DUNGEONS (PART II)

LEVEL	90	HP	1130-1413	WEIGHT	30	STRENGTH	58	INTELLECT	28	SPIRIT	72
VARIABLE LEVEL	YES	ABILITY SPEED	60	ATTACK ELEMENT	DARK LV.1	ATTACK	52	ACCURACY	150	DEFENSE	36
INFLICTS	—					MAGIC DEFENSE	34	EVASION	0	MAGIC EVASION	4

ELEMENTAL DEFENSE	FIRE	WATER	WIND	EARTH	LIGHT	DARK
	—	—	—	—	—	—

IMMUNE TO	CURSE

TAME (SCHOLAR)	YES	POT LUCK (PARTY HOST)	YES	FORBIDDEN ART (SHAMAN)	YES	CAPTURE (BEASTMASTER)	YES
ATTACK PROFICIENCY	A	MAGIC PROFICIENCY	A	EVASION CORRECTION	A	MAGIC EVASION CORRECTION	A

ABILITIES	WALLOP			
EXPERIENCE POINTS	100	STEAL	POTION (40%)/HI-POTION (25%)/RAVEN'S YAWN (5%)	
DROP	RUBY (37.6%)	POTION (7.8%)	PHOENIX DOWN (3.9%)	EMERALD (2%)

MINOTAUR [A]

ENCOUNTERED	MT. GULG(PART II) QUICKSAND CASTLE(PART II)						
LEVEL	30	HP	240-300	WEIGHT	10	STRENGTH 13	INTELLECT 5	SPIRIT 5
VARIABLE LEVEL	YES	ABILITY SPEED	50	ATTACK ELEMENT	EARTH LV.2	ATTACK 9	ACCURACY 5	DEFENSE 14
INFLICTS	—					MAGIC DEFENSE 12	EVASION 0	MAGIC EVASION 0

ELEMENTAL DEFENSE	FIRE	WATER	WIND	EARTH	LIGHT	DARK
	—	—	—	NO EFFECT	—	DARK

IMMUNE TO: PETRIFY / CURSE / DEATH

TAME (SCHOLAR)	YES	POT LUCK (PARTY HOST)	YES	FORBIDDEN ART (SHAMAN)	—	CAPTURE (BEASTMASTER)	—
ATTACK PROFICIENCY	A	MAGIC PROFICIENCY	C	EVASION CORRECTION	B	MAGIC EVASION CORRECTION	C

ABILITIES: FULL SWING

EXPERIENCE POINTS	14	STEAL	—		
DROP	RUBY (100%)	EMERALD (100%)	EMERALD (100%)	POWER RING (2%)	

MUNINN

FLYING

ENCOUNTERED	STAR CHAMBER(PART II) GREAT TREE(PART II)						
LEVEL	25	HP	130-163	WEIGHT	—	STRENGTH 13	INTELLECT 18	SPIRIT 18
VARIABLE LEVEL	YES	ABILITY SPEED	55	ATTACK ELEMENT	LIGHT LV.1	ATTACK 7	ACCURACY 3	DEFENSE 4
INFLICTS	—					MAGIC DEFENSE 6	EVASION 70	MAGIC EVASION 7

ELEMENTAL DEFENSE	FIRE	WATER	WIND	EARTH	LIGHT	DARK
	—	—	WEAK	—	HALF	WEAK

IMMUNE TO: —

TAME (SCHOLAR)	YES	POT LUCK (PARTY HOST)	YES	FORBIDDEN ART (SHAMAN)	YES	CAPTURE (BEASTMASTER)	YES
ATTACK PROFICIENCY	B	MAGIC PROFICIENCY	B	EVASION CORRECTION	A	MAGIC EVASION CORRECTION	B

ABILITIES: WOOD BLAST/SILENCE/FLASH

EXPERIENCE POINTS	14	STEAL	PHOENIX DOWN (40%)/EYE DROPS (25%)/GREAT TREE LOG (5%)		
DROP	SAPPHIRE (37.6%)	LAPIS (3.9%)	PHOENIX DOWN (10.2%)	GALE GAUNTLET (5.1%)	

MYCONID [A]

ENCOUNTERED	NORTHERN CAVES(PART I) ANIMAL BURROW(PART I)						
LEVEL	4	HP	10-13	WEIGHT	—	STRENGTH 3	INTELLECT 2	SPIRIT 2
VARIABLE LEVEL	—	ABILITY SPEED	30	ATTACK ELEMENT	EARTH LV.1	ATTACK 3	ACCURACY 96	DEFENSE 1
INFLICTS	—					MAGIC DEFENSE 4	EVASION 1	MAGIC EVASION 10

ELEMENTAL DEFENSE	FIRE	WATER	WIND	EARTH	LIGHT	DARK
	—	—	—	HALF	—	DARK

IMMUNE TO: —

TAME (SCHOLAR)	YES	POT LUCK (PARTY HOST)	YES	FORBIDDEN ART (SHAMAN)	YES	CAPTURE (BEASTMASTER)	YES
ATTACK PROFICIENCY	B	MAGIC PROFICIENCY	C	EVASION CORRECTION	B	MAGIC EVASION CORRECTION	C

ABILITIES:

EXPERIENCE POINTS	3	STEAL	POTION (40%)/HI-POTION (25%)/RAVEN'S YAWN (5%)		
DROP	RUBY (37.6%)	TOPAZ (3.9%)	POTION (10.2%)	ANTIDOTE (5.1%)	

MYCONID [B]

ENCOUNTERED	HUNTING CAVES(PART I) GREAT TREE ROOTS(PART I)						
LEVEL	13	HP	50-63	WEIGHT	—	STRENGTH 8	INTELLECT 4	SPIRIT 4
VARIABLE LEVEL	—	ABILITY SPEED	40	ATTACK ELEMENT	WIND LV.1	ATTACK 6	ACCURACY 98	DEFENSE 2
INFLICTS	—					MAGIC DEFENSE 8	EVASION 5	MAGIC EVASION 1

ELEMENTAL DEFENSE	FIRE	WATER	WIND	EARTH	LIGHT	DARK
	WEAK	—	HALF	—	—	DARK

IMMUNE TO: —

TAME (SCHOLAR)	YES	POT LUCK (PARTY HOST)	YES	FORBIDDEN ART (SHAMAN)	YES	CAPTURE (BEASTMASTER)	YES
ATTACK PROFICIENCY	B	MAGIC PROFICIENCY	C	EVASION CORRECTION	B	MAGIC EVASION CORRECTION	C

ABILITIES: SPORE

EXPERIENCE POINTS	7	STEAL	HI-POTION (40%)/X-POTION (25%)/GAIA DRUM (5%)		
DROP	LAPIS (37.6%)	SAPPHIRE (10.2%)	POTION (7.8%)	ANTIDOTE (3.9%)	

MYCONID [C]

2 ACTIONS

ENCOUNTERED	TRIAL TOWER (PART II)						
LEVEL	90	HP	836-1045	WEIGHT	30	STRENGTH 67	INTELLECT 92	SPIRIT 12
VARIABLE LEVEL	YES	ABILITY SPEED	60	ATTACK ELEMENT	—	ATTACK 54	ACCURACY 150	DEFENSE 38
INFLICTS	SLEEP (25%)					MAGIC DEFENSE 33	EVASION 0	MAGIC EVASION 6

ELEMENTAL DEFENSE	FIRE	WATER	WIND	EARTH	LIGHT	DARK
	—	—	—	—	—	DARK

IMMUNE TO: CURSE

TAME (SCHOLAR)	YES	POT LUCK (PARTY HOST)	YES	FORBIDDEN ART (SHAMAN)	YES	CAPTURE (BEASTMASTER)	YES
ATTACK PROFICIENCY	A	MAGIC PROFICIENCY	A	EVASION CORRECTION	A	MAGIC EVASION CORRECTION	A

ABILITIES:

EXPERIENCE POINTS	100	STEAL	POTION (40%)/HI-POTION (25%)/RAVEN'S YAWN (5%)		
DROP	RUBY (37.6%)	POTION (7.8%)	—	—	

MYTHRITOISE

ENCOUNTERED	URBETH AREA (PART I)								
LEVEL	15	HP	62-78	WEIGHT	—	STRENGTH	6	INTELLECT	24	SPIRIT	14
VARIABLE LEVEL	—	ABILITY SPEED	8	ATTACK ELEMENT	WATER LV.1	ATTACK	4	ACCURACY	97	DEFENSE	8
INFLICTS	—					MAGIC DEFENSE	3	EVASION	1	MAGIC EVASION	7

ELEMENTAL DEFENSE	FIRE	WATER	WIND	EARTH	LIGHT	DARK
		NO EFFECT		WEAK	—	—

IMMUNE TO: CURSE

TAME (SCHOLAR)	YES	POT LUCK (PARTY HOST)	YES	FORBIDDEN ART (SHAMAN)	YES	CAPTURE (BEASTMASTER)	YES
ATTACK PROFICIENCY	A	MAGIC PROFICIENCY	A	EVASION CORRECTION	A	MAGIC EVASION CORRECTION	A

ABILITIES: UNBREAKABLE

EXPERIENCE POINTS	9	STEAL	MYTHRIL (40%)/TURTLE SHELL (25%)/ANTARCTIC WIND (5%)		
DROP	SAPPHIRE (37.6%)	TURTLE SHELL (8.6%)	PHOENIX DOWN (7.8%)	AQUAMARINE (2%)

NEKO NATTER

FLYING

ENCOUNTERED	QUICKSAND CASTLE(PART II) STAR CHAMBER(PART II)								
LEVEL	25	HP	129-156	WEIGHT	—	STRENGTH	10	INTELLECT	30	SPIRIT	15
VARIABLE LEVEL	YES	ABILITY SPEED	40	ATTACK ELEMENT	LIGHT LV.1	ATTACK	6	ACCURACY	3	DEFENSE	4
INFLICTS	CONFUSION (10%)					MAGIC DEFENSE	6	EVASION	5	MAGIC EVASION	6

ELEMENTAL DEFENSE	FIRE	WATER	WIND	EARTH	LIGHT	DARK
					HALF	WEAK

IMMUNE TO: —

TAME (SCHOLAR)	YES	POT LUCK (PARTY HOST)	YES	FORBIDDEN ART (SHAMAN)	YES	CAPTURE (BEASTMASTER)	YES
ATTACK PROFICIENCY	B	MAGIC PROFICIENCY	A	EVASION CORRECTION	B	MAGIC EVASION CORRECTION	B

ABILITIES: QUAKRA/EARTH BLAST/PROTECT/POISON

EXPERIENCE POINTS	14	STEAL	SACRED TREE STAFF (40%)/SHINING STAFF (25%)/GAIA DRUM (5%)		
DROP	EMERALD (37.6%)	TOPAZ (3.9%)	PHOENIX DOWN (10.2%)	TERRA STAVE (5.1%)

NIDHOGG

FLYING

ENCOUNTERED	SPELVIA DUNGEONS(PART II) INVIDIA UNDERGROUND(PART II)								
LEVEL	25	HP	140-175	WEIGHT	—	STRENGTH	14	INTELLECT	18	SPIRIT	18
VARIABLE LEVEL	YES	ABILITY SPEED	55	ATTACK ELEMENT		ATTACK	8	ACCURACY	3	DEFENSE	8
INFLICTS						MAGIC DEFENSE	10	EVASION	5	MAGIC EVASION	7

ELEMENTAL DEFENSE	FIRE	WATER	WIND	EARTH	LIGHT	DARK
	—	—	WEAK	—	—	—

IMMUNE TO: —

TAME (SCHOLAR)	YES	POT LUCK (PARTY HOST)	YES	FORBIDDEN ART (SHAMAN)	YES	CAPTURE (BEASTMASTER)	YES
ATTACK PROFICIENCY	A	MAGIC PROFICIENCY	B	EVASION CORRECTION	B	MAGIC EVASION CORRECTION	B

ABILITIES: MIGHTY SLAP

EXPERIENCE POINTS	14	STEAL	ANTIDOTE (40%)/HI-POTION (25%)/HOLY BREATH (5%)		
DROP	AQUAMARINE (37.6%)	LAPIS (3.9%)	HI-POTION (10.2%)	—

NUE [A]

2 ACTIONS, FLYING

ENCOUNTERED	INVIDIA AREA (PART II) MT. GULG(PART II)								
LEVEL	25	HP	140-175	WEIGHT	10	STRENGTH	13	INTELLECT	20	SPIRIT	18
VARIABLE LEVEL	YES	ABILITY SPEED	30	ATTACK ELEMENT	DARK LV.1	ATTACK	7	ACCURACY	3	DEFENSE	4
INFLICTS	PARALYSIS SILENCE BLINDNESS (10%)					MAGIC DEFENSE	6	EVASION	5	MAGIC EVASION	7

ELEMENTAL DEFENSE	FIRE	WATER	WIND	EARTH	LIGHT	DARK
	—	—	—	—	—	HALF

IMMUNE TO: —

TAME (SCHOLAR)	YES	POT LUCK (PARTY HOST)	YES	FORBIDDEN ART (SHAMAN)	YES	CAPTURE (BEASTMASTER)	YES
ATTACK PROFICIENCY	B	MAGIC PROFICIENCY	A	EVASION CORRECTION	B	MAGIC EVASION CORRECTION	B

ABILITIES: CURSE/QUAKRA/FIRA/FLAME BLAST [A]

EXPERIENCE POINTS	14	STEAL	DRAGON WING (40%)/STUN RING (25%)/BOMB FRAGMENT (5%)		
DROP	LAPIS (37.6%)	EMERALD (3.9%)	DRAGON WING (10.2%)	BOMB FRAGMENT (5.1%)

OCEANUS

FLYING

ENCOUNTERED	PIRATE HIDEOUT(PART II) STAR CHAMBER(PART II)								
LEVEL	25	HP	129-161	WEIGHT	—	STRENGTH	12	INTELLECT	18	SPIRIT	18
VARIABLE LEVEL	YES	ABILITY SPEED	55	ATTACK ELEMENT	WATER LV.1	ATTACK	6	ACCURACY	3	DEFENSE	5
INFLICTS	—					MAGIC DEFENSE	5	EVASION	70	MAGIC EVASION	7

ELEMENTAL DEFENSE	FIRE	WATER	WIND	EARTH	LIGHT	DARK
	WEAK	NO EFFECT				

IMMUNE TO: —

TAME (SCHOLAR)	YES	POT LUCK (PARTY HOST)	YES	FORBIDDEN ART (SHAMAN)	YES	CAPTURE (BEASTMASTER)	YES
ATTACK PROFICIENCY	B	MAGIC PROFICIENCY	B	EVASION CORRECTION	A	MAGIC EVASION CORRECTION	B

ABILITIES: WATER BLAST

EXPERIENCE POINTS	14	STEAL	HI-POTION (40%)/ETHER (25%)/ANTARCTIC WIND (5%)		
DROP	TOPAZ (37.6%)	SAPPHIRE (3.9%)	HI-POTION (10.2%)	SPRING GAUNTLETS (5.1%)

ORC [A]

ENCOUNTERED	WITCH'S MANSION(PART I)											
LEVEL	6	HP	12-15	WEIGHT	—		STRENGTH	4	INTELLECT	2	SPIRIT	2
VARIABLE LEVEL	—	ABILITY SPEED	20	ATTACK ELEMENT	—		ATTACK	3	ACCURACY	97	DEFENSE	3
INFLICTS	—						MAGIC DEFENSE	2	EVASION	2	MAGIC EVASION	10

ELEMENTAL DEFENSE	FIRE	WATER	WIND	EARTH	LIGHT	DARK
	—	—	—	—	—	—

IMMUNE TO	—

TAME (SCHOLAR)	YES	POT LUCK (PARTY HOST)	YES	FORBIDDEN ART (SHAMAN)	YES	CAPTURE (BEASTMASTER)	YES
ATTACK PROFICIENCY		MAGIC PROFICIENCY		EVASION CORRECTION		MAGIC EVASION CORRECTION	

ABILITIES	ORC STRIKE				
EXPERIENCE POINTS	4	STEAL	POTION (40%)/STEEL SPEAR (25%)/RAVEN'S YAWN (5%)		
DROP	RUBY (37.6%)		RUBY (3.9%)	POTION (10.2%)	STEEL SPEAR (5.1%)

ORC [B]

ENCOUNTERED	INVIDIA UNDERGROUND(PART I) TOWER OF THE SKY(PART I)											
LEVEL	6	HP	58-73	WEIGHT	—		STRENGTH	9	INTELLECT	4	SPIRIT	4
VARIABLE LEVEL	—	ABILITY SPEED	30	ATTACK ELEMENT	WIND LV.1		ATTACK	8	ACCURACY	99	DEFENSE	4
INFLICTS	—						MAGIC DEFENSE	4	EVASION	2	MAGIC EVASION	1

ELEMENTAL DEFENSE	FIRE	WATER	WIND	EARTH	LIGHT	DARK
	HALF	—	—	—	—	—

IMMUNE TO	—

TAME (SCHOLAR)	YES	POT LUCK (PARTY HOST)	YES	FORBIDDEN ART (SHAMAN)	YES	CAPTURE (BEASTMASTER)	YES
ATTACK PROFICIENCY	B	MAGIC PROFICIENCY	C	EVASION CORRECTION	B	MAGIC EVASION CORRECTION	C

ABILITIES	ORC STRIKE				
EXPERIENCE POINTS	7	STEAL	SHARK LANCE (40%)/X-POTION (25%)/BOMB FRAGMENT (5%)		
DROP	SAPPHIRE (37.6%)		AQUAMARINE (10.2%)	POTION (7.8%)	STEEL SPEAR (3.9%)

ORC [C]

2 ACTIONS

ENCOUNTERED	MYSTERIOUS LIGHTHOUSE(PART II)
	TRIAL TOWER(PART II)

LEVEL	70	HP	622-778	WEIGHT	60		STRENGTH	40	INTELLECT	11	SPIRIT	12
VARIABLE LEVEL	YES	ABILITY SPEED	100	ATTACK ELEMENT	—		ATTACK	44	ACCURACY	150	DEFENSE	27
INFLICTS	—						MAGIC DEFENSE	26	EVASION	2	MAGIC EVASION	6

ELEMENTAL DEFENSE	FIRE	WATER	WIND	EARTH	LIGHT	DARK
	—	—	—	—	—	

IMMUNE TO	CURSE

TAME (SCHOLAR)	YES	POT LUCK (PARTY HOST)	YES	FORBIDDEN ART (SHAMAN)	YES	CAPTURE (BEASTMASTER)	YES
ATTACK PROFICIENCY	A	MAGIC PROFICIENCY	A	EVASION CORRECTION	A	MAGIC EVASION CORRECTION	A

ABILITIES	ORC STRIKE		
EXPERIENCE POINTS	100	STEAL	POTION (40%)/HI-POTION (25%)/RAVEN'S YAWN (5%)
DROP	RUBY (37.6%)	POTION (7.8%)	—	STEEL SPEAR (2%)

ORC LORD

ENCOUNTERED	LIBERTE AREA (PART II)
	HUNTING CAVES(PART II)

LEVEL	25	HP	138-173	WEIGHT	—		STRENGTH	13	INTELLECT	11	SPIRIT	12
VARIABLE LEVEL	YES	ABILITY SPEED	25	ATTACK ELEMENT	—		ATTACK	7	ACCURACY	5	DEFENSE	9
INFLICTS	—						MAGIC DEFENSE	5	EVASION	5	MAGIC EVASION	5

ELEMENTAL DEFENSE	FIRE	WATER	WIND	EARTH	LIGHT	DARK
	—	—	WEAK	—	—	

IMMUNE TO	—

TAME (SCHOLAR)	YES	POT LUCK (PARTY HOST)	YES	FORBIDDEN ART (SHAMAN)	YES	CAPTURE (BEASTMASTER)	YES
ATTACK PROFICIENCY	A	MAGIC PROFICIENCY	B	EVASION CORRECTION	B	MAGIC EVASION CORRECTION	B

ABILITIES	ORC STRIKE			
EXPERIENCE POINTS	14	STEAL	STEEL SPEAR (40%)/TEMPEST PIKE (25%)/RAVEN'S YAWN (5%)	
DROP	RUBY (37.6%)	RUBY (3.9%)	HI-POTION (10.2%)	STEEL SPEAR (5.1%)

PUMPKING

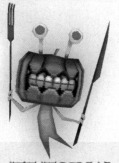

ENCOUNTERED	GUERA AREA (PART II)
	GREAT TREE ROOTS(PART II)

LEVEL	25	HP	122-153	WEIGHT	—		STRENGTH	11	INTELLECT	15	SPIRIT	15
VARIABLE LEVEL	YES	ABILITY SPEED	35	ATTACK ELEMENT	FIRE LV.1		ATTACK	6	ACCURACY	3	DEFENSE	4
INFLICTS	—						MAGIC DEFENSE	6	EVASION	5	MAGIC EVASION	6

ELEMENTAL DEFENSE	FIRE	WATER	WIND	EARTH	LIGHT	DARK
	HALF	WEAK	—	—	—	

IMMUNE TO	—

TAME (SCHOLAR)	YES	POT LUCK (PARTY HOST)	YES	FORBIDDEN ART (SHAMAN)	YES	CAPTURE (BEASTMASTER)	YES
ATTACK PROFICIENCY	B	MAGIC PROFICIENCY	A	EVASION CORRECTION	B	MAGIC EVASION CORRECTION	B

ABILITIES	IMPALE/FIRA		
EXPERIENCE POINTS	14	STEAL	HI-POTION (40%)/ETHER (25%)/RAVEN'S YAWN (5%)
DROP	RUBY (37.6%)	SAPPHIRE (3.9%)	HI-POTION (10.2%)	—

RATTATOX [A]

FLYING

ENCOUNTERED	GREAT TREE(PART I)
	GREAT TREE: TO THE SUMMIT (PART I)

LEVEL	15	HP	51-64	WEIGHT	—		STRENGTH	8	INTELLECT	15	SPIRIT	12
VARIABLE LEVEL	—	ABILITY SPEED	55	ATTACK ELEMENT	—		ATTACK	4	ACCURACY	98	DEFENSE	1
INFLICTS	—						MAGIC DEFENSE	9	EVASION	8	MAGIC EVASION	10

ELEMENTAL DEFENSE	FIRE	WATER	WIND	EARTH	LIGHT	DARK
	WEAK	—	—	—	—	

IMMUNE TO	—

TAME (SCHOLAR)	YES	POT LUCK (PARTY HOST)	YES	FORBIDDEN ART (SHAMAN)	YES	CAPTURE (BEASTMASTER)	YES
ATTACK PROFICIENCY	C	MAGIC PROFICIENCY	B	EVASION CORRECTION	A	MAGIC EVASION CORRECTION	A

ABILITIES	WOOD BLAST/CURE/SILENCE/SLEEP/PROTECT			
EXPERIENCE POINTS	9	STEAL	PHOENIX DOWN (40%)/HI-POTION (25%)/GREAT TREE LOG (5%)	
DROP	LAPIS (37.6%)	SAPPHIRE (3.9%)	HI-POTION (10.2%)	WIND DAGGER (5.1%)

RATTATOX [B]

2 ACTIONS, FLYING

ENCOUNTERED	TRIAL TOWER (PART II)

LEVEL	90	HP	848-1060	WEIGHT	30		STRENGTH	65	INTELLECT	184	SPIRIT	72
VARIABLE LEVEL	YES	ABILITY SPEED	60	ATTACK ELEMENT	—		ATTACK	52	ACCURACY	150	DEFENSE	29
INFLICTS	—						MAGIC DEFENSE	37	EVASION	5	MAGIC EVASION	36

ELEMENTAL DEFENSE	FIRE	WATER	WIND	EARTH	LIGHT	DARK
	WEAK	—	—	NO EFFECT	—	

IMMUNE TO	CURSE

TAME (SCHOLAR)	YES	POT LUCK (PARTY HOST)	YES	FORBIDDEN ART (SHAMAN)	YES	CAPTURE (BEASTMASTER)	YES
ATTACK PROFICIENCY	A	MAGIC PROFICIENCY	A	EVASION CORRECTION	A	MAGIC EVASION CORRECTION	A

ABILITIES	WOOD BLAST/CURE/SILENCE/SLEEP/PROTECT		
EXPERIENCE POINTS	100	STEAL	POTION (40%)/HI-POTION (25%)/GREAT TREE LOG (5%)
DROP	SAPPHIRE (37.6%)	HI-POTION (7.8%)	—	—

RED JELLY

ENCOUNTERED	URBETH AREA (PART II) MT. GULG (PART II)										
LEVEL	25	HP	138-173	WEIGHT	—	STRENGTH	11	INTELLECT	18	SPIRIT	18
VARIABLE LEVEL	YES	ABILITY SPEED	40	ATTACK ELEMENT	FIRE LV.1	ATTACK	6	ACCURACY	3	DEFENSE	3
INFLICTS	—					MAGIC DEFENSE	6	EVASION	70	MAGIC EVASION	7

ELEMENTAL DEFENSE	FIRE	WATER	WIND	EARTH	LIGHT	DARK
	HALF	WEAK	—	—	—	

IMMUNE TO	—

TAME (SCHOLAR)	YES	POT LUCK (PARTY HOST)	YES	FORBIDDEN ART (SHAMAN)	YES	CAPTURE (BEASTMASTER)	YES
ATTACK PROFICIENCY	B	MAGIC PROFICIENCY	B	EVASION CORRECTION	A	MAGIC EVASION CORRECTION	B

ABILITIES	MERGE			
EXPERIENCE POINTS	14	STEAL	ETHER (40%)/HI-ETHER (25%)/ANTARCTIC WIND (5%)	
DROP	TOPAZ (37.6%)	RUBY (3.9%)	HI-POTION (10.2%)	ETHER (5.1%)

ROCK GOLEM [A]

ENCOUNTERED	TOWER OF THE SKY (PART I)										
LEVEL	16	HP	55-69	WEIGHT	—	STRENGTH	11	INTELLECT	5	SPIRIT	5
VARIABLE LEVEL		ABILITY SPEED	5	ATTACK ELEMENT	EARTH LV.1	ATTACK	7	ACCURACY	98	DEFENSE	8
INFLICTS	—					MAGIC DEFENSE	4	EVASION	0	MAGIC EVASION	10

ELEMENTAL DEFENSE	FIRE	WATER	WIND	EARTH	LIGHT	DARK
	—	—	WEAK	REFLECT	—	—

IMMUNE TO	—

TAME (SCHOLAR)	YES	POT LUCK (PARTY HOST)	YES	FORBIDDEN ART (SHAMAN)	YES	CAPTURE (BEASTMASTER)	YES
ATTACK PROFICIENCY	A	MAGIC PROFICIENCY	B	EVASION CORRECTION	C	MAGIC EVASION CORRECTION	B

ABILITIES	WHIRL BLUDGEON [B]			
EXPERIENCE POINTS	9	STEAL	POTION (40%)/BOMB FRAGMENT (25%)/MYTHRIL (5%)	
DROP	SAPPHIRE (37.6%)	EMERALD (3.9%)	MYTHRIL (5.1%)	EARTH AXE (2%)

ROCK GOLEM [B]

2 ACTIONS

ENCOUNTERED	MYSTERIOUS LIGHTHOUSE (PART II) TRIAL TOWER (PART II)										
LEVEL	70	HP	712-890	WEIGHT	60	STRENGTH	43	INTELLECT	20	SPIRIT	18
VARIABLE LEVEL	YES	ABILITY SPEED	100	ATTACK ELEMENT	EARTH LV.1	ATTACK	50	ACCURACY	150	DEFENSE	31
INFLICTS	—					MAGIC DEFENSE	24	EVASION	1	MAGIC EVASION	9

ELEMENTAL DEFENSE	FIRE	WATER	WIND	EARTH	LIGHT	DARK
	—	—	WEAK	NO EFFECT	—	—

IMMUNE TO	CURSE

TAME (SCHOLAR)	YES	POT LUCK (PARTY HOST)	YES	FORBIDDEN ART (SHAMAN)	YES	CAPTURE (BEASTMASTER)	YES
ATTACK PROFICIENCY	A	MAGIC PROFICIENCY	A	EVASION CORRECTION	A	MAGIC EVASION CORRECTION	A

ABILITIES	WHIRL BLUDGEON [B]			
EXPERIENCE POINTS	100	STEAL	POTION (40%)/HI-POTION (25%)/BOMB FRAGMENT (5%)	
DROP	LAPIS (37.6%)	PHOENIX DOWN (7.8%)	HI-POTION (3.9%)	EARTH GAUNTLET (2%)

SCYLLA

ENCOUNTERED	PIRATE HIDEOUT (PART II) INVIDIA UNDERGROUND (PART II)										
LEVEL	25	HP	126-158	WEIGHT	—	STRENGTH	12	INTELLECT	20	SPIRIT	18
VARIABLE LEVEL	YES	ABILITY SPEED	60	ATTACK ELEMENT	LIGHT/WATER LV.1	ATTACK	7	ACCURACY	3	DEFENSE	4
INFLICTS	—					MAGIC DEFENSE	8	EVASION	5	MAGIC EVASION	7

ELEMENTAL DEFENSE	FIRE	WATER	WIND	EARTH	LIGHT	DARK
	WEAK	NO EFFECT	—	—	HALF	

IMMUNE TO	—

TAME (SCHOLAR)	YES	POT LUCK (PARTY HOST)	YES	FORBIDDEN ART (SHAMAN)	YES	CAPTURE (BEASTMASTER)	YES
ATTACK PROFICIENCY	B	MAGIC PROFICIENCY	A	EVASION CORRECTION	B	MAGIC EVASION CORRECTION	B

ABILITIES	CURAGA/DRAIN/ENTICE [B]			
EXPERIENCE POINTS	14	STEAL	PHOENIX DOWN (40%)/HI-POTION (25%)/ANTARCTIC WIND (5%)	
DROP	TOPAZ (37.6%)	SAPPHIRE (3.9%)	PHOENIX DOWN (10.2%)	SLEEP RING (5.1%)

SELCHIE

ENCOUNTERED	INVIDIA AREA (PART II) MYSTERIOUS LIGHTHOUSE (PART II)										
LEVEL	25	HP	138-173	WEIGHT	—	STRENGTH	13	INTELLECT	18	SPIRIT	18
VARIABLE LEVEL	YES	ABILITY SPEED	10	ATTACK ELEMENT	WATER LV.1	ATTACK	7	ACCURACY	5	DEFENSE	4
INFLICTS	—					MAGIC DEFENSE	7	EVASION	0	MAGIC EVASION	7

ELEMENTAL DEFENSE	FIRE	WATER	WIND	EARTH	LIGHT	DARK
	—	HALF	—	—	—	

IMMUNE TO	—

TAME (SCHOLAR)	YES	POT LUCK (PARTY HOST)	YES	FORBIDDEN ART (SHAMAN)	YES	CAPTURE (BEASTMASTER)	YES
ATTACK PROFICIENCY	B	MAGIC PROFICIENCY	B	EVASION CORRECTION	B	MAGIC EVASION CORRECTION	B

ABILITIES	MASH			
EXPERIENCE POINTS	14	STEAL	HI-POTION (40%)/X-POTION (25%)/DARK SIGH (5%)	
DROP	AQUAMARINE (37.6%)	SAPPHIRE (3.9%)	HI-POTION (10.2%)	—

SHADE TROLLUD

ENCOUNTERED	INVIDIA UNDERGROUND (PART II) / SUN TEMPLE (PART II)						
LEVEL	25	HP	136-170	WEIGHT	—	STRENGTH 14	INTELLECT 18	SPIRIT 18
VARIABLE LEVEL	YES	ABILITY SPEED	10	ATTACK ELEMENT	EARTH LV.1	ATTACK 7	ACCURACY 5	DEFENSE 7
INFLICTS	—					MAGIC DEFENSE 5	EVASION 0	MAGIC EVASION 7

ELEMENTAL DEFENSE	FIRE	WATER	WIND	EARTH	LIGHT	DARK
	—	—	HALF	—	—	

IMMUNE TO: —

TAME (SCHOLAR)	YES	POT LUCK (PARTY HOST)	YES	FORBIDDEN ART (SHAMAN)	YES	CAPTURE (BEASTMASTER)	YES
ATTACK PROFICIENCY	A	MAGIC PROFICIENCY	B	EVASION CORRECTION	B	MAGIC EVASION CORRECTION	B

ABILITIES: BERSERK/WHIRL BLUDGEON [D]

EXPERIENCE POINTS	14	STEAL	HI-POTION (40%)/HYDRAXE (25%)/DARK SIGH (5%)		
DROP	AQUAMARINE (37.6%)		RUBY (3.9%)	HI-POTION (10.2%)	—

SILKY [A] — FLYING

ENCOUNTERED	INVIDIA AREA (PART I) / ICE CAVERNS (PART I)						
LEVEL	22	HP	30-38	WEIGHT	—	STRENGTH 8	INTELLECT 16	SPIRIT 15
VARIABLE LEVEL	—	ABILITY SPEED	55	ATTACK ELEMENT	DARK LV.1	ATTACK 6	ACCURACY 98	DEFENSE 2
INFLICTS	SILENCE (12%)					MAGIC DEFENSE 4	EVASION 70	MAGIC EVASION 6

ELEMENTAL DEFENSE	FIRE	WATER	WIND	EARTH	LIGHT	DARK
	—	—	—	—	WEAK	NO EFFECT

IMMUNE TO: —

TAME (SCHOLAR)	YES	POT LUCK (PARTY HOST)	YES	FORBIDDEN ART (SHAMAN)	YES	CAPTURE (BEASTMASTER)	YES
ATTACK PROFICIENCY	B	MAGIC PROFICIENCY	B	EVASION CORRECTION	A	MAGIC EVASION CORRECTION	B

ABILITIES: ICE BLAST/DARK/SUPPRESS

EXPERIENCE POINTS	12	STEAL	POTION (40%)/HI-POTION (25%)/DARK SIGH (5%)		
DROP	AQUAMARINE (37.6%)		EMERALD (3.9%)	ANIMATE TONIC (5.1%)	SILENCE RING (2%)

SILKY [B] — 2 ACTIONS, FLYING

ENCOUNTERED	HOLY TREE TOWER (PART II)						
LEVEL	60	HP	325-406	WEIGHT	30	STRENGTH 20	INTELLECT 117	SPIRIT 48
VARIABLE LEVEL	YES	ABILITY SPEED	80	ATTACK ELEMENT	DARK LV.1	ATTACK 36	ACCURACY 150	DEFENSE 5
INFLICTS	SILENCE (12%)					MAGIC DEFENSE 17	EVASION 99	MAGIC EVASION 24

ELEMENTAL DEFENSE	FIRE	WATER	WIND	EARTH	LIGHT	DARK
	—	—	—	NO EFFECT	WEAK	NO EFFECT

IMMUNE TO: CURSE

TAME (SCHOLAR)	YES	POT LUCK (PARTY HOST)	YES	FORBIDDEN ART (SHAMAN)	YES	CAPTURE (BEASTMASTER)	YES
ATTACK PROFICIENCY	A	MAGIC PROFICIENCY	A	EVASION CORRECTION	A	MAGIC EVASION CORRECTION	A

ABILITIES: ICE BLAST/DARK/SUPPRESS

EXPERIENCE POINTS	100	STEAL	POTION (40%)/HI-POTION (25%)/DARK SIGH (5%)		
DROP	SAPPHIRE (37.6%)		HI-POTION (7.8%)	ECHO HERBS (3.9%)	SILENCE RING (2%)

SKELETON [A]

ENCOUNTERED	INVIDIA UNDERGROUND (PART I)						
LEVEL	21	HP	62-78	WEIGHT	—	STRENGTH 10	INTELLECT 10	SPIRIT 13
VARIABLE LEVEL	—	ABILITY SPEED	10	ATTACK ELEMENT	DARK LV.1	ATTACK 7	ACCURACY 98	DEFENSE 3
INFLICTS	POISON (10%)					MAGIC DEFENSE 7	EVASION 6	MAGIC EVASION 4

ELEMENTAL DEFENSE	FIRE	WATER	WIND	EARTH	LIGHT	DARK
	—	—	—	—	WEAK	HALF

IMMUNE TO: —

ATTACK PROFICIENCY	B	MAGIC PROFICIENCY	B	EVASION CORRECTION	C	MAGIC EVASION CORRECTION	C

ABILITIES: WHIRL BLUDGEON [A]

EXPERIENCE POINTS	12	STEAL	POTION (40%)/DARKNESS AXE (25%)/DARK SIGH (5%)		
DROP	AQUAMARINE (37.6%)		RUBY (3.9%)	ANTIDOTE (5.1%)	DUSK GAUNTLET (2%)

SKELETON [B] — 2 ACTIONS

ENCOUNTERED	MYSTERIOUS LIGHTHOUSE (PART II) / TRIAL TOWER (PART II)						
LEVEL	70	HP	526-658	WEIGHT	60	STRENGTH 40	INTELLECT 56	SPIRIT 56
VARIABLE LEVEL	YES	ABILITY SPEED	100	ATTACK ELEMENT	DARK LV.1	ATTACK 43	ACCURACY 150	DEFENSE 28
INFLICTS	POISON (10%)					MAGIC DEFENSE 20	EVASION 0	MAGIC EVASION 28

ELEMENTAL DEFENSE	FIRE	WATER	WIND	EARTH	LIGHT	DARK
	—	—	—	—	WEAK	NO EFFECT

IMMUNE TO: CURSE

TAME (SCHOLAR)	YES	POT LUCK (PARTY HOST)	YES	FORBIDDEN ART (SHAMAN)	YES	CAPTURE (BEASTMASTER)	YES
ATTACK PROFICIENCY	A	MAGIC PROFICIENCY	A	EVASION CORRECTION	A	MAGIC EVASION CORRECTION	A

ABILITIES: WHIRL BLUDGEON [A]

EXPERIENCE POINTS	100	STEAL	POTION (40%)/DARKNESS AXE (25%)/DARK SIGH (5%)		
DROP	SAPPHIRE (37.6%)		PHOENIX DOWN (7.8%)	ANTIDOTE (3.9%)	DUSK GAUNTLET (2%)

SLIME [A]

ENCOUNTERED	LIBERTE AREA (PART I)							
	PIRATE HIDEOUT (PART I)							

LEVEL	8	HP	35-44	WEIGHT	—	STRENGTH	6	INTELLECT	4	SPIRIT	0
VARIABLE LEVEL	—	ABILITY SPEED	35	ATTACK ELEMENT	WATER LV.1	ATTACK	4	ACCURACY	97	DEFENSE	2
INFLICTS	—					MAGIC DEFENSE	4	EVASION	3	MAGIC EVASION	10

ELEMENTAL DEFENSE	FIRE	WATER	WIND	EARTH	LIGHT	DARK
	WEAK	NO EFFECT				

IMMUNE TO	—

TAME (SCHOLAR)	YES	POT LUCK (PARTY HOST)	YES	FORBIDDEN ART (SHAMAN)	YES	CAPTURE (BEASTMASTER)	YES
ATTACK PROFICIENCY	B	MAGIC PROFICIENCY	B	EVASION CORRECTION	B	MAGIC EVASION CORRECTION	B

ABILITIES	MERGE			
EXPERIENCE POINTS	5	STEAL	POTION (40%)/HI-POTION (25%)/ANTARCTIC WIND (5%)	
DROP	TOPAZ (37.6%)	EMERALD (3.9%)	POTION (10.2%)	HI-POTION (5.1%)

SLIME [B]

ENCOUNTERED	HOLY TREE TOWER (PART II)

LEVEL	60	HP	340-425	WEIGHT	—	STRENGTH	22	INTELLECT	48	SPIRIT	48
VARIABLE LEVEL	YES	ABILITY SPEED	80	ATTACK ELEMENT	WATER LV.1	ATTACK	28	ACCURACY	150	DEFENSE	5
INFLICTS	—					MAGIC DEFENSE	18	EVASION	99	MAGIC EVASION	24

ELEMENTAL DEFENSE	FIRE	WATER	WIND	EARTH	LIGHT	DARK
	—	HALF	—	WEAK	—	—

IMMUNE TO	CURSE

TAME (SCHOLAR)	YES	POT LUCK (PARTY HOST)	YES	FORBIDDEN ART (SHAMAN)	YES	CAPTURE (BEASTMASTER)	YES
ATTACK PROFICIENCY	A	MAGIC PROFICIENCY	A	EVASION CORRECTION	A	MAGIC EVASION CORRECTION	A

ABILITIES	MERGE			
EXPERIENCE POINTS	100	STEAL	POTION (40%)/HI-POTION (25%)/ANTARCTIC WIND (5%)	
DROP	TOPAZ (37.6%)	POTION (7.8%)	HI-POTION (3.9%)	—

SUCCUBUS [A]

FLYING

ENCOUNTERED	URBETH AREA (PART I)							
	TOWER OF THE SKY (PART I)							

LEVEL	15	HP	47-59	WEIGHT	—	STRENGTH	8	INTELLECT	14	SPIRIT	11
VARIABLE LEVEL	—	ABILITY SPEED	55	ATTACK ELEMENT	—	ATTACK	6	ACCURACY	98	DEFENSE	2
INFLICTS	—					MAGIC DEFENSE	5	EVASION	6	MAGIC EVASION	10

ELEMENTAL DEFENSE	FIRE	WATER	WIND	EARTH	LIGHT	DARK
	—	—	—	—	—	—

IMMUNE TO	—

TAME (SCHOLAR)	YES	POT LUCK (PARTY HOST)	YES	FORBIDDEN ART (SHAMAN)	YES	CAPTURE (BEASTMASTER)	YES
ATTACK PROFICIENCY	B	MAGIC PROFICIENCY	B	EVASION CORRECTION	B	MAGIC EVASION CORRECTION	B

ABILITIES	ENTICE [A]			
EXPERIENCE POINTS	9	STEAL	PHOENIX DOWN (40%)/HI-POTION (25%)/BOMB FRAGMENT (5%)	
DROP	SAPPHIRE (37.6%)	AQUAMARINE (3.9%)	PHOENIX DOWN (10.2%)	CONFUSE RING (5.1%)

SUCCUBUS [B]

2 ACTIONS, FLYING

ENCOUNTERED	TRIAL TOWER (PART II)

LEVEL	90	HP	834-1043	WEIGHT	30	STRENGTH	65	INTELLECT	192	SPIRIT	37
VARIABLE LEVEL	YES	ABILITY SPEED	60	ATTACK ELEMENT	—	ATTACK	58	ACCURACY	150	DEFENSE	38
INFLICTS	—					MAGIC DEFENSE	37	EVASION	5	MAGIC EVASION	19

ELEMENTAL DEFENSE	FIRE	WATER	WIND	EARTH	LIGHT	DARK
	—	—	—	NO EFFECT	—	—

IMMUNE TO	CURSE

TAME (SCHOLAR)	YES	POT LUCK (PARTY HOST)	YES	FORBIDDEN ART (SHAMAN)	YES	CAPTURE (BEASTMASTER)	YES
ATTACK PROFICIENCY	A	MAGIC PROFICIENCY	A	EVASION CORRECTION	A	MAGIC EVASION CORRECTION	A

ABILITIES	ENTICE [A]			
EXPERIENCE POINTS	100	STEAL	PHOENIX DOWN (40%)/HI-POTION (25%)/BOMB FRAGMENT (5%)	
DROP	LAPIS (37.6%)	PHOENIX DOWN (7.8%)	—	CONFUSE RING (2%)

TOKKAKU

FLYING

ENCOUNTERED	INVIDIA AREA (PART II)							
	STAR CHAMBER (PART II)							

LEVEL	25	HP	138-173	WEIGHT	—	STRENGTH	13	INTELLECT	17	SPIRIT	18
VARIABLE LEVEL	YES	ABILITY SPEED	50	ATTACK ELEMENT	WATER LV.2	ATTACK	6	ACCURACY	3	DEFENSE	7
INFLICTS	PARALYSIS (10%)					MAGIC DEFENSE	5	EVASION	5	MAGIC EVASION	7

ELEMENTAL DEFENSE	FIRE	WATER	WIND	EARTH	LIGHT	DARK
	WEAK	NO EFFECT	—	—	—	—

IMMUNE TO	—

TAME (SCHOLAR)	YES	POT LUCK (PARTY HOST)	YES	FORBIDDEN ART (SHAMAN)	YES	CAPTURE (BEASTMASTER)	YES
ATTACK PROFICIENCY	B	MAGIC PROFICIENCY	A	EVASION CORRECTION	B	MAGIC EVASION CORRECTION	B

ABILITIES	LIGHTNING BOLT [A]			
EXPERIENCE POINTS	14	STEAL	ANIMATE TONIC (40%)/ETHER (25%)/ANTARCTIC WIND (5%)	
DROP	TOPAZ (37.6%)	AQUAMARINE (3.9%)	HI-POTION (10.2%)	DEATH RING (5.1%)

TROLLUD [A]

ENCOUNTERED	ICE CAVERNS(PART I)								
LEVEL	20	HP	63-79	WEIGHT	—	STRENGTH	11	INTELLECT	10	SPIRIT	6
VARIABLE LEVEL	—	ABILITY SPEED	15	ATTACK ELEMENT	EARTH LV.1	ATTACK	6	ACCURACY	98	DEFENSE	5
INFLICTS	—					MAGIC DEFENSE	4	EVASION	3	MAGIC EVASION	5

ELEMENTAL DEFENSE	FIRE	WATER	WIND	EARTH	LIGHT	DARK
	—	—	—	HALF	—	—

IMMUNE TO	—

TAME (SCHOLAR)	YES	POT LUCK (PARTY HOST)	YES	FORBIDDEN ART (SHAMAN)	YES	CAPTURE (BEASTMASTER)	YES
ATTACK PROFICIENCY	A	MAGIC PROFICIENCY	C	EVASION CORRECTION	C	MAGIC EVASION CORRECTION	C

ABILITIES	BERSERK/WHIRL BLUDGEON [D]

EXPERIENCE POINTS	11	STEAL	PHOENIX DOWN (40%)/HYDRAXE (25%)/DARK SIGH (5%)	
DROP	AQUAMARINE (37.6%)	SAPPHIRE (3.9%)	EYE DROPS (5.1%)	—

TROLLUD [B]

2 ACTIONS

ENCOUNTERED	MYSTERIOUS LIGHTHOUSE(PART II) / TRIAL TOWER(PART II)								
LEVEL	70	HP	610-763	WEIGHT	60	STRENGTH	41	INTELLECT	56	SPIRIT	56
VARIABLE LEVEL	YES	ABILITY SPEED	100	ATTACK ELEMENT	—	ATTACK	43	ACCURACY	150	DEFENSE	28
INFLICTS	—					MAGIC DEFENSE	21	EVASION	3	MAGIC EVASION	5

ELEMENTAL DEFENSE	FIRE	WATER	WIND	EARTH	LIGHT	DARK
	—	—	—	—	—	—

IMMUNE TO	CURSE

TAME (SCHOLAR)	YES	POT LUCK (PARTY HOST)	YES	FORBIDDEN ART (SHAMAN)	YES	CAPTURE (BEASTMASTER)	YES
ATTACK PROFICIENCY	A	MAGIC PROFICIENCY	A	EVASION CORRECTION	A	MAGIC EVASION CORRECTION	A

ABILITIES	BERSERK/WHIRL BLUDGEON [D]

EXPERIENCE POINTS	100	STEAL	POTION (40%)/HYDRAXE (25%)/DARK SIGH (5%)	
DROP	TOPAZ (37.6%)	HI-POTION (7.8%)	EYE DROPS (3.9%)	HATCHET (2%)

TROLLUD ZOMBIE

ENCOUNTERED	INVIDIA UNDERGROUND(PART II) / SUN TEMPLE(PART II)								
LEVEL	25	HP	138-173	WEIGHT	—	STRENGTH	13	INTELLECT	18	SPIRIT	18
VARIABLE LEVEL	YES	ABILITY SPEED	10	ATTACK ELEMENT	WATER LV.1	ATTACK	7	ACCURACY	5	DEFENSE	4
INFLICTS	CURSE (10%)					MAGIC DEFENSE	6	EVASION	5	MAGIC EVASION	7

ELEMENTAL DEFENSE	FIRE	WATER	WIND	EARTH	LIGHT	DARK
	—	HALF	—	WEAK	—	—

IMMUNE TO	—

TAME (SCHOLAR)	YES	POT LUCK (PARTY HOST)	YES	FORBIDDEN ART (SHAMAN)	YES	CAPTURE (BEASTMASTER)	YES
ATTACK PROFICIENCY	A	MAGIC PROFICIENCY	B	EVASION CORRECTION	B	MAGIC EVASION CORRECTION	B

ABILITIES	WHIRL BLUDGEON [A]

EXPERIENCE POINTS	14	STEAL	HI-POTION (40%)/DARKNESS AXE (25%)/HOLY BREATH (5%)	
DROP	AQUAMARINE (37.6%)	TOPAZ (3.9%)	HI-POTION (10.2%)	DUSK GAUNTLET (5.1%)

VAMPIRE BAT [A]

FLYING

ENCOUNTERED	GREAT TREE ROOTS(PART II) / MT. GULG(PART II)								
LEVEL	25	HP	129-161	WEIGHT	—	STRENGTH	11	INTELLECT	9	SPIRIT	12
VARIABLE LEVEL	YES	ABILITY SPEED	30	ATTACK ELEMENT	—	ATTACK	6	ACCURACY	5	DEFENSE	4
INFLICTS	—					MAGIC DEFENSE	6	EVASION	5	MAGIC EVASION	5

ELEMENTAL DEFENSE	FIRE	WATER	WIND	EARTH	LIGHT	DARK
	—	—	—	—	—	—

IMMUNE TO	—

TAME (SCHOLAR)	YES	POT LUCK (PARTY HOST)	YES	FORBIDDEN ART (SHAMAN)	YES	CAPTURE (BEASTMASTER)	YES
ATTACK PROFICIENCY	B	MAGIC PROFICIENCY	A	EVASION CORRECTION	B	MAGIC EVASION CORRECTION	B

ABILITIES	BLOODFEAST

EXPERIENCE POINTS	14	STEAL	HI-POTION (40%)/ETHER (25%)/RAVEN'S YAWN (5%)	
DROP	RUBY (37.6%)	TOPAZ (3.9%)	POTION (10.2%)	BLOODY RING (0.8%)

VAMPIRE BAT [B]

FLYING

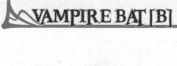

ENCOUNTERED	MOONSAND RUINS(PART II)								
LEVEL	50	HP	278-348	WEIGHT	—	STRENGTH	21	INTELLECT	40	SPIRIT	40
VARIABLE LEVEL	YES	ABILITY SPEED	60	ATTACK ELEMENT	—	ATTACK	21	ACCURACY	150	DEFENSE	6
INFLICTS	—					MAGIC DEFENSE	8	EVASION	5	MAGIC EVASION	10

ELEMENTAL DEFENSE	FIRE	WATER	WIND	EARTH	LIGHT	DARK
	WEAK	—	—	NO EFFECT	—	—

IMMUNE TO	PETRIFY / CURSE / DEATH

TAME (SCHOLAR)	YES	POT LUCK (PARTY HOST)	YES	FORBIDDEN ART (SHAMAN)	YES	CAPTURE (BEASTMASTER)	YES
ATTACK PROFICIENCY	A	MAGIC PROFICIENCY	A	EVASION CORRECTION	A	MAGIC EVASION CORRECTION	A

ABILITIES	BLOODFEAST

EXPERIENCE POINTS	100	STEAL	POTION (40%)/HI-POTION (25%)/X-POTION (5%)	
DROP	RUBY (9.8%)	POTION (7.8%)	—	—

VULTURE

											FLYING
ENCOUNTERED	ARBOR SOUTH AREA (PART II)										
	GREAT TREE(PART II)										
LEVEL	25	HP	131-164	WEIGHT	—	STRENGTH	12	INTELLECT	13	SPIRIT	13
VARIABLE LEVEL	YES	ABILITY SPEED	40	ATTACK ELEMENT	—	ATTACK	6	ACCURACY	3	DEFENSE	3
INFLICTS						MAGIC DEFENSE	6	EVASION	70	MAGIC EVASION	5

	FIRE	WATER	WIND	EARTH	LIGHT	DARK
ELEMENTAL DEFENSE	—	—	WEAK	—	—	—
IMMUNE TO	—					

TAME (SCHOLAR)	YES	POT LUCK (PARTY HOST)	YES	FORBIDDEN ART (SHAMAN)	YES	CAPTURE (BEASTMASTER)	YES
ATTACK PROFICIENCY	B	MAGIC PROFICIENCY	B	EVASION CORRECTION	A	MAGIC EVASION CORRECTION	B

ABILITIES	DIVE			
EXPERIENCE POINTS	14	STEAL	HI-POTION (40%)/ETHER (25%)/GAIA DRUM (5%)	
DROP	EMERALD (37.6%)	HI-POTION (3.9%)	PHOENIX DOWN (5.1%)	GALE GAUNTLET (2%)

WIGHT [A]

											FLYING
ENCOUNTERED	MOONLIGHT TOWER(PART I)										
	QUICKSAND CASTLE(PART I)										
LEVEL	11	HP	58-73	WEIGHT	—	STRENGTH	9	INTELLECT	8	SPIRIT	8
VARIABLE LEVEL	—	ABILITY SPEED	35	ATTACK ELEMENT	DARK LV.1	ATTACK	4	ACCURACY	97	DEFENSE	2
INFLICTS	BLINDNESS (10%)					MAGIC DEFENSE	4	EVASION	4	MAGIC EVASION	10

	FIRE	WATER	WIND	EARTH	LIGHT	DARK
ELEMENTAL DEFENSE	—	—	—	—	—	NO EFFECT
IMMUNE TO	—					

TAME (SCHOLAR)	YES	POT LUCK (PARTY HOST)	YES	FORBIDDEN ART (SHAMAN)	YES	CAPTURE (BEASTMASTER)	YES
ATTACK PROFICIENCY	B	MAGIC PROFICIENCY	B	EVASION CORRECTION	B	MAGIC EVASION CORRECTION	B

ABILITIES	FLASH			
EXPERIENCE POINTS	7	STEAL	HI-POTION (40%)/CROSS (25%)/GAIA DRUM (5%)	
DROP	EMERALD (37.6%)	SAPPHIRE (3.9%)	ANIMATE TONIC (5.1%)	DEATH RING (1.2%)

WIGHT [B]

											FLYING
ENCOUNTERED	INVIDIA UNDERGROUND(PART I)										
	SPELVIA DUNGEONS(PART I)										
LEVEL	1	HP	68-85	WEIGHT	—	STRENGTH	10	INTELLECT	10	SPIRIT	7
VARIABLE LEVEL	—	ABILITY SPEED	40	ATTACK ELEMENT		ATTACK	7	ACCURACY	98	DEFENSE	3
INFLICTS	PARALYSIS (25%)					MAGIC DEFENSE	9	EVASION	5	MAGIC EVASION	3

	FIRE	WATER	WIND	EARTH	LIGHT	DARK
ELEMENTAL DEFENSE	—	—	—	—	WEAK	HALF
IMMUNE TO	PETRIFY / CURSE / DEATH					

TAME (SCHOLAR)	YES	POT LUCK (PARTY HOST)	YES	FORBIDDEN ART (SHAMAN)	YES	CAPTURE (BEASTMASTER)	YES
ATTACK PROFICIENCY	B	MAGIC PROFICIENCY	B	EVASION CORRECTION	B	MAGIC EVASION CORRECTION	B

ABILITIES	SILENCE/DARK BLAST			
EXPERIENCE POINTS	12	STEAL	HI-POTION (40%)/X-POTION (25%)/BOMB FRAGMENT (5%)	
DROP	AQUAMARINE (37.6%)	LAPIS (10.2%)	POTION (7.8%)	DEATH RING (3.9%)

WIGHT [C]

											2 ACTIONS, FLYING
ENCOUNTERED	HOLY TREE TOWER (PART II)										
LEVEL	60	HP	410-513	WEIGHT	30	STRENGTH	24	INTELLECT	116	SPIRIT	18
VARIABLE LEVEL	YES	ABILITY SPEED	80	ATTACK ELEMENT		ATTACK	24	ACCURACY	150	DEFENSE	19
INFLICTS	BLINDNESS (10%)					MAGIC DEFENSE	18	EVASION	10	MAGIC EVASION	9

	FIRE	WATER	WIND	EARTH	LIGHT	DARK
ELEMENTAL DEFENSE	—	—	—	NO EFFECT	—	—
IMMUNE TO	CURSE					

TAME (SCHOLAR)	YES	POT LUCK (PARTY HOST)	YES	FORBIDDEN ART (SHAMAN)	YES	CAPTURE (BEASTMASTER)	YES
ATTACK PROFICIENCY	A	MAGIC PROFICIENCY	A	EVASION CORRECTION	A	MAGIC EVASION CORRECTION	A

ABILITIES	FLASH			
EXPERIENCE POINTS	100	STEAL	POTION (40%)/HI-POTION (25%)/GAIA DRUM (5%)	
DROP	EMERALD (37.6%)	POTION (7.8%)	ANIMATE TONIC (3.9%)	DEATH RING (2%)

WRAITH [A]

											FLYING
ENCOUNTERED	ROLAN'S SOUL(PART II)										
	STAR CHAMBER(PART II)										
LEVEL	25	HP	120-150	WEIGHT	—	STRENGTH	11	INTELLECT	20	SPIRIT	18
VARIABLE LEVEL	YES	ABILITY SPEED	40	ATTACK ELEMENT	DARK LV.1	ATTACK	6	ACCURACY	3	DEFENSE	4
INFLICTS	PARALYSIS (10%)					MAGIC DEFENSE	6	EVASION	70	MAGIC EVASION	7

	FIRE	WATER	WIND	EARTH	LIGHT	DARK
ELEMENTAL DEFENSE	—	—	—	—	WEAK	NO EFFECT
IMMUNE TO	—					

TAME (SCHOLAR)	YES	POT LUCK (PARTY HOST)	YES	FORBIDDEN ART (SHAMAN)	YES	CAPTURE (BEASTMASTER)	YES
ATTACK PROFICIENCY	B	MAGIC PROFICIENCY	A	EVASION CORRECTION	A	MAGIC EVASION CORRECTION	B

ABILITIES	ICE BLAST/DARK/SUPPRESS/BREAK			
EXPERIENCE POINTS	14	STEAL	ANIMATE TONIC (40%)/X-POTION (25%)/DARK SIGH (5%)	
DROP	AQUAMARINE (37.6%)	RUBY (3.9%)	CROSS (10.2%)	SILENCE RING (5.1%)

WYORM

ENCOUNTERED	GUERA AREA (PART II)									
	MOONLIGHT TOWER(PART II)									
LEVEL	25	HP	137-171	WEIGHT	—	STRENGTH	13	INTELLECT	11	SPIRIT	10
VARIABLE LEVEL	YES	ABILITY SPEED	40	ATTACK ELEMENT	EARTH LV.2	ATTACK	7	ACCURACY	3	DEFENSE	4
INFLICTS	PARALYSIS (10%)					MAGIC DEFENSE	6	EVASION	4	MAGIC EVASION	4

ELEMENTAL DEFENSE	FIRE	WATER	WIND	EARTH	LIGHT	DARK
	—	—	—	NO EFFECT	—	—

IMMUNE TO	—

TAME (SCHOLAR)	YES	POT LUCK (PARTY HOST)	YES	FORBIDDEN ART (SHAMAN)	YES	CAPTURE (BEASTMASTER)	YES
ATTACK PROFICIENCY	B	MAGIC PROFICIENCY	B	EVASION CORRECTION	C	MAGIC EVASION CORRECTION	B
ABILITIES	VITRIOL						
EXPERIENCE POINTS	14	STEAL		HI-POTION (40%)/REMEDY (25%)/GAIA DRUM (5%)			
DROP		EMERALD (37.6%)		TOPAZ (3.9%)		ANIMATE TONIC (10.2%)	EARTH GAUNTLET (5.1%)

WYVERN [A]

ENCOUNTERED	SPELVIA DUNGEONS(PART I)									
LEVEL	21	HP	71-89	WEIGHT	—	STRENGTH	13	INTELLECT	10	SPIRIT	15
VARIABLE LEVEL		ABILITY SPEED	30	ATTACK ELEMENT	—	ATTACK	7	ACCURACY	98	DEFENSE	4
INFLICTS	PARALYSIS (10%)					MAGIC DEFENSE	4	EVASION	9	MAGIC EVASION	6

ELEMENTAL DEFENSE	FIRE	WATER	WIND	EARTH	LIGHT	DARK
	—	—	—	—	—	WEAK

IMMUNE TO	—

TAME (SCHOLAR)	YES	POT LUCK (PARTY HOST)	YES	FORBIDDEN ART (SHAMAN)	YES	CAPTURE (BEASTMASTER)	YES
ATTACK PROFICIENCY	A	MAGIC PROFICIENCY	B	EVASION CORRECTION	B	MAGIC EVASION CORRECTION	B
ABILITIES	MIGHTY SLAP						
EXPERIENCE POINTS	12	STEAL		POTION (40%)/HI-POTION (25%)/HOLY BREATH (5%)			
DROP		AQUAMARINE (37.6%)		EMERALD (3.9%)		GOLD NEEDLE (5.1%)	—

WYVERN [B]

2 ACTIONS

ENCOUNTERED	MYSTERIOUS LIGHTHOUSE(PART II)									
	TRIAL TOWER(PART II)									
LEVEL	70	HP	680-850	WEIGHT	60	STRENGTH	40	INTELLECT	28	SPIRIT	56
VARIABLE LEVEL	YES	ABILITY SPEED	100	ATTACK ELEMENT	—	ATTACK	46	ACCURACY	150	DEFENSE	25
INFLICTS	PARALYSIS (10%)					MAGIC DEFENSE	26	EVASION	6	MAGIC EVASION	28

ELEMENTAL DEFENSE	FIRE	WATER	WIND	EARTH	LIGHT	DARK
	—	—	—	NO EFFECT	—	—

IMMUNE TO	CURSE

TAME (SCHOLAR)	YES	POT LUCK (PARTY HOST)	YES	FORBIDDEN ART (SHAMAN)	YES	CAPTURE (BEASTMASTER)	YES
ATTACK PROFICIENCY	A	MAGIC PROFICIENCY	A	EVASION CORRECTION	A	MAGIC EVASION CORRECTION	A
ABILITIES	MIGHTY SLAP						
EXPERIENCE POINTS	100	STEAL		POTION (40%)/HI-POTION (25%)/HOLY BREATH (5%)			
DROP		AMETHYST (37.6%)		HI-POTION (7.8%)		GOLD NEEDLE (3.9%)	HOLY LANCE (2%)

YOTON [A]

ENCOUNTERED	INVIDIA AREA (PART I)									
	ICE CAVERNS(PART I)									
LEVEL	21	HP	60-75	WEIGHT	—	STRENGTH	9	INTELLECT	10	SPIRIT	14
VARIABLE LEVEL		ABILITY SPEED	10	ATTACK ELEMENT	WATER LV.1	ATTACK	6	ACCURACY	98	DEFENSE	3
INFLICTS	—					MAGIC DEFENSE	5	EVASION	1	MAGIC EVASION	6

ELEMENTAL DEFENSE	FIRE	WATER	WIND	EARTH	LIGHT	DARK
	—	HALF	—	WEAK	—	—

IMMUNE TO	—

TAME (SCHOLAR)	YES	POT LUCK (PARTY HOST)	YES	FORBIDDEN ART (SHAMAN)	YES	CAPTURE (BEASTMASTER)	YES
ATTACK PROFICIENCY	B	MAGIC PROFICIENCY	B	EVASION CORRECTION	C	MAGIC EVASION CORRECTION	B
ABILITIES	MASH						
EXPERIENCE POINTS	11	STEAL		POTION (40%)/HI-POTION (25%)/DARK SIGH (5%)			
DROP		AQUAMARINE (37.6%)		SAPPHIRE (3.9%)		ANIMATE TONIC (10.2%)	—

YOTON [B]

2 ACTIONS

ENCOUNTERED	MYSTERIOUS TOWER (PART II)									
LEVEL	70	HP	544-680	WEIGHT	60	STRENGTH	39	INTELLECT	56	SPIRIT	56
VARIABLE LEVEL	YES	ABILITY SPEED	100	ATTACK ELEMENT	WATER LV.1	ATTACK	36	ACCURACY	150	DEFENSE	29
INFLICTS	—					MAGIC DEFENSE	22	EVASION	1	MAGIC EVASION	28

ELEMENTAL DEFENSE	FIRE	WATER	WIND	EARTH	LIGHT	DARK
	—	HALF	—	WEAK	—	—

IMMUNE TO	CURSE

TAME (SCHOLAR)	YES	POT LUCK (PARTY HOST)	YES	FORBIDDEN ART (SHAMAN)	YES	CAPTURE (BEASTMASTER)	YES
ATTACK PROFICIENCY	A	MAGIC PROFICIENCY	A	EVASION CORRECTION	A	MAGIC EVASION CORRECTION	A
ABILITIES	MASH						
EXPERIENCE POINTS	100	STEAL		POTION (40%)/HI-POTION (25%)/DARK SIGH (5%)			
DROP		TOPAZ (37.6%)		ANIMATE TONIC (7.8%)	—		DARKENING HARP (2%)

BOSSES

MINOTAUR [B]

ENCOUNTERED	NORTHERN CAVES								
LEVEL	4	HP	120	WEIGHT	—	STRENGTH	3	INTELLECT	2	SPIRIT	1
VARIABLE LEVEL	—	ABILITY SPEED	5	ATTACK ELEMENT	—	ATTACK	4	ACCURACY	95	DEFENSE	2
INFLICTS						MAGIC DEFENSE	1	EVASION	5	MAGIC EVASION	2

ELEMENTAL DEFENSE	FIRE	WATER	WIND	EARTH	LIGHT	DARK
	WEAK	—	—	—	—	

IMMUNE TO: PETRIFY / CURSE / DEATH

TAME (SCHOLAR)	—	POT LUCK (PARTY HOST)	—	FORBIDDEN ART (SHAMAN)	—	CAPTURE (BEASTMASTER)	—
ATTACK PROFICIENCY	A	MAGIC PROFICIENCY	C	EVASION CORRECTION	C	MAGIC EVASION CORRECTION	C

ABILITIES: FULL SWING

EXPERIENCE POINTS	20	STEAL	—		
DROP	RUBY (100%)	RUBY (100%)	AMETHYST (100%)	POWER RING (2%)

GREAPS [A]

ENCOUNTERED	WITCH'S MANSION								
LEVEL	8	HP	260	WEIGHT	—	STRENGTH	4	INTELLECT	5	SPIRIT	4
VARIABLE LEVEL	—	ABILITY SPEED	15	ATTACK ELEMENT	WIND LV.1	ATTACK	7	ACCURACY	98	DEFENSE	3
INFLICTS						MAGIC DEFENSE	2	EVASION	3	MAGIC EVASION	10

ELEMENTAL DEFENSE	FIRE	WATER	WIND	EARTH	LIGHT	DARK
	WEAK	—	HALF	—	—	

IMMUNE TO: PETRIFY / CURSE / DEATH

TAME (SCHOLAR)	—	POT LUCK (PARTY HOST)	—	FORBIDDEN ART (SHAMAN)	—	CAPTURE (BEASTMASTER)	—
ATTACK PROFICIENCY	B	MAGIC PROFICIENCY	B	EVASION CORRECTION	B	MAGIC EVASION CORRECTION	B

ABILITIES: BLAST OF AIR

EXPERIENCE POINTS	72	STEAL	—		
DROP	RUBY (100%)	RUBY (100%)	AMETHYST (100%)	AMETHYST (100%)

SAND DEVIL [A]

ENCOUNTERED	QUICKSAND CASTLE								
LEVEL	14	HP	600	WEIGHT	—	STRENGTH	7	INTELLECT	9	SPIRIT	6
VARIABLE LEVEL	—	ABILITY SPEED	140	ATTACK ELEMENT	EARTH LV.1	ATTACK	9	ACCURACY	96	DEFENSE	99
INFLICTS						MAGIC DEFENSE	6	EVASION	6	MAGIC EVASION	10

ELEMENTAL DEFENSE	FIRE	WATER	WIND	EARTH	LIGHT	DARK
	—	WEAK	—	HALF	—	

IMMUNE TO: PETRIFY / CURSE / DEATH

TAME (SCHOLAR)	—	POT LUCK (PARTY HOST)	—	FORBIDDEN ART (SHAMAN)	—	CAPTURE (BEASTMASTER)	—
ATTACK PROFICIENCY	B	MAGIC PROFICIENCY	A	EVASION CORRECTION	B	MAGIC EVASION CORRECTION	B

ABILITIES: SANDSTORM

EXPERIENCE POINTS	210	STEAL	—		
DROP	EMERALD (100%)	EMERALD (100%)	AMETHYST (100%)	EARTH SWORD (100%)

TROLLUD [C]

ENCOUNTERED	PIRATE HIDEOUT								
LEVEL	13	HP	400	WEIGHT	—	STRENGTH	6	INTELLECT	6	SPIRIT	6
VARIABLE LEVEL	—	ABILITY SPEED	40	ATTACK ELEMENT	—	ATTACK	6	ACCURACY	98	DEFENSE	7
INFLICTS						MAGIC DEFENSE	9	EVASION	3	MAGIC EVASION	5

ELEMENTAL DEFENSE	FIRE	WATER	WIND	EARTH	LIGHT	DARK
	—	—	—	—	—	

IMMUNE TO:

TAME (SCHOLAR)	—	POT LUCK (PARTY HOST)	—	FORBIDDEN ART (SHAMAN)	—	CAPTURE (BEASTMASTER)	—
ATTACK PROFICIENCY	A	MAGIC PROFICIENCY	C	EVASION CORRECTION	C	MAGIC EVASION CORRECTION	C

ABILITIES: BERSERK, WHIRL BLUDGEON [D]

EXPERIENCE POINTS	182	STEAL	HI-POTION (40%)/X-POTION (25%)/ANTARCTIC WIND (5%)		
DROP	TOPAZ (100%)	TOPAZ (10.2%)	TOPAZ (100%)	TOPAZ (100%)

OGRE BEAR

3 ACTIONS

ENCOUNTERED	ANIMAL BURROW								
LEVEL	99	HP	9999-12499	WEIGHT	30	STRENGTH	99	INTELLECT	99	SPIRIT	255
VARIABLE LEVEL	—	ABILITY SPEED	200	ATTACK ELEMENT	—	ATTACK	333	ACCURACY	999	DEFENSE	99
INFLICTS	DEATH (8%)					MAGIC DEFENSE	99	EVASION	0	MAGIC EVASION	99

ELEMENTAL DEFENSE	FIRE	WATER	WIND	EARTH	LIGHT	DARK
	—	—	—	—	—	

IMMUNE TO: PETRIFY / DEATH

TAME (SCHOLAR)	YES	POT LUCK (PARTY HOST)	YES	FORBIDDEN ART (SHAMAN)	—	CAPTURE (BEASTMASTER)	—
ATTACK PROFICIENCY	B	MAGIC PROFICIENCY	C	EVASION CORRECTION	B	MAGIC EVASION CORRECTION	C

ABILITIES: WHIRL BLUDGEON

EXPERIENCE POINTS	1000	STEAL	RIBBON		
DROP	DIAMOND (100%)	DIAMOND (100%)	DIAMOND (100%)	DIAMOND (100%)

BRAINSHARK [B]

ENCOUNTERED	???								
LEVEL	14	HP	550	WEIGHT	—	STRENGTH	8	INTELLECT	9	SPIRIT	12
VARIABLE LEVEL	—	ABILITY SPEED	30	ATTACK ELEMENT	WATER LV.1	ATTACK	6	ACCURACY	96	DEFENSE	4
INFLICTS						MAGIC DEFENSE	7	EVASION	6	MAGIC EVASION	10

ELEMENTAL DEFENSE	FIRE	WATER	WIND	EARTH	LIGHT	DARK
	WEAK	HALF				

IMMUNE TO: PETRIFY / CURSE / DEATH

TAME (SCHOLAR)	—	POT LUCK (PARTY HOST)	—	FORBIDDEN ART (SHAMAN)	—	CAPTURE (BEASTMASTER)	—
ATTACK PROFICIENCY	B	MAGIC PROFICIENCY	A	EVASION CORRECTION	B	MAGIC EVASION CORRECTION	B

ABILITIES: CONFUSE, POISON, SILENCE, WATER, WATERSPOUT

EXPERIENCE POINTS	210	STEAL	—
DROP	AQUAMARINE (100%)	AMETHYST (100%)	AMETHYST (100%)	SHARK LANCE (2%)

DEMON [B]

ENCOUNTERED	TOWN OF URBETH								
LEVEL	15	HP	500	WEIGHT	—	STRENGTH	8	INTELLECT	11	SPIRIT	10
VARIABLE LEVEL	—	ABILITY SPEED	30	ATTACK ELEMENT	DARK LV.1	ATTACK	7	ACCURACY	95	DEFENSE	4
INFLICTS	CURSE (13%)					MAGIC DEFENSE	6	EVASION	6	MAGIC EVASION	5

ELEMENTAL DEFENSE	FIRE	WATER	WIND	EARTH	LIGHT	DARK
	HALF	—	—	—	WEAK	ABSORB

IMMUNE TO: PETRIFY / CURSE / DEATH

TAME (SCHOLAR)	—	POT LUCK (PARTY HOST)	—	FORBIDDEN ART (SHAMAN)	—	CAPTURE (BEASTMASTER)	—
ATTACK PROFICIENCY		MAGIC PROFICIENCY		EVASION CORRECTION		MAGIC EVASION CORRECTION	

ABILITIES: BLADEBLITZ, CURA, DARKRA, PROTECT

EXPERIENCE POINTS	60	STEAL	HI-POTION (40%)/ETHER (25%)
DROP	SAPPHIRE (100%)	SAPPHIRE (100%)	SAPPHIRE (100%)	EMERALD (100%)

ARBAROC

ENCOUNTERED	THE GREAT TREE								
LEVEL	18	HP	490	WEIGHT	20	STRENGTH	8	INTELLECT	5	SPIRIT	20
VARIABLE LEVEL	—	ABILITY SPEED	30	ATTACK ELEMENT	—	ATTACK	10	ACCURACY	125	DEFENSE	3
INFLICTS	—					MAGIC DEFENSE	20	EVASION	0	MAGIC EVASION	10

ELEMENTAL DEFENSE	FIRE	WATER	WIND	EARTH	LIGHT	DARK
	—	—	—	—	—	—

IMMUNE TO: PETRIFY / CURSE / DEATH

TAME (SCHOLAR)	—	POT LUCK (PARTY HOST)	—	FORBIDDEN ART (SHAMAN)	—	CAPTURE (BEASTMASTER)	—
ATTACK PROFICIENCY	B	MAGIC PROFICIENCY	A	EVASION CORRECTION	B	MAGIC EVASION CORRECTION	A

ABILITIES: LEAFRA, LEAFAGA, THUNDAGA, AIRSTORM

EXPERIENCE POINTS	342	STEAL	PHOENIX DOWN (40%)/WIND CAPE (5%)/GALE GAUNTLET (5%)
DROP	TOPAZ (100%)	TOPAZ (100%)	AMETHYST (100%)	AMETHYST (100%)

SORCERER

ENCOUNTERED	ICE CAVERNS								
LEVEL	20	HP	160	WEIGHT	—	STRENGTH	5	INTELLECT	12	SPIRIT	12
VARIABLE LEVEL	—	ABILITY SPEED	50	ATTACK ELEMENT	—	ATTACK	3	ACCURACY	97	DEFENSE	3
INFLICTS						MAGIC DEFENSE	4	EVASION	8	MAGIC EVASION	5

ELEMENTAL DEFENSE	FIRE	WATER	WIND	EARTH	LIGHT	DARK
	—	—	—	—	—	—

IMMUNE TO: PETRIFY / CURSE / DEATH

TAME (SCHOLAR)	YES	POT LUCK (PARTY HOST)	YES	FORBIDDEN ART (SHAMAN)	YES	CAPTURE (BEASTMASTER)	—
ATTACK PROFICIENCY	B	MAGIC PROFICIENCY	B	EVASION CORRECTION	B	MAGIC EVASION CORRECTION	B

ABILITIES: POISON, BLIZZARD, CONFUSE

EXPERIENCE POINTS	30	STEAL	POTION (40%)/HI-POTION (25%)/X-POTION (5%)
DROP	AQUAMARINE (9.8%)	—	—	—

BEHUGEMOTH [A]

ENCOUNTERED	ICE CAVERNS								
LEVEL	16	HP	500	WEIGHT	—	STRENGTH	9	INTELLECT	10	SPIRIT	11
VARIABLE LEVEL	—	ABILITY SPEED	30	ATTACK ELEMENT	LIGHT LV.1	ATTACK	9	ACCURACY	97	DEFENSE	8
INFLICTS						MAGIC DEFENSE	8	EVASION	5	MAGIC EVASION	4

ELEMENTAL DEFENSE	FIRE	WATER	WIND	EARTH	LIGHT	DARK
	—	—	—	—	HALF	

IMMUNE TO: PETRIFY / CURSE / DEATH

TAME (SCHOLAR)	—	POT LUCK (PARTY HOST)	—	FORBIDDEN ART (SHAMAN)	—	CAPTURE (BEASTMASTER)	—
ATTACK PROFICIENCY	A	MAGIC PROFICIENCY	B	EVASION CORRECTION	C	MAGIC EVASION CORRECTION	B

ABILITIES: LIGHTNING BOLT, THUNDARA

EXPERIENCE POINTS	272	STEAL	HI-POTION (40%)/GLIMMER GAUNTLET (25%)/SHINE CAPE (5%)
DROP	AMETHYST (100%)	AMETHYST (100%)	AQUAMARINE (100%)	HI-POTION (2%)

ICE DRAGON [A]

ENCOUNTERED	INVIDIA UNDERGROUND								2 ACTIONS
LEVEL	30	HP	520	WEIGHT	20	STRENGTH	11	INTELLECT	16	SPIRIT	24

LEVEL	30	HP	520	WEIGHT	20	STRENGTH	11	INTELLECT	16	SPIRIT	24
VARIABLE LEVEL	—	ABILITY SPEED	100	ATTACK ELEMENT	WATER LV.2	ATTACK	11	ACCURACY	98	DEFENSE	6
INFLICTS	—					MAGIC DEFENSE	12	EVASION	0	MAGIC EVASION	12

ELEMENTAL DEFENSE	FIRE	WATER	WIND	EARTH	LIGHT	DARK
	WEAK	REFLECT	HALF	HALF	HALF	HALF

IMMUNE TO	PARALYZE/PETRIFY/CURSE/CONFUSE/DEATH

TAME (SCHOLAR)	—	POT LUCK (PARTY HOST)	—	FORBIDDEN ART (SHAMAN)	—	CAPTURE (BEASTMASTER)	—
ATTACK PROFICIENCY	A	MAGIC PROFICIENCY	A	EVASION CORRECTION	A	MAGIC EVASION CORRECTION	A

ABILITIES	ICE BREATH

EXPERIENCE POINTS	465	STEAL	POTION (40%)/STREAM CAPE (25%)/DARK SIGH (5%)
DROP	AMETHYST (100%)		SAPPHIRE (3.9%)	AMETHYST (100%)	AQUAMARINE (100%)

GERI [A]

ENCOUNTERED	ROLAN'S SOUL								

LEVEL	25	HP	450	WEIGHT	—	STRENGTH	17	INTELLECT	14	SPIRIT	12
VARIABLE LEVEL	—	ABILITY SPEED	30	ATTACK ELEMENT	FIRE LV.1	ATTACK	7	ACCURACY	90	DEFENSE	9
INFLICTS	—					MAGIC DEFENSE	8	EVASION	13	MAGIC EVASION	6

ELEMENTAL DEFENSE	FIRE	WATER	WIND	EARTH	LIGHT	DARK
	HALF	WEAK	—	—	—	—

IMMUNE TO	PETRIFY / CURSE / DEATH

TAME (SCHOLAR)	—	POT LUCK (PARTY HOST)	—	FORBIDDEN ART (SHAMAN)	—	CAPTURE (BEASTMASTER)	—
ATTACK PROFICIENCY	A	MAGIC PROFICIENCY	B	EVASION CORRECTION	A	MAGIC EVASION CORRECTION	B

ABILITIES	FIRE BREATH [B], BERSERK

EXPERIENCE POINTS	260	STEAL	HI-POTION (40%)/X-POTION (25%)/BOMB FRAGMENT (5%)
DROP	RUBY (100%)		AMETHYST (100%)	FLAME GAUNTLETS (3.9%)	FLAME CAPE (3.9%)

FREKI [A]

ENCOUNTERED	ROLAN'S SOUL								

LEVEL	25	HP	450	WEIGHT	—	STRENGTH	14	INTELLECT	19	SPIRIT	12
VARIABLE LEVEL	—	ABILITY SPEED	30	ATTACK ELEMENT	WATER LV.1	ATTACK	7	ACCURACY	98	DEFENSE	6
INFLICTS	—					MAGIC DEFENSE	10	EVASION	10	MAGIC EVASION	6

ELEMENTAL DEFENSE	FIRE	WATER	WIND	EARTH	LIGHT	DARK
	WEAK	HALF	—	—	—	—

IMMUNE TO	PETRIFY / CURSE / DEATH

TAME (SCHOLAR)	—	POT LUCK (PARTY HOST)	—	FORBIDDEN ART (SHAMAN)	—	CAPTURE (BEASTMASTER)	—
ATTACK PROFICIENCY	B	MAGIC PROFICIENCY	A	EVASION CORRECTION	B	MAGIC EVASION CORRECTION	A

ABILITIES	ICE BREATH [B], BLIZZARA, MAGICK

EXPERIENCE POINTS	260	STEAL	HI-POTION (40%)/X-POTION (25%)/ANTARCTIC WIND (5%)
DROP	LAPIS (100%)		AMETHYST (100%)	SPRING GAUNTLETS (3.9%)	STREAM CAPE (3.9%)

ROLAN [A]

ENCOUNTERED	ROLAN'S SOUL								2 ACTIONS

LEVEL	27	HP	800	WEIGHT	10	STRENGTH	13	INTELLECT	20	SPIRIT	25
VARIABLE LEVEL	—	ABILITY SPEED	80	ATTACK ELEMENT	DARK LV.1	ATTACK	11	ACCURACY	98	DEFENSE	10
INFLICTS	—					MAGIC DEFENSE	10	EVASION	5	MAGIC EVASION	10

ELEMENTAL DEFENSE	FIRE	WATER	WIND	EARTH	LIGHT	DARK
	HALF	HALF	HALF	HALF	HALF	ABSORB

IMMUNE TO	ALL

TAME (SCHOLAR)	—	POT LUCK (PARTY HOST)	—	FORBIDDEN ART (SHAMAN)	—	CAPTURE (BEASTMASTER)	—
ATTACK PROFICIENCY	A	MAGIC PROFICIENCY	A	EVASION CORRECTION	A	MAGIC EVASION CORRECTION	A

ABILITIES	DARKAGA, THUNDARA, THUNDAGA

EXPERIENCE POINTS	756	STEAL	X-POTION (40%)/LIGHTBRINGER (25%)/HOLY BREATH (5%)
DROP	DIAMOND (100%)		DIAMOND (100%)	AMETHYST (100%)	AMETHYST (100%)

BELPHEGOR [A]

ENCOUNTERED	MT. GULG								2 ACTIONS, FLYING

LEVEL	27	HP	2000-2500	WEIGHT	20	STRENGTH	16	INTELLECT	30	SPIRIT	19
VARIABLE LEVEL	YES	ABILITY SPEED	20	ATTACK ELEMENT	FIRE LV.1	ATTACK	18	ACCURACY	98	DEFENSE	9
INFLICTS	SLEEP (15%)					MAGIC DEFENSE	12	EVASION	5	MAGIC EVASION	8

ELEMENTAL DEFENSE	FIRE	WATER	WIND	EARTH	LIGHT	DARK
	ABSORB	WEAK	NO EFFECT	NO EFFECT	NO EFFECT	NO EFFECT

IMMUNE TO	PETRIFY / CURSE / DEATH

TAME (SCHOLAR)	—	POT LUCK (PARTY HOST)	—	FORBIDDEN ART (SHAMAN)	—	CAPTURE (BEASTMASTER)	—
ATTACK PROFICIENCY	B	MAGIC PROFICIENCY	A	EVASION CORRECTION	C	MAGIC EVASION CORRECTION	B

ABILITIES	FIRAGA, FIRA, CURA, BALL OF FIRE

EXPERIENCE POINTS	756	STEAL	BOMB FRAGMENT (40%)/PHOENIX DOWN (25%)/FLAME CAPE (5%)
DROP	AMETHYST (100%)		AMETHYST (100%)	AMETHYST (100%)	DIAMOND (100%)

CUBES [A]

FLYING

ENCOUNTERED	MT. GULG								
LEVEL	27	HP	500-625	WEIGHT	—	STRENGTH	6	INTELLECT	10	SPIRIT	6
VARIABLE LEVEL	YES	ABILITY SPEED	80	ATTACK ELEMENT	FIRE LV.1	ATTACK	10	ACCURACY	98	DEFENSE	6
INFLICTS	—					MAGIC DEFENSE	12	EVASION	11	MAGIC EVASION	2

ELEMENTAL DEFENSE	FIRE	WATER	WIND	EARTH	LIGHT	DARK
	ABSORB	WEAK	NO EFFECT	NO EFFECT	NO EFFECT	NO EFFECT

IMMUNE TO: PETRIFY / CURSE / DEATH

TAME (SCHOLAR)	—	POT LUCK (PARTY HOST)	—	FORBIDDEN ART (SHAMAN)	—	CAPTURE (BEASTMASTER)	—
ATTACK PROFICIENCY	B	MAGIC PROFICIENCY	A	EVASION CORRECTION	B	MAGIC EVASION CORRECTION	B

ABILITIES: FIRAGA, FIRA, WATERGA, WATERA, AEROGA, AERORA

EXPERIENCE POINTS	0	STEAL	BOMB FRAGMENT (40%)/PHOENIX DOWN (25%)
DROP	AMETHYST (100%)	AMETHYST (100%)	AMETHYST (100%)	DIAMOND (100%)

LUCIFER [A]

2 ACTIONS

ENCOUNTERED	ROLAN'S SOUL								
LEVEL	27	HP	2000-2500	WEIGHT	20	STRENGTH	18	INTELLECT	31	SPIRIT	19
VARIABLE LEVEL	YES	ABILITY SPEED	90	ATTACK ELEMENT	LIGHT LV.1	ATTACK	18	ACCURACY	98	DEFENSE	8
INFLICTS	SILENCE (10%)					MAGIC DEFENSE	12	EVASION	10	MAGIC EVASION	15

ELEMENTAL DEFENSE	FIRE	WATER	WIND	EARTH	LIGHT	DARK
	—	—	—	—	NO EFFECT	WEAK

IMMUNE TO: PETRIFY / CURSE / DEATH

TAME (SCHOLAR)	—	POT LUCK (PARTY HOST)	—	FORBIDDEN ART (SHAMAN)	—	CAPTURE (BEASTMASTER)	—
ATTACK PROFICIENCY	A	MAGIC PROFICIENCY	A	EVASION CORRECTION	B	MAGIC EVASION CORRECTION	B

ABILITIES: THUNDARA, THUNDAGA, AEROGA, JUDGEMENT BOLT, CURA

EXPERIENCE POINTS	756	STEAL	HOLY BREATH (40%)/HOLY BREATH (25%)/LIGHTBRINGER (5%)
DROP	AMETHYST (100%)	AMETHYST (100%)	AMETHYST (100%)	DIAMOND (100%)

SEADEVIL [A]

2 ACTIONS, FLYING

ENCOUNTERED	PIRATE'S HIDEOUT / STAR CHAMBER								
LEVEL	30	HP	700-875	WEIGHT	20	STRENGTH	16	INTELLECT	16	SPIRIT	13
VARIABLE LEVEL	YES	ABILITY SPEED	30	ATTACK ELEMENT	FIRE LV.1	ATTACK	9	ACCURACY	5	DEFENSE	10
INFLICTS	SILENCE (25%)					MAGIC DEFENSE	12	EVASION	12	MAGIC EVASION	5

ELEMENTAL DEFENSE	FIRE	WATER	WIND	EARTH	LIGHT	DARK
	HALF	WEAK	—	—	—	—

IMMUNE TO: PETRIFY / CURSE / DEATH

TAME (SCHOLAR)	YES	POT LUCK (PARTY HOST)	YES	FORBIDDEN ART (SHAMAN)	YES	CAPTURE (BEASTMASTER)	—
ATTACK PROFICIENCY	B	MAGIC PROFICIENCY	A	EVASION CORRECTION	B	MAGIC EVASION CORRECTION	B

ABILITIES: POISON, SILENCE, CONFUSE, FIRAGA, WATER BLAST

EXPERIENCE POINTS	14	STEAL	
DROP	AQUAMARINE (100%)	AMETHYST (100%)	AMETHYST (100%)	SHARK LANCE (2%)

LEVIATHAN [A]

2 ACTIONS, FLYING

ENCOUNTERED	WORLD MAP								
LEVEL	27	HP	3500-4375	WEIGHT	20	STRENGTH	22	INTELLECT	22	SPIRIT	19
VARIABLE LEVEL	YES	ABILITY SPEED	40	ATTACK ELEMENT	WATER LV.1	ATTACK	10	ACCURACY	98	DEFENSE	6
INFLICTS	DEATH (12%)					MAGIC DEFENSE	10	EVASION	8	MAGIC EVASION	8

ELEMENTAL DEFENSE	FIRE	WATER	WIND	EARTH	LIGHT	DARK
	WEAK	ABSORB	—	NO EFFECT	—	—

IMMUNE TO: PETRIFY / CURSE / DEATH

TAME (SCHOLAR)	—	POT LUCK (PARTY HOST)	—	FORBIDDEN ART (SHAMAN)	—	CAPTURE (BEASTMASTER)	—
ATTACK PROFICIENCY	A	MAGIC PROFICIENCY	A	EVASION CORRECTION	C	MAGIC EVASION CORRECTION	B

ABILITIES: WATER, WATERA, THUNDARA, THUNDAGA, CHARGE, TIDAL WAVE

EXPERIENCE POINTS	756	STEAL	PHOENIX DOWN (40%)/PHOENIX DOWN (25%)/DEATH RING (5%)
DROP	AMETHYST (100%)	AMETHYST (100%)	AMETHYST (100%)	DIAMOND (100%)

BEELZEBUB

2 ACTIONS

ENCOUNTERED	TOWER OF THE SKY								
LEVEL	27	HP	3000-3750	WEIGHT	20	STRENGTH	13	INTELLECT	22	SPIRIT	22
VARIABLE LEVEL	YES	ABILITY SPEED	40	ATTACK ELEMENT	—	ATTACK	16	ACCURACY	98	DEFENSE	25
INFLICTS	POISON, PARALYSIS, SILENCE, CURSE, BLIND (9%)					MAGIC DEFENSE	25	EVASION	0	MAGIC EVASION	30

ELEMENTAL DEFENSE	FIRE	WATER	WIND	EARTH	LIGHT	DARK
	HALF	HALF	HALF	HALF	HALF	HALF

IMMUNE TO: PETRIFY / CURSE / DEATH

TAME (SCHOLAR)	—	POT LUCK (PARTY HOST)	—	FORBIDDEN ART (SHAMAN)	—	CAPTURE (BEASTMASTER)	—
ATTACK PROFICIENCY	B	MAGIC PROFICIENCY	B	EVASION CORRECTION	B	MAGIC EVASION CORRECTION	A

ABILITIES: FIRAGA, FIRA, BEZETEOR, FALL OF ANGELS

EXPERIENCE POINTS	756	STEAL	X-POTION (40%)/X-POTION (25%)/X-POTION (5%)
DROP	AMETHYST (100%)	AMETHYST (100%)	AMETHYST (100%)	DIAMOND (100%)

ICE DRAGON [B]

ENCOUNTERED	INVIDIA UNDERGROUND									2 ACTIONS	
LEVEL	30	HP	1200-1500	WEIGHT	10	STRENGTH	15	INTELLECT	22	SPIRIT	26
VARIABLE LEVEL	YES	ABILITY SPEED	100	ATTACK ELEMENT	WATER LV.2	ATTACK	15	ACCURACY	5	DEFENSE	8
INFLICTS	—					MAGIC DEFENSE	12	EVASION	0	MAGIC EVASION	12

ELEMENTAL DEFENSE	FIRE	WATER	WIND	EARTH	LIGHT	DARK
	WEAK		HALF	HALF	HALF	HALF

IMMUNE TO: PETRIFY / CURSE / DEATH / PARALYSIS / CONFUSE

TAME (SCHOLAR)	—	POT LUCK (PARTY HOST)	—	FORBIDDEN ART (SHAMAN)	—	CAPTURE (BEASTMASTER)	—
ATTACK PROFICIENCY	A	MAGIC PROFICIENCY	A	EVASION CORRECTION	A	MAGIC EVASION CORRECTION	A

ABILITIES: ICE BREATH [B]

465		STEAL	POTION (40%)/STREAM CAPE (25%)/X-POTION (5%)		
AMETHYST (100%)			AMETHYST (100%)	AQUAMARINE (100%)	AQUAMARINE (100%)

MAMMON [A]

ENCOUNTERED	SUN TEMPLE									4 ACTIONS, FLYING	
LEVEL	27	HP	1500-1875	WEIGHT	40	STRENGTH	12	INTELLECT	16	SPIRIT	15
VARIABLE LEVEL	YES	ABILITY SPEED	90	ATTACK ELEMENT	WATER LV.1	ATTACK	9	ACCURACY	94	DEFENSE	65
INFLICTS	—					MAGIC DEFENSE	65	EVASION	15	MAGIC EVASION	20

ELEMENTAL DEFENSE	FIRE	WATER	WIND	EARTH	LIGHT	DARK
	WEAK	ABSORB				

IMMUNE TO: PETRIFY / CURSE / DEATH

TAME (SCHOLAR)	—	POT LUCK (PARTY HOST)	—	FORBIDDEN ART (SHAMAN)	—	CAPTURE (BEASTMASTER)	—
ATTACK PROFICIENCY	B	MAGIC PROFICIENCY	A	EVASION CORRECTION	A	MAGIC EVASION CORRECTION	A

ABILITIES: PROTECT, SHELL, POISON, CONFUSE, DIAMOND DUST, BLIZZARD DANCE

EXPERIENCE POINTS	756	STEAL	ANTARCTIC WIND (40%)/ANTARCTIC WIND (25%)/CLAUSTRUM (5%)		
DROP	AMETHYST (100%)		AMETHYST (100%)	AMETHYST (100%)	DIAMOND (100%)

KING GUERA

ENCOUNTERED	QUICKSAND CASTLE									2 ACTIONS	
LEVEL	27	HP	400-500	WEIGHT	10	STRENGTH	10	INTELLECT	20	SPIRIT	30
VARIABLE LEVEL	YES	ABILITY SPEED	50	ATTACK ELEMENT	—	ATTACK	8	ACCURACY	98	DEFENSE	8
INFLICTS	—					MAGIC DEFENSE	20	EVASION	0	MAGIC EVASION	20

ELEMENTAL DEFENSE	FIRE	WATER	WIND	EARTH	LIGHT	DARK
	—	—	—	—	—	—

IMMUNE TO: PETRIFY / CURSE / DEATH

TAME (SCHOLAR)	YES	POT LUCK (PARTY HOST)	YES	FORBIDDEN ART (SHAMAN)	—	CAPTURE (BEASTMASTER)	—
ATTACK PROFICIENCY	B	MAGIC PROFICIENCY	A	EVASION CORRECTION	B	MAGIC EVASION CORRECTION	A

ABILITIES: QUAKRA, FIRAGA

EXPERIENCE POINTS	100	STEAL	POTION (40%)/HI-POTION (25%)/X-POTION (5%)		
DROP	AMETHYST (9.8%)		—	—	—

ASMODEUS [A]

ENCOUNTERED	QUICKSAND CASTLE									2 ACTIONS, FLYING	
LEVEL	27	HP	2400-3000	WEIGHT	30	STRENGTH	14	INTELLECT	25	SPIRIT	19
VARIABLE LEVEL	YES	ABILITY SPEED	100	ATTACK ELEMENT	EARTH LV.1	ATTACK	11	ACCURACY	100	DEFENSE	6
INFLICTS	POISON (100%)					MAGIC DEFENSE	7	EVASION	5	MAGIC EVASION	8

ELEMENTAL DEFENSE	FIRE	WATER	WIND	EARTH	LIGHT	DARK
	—	WEAK	—	ABSORB	—	—

IMMUNE TO: PETRIFY / CURSE / DEATH

TAME (SCHOLAR)	—	POT LUCK (PARTY HOST)	—	FORBIDDEN ART (SHAMAN)	—	CAPTURE (BEASTMASTER)	—
ATTACK PROFICIENCY	B	MAGIC PROFICIENCY	A	EVASION CORRECTION	B	MAGIC EVASION CORRECTION	B

ABILITIES: FIRA, AERORA, AEROGA, QUAKRA, QUAGA, SIDEWINDER, MOONLIGHT CURSE, FLASH, SILENCE, BREAK, SLEEP

EXPERIENCE POINTS	756	STEAL	ANTARCTIC WIND (40%)/PHOENIX DOWN (25%)/POISON RING (5%)		
DROP	AMETHYST (100%)		AMETHYST (100%)	AMETHYST (100%)	DIAMOND (100%)

GREAPS [B]

ENCOUNTERED	WITCH'S MANSION / HOLY TREE TOWER									2 ACTIONS	
LEVEL	8	HP	800-1000	WEIGHT	10	STRENGTH	12	INTELLECT	15	SPIRIT	15
VARIABLE LEVEL	YES	ABILITY SPEED	100	ATTACK ELEMENT	WIND LV.1	ATTACK	7	ACCURACY	5	DEFENSE	9
INFLICTS	—					MAGIC DEFENSE	10	EVASION	3	MAGIC EVASION	10

ELEMENTAL DEFENSE	FIRE	WATER	WIND	EARTH	LIGHT	DARK
	WEAK	—	HALF	—	—	—

IMMUNE TO: PETRIFY / CURSE / DEATH

TAME (SCHOLAR)	YES	POT LUCK (PARTY HOST)	YES	FORBIDDEN ART (SHAMAN)	YES	CAPTURE (BEASTMASTER)	—
ATTACK PROFICIENCY	B	MAGIC PROFICIENCY	A	EVASION CORRECTION	B	MAGIC EVASION CORRECTION	B

ABILITIES: THUNDARA, AEROGA, CURA

EXPERIENCE POINTS	14	STEAL			
DROP	RUBY (100%)		RUBY (100%)	AMETHYST (100%)	AMETHYST (100%)

DOPPELGANGER [AIRE C]

2 ACTIONS

ENCOUNTERED	WITCH'S MANSION							
	MOONSAND RUINS							
LEVEL	50	HP	390-488	WEIGHT	30	STRENGTH	22	INTELLECT	106	SPIRIT	98

LEVEL	50	HP	390-488	WEIGHT	30
VARIABLE LEVEL	YES	ABILITY SPEED	60	ATTACK ELEMENT	DARK LV.1
INFLICTS	CURSE, STATUS DOWN (15%)				

STRENGTH	22	INTELLECT	106	SPIRIT	98
ATTACK	36	ACCURACY	150	DEFENSE	17
MAGIC DEFENSE	28	EVASION	5	MAGIC EVASION	49

ELEMENTAL DEFENSE	FIRE	WATER	WIND	EARTH	LIGHT	DARK
	—	—	—	—	WEAK	NO EFFECT

IMMUNE TO	CURSE

TAME (SCHOLAR)	YES	POT LUCK (PARTY HOST)	YES	FORBIDDEN ART (SHAMAN)	YES	CAPTURE (BEASTMASTER)	—
ATTACK PROFICIENCY	A	MAGIC PROFICIENCY	A	EVASION CORRECTION	A	MAGIC EVASION CORRECTION	A

ABILITIES	CURA, CURAGA, SLEEP, SILENCE, FLASH			
EXPERIENCE POINTS	100	STEAL	HI-POTION (40%)/PHOENIX DOWN (25%)/CURSE RING (5%)	
DROP	AMETHYST (37.6%)	CROSS (7.8%)	—	CURSED BLADE (2%)

DOPPELGANGER [BRANDT C]

2 ACTIONS

ENCOUNTERED	WITCH'S MANSION
	MOONSAND RUINS

LEVEL	50	HP	470-588	WEIGHT	30
VARIABLE LEVEL	YES	ABILITY SPEED	60	ATTACK ELEMENT	DARK LV.1
INFLICTS	CURSE, STATUS DOWN (15%)				

STRENGTH	28	INTELLECT	92	SPIRIT	40
ATTACK	45	ACCURACY	150	DEFENSE	20
MAGIC DEFENSE	26	EVASION	5	MAGIC EVASION	20

ELEMENTAL DEFENSE	FIRE	WATER	WIND	EARTH	LIGHT	DARK
	—	—	—	—	WEAK	NO EFFECT

IMMUNE TO	CURSE

TAME (SCHOLAR)	YES	POT LUCK (PARTY HOST)	YES	FORBIDDEN ART (SHAMAN)	YES	CAPTURE (BEASTMASTER)	—
ATTACK PROFICIENCY	A	MAGIC PROFICIENCY	A	EVASION CORRECTION	A	MAGIC EVASION CORRECTION	A

ABILITIES	CURA, BERSERK			
EXPERIENCE POINTS	100	STEAL	HI-POTION (40%)/PHOENIX DOWN (25%)/CURSE RING (5%)	
DROP	AMETHYST (37.6%)	CROSS (7.8%)	—	CURSED BLADE (2%)

DOPPELGANGER [JUSQUA C]

2 ACTIONS

ENCOUNTERED	WITCH'S MANSION
	MOONSAND RUINS

LEVEL	50	HP	440-550	WEIGHT	30
VARIABLE LEVEL	YES	ABILITY SPEED	60	ATTACK ELEMENT	DARK LV.1
INFLICTS	CURSE, STATUS DOWN (15%)				

STRENGTH	23	INTELLECT	108	SPIRIT	90
ATTACK	42	ACCURACY	150	DEFENSE	18
MAGIC DEFENSE	24	EVASION	10	MAGIC EVASION	45

ELEMENTAL DEFENSE	FIRE	WATER	WIND	EARTH	LIGHT	DARK
	—	—	—	—	WEAK	NO EFFECT

IMMUNE TO	CURSE

TAME (SCHOLAR)	YES	POT LUCK (PARTY HOST)	YES	FORBIDDEN ART (SHAMAN)	YES	CAPTURE (BEASTMASTER)	—
ATTACK PROFICIENCY	A	MAGIC PROFICIENCY	A	EVASION CORRECTION	A	MAGIC EVASION CORRECTION	A

ABILITIES	DARKRA, DARKAGA			
EXPERIENCE POINTS	100	STEAL	HI-POTION (40%)/PHOENIX DOWN (25%)/CURSE RING (5%)	
DROP	AMETHYST (37.6%)	CROSS (7.8%)	—	CURSED BLADE (2%)

DOPPELGANGER [YUNITA C]

2 ACTIONS

ENCOUNTERED	WITCH'S MANSION
	MOONSAND RUINS

LEVEL	50	HP	410-513	WEIGHT	30
VARIABLE LEVEL	YES	ABILITY SPEED	60	ATTACK ELEMENT	DARK LV.1
INFLICTS	CURSE, STATUS DOWN (15%)				

STRENGTH	25	INTELLECT	125	SPIRIT	40
ATTACK	36	ACCURACY	150	DEFENSE	18
MAGIC DEFENSE	20	EVASION	5	MAGIC EVASION	20

ELEMENTAL DEFENSE	FIRE	WATER	WIND	EARTH	LIGHT	DARK
	—	—	—	—	WEAK	NO EFFECT

IMMUNE TO	CURSE

TAME (SCHOLAR)	YES	POT LUCK (PARTY HOST)	YES	FORBIDDEN ART (SHAMAN)	YES	CAPTURE (BEASTMASTER)	—
ATTACK PROFICIENCY	A	MAGIC PROFICIENCY	A	EVASION CORRECTION	A	MAGIC EVASION CORRECTION	A

ABILITIES	CURA			
EXPERIENCE POINTS	100	STEAL	HI-POTION (40%)/PHOENIX DOWN (25%)/CURSE RING (5%)	
DROP	AMETHYST (37.6%)	CROSS (7.8%)	—	CURSED BLADE (2%)

SATAN [A]

4 ACTIONS

ENCOUNTERED	MAGIC LABORATORY

LEVEL	27	HP	3000-3750	WEIGHT	100
VARIABLE LEVEL	YES	ABILITY SPEED	160	ATTACK ELEMENT	DARK LV.2
INFLICTS	—				

STRENGTH	18	INTELLECT	18	SPIRIT	25
ATTACK	18	ACCURACY	100	DEFENSE	22
MAGIC DEFENSE	18	EVASION	10	MAGIC EVASION	10

ELEMENTAL DEFENSE	FIRE	WATER	WIND	EARTH	LIGHT	DARK
	—	—	—	—	WEAK	ABSORB

IMMUNE TO	PETRIFY / CURSE / DEATH

TAME (SCHOLAR)	—	POT LUCK (PARTY HOST)	—	FORBIDDEN ART (SHAMAN)	—	CAPTURE (BEASTMASTER)	—
ATTACK PROFICIENCY	A	MAGIC PROFICIENCY	A	EVASION CORRECTION	C	MAGIC EVASION CORRECTION	B

ABILITIES	ARCANE FOCUS, DARKRA, DARKAGA, CURA			
EXPERIENCE POINTS	756	STEAL	X-POTION (40%)/PHOENIX DOWN (25%)/DARKBRINGER (5%)	
DROP	AMETHYST (100%)	AMETHYST (100%)	AMETHYST (100%)	DIAMOND (100%)

BELPHEGOR [B]

2 ACTIONS, FLYING

ENCOUNTERED	STAR CHAMBER							
LEVEL	40	HP	3400-4250	WEIGHT	20	STRENGTH	26	INTELLECT 68 / SPIRIT 27
VARIABLE LEVEL	YES	ABILITY SPEED	30	ATTACK ELEMENT	FIRE LV.1	ATTACK	32	ACCURACY 160 / DEFENSE 15
INFLICTS	SLEEP (15%)					MAGIC DEFENSE	16	EVASION 8 / MAGIC EVASION 8

ELEMENTAL DEFENSE	FIRE	WATER	WIND	EARTH	LIGHT	DARK
	ABSORB	WEAK	NO EFFECT	NO EFFECT	NO EFFECT	NO EFFECT

IMMUNE TO	PETRIFY / CURSE / DEATH		
TAME (SCHOLAR)	—	POT LUCK (PARTY HOST)	—
FORBIDDEN ART (SHAMAN)	—	CAPTURE (BEASTMASTER)	—

ATTACK PROFICIENCY	B	MAGIC PROFICIENCY	A	EVASION CORRECTION	B	MAGIC EVASION CORRECTION	B

ABILITIES	FIRAGA, FIRA, CURA, BALLS OF FIRE

EXPERIENCE POINTS	756	STEAL	BOMB FRAGMENT (40%)/PHOENIX DOWN (25%)/ FLAME CAPE (5%)
DROP	AMETHYST (100%)	AMETHYST (100%) / AMETHYST (100%)	DIAMOND (100%)

CUBES [B]

FLYING

ENCOUNTERED	STAR CHAMBER							
LEVEL	40	HP	1200-1500	WEIGHT	—	STRENGTH	12	INTELLECT 30 / SPIRIT 15
VARIABLE LEVEL	YES	ABILITY SPEED	100	ATTACK ELEMENT	FIRE LV.1	ATTACK	12	ACCURACY 98 / DEFENSE 13
INFLICTS	—					MAGIC DEFENSE	11	EVASION 11 / MAGIC EVASION 2

ELEMENTAL DEFENSE	FIRE	WATER	WIND	EARTH	LIGHT	DARK
	ABSORB	WEAK	NO EFFECT	NO EFFECT	NO EFFECT	NO EFFECT

IMMUNE TO	PETRIFY / CURSE / DEATH		
TAME (SCHOLAR)	—	POT LUCK (PARTY HOST)	—
FORBIDDEN ART (SHAMAN)	—	CAPTURE (BEASTMASTER)	—

ATTACK PROFICIENCY	B	MAGIC PROFICIENCY	A	EVASION CORRECTION	B	MAGIC EVASION CORRECTION	B

ABILITIES	FIRAGA, FIRA, WATERA, WATERGA, AERORA, AEROGA

EXPERIENCE POINTS	0	STEAL	BOMB FRAGMENT (40%)
DROP	AMETHYST (100%)	AMETHYST (100%) / AMETHYST (100%)	DIAMOND (100%)

ASMODEUS [B]

4 ACTIONS, FLYING

ENCOUNTERED	STAR CHAMBER							
LEVEL	40	HP	3500-4375	WEIGHT	30	STRENGTH	24	INTELLECT 58 / SPIRIT 26
VARIABLE LEVEL	YES	ABILITY SPEED	100	ATTACK ELEMENT	EARTH LV.1	ATTACK	23	ACCURACY 150 / DEFENSE 14
INFLICTS	POISON (100%)					MAGIC DEFENSE	16	EVASION 0 / MAGIC EVASION 8

ELEMENTAL DEFENSE	FIRE	WATER	WIND	EARTH	LIGHT	DARK
	—	WEAK	—	ABSORB	—	—

IMMUNE TO	PETRIFY / CURSE / DEATH		
TAME (SCHOLAR)	—	POT LUCK (PARTY HOST)	—
FORBIDDEN ART (SHAMAN)	—	CAPTURE (BEASTMASTER)	—

ATTACK PROFICIENCY	B	MAGIC PROFICIENCY	A	EVASION CORRECTION	B	MAGIC EVASION CORRECTION	B

ABILITIES	FIRA, AERORA, AEROGA, QUAKRA, QUAGA, SIDEWINDER, MOONLIGHT CURSE, FLASH, SILENCE, BREAK, SLEEP

EXPERIENCE POINTS	756	STEAL	HI-POTION (40%)
DROP	AMETHYST (100%)	AMETHYST (100%) / AMETHYST (100%)	DIAMOND (100%)

LEVIATHAN [B]

4 ACTIONS, FLYING

ENCOUNTERED	STAR CHAMBER							
LEVEL	40	HP	4400-5500	WEIGHT	50	STRENGTH	21	INTELLECT 52 / SPIRIT 26
VARIABLE LEVEL	YES	ABILITY SPEED	150	ATTACK ELEMENT	WATER LV.1	ATTACK	30	ACCURACY 120 / DEFENSE 14
INFLICTS	DEATH (6%)					MAGIC DEFENSE	20	EVASION 8 / MAGIC EVASION 8

ELEMENTAL DEFENSE	FIRE	WATER	WIND	EARTH	LIGHT	DARK
	WEAK	—	—	—	—	—

IMMUNE TO	PETRIFY / CURSE / DEATH		
TAME (SCHOLAR)	—	POT LUCK (PARTY HOST)	—
FORBIDDEN ART (SHAMAN)	—	CAPTURE (BEASTMASTER)	—

ATTACK PROFICIENCY	A	MAGIC PROFICIENCY	A	EVASION CORRECTION	B	MAGIC EVASION CORRECTION	B

ABILITIES	WATERA, THUNDARA, THUNDAGA, CHARGE, TIDAL WAVE

EXPERIENCE POINTS	756	STEAL	HI-POTION (40%)
DROP	AMETHYST (100%)	AMETHYST (100%) / AMETHYST (100%)	DIAMOND (100%)

LUCIFER [B]

2 ACTIONS

ENCOUNTERED	STAR CHAMBER							
LEVEL	40	HP	3600-4500	WEIGHT	20	STRENGTH	22	INTELLECT 66 / SPIRIT 28
VARIABLE LEVEL	YES	ABILITY SPEED	150	ATTACK ELEMENT	LIGHT LV.1	ATTACK	32	ACCURACY 200 / DEFENSE 15
INFLICTS	SILENCE (9%)					MAGIC DEFENSE	16	EVASION 10 / MAGIC EVASION 8

ELEMENTAL DEFENSE	FIRE	WATER	WIND	EARTH	LIGHT	DARK
	—	—	—	—	ABSORB	WEAK

IMMUNE TO	PETRIFY / CURSE / DEATH		
TAME (SCHOLAR)	—	POT LUCK (PARTY HOST)	—
FORBIDDEN ART (SHAMAN)	—	CAPTURE (BEASTMASTER)	—

ATTACK PROFICIENCY	A	MAGIC PROFICIENCY	A	EVASION CORRECTION	B	MAGIC EVASION CORRECTION	B

ABILITIES	THUNDARA, THUNDAGA, AEROGA, JUDGEMENT BOLT, CURA

EXPERIENCE POINTS	756	STEAL	HI-POTION (40%)/LIGHTBRINGER (5%)
DROP	AMETHYST (100%)	AMETHYST (100%) / AMETHYST (100%)	DIAMOND (100%)

SATAN [B]

4 ACTIONS

ENCOUNTERED	STAR CHAMBER								
LEVEL	40	HP	3700-4625	WEIGHT	40	STRENGTH	26	INTELLECT	18	SPIRIT	28

					STRENGTH	26	INTELLECT	18	SPIRIT	28
LEVEL	40	HP 3700-4625	WEIGHT 40						
VARIABLE LEVEL	YES	ABILITY SPEED 190	ATTACK ELEMENT DARK LV.2		ATTACK	30	ACCURACY	400	DEFENSE	17
INFLICTS	—				MAGIC DEFENSE	15	EVASION	10	MAGIC EVASION	10

ELEMENTAL DEFENSE	FIRE	WATER	WIND	EARTH	LIGHT	DARK
	—	—	—	—	WEAK	ABSORB

IMMUNE TO: PETRIFY / CURSE / DEATH

TAME (SCHOLAR)	—	POT LUCK (PARTY HOST)	—	FORBIDDEN ART (SHAMAN)	—	CAPTURE (BEASTMASTER)	—
ATTACK PROFICIENCY	A	MAGIC PROFICIENCY	A	EVASION CORRECTION	C	MAGIC EVASION CORRECTION	B

ABILITIES: ARCANE FOCUS, DARKRA, DARKAGA, CURA

EXPERIENCE POINTS	756	STEAL	HI-POTION (40%)/DARKBRINGER (5%)
DROP	AMETHYST (100%)	AMETHYST (100%)	AMETHYST (100%)	DIAMOND (100%)

MAMMON [B]

4 ACTIONS, FLYING

					STRENGTH	24	INTELLECT	50	SPIRIT	28
ENCOUNTERED	STAR CHAMBER								
LEVEL	40	HP 3400-4250	WEIGHT 30						
VARIABLE LEVEL	YES	ABILITY SPEED 120	ATTACK ELEMENT WATER LV.1		ATTACK	24	ACCURACY	200	DEFENSE	90
INFLICTS	—				MAGIC DEFENSE	90	EVASION	15	MAGIC EVASION	15

ELEMENTAL DEFENSE	FIRE	WATER	WIND	EARTH	LIGHT	DARK
	WEAK	ABSORB	—	—	—	—

IMMUNE TO: PETRIFY / CURSE / DEATH

TAME (SCHOLAR)	—	POT LUCK (PARTY HOST)	—	FORBIDDEN ART (SHAMAN)	—	CAPTURE (BEASTMASTER)	—
ATTACK PROFICIENCY	B	MAGIC PROFICIENCY	A	EVASION CORRECTION	A	MAGIC EVASION CORRECTION	A

ABILITIES: PROTECT, SHELL, POISON, CONFUSE, DIAMOND DUST, BLIZZARD DANCE

EXPERIENCE POINTS	756	STEAL	HI-POTION (40%)/MAMMON'S SPEAR (5%)
DROP	AMETHYST (100%)	AMETHYST (100%)	AMETHYST (100%)	DIAMOND (100%)

BEELZEBUB [B]

4 ACTIONS

					STRENGTH	36	INTELLECT	58	SPIRIT	30
ENCOUNTERED	STAR CHAMBER								
LEVEL	40	HP 4200-5250	WEIGHT 20						
VARIABLE LEVEL	YES	ABILITY SPEED 80	ATTACK ELEMENT —		ATTACK	35	ACCURACY	200	DEFENSE	35
INFLICTS	PARALYSIS, POISON, CURSE, BLIND, SILENCE (8%)				MAGIC DEFENSE	35	EVASION	0	MAGIC EVASION	50

ELEMENTAL DEFENSE	FIRE	WATER	WIND	EARTH	LIGHT	DARK
	HALF	HALF	HALF	HALF	HALF	HALF

IMMUNE TO: PETRIFY / CURSE / DEATH

TAME (SCHOLAR)	—	POT LUCK (PARTY HOST)	—	FORBIDDEN ART (SHAMAN)	—	CAPTURE (BEASTMASTER)	—
ATTACK PROFICIENCY	B	MAGIC PROFICIENCY	B	EVASION CORRECTION	B	MAGIC EVASION CORRECTION	A

ABILITIES: FIRAGA, FIRA, BEZETEOR, FALL OF ANGELS

EXPERIENCE POINTS	756	STEAL	HI-POTION (40%)/NECRONOMICON (5%)
DROP	AMETHYST (100%)	AMETHYST (100%)	AMETHYST (100%)	DIAMOND (100%)

CHAOS [FIRST FORM]

2 ACTIONS, FLYING

					STRENGTH	38	INTELLECT	100	SPIRIT	66
ENCOUNTERED	STAR CHAMBER								
LEVEL	50	HP 6000-7500	WEIGHT 40						
VARIABLE LEVEL	YES	ABILITY SPEED 180	ATTACK ELEMENT —		ATTACK	26	ACCURACY	300	DEFENSE	18
INFLICTS	—				MAGIC DEFENSE	20	EVASION	10	MAGIC EVASION	50

ELEMENTAL DEFENSE	FIRE	WATER	WIND	EARTH	LIGHT	DARK
	—	—	—	—	—	—

IMMUNE TO: PETRIFY / CURSE / DEATH

TAME (SCHOLAR)	—	POT LUCK (PARTY HOST)	—	FORBIDDEN ART (SHAMAN)	—	CAPTURE (BEASTMASTER)	—
ATTACK PROFICIENCY	A	MAGIC PROFICIENCY	A	EVASION CORRECTION	A	MAGIC EVASION CORRECTION	A

ABILITIES: ESUNA, DARKRA, DARKAGA, MAGICK, SHELL, PROTECT, BANISHRA, BANISHGA, HASTE, SLOW, STOP

EXPERIENCE POINTS	666	STEAL	HI-ETHER (40%)/REMEDY (25%)/PHOENIX DOWN (15%)
DROP			

CHAOS [SECOND FORM]

2 ACTIONS, FLYING

					STRENGTH	40	INTELLECT	100	SPIRIT	40
ENCOUNTERED	STAR CHAMBER								
LEVEL	50	HP 8000-10000	WEIGHT 30						
VARIABLE LEVEL	YES	ABILITY SPEED 160	ATTACK ELEMENT —		ATTACK	26	ACCURACY	300	DEFENSE	18
INFLICTS	—				MAGIC DEFENSE	14	EVASION	5	MAGIC EVASION	50

ELEMENTAL DEFENSE	FIRE	WATER	WIND	EARTH	LIGHT	DARK
	—	—	—	—	—	—

IMMUNE TO: PETRIFY / CURSE / DEATH

TAME (SCHOLAR)	—	POT LUCK (PARTY HOST)	—	FORBIDDEN ART (SHAMAN)	—	CAPTURE (BEASTMASTER)	—
ATTACK PROFICIENCY	A	MAGIC PROFICIENCY	A	EVASION CORRECTION	A	MAGIC EVASION CORRECTION	A

ABILITIES: FLY SWAT, BLAZE, EARTHQUAKE, TSUNAMI, LIGHTNING

EXPERIENCE POINTS	777	STEAL	HI-ETHER (40%)/REMEDY (25%)/PHOENIX DOWN (15%)
DROP			

CHAOS [THIRD FORM]

2 ACTIONS, FLYING

ENCOUNTERED	STAR CHAMBER							
LEVEL	50	HP	9999-12498	WEIGHT	50	STRENGTH	40	INTELLECT 100 SPIRIT 255
VARIABLE LEVEL	YES	ABILITY SPEED	200	ATTACK ELEMENT	—	ATTACK	30	ACCURACY 300 DEFENSE 16
INFLICTS	—					MAGIC DEFENSE	16	EVASION 0 MAGIC EVASION 50

ELEMENTAL DEFENSE	FIRE	WATER	WIND	EARTH	LIGHT	DARK
	—	—	—	—	—	—

IMMUNE TO	PETRIFY / CURSE / DEATH

TAME (SCHOLAR)	—	POT LUCK (PARTY HOST)	—	FORBIDDEN ART (SHAMAN)	—	CAPTURE (BEASTMASTER)	—
ATTACK PROFICIENCY	A	MAGIC PROFICIENCY	A	EVASION CORRECTION	A	MAGIC EVASION CORRECTION	A
ABILITIES	BIG BANG, BANISHRA, DARKRA, DARKAGA, TSUNAMI, EARTHQUAKE, BLACK HOLE, CURA, BLAZE						
EXPERIENCE POINTS	999	STEAL	HI-ETHER (40%)/REMEDY (25%)/PHOENIX DOWN (15%)				
DROP	—		—	—	—	—	

LEFT ARM

FLYING

ENCOUNTERED	STAR CHAMBER							
LEVEL	50	HP	4000-5000	WEIGHT	—	STRENGTH	40	INTELLECT 110 SPIRIT 60
VARIABLE LEVEL	YES	ABILITY SPEED	170	ATTACK ELEMENT	—	ATTACK	32	ACCURACY 300 DEFENSE 15
INFLICTS	—					MAGIC DEFENSE	17	EVASION 0 MAGIC EVASION 50

ELEMENTAL DEFENSE	FIRE	WATER	WIND	EARTH	LIGHT	DARK
	—	—	—	—	—	—

IMMUNE TO	PETRIFY / CURSE / DEATH

TAME (SCHOLAR)	YES	POT LUCK (PARTY HOST)	YES	FORBIDDEN ART (SHAMAN)	—	CAPTURE (BEASTMASTER)	—
ATTACK PROFICIENCY	A	MAGIC PROFICIENCY	A	EVASION CORRECTION	A	MAGIC EVASION CORRECTION	A
ABILITIES	CURAGA, CURSE, HASTE, SLOW, STOP, FLASH, CONFUSE, POISON, DEATH						
EXPERIENCE POINTS	0	STEAL	HI-ETHER (40%)/REMEDY (25%)/PHOENIX DOWN (15%)				
DROP	—		—	—	—	—	

RIGHT ARM

FLYING

ENCOUNTERED	STAR CHAMBER							
LEVEL	50	HP	4000-5000	WEIGHT	—	STRENGTH	48	INTELLECT 110 SPIRIT 60
VARIABLE LEVEL	YES	ABILITY SPEED	170	ATTACK ELEMENT	—	ATTACK	34	ACCURACY 300 DEFENSE 17
INFLICTS	CONFUSE, CURSE, SILENCE, BLINDNESS, SLEEP, POISON, PETRIFY, DEATH, STATUS DOWN (5%)					MAGIC DEFENSE	15	EVASION 0 MAGIC EVASION 50

ELEMENTAL DEFENSE	FIRE	WATER	WIND	EARTH	LIGHT	DARK
	—	—	—	—	—	—

IMMUNE TO	PETRIFY / CURSE / DEATH

TAME (SCHOLAR)	YES	POT LUCK (PARTY HOST)	YES	FORBIDDEN ART (SHAMAN)	—	CAPTURE (BEASTMASTER)	—
ATTACK PROFICIENCY	A	MAGIC PROFICIENCY	A	EVASION CORRECTION	A	MAGIC EVASION CORRECTION	A
ABILITIES	HURL						
EXPERIENCE POINTS	0	STEAL	HI-ETHER (40%)/REMEDY (25%)/PHOENIX DOWN (15%)				
DROP	—		—	—	—	—	

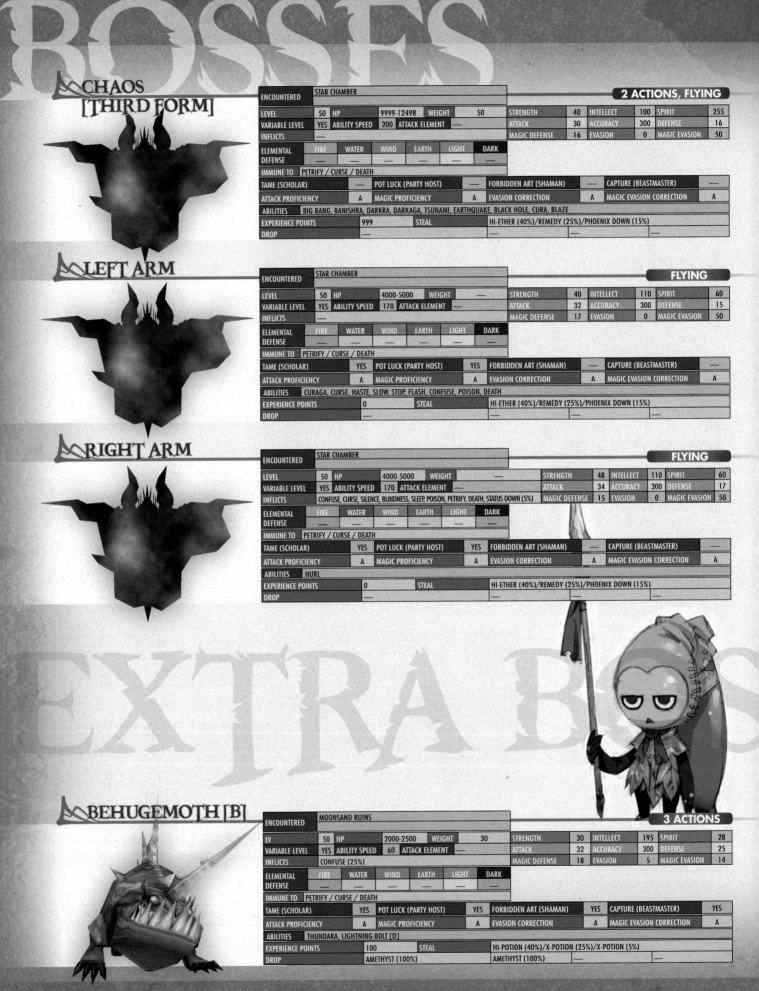

BEHUGEMOTH [B]

3 ACTIONS

ENCOUNTERED	MOONSAND RUINS							
LV	50	HP	2000-2500	WEIGHT	30	STRENGTH	30	INTELLECT 195 SPIRIT 28
VARIABLE LEVEL	YES	ABILITY SPEED	60	ATTACK ELEMENT	—	ATTACK	32	ACCURACY 300 DEFENSE 25
INFLICTS	CONFUSE (25%)					MAGIC DEFENSE	18	EVASION 5 MAGIC EVASION 14

ELEMENTAL DEFENSE	FIRE	WATER	WIND	EARTH	LIGHT	DARK
	—	—	—	—	—	—

IMMUNE TO	PETRIFY / CURSE / DEATH

TAME (SCHOLAR)	YES	POT LUCK (PARTY HOST)	YES	FORBIDDEN ART (SHAMAN)	YES	CAPTURE (BEASTMASTER)	YES
ATTACK PROFICIENCY	A	MAGIC PROFICIENCY	A	EVASION CORRECTION	A	MAGIC EVASION CORRECTION	A
ABILITIES	THUNDARA, LIGHTNING BOLT [D]						
EXPERIENCE POINTS	100	STEAL	HI-POTION (40%)/X-POTION (25%)/X-POTION (5%)				
DROP	AMETHYST (100%)		AMETHYST (100%)	—	—		

DEMON LORD

3 ACTIONS

ENCOUNTERED	MOONSAND RUINS							
LV	50	HP	2500-3125	WEIGHT	30	STRENGTH	38	INTELLECT 195 · SPIRIT 28
VARIABLE LEVEL	YES	ABILITY SPEED	60	ATTACK ELEMENT	DARK LV.2	ATTACK	31	ACCURACY 300 · DEFENSE 24
INFLICTS	CURSE (25%)					MAGIC DEFENSE	21	EVASION 25 · MAGIC EVASION 14

ELEMENTAL DEFENSE	FIRE	WATER	WIND	EARTH	LIGHT	DARK
	—	WEAK	—	—	HALF	NO EFFECT

IMMUNE TO	PETRIFY / CURSE / DEATH

TAME (SCHOLAR)	YES	POT LUCK (PARTY HOST)	YES	FORBIDDEN ART (SHAMAN)	—	CAPTURE (BEASTMASTER)	—
ATTACK PROFICIENCY	A	MAGIC PROFICIENCY	A	EVASION CORRECTION	A	MAGIC EVASION CORRECTION	A

ABILITIES	BLADEBLITZ, WORLD OF DARK			
EXPERIENCE POINTS	100	STEAL	HI-POTION (40%)/X-POTION (25%)/X-POTION (5%)	
DROP	AMETHYST (100%)	AMETHYST (100%)	AMETHYST (100%)	DIAMOND (100%)

SAND DEVIL [B]

2 ACTIONS

ENCOUNTERED	MOONSAND RUINS							
LV	55	HP	3000-3750	WEIGHT	30	STRENGTH	40	INTELLECT 190 · SPIRIT 66
VARIABLE LEVEL	YES	ABILITY SPEED	100	ATTACK ELEMENT	EARTH LV.2	ATTACK	30	ACCURACY 300 · DEFENSE 52
INFLICTS	PETRIFY (5%)					MAGIC DEFENSE	19	EVASION 28 · MAGIC EVASION 10

ELEMENTAL DEFENSE	FIRE	WATER	WIND	EARTH	LIGHT	DARK
	HALF	WEAK	—	NO EFFECT	—	—

IMMUNE TO	PETRIFY / CURSE / DEATH

TAME (SCHOLAR)	—	POT LUCK (PARTY HOST)	—	FORBIDDEN ART (SHAMAN)	—	CAPTURE (BEASTMASTER)	—
ATTACK PROFICIENCY	A	MAGIC PROFICIENCY	A	EVASION CORRECTION	A	MAGIC EVASION CORRECTION	A

ABILITIES	SANDSTORM, QUAKRA			
EXPERIENCE POINTS	756	STEAL	—	
DROP	DIAMOND (100%)	DIAMOND (100%)	DIAMOND (100%)	—

BAHAMUT

ENCOUNTERED	MOONSAND RUINS							
LV	55	HP	5000-6250	WEIGHT	60	STRENGTH	29	INTELLECT 120 · SPIRIT 55
VARIABLE LEVEL	YES	ABILITY SPEED	100	ATTACK ELEMENT	LIGHT LV.2	ATTACK	37	ACCURACY 300 · DEFENSE 25
INFLICTS	—					MAGIC DEFENSE	21	EVASION 0 · MAGIC EVASION 28

ELEMENTAL DEFENSE	FIRE	WATER	WIND	EARTH	LIGHT	DARK
	—	—	—	—	ABSORBS	—

IMMUNE TO	PETRIFY / CURSE / DEATH

TAME (SCHOLAR)	YES	POT LUCK (PARTY HOST)	YES	FORBIDDEN ART (SHAMAN)	YES	CAPTURE (BEASTMASTER)	—
ATTACK PROFICIENCY	A	MAGIC PROFICIENCY	A	EVASION CORRECTION	A	MAGIC EVASION CORRECTION	A

ABILITIES	FIRE BREATH [C], CURA, FLASH, BANISHGA			
EXPERIENCE POINTS	800	STEAL	—	
DROP	ORIHALCON (100%)	—	—	—

KRINJH

3 ACTIONS

ENCOUNTERED	MOONSAND RUINS							
LV	99	HP	8000-10000	WEIGHT	150	STRENGTH	66	INTELLECT 250 · SPIRIT 63
VARIABLE LEVEL	YES	ABILITY SPEED	250	ATTACK ELEMENT	EARTH LV.2	ATTACK	66	ACCURACY 300 · DEFENSE 45
INFLICTS	BLINDNESS (25%)					MAGIC DEFENSE	65	EVASION 50 · MAGIC EVASION 10

ELEMENTAL DEFENSE	FIRE	WATER	WIND	EARTH	LIGHT	DARK
	—	—	WEAK	HALF	—	—

IMMUNE TO	PETRIFY / CURSE / DEATH

TAME (SCHOLAR)	—	POT LUCK (PARTY HOST)	—	FORBIDDEN ART (SHAMAN)	—	CAPTURE (BEASTMASTER)	—
ATTACK PROFICIENCY	A	MAGIC PROFICIENCY	A	EVASION CORRECTION	A	MAGIC EVASION CORRECTION	A

ABILITIES	QUAGA, WATERA, CURA, SILENCE			
EXPERIENCE POINTS	756	STEAL	POTION (40%)/KRINJH'S ROBE (25%)/HOLY BREATH (5%)	
DROP	DIAMOND (100%)	DIAMOND (100%)	DIAMOND (100%)	KRINJH'S ROBE (15%)

SEADEVIL [B]

3 ACTIONS, FLYING

ENCOUNTERED	HOLY TREE TOWER							
LV	60	HP	3000-3750	WEIGHT	30	STRENGTH	33	INTELLECT 195 · SPIRIT 55
VARIABLE LEVEL	YES	ABILITY SPEED	60	ATTACK ELEMENT	WATER LV.2	ATTACK	36	ACCURACY 300 · DEFENSE 19
INFLICTS	SILENCE / CURSE (50%)					MAGIC DEFENSE	17	EVASION 3 · MAGIC EVASION 28

ELEMENTAL DEFENSE	FIRE	WATER	WIND	EARTH	LIGHT	DARK
	WEAK	ABSORBS	—	—	—	—

IMMUNE TO	PETRIFY / CURSE / DEATH

TAME (SCHOLAR)	YES	POT LUCK (PARTY HOST)	YES	FORBIDDEN ART (SHAMAN)	—	CAPTURE (BEASTMASTER)	—
ATTACK PROFICIENCY	A	MAGIC PROFICIENCY	A	EVASION CORRECTION	A	MAGIC EVASION CORRECTION	A

ABILITIES	WATERSPRAY, SILENCE, CONFUSE, POISON			
EXPERIENCE POINTS	100	STEAL	HI-POTION (40%)/X-POTION (25%)/X-POTION (5%)	
DROP	AMETHYST (100%)	AMETHYST (100%)	—	—

⚤ NUE [B]

3 ACTIONS, FLYING

ENCOUNTERED	HOLY TREE TOWER								
LV	60	HP	3500-4375	WEIGHT	40	STRENGTH	35	INTELLECT	150	SPIRIT	52
VARIABLE LEVEL	YES	ABILITY SPEED	100	ATTACK ELEMENT	—	ATTACK	38	ACCURACY	300	DEFENSE	28
INFLICTS	POISON					MAGIC DEFENSE	25	EVASION	10	MAGIC EVASION	26

ELEMENTAL DEFENSE	FIRE	WATER	WIND	EARTH	LIGHT	DARK
	—	—	—	—	—	

IMMUNE TO	PETRIFY / CURSE / DEATH

TAME (SCHOLAR)	YES	POT LUCK (PARTY HOST)	YES	FORBIDDEN ART (SHAMAN)	YES	CAPTURE (BEASTMASTER)	YES
ATTACK PROFICIENCY	A	MAGIC PROFICIENCY	A	EVASION CORRECTION	A	MAGIC EVASION CORRECTION	A
ABILITIES	FLAME BLAST, CURSE, SUPPRESS, BREAK						
EXPERIENCE POINTS	100	STEAL		POTION (40%)/HI-POTION (25%)/X-POTION (5%)			
DROP	AMETHYST (100%)		DIAMOND (100%)	—	—		

⚤ WRAITH [B]

2 ACTIONS, FLYING

ENCOUNTERED	HOLY TREE TOWER								
LV	65	HP	2000-2500	WEIGHT	60	STRENGTH	31	INTELLECT	100	SPIRIT	64
VARIABLE LEVEL	YES	ABILITY SPEED	150	ATTACK ELEMENT	—	ATTACK	33	ACCURACY	300	DEFENSE	5
INFLICTS	CURSE (10%)					MAGIC DEFENSE	16	EVASION	90	MAGIC EVASION	32

ELEMENTAL DEFENSE	FIRE	WATER	WIND	EARTH	LIGHT	DARK
	—	—	—	—	—	

IMMUNE TO	PETRIFY / CURSE / DEATH

TAME (SCHOLAR)	YES	POT LUCK (PARTY HOST)	YES	FORBIDDEN ART (SHAMAN)	YES	CAPTURE (BEASTMASTER)	YES
ATTACK PROFICIENCY	A	MAGIC PROFICIENCY	A	EVASION CORRECTION	A	MAGIC EVASION CORRECTION	A
ABILITIES	ICE BLAST, SILENCE, DEATH, CURSE						
EXPERIENCE POINTS	100	STEAL		POTION (40%)/HI-POTION (25%)/X-POTION (5%)			
DROP	AMETHYST (100%)		AMETHYST (100%)	—	—		

⚤ GOBLIN LORD

2 ACTIONS

ENCOUNTERED	HOLY TREE TOWER								
LV	65	HP	3500-4375	WEIGHT	100	STRENGTH	43	INTELLECT	174	SPIRIT	35
VARIABLE LEVEL	YES	ABILITY SPEED	150	ATTACK ELEMENT	—	ATTACK	39	ACCURACY	300	DEFENSE	23
INFLICTS	—					MAGIC DEFENSE	45	EVASION	0	MAGIC EVASION	18

ELEMENTAL DEFENSE	FIRE	WATER	WIND	EARTH	LIGHT	DARK
	—	—	—	—	—	

IMMUNE TO	PETRIFY / CURSE / DEATH

TAME (SCHOLAR)	YES	POT LUCK (PARTY HOST)	YES	FORBIDDEN ART (SHAMAN)	YES	CAPTURE (BEASTMASTER)	YES
ATTACK PROFICIENCY	A	MAGIC PROFICIENCY	A	EVASION CORRECTION	A	MAGIC EVASION CORRECTION	A
ABILITIES	GOBLIN STRIKE, LEAFRA						
EXPERIENCE POINTS	100	STEAL		POTION (40%)/HI-POTION (25%)/X-POTION (5%)			
DROP	DIAMOND (100%)		DIAMOND (100%)	DIAMOND (100%)	—		

⚤ RED DRAGON

2 ACTIONS

ENCOUNTERED	HOLY TREE TOWER								
LV	65	HP	5000-6250	WEIGHT	20	STRENGTH	42	INTELLECT	160	SPIRIT	55
VARIABLE LEVEL	YES	ABILITY SPEED	100	ATTACK ELEMENT	FIRE LV.2	ATTACK	51	ACCURACY	300	DEFENSE	26
INFLICTS	—					MAGIC DEFENSE	24	EVASION	0	MAGIC EVASION	10

ELEMENTAL DEFENSE	FIRE	WATER	WIND	EARTH	LIGHT	DARK
	ABSORBS	—	—	—	—	

IMMUNE TO	PETRIFY / CURSE / DEATH

TAME (SCHOLAR)	YES	POT LUCK (PARTY HOST)	YES	FORBIDDEN ART (SHAMAN)	YES	CAPTURE (BEASTMASTER)	—
ATTACK PROFICIENCY	A	MAGIC PROFICIENCY	A	EVASION CORRECTION	A	MAGIC EVASION CORRECTION	A
ABILITIES	FLAME BREATH [C], CURA						
EXPERIENCE POINTS	800	STEAL		—			
DROP	ORIHALCON (100%)		—	—	—		

⚤ TORTE

3 ACTIONS

ENCOUNTERED	HOLY TREE TOWER								
LV	99	HP	8000-10000	WEIGHT	80	STRENGTH	35	INTELLECT	240	SPIRIT	90
VARIABLE LEVEL	YES	ABILITY SPEED	150	ATTACK ELEMENT	WIND LV.2	ATTACK	46	ACCURACY	300	DEFENSE	50
INFLICTS	SILENCE (25%)					MAGIC DEFENSE	99	EVASION	5	MAGIC EVASION	100

ELEMENTAL DEFENSE	FIRE	WATER	WIND	EARTH	LIGHT	DARK
	—	—	WEAK	HALF	—	

IMMUNE TO	PETRIFY / CURSE / DEATH

TAME (SCHOLAR)	—	POT LUCK (PARTY HOST)	—	FORBIDDEN ART (SHAMAN)	—	CAPTURE (BEASTMASTER)	—
ATTACK PROFICIENCY	A	MAGIC PROFICIENCY	A	EVASION CORRECTION	A	MAGIC EVASION CORRECTION	A
ABILITIES	SHELL, LEAFRA, LEAFAGA, MAGICK, CURA						
EXPERIENCE POINTS	756	STEAL		POTION (40%)/TORTE'S CLOTHES (25%)/HOLY BREATH (5%)			
DROP	DIAMOND (100%)		DIAMOND (100%)	DIAMOND (100%)	TORTE'S CLOTHES (15%)		

MINOTAUR [C]

3 ACTIONS

ENCOUNTERED	MYSTERIOUS TOWER						
LV	70	HP	3500-4375	WEIGHT	60		
VARIABLE LEVEL	YES	ABILITY SPEED	120	ATTACK ELEMENT	EARTH LV.2		
INFLICTS							

STRENGTH	42	INTELLECT	11	SPIRIT	28
ATTACK	60	ACCURACY	300	DEFENSE	33
MAGIC DEFENSE	28	EVASION	0	MAGIC EVASION	0

ELEMENTAL DEFENSE	FIRE	WATER	WIND	EARTH	LIGHT	DARK
		WEAK	NO EFFECT			

IMMUNE TO	PETRIFY / CURSE / DEATH

TAME (SCHOLAR)	YES	POT LUCK (PARTY HOST)	YES	FORBIDDEN ART (SHAMAN)	YES	CAPTURE (BEASTMASTER)	YES
ATTACK PROFICIENCY	A	MAGIC PROFICIENCY	A	EVASION CORRECTION	A	MAGIC EVASION CORRECTION	A
ABILITIES	FULL SWING						
EXPERIENCE POINTS	100		STEAL	HI-POTION (40%)/X-POTION (25%)/X-POTION (5%)			
DROP		AMETHYST (100%)		AMETHYST (100%)			

MYTHRIL GOLEM

3 ACTIONS

ENCOUNTERED	MYSTERIOUS TOWER						
LV	70	HP	4500-5625	WEIGHT	60		
VARIABLE LEVEL	YES	ABILITY SPEED	120	ATTACK ELEMENT	EARTH LV.2		
INFLICTS	—						

STRENGTH	43	INTELLECT	10	SPIRIT	66
ATTACK	63	ACCURACY	300	DEFENSE	99
MAGIC DEFENSE	20	EVASION	0	MAGIC EVASION	5

ELEMENTAL DEFENSE	FIRE	WATER	WIND	EARTH	LIGHT	DARK
	—	—	—	REFLECT	—	—

IMMUNE TO	PETRIFY / CURSE / DEATH

TAME (SCHOLAR)	YES	POT LUCK (PARTY HOST)	YES	FORBIDDEN ART (SHAMAN)	YES	CAPTURE (BEASTMASTER)	—
ATTACK PROFICIENCY	A	MAGIC PROFICIENCY	A	EVASION CORRECTION	A	MAGIC EVASION CORRECTION	A
ABILITIES	WHIRL BLUDGEON [B]						
EXPERIENCE POINTS	100		STEAL	MYTHRIL (40%)			
DROP		AMETHYST (100%)		DIAMOND (100%)	AMETHYST (100%)	DIAMOND (100%)	

GERI [B]

2 ACTIONS

ENCOUNTERED	MYSTERIOUS TOWER						
LV	75	HP	3500-4375	WEIGHT	80		
VARIABLE LEVEL	YES	ABILITY SPEED	120	ATTACK ELEMENT	FIRE LV.2		
INFLICTS	—						

STRENGTH	45	INTELLECT	220	SPIRIT	100
ATTACK	68	ACCURACY	300	DEFENSE	28
MAGIC DEFENSE	30	EVASION	5	MAGIC EVASION	6

ELEMENTAL DEFENSE	FIRE	WATER	WIND	EARTH	LIGHT	DARK
	ABSORBS	WEAK	—	—	—	—

IMMUNE TO	PETRIFY / CURSE / DEATH

TAME (SCHOLAR)	—	POT LUCK (PARTY HOST)	—	FORBIDDEN ART (SHAMAN)		CAPTURE (BEASTMASTER)	—
ATTACK PROFICIENCY	A	MAGIC PROFICIENCY	A	EVASION CORRECTION	A	MAGIC EVASION CORRECTION	A
ABILITIES	FIRE BREATH, BERSERK						
EXPERIENCE POINTS	2280		STEAL	HI-POTION (40%)/X-POTION (25%)/BOMB FRAGMENT (5%)			
DROP		DIAMOND (100%)		DIAMOND (100%)			

FREKI [B]

2 ACTIONS

ENCOUNTERED	MYSTERIOUS TOWER						
LV	75	HP	3500-4375	WEIGHT	80		
VARIABLE LEVEL	YES	ABILITY SPEED	120	ATTACK ELEMENT	WATER LV.2		
INFLICTS	—						

STRENGTH	40	INTELLECT	240	SPIRIT	100
ATTACK	58	ACCURACY	300	DEFENSE	26
MAGIC DEFENSE	34	EVASION	5	MAGIC EVASION	50

ELEMENTAL DEFENSE	FIRE	WATER	WIND	EARTH	LIGHT	DARK
	WEAK	ABSORBS	—	—	—	—

IMMUNE TO	PETRIFY / CURSE / DEATH

TAME (SCHOLAR)	—	POT LUCK (PARTY HOST)	—	FORBIDDEN ART (SHAMAN)		CAPTURE (BEASTMASTER)	—
ATTACK PROFICIENCY	A	MAGIC PROFICIENCY	A	EVASION CORRECTION	A	MAGIC EVASION CORRECTION	A
ABILITIES	ICE BREATH, MAGICK						
EXPERIENCE POINTS	2280		STEAL	HI-POTION (40%)/X-POTION (25%)/ANTARCTIC WIND (5%)			
DROP		DIAMOND (100%)					

DRAGON

2 ACTIONS

ENCOUNTERED	MYSTERIOUS TOWER						
LV	75	HP	5200-6500	WEIGHT	60		
VARIABLE LEVEL	YES	ABILITY SPEED	120	ATTACK ELEMENT			
INFLICTS	—						

STRENGTH	46	INTELLECT	200	SPIRIT	58
ATTACK	65	ACCURACY	300	DEFENSE	35
MAGIC DEFENSE	31	EVASION	0	MAGIC EVASION	29

ELEMENTAL DEFENSE	FIRE	WATER	WIND	EARTH	LIGHT	DARK
	HALF	HALF	HALF	HALF	—	—

IMMUNE TO	PETRIFY / CURSE / DEATH

TAME (SCHOLAR)	YES	POT LUCK (PARTY HOST)	YES	FORBIDDEN ART (SHAMAN)	YES	CAPTURE (BEASTMASTER)	A
ATTACK PROFICIENCY	A	MAGIC PROFICIENCY	A	EVASION CORRECTION	A	MAGIC EVASION CORRECTION	A
ABILITIES	FIRE BREATH						
EXPERIENCE POINTS	800		STEAL	—			
DROP		ORIHALCON (100%)		—	—	—	

REKOTEH

ENCOUNTERED	MYSTERIOUS TOWER								2 ACTIONS
LV	99	HP	6500-8125	WEIGHT	150	STRENGTH	60	INTELLECT	250	SPIRIT	66
VARIABLE LEVEL	YES	ABILITY SPEED	200	ATTACK ELEMENT	WATER LV.2	ATTACK	55	ACCURACY	300	DEFENSE	52
INFLICTS						MAGIC DEFENSE	70	EVASION	30	MAGIC EVASION	10

ELEMENTAL DEFENSE	FIRE	WATER	WIND	EARTH	LIGHT	DARK
	WEAK	HALF	—	—	—	—

IMMUNE TO: PETRIFY / CURSE / DEATH

TAME (SCHOLAR)	—	POT LUCK (PARTY HOST)	—	FORBIDDEN ART (SHAMAN)	—	CAPTURE (BEASTMASTER)	—
ATTACK PROFICIENCY	A	MAGIC PROFICIENCY	A	EVASION CORRECTION	A	MAGIC EVASION CORRECTION	A

ABILITIES: THUNDAGA, CURA, BLIZZARA, BLIZZAGA, SILENCE, SHELL, PROTECT

EXPERIENCE POINTS	756	STEAL	POTION (40%)/REKOTEH'S CLOTHES (25%)/HOLY BREATH (5%)
DROP	DIAMOND (100%)	DIAMOND (100%)	DIAMOND (100%)	REKOTEH'S CLOTHES (15%)

ROLAN [B]

ENCOUNTERED	MYSTERIOUS TOWER								2 ACTIONS
LV	99	HP	8500-10625	WEIGHT	100	STRENGTH	77	INTELLECT	250	SPIRIT	38
VARIABLE LEVEL	YES	ABILITY SPEED	150	ATTACK ELEMENT	LIGHT LV.2	ATTACK	87	ACCURACY	300	DEFENSE	68
INFLICTS						MAGIC DEFENSE	55	EVASION	5	MAGIC EVASION	10

ELEMENTAL DEFENSE	FIRE	WATER	WIND	EARTH	LIGHT	DARK
	—	—	—	—	HALF	—

IMMUNE TO: PETRIFY / CURSE / DEATH

TAME (SCHOLAR)	—	POT LUCK (PARTY HOST)	—	FORBIDDEN ART (SHAMAN)	—	CAPTURE (BEASTMASTER)	—
ATTACK PROFICIENCY	A	MAGIC PROFICIENCY	A	EVASION CORRECTION	A	MAGIC EVASION CORRECTION	A

ABILITIES: THUNDARA, THUNDAGA, CURA, DARKRA, DARKAGA

EXPERIENCE POINTS	756	STEAL	POTION (40%)/ROLAN'S CLOTHES (25%)/HOLY BREATH (5%)
DROP	DIAMOND (100%)	DIAMOND (100%)	DIAMOND (100%)	ROLAN'S CLOTHES (15%)

DEMON PRINCE

ENCOUNTERED	TRIAL TOWER								3 ACTIONS
LV	90	HP	4300-5375	WEIGHT	80	STRENGTH	78	INTELLECT	200	SPIRIT	33
VARIABLE LEVEL	YES	ABILITY SPEED	150	ATTACK ELEMENT	DARK LV.2	ATTACK	67	ACCURACY	300	DEFENSE	48
INFLICTS	BLINDNESS, CURSE (15%)					MAGIC DEFENSE	36	EVASION	5	MAGIC EVASION	17

ELEMENTAL DEFENSE	FIRE	WATER	WIND	EARTH	LIGHT	DARK
	—	WEAK	—	—	—	—

IMMUNE TO: PETRIFY / CURSE / DEATH

TAME (SCHOLAR)	YES	POT LUCK (PARTY HOST)	YES	FORBIDDEN ART (SHAMAN)	—	CAPTURE (BEASTMASTER)	—
ATTACK PROFICIENCY	A	MAGIC PROFICIENCY	A	EVASION CORRECTION	A	MAGIC EVASION CORRECTION	A

ABILITIES: BLADEBLITZ, WORLD OF DARKNESS, FIRA, FIRAGA

EXPERIENCE POINTS	100	STEAL	HI-POTION (40%)/X-POTION (25%)/X-POTION (5%)
DROP	AMETHYST (100%)	AMETHYST (100%)	—	—

BUFFOHELM [B]

ENCOUNTERED	TRIAL TOWER								2 ACTIONS
LV	90	HP	4000-5000	WEIGHT	80	STRENGTH	81	INTELLECT	250	SPIRIT	68
VARIABLE LEVEL	YES	ABILITY SPEED	150	ATTACK ELEMENT	—	ATTACK	65	ACCURACY	300	DEFENSE	46
INFLICTS	CURSE, SILENCE (15%)					MAGIC DEFENSE	36	EVASION	5	MAGIC EVASION	36

ELEMENTAL DEFENSE	FIRE	WATER	WIND	EARTH	LIGHT	DARK
	WEAK	—	—	—	—	—

IMMUNE TO: PETRIFY / CURSE / DEATH

TAME (SCHOLAR)	YES	POT LUCK (PARTY HOST)	YES	FORBIDDEN ART (SHAMAN)	YES	CAPTURE (BEASTMASTER)	YES
ATTACK PROFICIENCY	A	MAGIC PROFICIENCY	A	EVASION CORRECTION	A	MAGIC EVASION CORRECTION	A

ABILITIES: CURSE, SILENCE, BREAK, POISON, FLASH, FIRAGA

EXPERIENCE POINTS	100	STEAL	POTION (40%)/HI-POTION (25%)/X-POTION (5%)
DROP	AMETHYST (100%)	AMETHYST (100%)	—	—

GHOUL [B]

ENCOUNTERED	TRIAL TOWER								2 ACTIONS
LV	90	HP	3500-4375	WEIGHT	80	STRENGTH	59	INTELLECT	250	SPIRIT	69
VARIABLE LEVEL	YES	ABILITY SPEED	150	ATTACK ELEMENT	—	ATTACK	65	ACCURACY	300	DEFENSE	48
INFLICTS	POISON, STATUS DOWN (15%)					MAGIC DEFENSE	45	EVASION	5	MAGIC EVASION	38

ELEMENTAL DEFENSE	FIRE	WATER	WIND	EARTH	LIGHT	DARK
	—	—	—	—	—	—

IMMUNE TO: PETRIFY / CURSE / DEATH

TAME (SCHOLAR)	YES	POT LUCK (PARTY HOST)	YES	FORBIDDEN ART (SHAMAN)	YES	CAPTURE (BEASTMASTER)	—
ATTACK PROFICIENCY	A	MAGIC PROFICIENCY	A	EVASION CORRECTION	A	MAGIC EVASION CORRECTION	A

ABILITIES: DARKRA, DARKAGA, SILENCE, DEATH, CURSE

EXPERIENCE POINTS	100	STEAL	POTION (40%)/HI-POTION (25%)/X-POTION (5%)
DROP	AMETHYST (100%)	DIAMOND (100%)	—	—

GREAPS [C]

ENCOUNTERED	TRIAL TOWER									3 ACTIONS	
LV	95	HP	5500-6875	WEIGHT	80		STRENGTH	77	INTELLECT	200	SPIRIT	58
VARIABLE LEVEL	YES	ABILITY SPEED	150	ATTACK ELEMENT	WIND LV.2		ATTACK	70	ACCURACY	300	DEFENSE	49
INFLICTS	SILENCE, SLEEP (15%)						MAGIC DEFENSE	38	EVASION	10	MAGIC EVASION	5

ELEMENTAL DEFENSE	FIRE	WATER	WIND	EARTH	LIGHT	DARK
	—	—	NO EFFECT	NO EFFECT	—	—

IMMUNE TO	PETRIFY / CURSE / DEATH						
TAME (SCHOLAR)		YES	POT LUCK (PARTY HOST)	YES	FORBIDDEN ART (SHAMAN)	YES	CAPTURE (BEASTMASTER)	YES
ATTACK PROFICIENCY	A	MAGIC PROFICIENCY	A	EVASION CORRECTION	A	MAGIC EVASION CORRECTION	A
ABILITIES	AEROGA, THUNDRA, CURA						
EXPERIENCE POINTS	100	STEAL		HI-POTION (40%)/X-POTION (25%)/X-POTION (5%)		
DROP	DIAMOND (100%)		DIAMOND (100%)	DIAMOND (100%)	—	

BLACK DRAGON

ENCOUNTERED	TRIAL TOWER									2 ACTIONS	
LV	95	HP	6500-8125	WEIGHT	80		STRENGTH	77	INTELLECT	240	SPIRIT	65
VARIABLE LEVEL	YES	ABILITY SPEED	150	ATTACK ELEMENT	DARK LV.2		ATTACK	79	ACCURACY	300	DEFENSE	58
INFLICTS							MAGIC DEFENSE	39	EVASION	0	MAGIC EVASION	10

ELEMENTAL DEFENSE	FIRE	WATER	WIND	EARTH	LIGHT	DARK
	—	—	—	—	—	NO EFFECT

IMMUNE TO	PETRIFY / CURSE / DEATH						
TAME (SCHOLAR)		YES	POT LUCK (PARTY HOST)	YES	FORBIDDEN ART (SHAMAN)	YES	CAPTURE (BEASTMASTER)	—
ATTACK PROFICIENCY	A	MAGIC PROFICIENCY	A	EVASION CORRECTION	A	MAGIC EVASION CORRECTION	A
ABILITIES	DARK BREATH, DARKAGA, SUPPRESS, CURA						
EXPERIENCE POINTS	800	STEAL				
DROP	ORIHALCON (100%)		—	—	—	

ADVENTURER

ENCOUNTERED	TRIAL TOWER									2 ACTIONS	
LV	99	HP	9000-11250	WEIGHT	150		STRENGTH	89	INTELLECT	250	SPIRIT	83
VARIABLE LEVEL	YES	ABILITY SPEED	200	ATTACK ELEMENT	—		ATTACK	88	ACCURACY	300	DEFENSE	76
INFLICTS	SILENCE, POISON (15%)						MAGIC DEFENSE	68	EVASION	15	MAGIC EVASION	10

ELEMENTAL DEFENSE	FIRE	WATER	WIND	EARTH	LIGHT	DARK
	—	—	—	—	—	—

IMMUNE TO	PETRIFY / CURSE / DEATH						
TAME (SCHOLAR)		—	POT LUCK (PARTY HOST)	—	FORBIDDEN ART (SHAMAN)	—	CAPTURE (BEASTMASTER)	—
ATTACK PROFICIENCY	A	MAGIC PROFICIENCY	A	EVASION CORRECTION	A	MAGIC EVASION CORRECTION	A
ABILITIES	BERSERK, PROTECT, SUPPRESS, CURA, CURAGA						
EXPERIENCE POINTS	756	STEAL		POTION (40%)/ADVENTURER'S GARB (25%)/HOLY BREATH (5%)		
DROP	DIAMOND (100%)		DIAMOND (100%)	DIAMOND (100%)	ADVENTURER'S GARB (15%)	

FAITHFUL FOX

ENCOUNTERED	TRIAL TOWER									2 ACTIONS	
LV	99	HP	5000-6250	WEIGHT	150		STRENGTH	59	INTELLECT	250	SPIRIT	255
VARIABLE LEVEL	YES	ABILITY SPEED	200	ATTACK ELEMENT	FIRE LV.2		ATTACK	60	ACCURACY	300	DEFENSE	55
INFLICTS	PARALYSIS, CONFUSION (15%)						MAGIC DEFENSE	88	EVASION	30	MAGIC EVASION	10

ELEMENTAL DEFENSE	FIRE	WATER	WIND	EARTH	LIGHT	DARK
	HALF	—	—	—	—	—

IMMUNE TO	PETRIFY / CURSE / DEATH						
TAME (SCHOLAR)		—	POT LUCK (PARTY HOST)	—	FORBIDDEN ART (SHAMAN)	—	CAPTURE (BEASTMASTER)	—
ATTACK PROFICIENCY	A	MAGIC PROFICIENCY	A	EVASION CORRECTION	A	MAGIC EVASION CORRECTION	A
ABILITIES	MAGICK, PROTECT, SHELL, BERSERK, CURSE, DEATH, BREAK, CONFUSE, FLASH, POISON, SILENCE, FIRA, CURA, CURAGA						
EXPERIENCE POINTS	14	STEAL		POTION (40%)/HI-POTION (25%)/RAVEN'S YAWN (5%)		
DROP	DIAMOND (100%)		DIAMOND (100%)	PHOENIX DOWN (3.9%)	X-POTION (2%)	

FINAL FANTASY
THE 4 HEROES OF LIGHT

OFFICIAL STRATEGY GUIDE

By Ken Schmidt and V.H. McCarty

© 2009, 2010 SQUARE ENIX CO., LTD. All Rights Reserved. CHARACTER DESIGN: Akihiko Yoshida.
THE 4 HEROES OF LIGHT is a registered trademark or trademark of Square Enix Co., Ltd. FINAL FANTASY, SQUARE ENIX and the SQUARE ENIX logo are registered trademarks or trademarks of Square Enix Holdings Co., Ltd.

DK/BradyGames, a division of Penguin Group (USA) Inc.
800 East 96th Street, 3rd Floor
Indianapolis, IN 46240

The ratings icon is a registered trademark of the Entertainment Software Association. All other trademarks and trade names are properties of their respective owners.

Please be advised that the ESRB ratings icons, "EC", "E", "E10+", "T", "M", "AO", and "RP" are trademarks owned by the Entertainment Software Association, and may only be used with their permission and authority. For information regarding whether a product has been rated by the ESRB, please visit www.esrb.org. For permission to use the ratings icons, please contact the ESA at esrblicenseinfo@theesa.com.

ISBN: 978-0-7440-1255-2

Printing Code: The rightmost double-digit number is the year of the book's printing; the rightmost single-digit number is the number of the book's printing. For example, 10-1 shows that the first printing of the book occurred in 2010.

13 12 11 10   4 3 2 1

Printed in the USA.

BRADYGAMES STAFF

Publisher
Mike Degler

Editor-In-Chief
H. Leigh Davis

Digital and Trade Publisher
Brian Saliba

Operations Manager
Stacey Beheler

CREDITS

Senior Development Editor
Chris Hausermann

Book Designer
Tim Amrhein

Production Designer
Tracy Wehmeyer